Spanish On Your Own

Spanish On Your Own

 Volume Two

Laurel H. Turk
DePauw University, Emeritus

Carlos A. Solé
University of Texas, Austin

Aurelio M. Espinosa, Jr.
Stanford University, Emeritus

Sheila McIntosh, Consulting Editor

HOUGHTON MIFFLIN COMPANY   Boston   New York

Director of Modern Language Programs: Kristina Baer
Development Manager: Beth Kramer
Project Editor: Kellie Cardone
Senior Production/Design Coordinator: Jennifer Waddell
Manufacturing Manager: Florence Cadran

Cover Designer: Rebecca Fagan, Rebecca Fagan Graphic Design

Printed in the U.S.A.

Library of Congress Catalog Card Number: 99-71896

ISBN: 0-395-96444-X

123456789-POO-03 02 01 00 99

Contents

Preface   viii

Lección 12

Viajando por España   2

Irregular verbs having **i**-stem preterits   3

Irregular forms and additional uses of the **-ndo** form   4

Position of object and reflexive pronouns with the **-ndo** form   6

Se + verb for the English passive voice   7

Se used as an indefinite subject   7

Forms and uses of prepositional pronouns   8

Cardinal numbers 100–1,000,000   9

Ordinal numbers   10

Dates   11

Lección 13

Regalos para todos   17

Irregular verbs having **u**-stem preterits   18

Verbs with spelling changes in the preterit and in formal commands   19

Direct and indirect object pronouns used together   20

Demonstrative pronouns   21

Use of **volver** and **devolver**   23

Acabar de + infinitive   23

Preterit indicative of **traer**   24

Lección 14

Unas vacaciones fantásticas   30

The past participle   31

The present perfect and pluperfect indicative   32

The past participle used as an adjective   35

Summary of other uses of **haber**   35

Hace meaning *ago, since*   36

Forms of **oír**   37

Lección 15

La Copa Mundial de Fútbol   44

The future indicative   45

The conditional indicative   46

Verbs irregular in the future and conditional   47

Uses of the future and the conditional   48

The future and conditional to express probability or conjecture   50

The future perfect and conditional perfect   51

Forms of **jugar**   52

Lección 16

En el hospital de la universidad   59

Stem-changing **-ir** verbs   60

More familiar singular (**tú**) command forms   62

Comparisons of inequality: Irregular comparative adjectives   64

Comparisons of inequality: Regular and irregular comparative adverbs   65

Comparisons of equality   67

The absolute superlative   68

Lección 17

Silvia y Alberto se casan   75

The present subjunctive of regular verbs   76

The present subjunctive of stem-changing verbs   77

The present subjunctive of irregular verbs and of verbs with special stem forms   78

Indicative vs. subjunctive mood   80

The subjunctive used with verbs expressing wish or volition, preference, advice, permission, request, or implied command   81

Indicative or subjunctive in noun clauses:
Reporting information or implied command
83

Lección 18

Un accidente de tráfico   89

The present subjunctive of verbs with spelling
changes   90

The subjunctive in noun clauses after verbs
expressing emotion   91

The subjunctive in noun clauses after verbs
expressing doubt or uncertainty   93

The infinitive or subjunctive after some verbs
of persuasion   95

Indirect commands and **nosotros** commands
95

The present perfect subjunctive   97

Lección 19

Miguel se gradúa y busca trabajo   104

Forms of verbs ending in **-ducir**   105

The subjunctive in noun clauses after
impersonal expressions   106

Adjective clauses and relative pronouns
107

Subjunctive or indicative in adjective clauses
109

Hacer in time clauses   110

Spanish equivalents for *to become* or *to get*
112

The infinitive after verbs of perception   112

Lección 20

Luna de miel en Suramérica   119

Forms of verbs ending in **-ger, -gir,** and **-iar,**
-uar   120

Subjunctive or indicative in adverbial clauses
121

Possessive pronouns   124

The definite article as a demonstrative
pronoun   125

The use of **pero** and **sino**   126

Lección 21

Hacen planes para un viaje   132

The imperfect subjunctive   133

The pluperfect subjunctive   136

Use of the subjunctive tenses   137

Si-clauses   139

Forms of **valer**   141

Lección 22

No digamos adiós, sino hasta luego   147

Familiar plural (**vosotros**) commands   148

The passive voice   149

Reflexives as reciprocal pronouns   151

Other uses of the subjunctive mood   151

Forms of **reunirse** and of verbs ending in **-uir**
153

Summary of uses of **para** and **por**   154

Appendix A

The Spanish alphabet   160

The sounds of Spanish vowels   160

The Spanish consonants   161

Diphthongs   162

Division of words into syllables   163

Word stress and use of the written accent
163

Intonation   163

Punctuation marks   165

Capitalization   166

Grammatical terms   166

Appendix B

Regular verbs   168

Irregular past participles of regular and
    stem-changing verbs   170

Comments concerning forms of verbs   170

Irregular verbs   171

Verbs with changes in spelling   175

Verbs with special changes   176

Stem-changing verbs   178

Appendix C

Repasos   181

Lecciones 12–15   181

Lecciones 16–19   183

Lecciones 20–22   186

Appendix D

Answer Keys   189

Appendix E

Tapescripts: *Actividades y práctica, Para
    comprender y escribir, Repaso* self-tests   203

Spanish-English Vocabulary   234

English-Spanish Vocabulary   257

Index   270

✹✹✹ *Preface*

Spanish has become firmly established as the foreign language of choice by language students in the United States. It's no wonder, considering that Spanish is spoken by some 300 million people in twenty countries whose role in international commerce and tourism continues to grow, as well as by more than 60 million native speakers in this country. While opportunities for persons fluent in Spanish have never been greater, many adults interested in learning the language are unable to attend a Spanish class that meets several times a week. If that group includes you, *Spanish On Your Own* can help you acquire the skills you need.

    Spanish On Your Own, a portable, flexible, use-anywhere introductory Spanish program designed for independent study or for use in courses with limited class time, is an ideal teaching tool for busy people. Whether you wish to learn Spanish for business or for pleasure, *Spanish On Your Own* will give you the support you need to begin communicating. The program's easy-to-follow format stresses the essential skills of listening, speaking, reading, and writing. It teaches essential vocabulary and grammatical structures in a logical sequence and reinforces them in subsequent lessons to help you retain what you learn. Each of the program's two volumes includes a text-correlated audio program that provides listening and speaking practice as it models Spanish as spoken by native speakers. To keep you motivated and on track, in-text review tests and answer keys allow you to chart your progress and target areas for review.

Contents of Volume Two

Volume II contains Lessons 12 through 22 of the *Spanish On Your Own* program. Each lesson contains the following sections:

Diálogos (*Dialogues*)

The lesson dialogues model conversational Spanish, introduce practical, everyday vocabulary, and provide a contextualized preview of each lesson's grammatical focus. Familiarizing yourself with the dialogues by listening to them on the Audio Program and reading them aloud will develop your listening skills and help you to practice the sounds of spoken Spanish. (As you progress through each lesson, listening to the dialogue without reading along in your text is a particularly valuable way to develop listening skills.) Follow-up **Preguntas sobre el diálogo** (*Questions on the dialogue*), found both in the text and on the Audio Program, allow you to check your understanding orally and in writing.

Notas gramaticales (*Grammatical notes*)

To facilitate independent study and review, all grammatical concepts are presented simply and completely. Information is often organized into helpful lists and charts. In addition, numerous examples, accompanied by English equivalents, illustrate each point as it is presented. Whenever applicable, a section called **¡Atención!** draws attention to potentially confusing differences between Spanish and English constructions.

    Written and oral exercises systematically reinforce the structures taught. In-text **Prácticas** (*Practice exercises*) supply structured reading and writing practice in a variety of formats, including question/answer drills, fill-in-the-blanks, sentence transformation, and sentence completion. The answer key in Appendix D allows you to check your work. **Actividades y práctica** (*Activities and practice*) exercises, signalled by a headphone icon in the text and found on the Audio Program, provide intensive listening and speaking practice for key structures. Correct answers are supplied on the recording so that you can verify your oral responses. Since listening without relying upon written words to read along provides the greatest listening challenge, consider doing these exercises more than once, even if you complete them successfully the first time. Returning to a previous lesson's exercises after you have moved ahead will help you to retain what you've learned and integrate material learned in different lessons.

The text's flexible format accommodates individual learning styles. While the lesson dialogue is presented first, some students may prefer to complete the grammar sections before turning to the dialogue, or read the grammar explanations, study the dialogue, and then turn to the grammar exercises. It's up to you!

Repaso (*Review*)

In this section, a vocabulary review exercise and a translation exercise related to the lesson dialogue serve as checkpoints to help you verify your mastery of the lesson's content before moving on to more open-ended self-expression in Spanish. Answer keys to this section are found in Appendix D.

Expansión (*Expansion*)

Here the stage is set for you to communicate in Spanish for your own needs. In each lesson, you'll use the vocabulary and structures you have learned to answer questions about your own life, and to complete dialogues in your own words or to write a letter or short composition. All activities are tailored to the abilities of beginners, but to make the most of this section, focus on your own communicative goals and challenge yourself to complete the activities as fully and creatively as you can.

Para comprender y escribir (*To listen and write*)

The listen-and-write section is designed for use with the Audio Program. In the first activity, you'll review vocabulary by selecting the best choice to answer a question or complete a statement. Next, grammar review activities have you answer questions in writing or create new statements based on cues provided. Then, you'll take dictation from a monologue, narrative, or advertisement featuring the lesson's vocabulary and structures. (To help you get it right, you'll hear the dictation three times.)

If completing the written portion of the activities seems too challenging, try listening all the way through first, then listen and write the second time. To enhance your writing accuracy, consult Appendix A for information on written accents, punctuation, and capitalization.

Vocabulario (*Vocabulary*)

Each end-of-lesson vocabulary section contains an alphabetical listing of the words and expressions presented in the dialogues, as well as related words and expressions. (For example, when the **Lección** dialogue features a discussion of career aspirations, the **Vocabulario** lists terms relevant to job seekers that are not used in the dialogue.) All vocabulary in these lists should be memorized since it will reappear throughout the text and the Audio Program. Be sure to learn the corresponding masculine or feminine definite article along with each noun, to help you remember its gender.

Reference Section

The text ends with a reference section. Appendix A includes the Spanish alphabet and concise summaries of the rules of syllabification, word stress and use of written accents, intonation, punctuation, and capitalization, as well as a list of grammatical terms. Appendix B contains verb charts for quick review of regular and irregular verb forms. Appendix C contains **Repaso** review tests to help you check your cumulative knowledge after every few lessons and target areas for further study. Scripts for the **Actividades y práctica** and **Para comprender y escribir** exercises, as well as the audio portions of the **Repaso** tests, are in Appendix E. Answer keys to the lesson exercises, as well as the audio portions of the **Repaso** tests, and the **Repaso** tests are found in Appendix D. The Spanish-English end vocabulary contains all words, expressions, and phrases that appear in *Spanish On Your Own*. The English-Spanish vocabulary lists the words and expressions needed to complete the translations in the **Repaso** section of each lesson, as well as the **Repaso** review tests in Appendix C.

A Final Word

You can do it! With consistent study and review, *Spanish On Your Own* will give you the basic communication tools you'll need to begin to understand and be understood by native speakers of Spanish. Your progress will accelerate if you seek out opportunities to hear and speak Spanish by watching Spanish-language television shows and movies, reading accessible short news pieces and advertisements in magazines and newspapers from Hispanic countries, and seeking opportunities to practice your emerging skills with native speakers or acquaintances who are fluent in Spanish. Remember, too, that language and culture go hand in hand; both in your language studies and your ability to relate to Spanish speakers in your professional or personal life will be enhanced by efforts you make to know and understand the way of life of people from the Hispanic world.

L.T.

Spanish On Your Own

Lección 12

❋❋❋

- ✿ Irregular verbs having **i**-stem preterits
- ✿ Irregular forms and additional uses of the **-ndo** form
- ✿ Position of object and reflexive pronouns with the **-ndo** form
- ✿ **Se** + verb for the English passive voice
- ✿ **Se** used as an indefinite subject
- ✿ Forms and uses of prepositional pronouns
- ✿ Cardinal numbers 100–1,000,000
- ✿ Ordinal numbers
- ✿ Dates

Viajando por España

En el mes de mayo de 1997,[1] los padres de Miguel Ramos hicieron un viaje a España. Yendo en coche desde Madrid a Granada, los señores Ramos[2] decidieron pasar la noche en un hotel de Córdoba, que durante los siglos diez y once fue la capital del Califato[3] de Córdoba, uno de los centros más brillantes de la civilización musulmana.

RECEPCIONISTA	—Buenas noches, señores. ¿Hicieron Uds. reservas?
SR. RAMOS	—No, señorita. Nos dijeron que, viniendo en este tiempo del año, no se necesita hacer reservas.
RECEPCIONISTA	—¡En Córdoba, siempre hay mucha gente de visita! Pero tienen Uds. mucha suerte… En el segundo piso[4] hay una habitación desocupada con dos camas sencillas y baño privado.
SR. RAMOS	—¿Y qué precio tiene esa habitación, por favor?
RECEPCIONISTA	—Con el desayuno completo cuesta doce mil pesetas al día para dos personas. Sin el desayuno, el precio de una habitación para dos es de diez mil pesetas.
SR. RAMOS	—Tienen Uds. estacionamiento para coches, ¿verdad?
RECEPCIONISTA	—Sí, tenemos un garaje pequeño pero se cobran mil pesetas. ¿Les interesa a Uds. la habitación?
SRA. RAMOS	—Sí, nos interesa mucho. Pero… ¿nos permite Ud. verla? Viéndola antes es más fácil decidir.
RECEPCIONISTA	—De acuerdo. Siempre conviene ver las habitaciones antes de tomarlas. Vengan conmigo, por favor.

La recepcionista y los señores Ramos toman el ascensor y suben al segundo piso.

SRA. RAMOS	—Me parece cómoda. No tiene aire acondicionado… pero en mayo todavía no hace mucho calor y no se necesita. (*Hablándole a su esposo.*) Además, hay dos ventanas grandes que dan a la plaza.
SR. RAMOS	(*Mirando la plaza.*) —La vista es agradable. Se ve mucha gente animada paseando y charlando… Me gusta; la tomamos.
RECEPCIONISTA	—¿Es la primera vez que vienen a Córdoba?
SRA. RAMOS	—No, es la segunda. Vinimos por primera vez in 1989.[5]
SR. RAMOS	—Pero esa vez hicimos el viaje de Madrid a Córdoba en avión. Ahora estamos viajando en coche porque así se conoce mejor el país.

---

1. Read: **mil novecientos noventa y siete.**
2. **Los señores Ramos** means *Mr. and Mrs. Ramos.* In direct address, **señores** means *gentlemen, madam and sir, ladies and gentlemen.*
3. A **Califato** is a caliphate, the dominion of a caliph, who was a successor of Muhammad as temporal and spiritual head of Islam.
4. **El segundo piso** (or **el piso segundo**) would be the third floor in the U.S. **El piso principal,** used in the next-to-the-last exchange of the dialogue, means *the first (main) floor*; **el primer piso** (or **el piso primero**) would be *the second floor,* and so on.
5. Read: **mil novecientos ochenta y nueve.**

SRA. RAMOS	—Para nosotros es muy importante conocer bien España. Los padres de mi esposo (*señalándolo*) eran españoles.
RECEPCIONISTA	—Aquí tienen Uds. la llave. La criada va a traerles más toallas, jabón…
SR. RAMOS	—Perdone Ud., pero ¿se puede todavía comer algo en el hotel? Ya es bastante tarde y tengo un poco de hambre.
RECEPCIONISTA	—Sí, claro… Bajen Uds. al piso principal, pues el comedor se cierra a las once. Luego pueden registrarse.
SRA. RAMOS	—Muchas gracias. Es Ud. muy amable, señorita. En seguida bajamos.

Preguntas sobre el diálogo

1. ¿Cuándo hicieron los padres de Miguel un viaje a España? _____

_____

2. ¿Cómo viajaban los señores Ramos a Granada? ¿Dónde decidieron pasar la noche? _____

_____

3. ¿Por qué no hicieron reservas los señores Ramos? _____

_____

4. ¿Qué les dice la recepcionista de Córdoba? ¿Por qué tienen ellos mucha suerte? _____

_____

5. ¿Cuánto cuesta la habitación al día para dos personas? _____

_____

6. ¿Adónde lleva la recepcionista a los señores Ramos? ¿Por qué los lleva allí? _____

_____

7. ¿Por qué no se necesita aire acondicionado en la habitación? _____

_____

8. ¿Qué hay en la habitación? ¿Por qué es agradable la vista a la plaza? _____

_____

9. ¿Por qué les gusta a los señores Ramos viajar en coche? ¿Es la primera vez que ellos visitan Córdoba?

_____

_____

10. ¿Por qué quiere el señor Ramos saber si hay un comedor en el hotel? _____

_____

Notas gramaticales

A. Irregular verbs having **i**-stem preterits
*(Verbos irregulares con **i** en la raíz del pretérito)*

	decir	hacer	querer	venir
Singular	dije	hice	quise	vine
	dijiste	hiciste	quisiste	viniste
	dijo	hizo	quiso	vino
Plural	dijimos	hicimos	quisimos	vinimos
	dijisteis	hicisteis	quisisteis	vinisteis
	dijeron	hicieron	quisieron	vinieron

- The preterit tense of these verbs has an **i** in the stem. Observe the spelling of **dijeron** and **hizo**.[1]
- In the first- and third-person singular forms, the stress falls on the stem instead of the ending; therefore, final **-e** and **-o** are not accented: **dije, dijo**.
- The English equivalents are **dije**, *I said, I did say, I told, I did tell*; **hice**, *I made, I did make, I did*; **quise**, *I wanted, I did want, I wished, I did wish*; **vine**, *I came, I did come*.

Práctica 1   Complete each sentence with the corresponding form of the preterit indicative tense of the verb.

(decir) 1. ¿Qué _____ Ud.?   2. Yo _____ que no quería ir al cine.   3. Y Uds., ¿qué _____?   4. Nosotros _____ que íbamos al teatro.

(hacer) 5. Jaime _____ dos viajes el año pasado.   6. ¿Cuántos viajes _____ Uds.?   7. Nosotros _____ tres viajes.   8. No olviden que yo _____ un viaje a España.

(querer) 9. Yo no _____ subir.   10. ¿_____ Uds. subir?   11. No, nosotros no _____ subir tampoco.   12. Y yo sé que tú no _____ subir.

(venir) 13. Yo _____ a tiempo.   14. ¿_____ Uds. a tiempo?   15. Sí, nosotros _____ a tiempo.   16. Pero Elena no _____ a tiempo.

Actividades y práctica: A

B. Irregular forms and additional uses of the **-ndo** form
(Formas irregulares y otros usos de la forma en -ndo)

Irregular -ndo Forms					
decir	**diciendo**	saying, telling	creer	**creyendo**	believing
ir	**yendo**	going	leer	**leyendo**	reading
poder	**pudiendo**	being able to	traer	**trayendo**	bringing
venir	**viniendo**	coming			

---

1. The **z** of **hizo** is an orthographic change to maintain the stem sound.

In addition to its use with **estar** in the progressive constructions, the **-ndo** form is also used alone in the following cases.

■ To describe the cause of an action or event

No hice reservas, **pensando** que no era
   necesario en este tiempo del año.

I did not make reservations,
   thinking that it wasn't necessary
   this time of the year.

■ To describe the time or moment of an event

Llegando temprano, se puede
   encontrar un hotel cómodo.
Los vi **subir** al comedor.

By arriving early, one can find a
   comfortable hotel.
I saw them going up to the dining
   room.

■ To relate the manner in which an action is carried out

Pagando con tarjeta de credito, es
   más caro.

By paying with a credit card, it is
   more expensive.

■ In these sentences, the English equivalents of the Spanish **-ndo** form are the English present participle (*-ing* form) or *by + -ing*, or a clause introduced by *since, when, as*.

¡Atención!   Remember that the infinitive, not the **-ndo** form, is used in Spanish after a preposition: **Descansaron un rato antes de bajar al comedor**, *They rested for a while before going down to the dining room.*

Práctica 2   Rewrite the sentences, changing the **si**-clause to the **-ndo** construction (if the subject of the **-ndo** form is different from that of the main verb, it follows the **-ndo** form, as in the model).

MODEL: Si llegas tarde, no te permiten entrar. → **Llegando (tú) tarde, no te permiten entrar.**

1. Si haces reservas, tienes cuarto en los hoteles.

   _____

2. Si vienes temprano, no necesitas boleto.

   _____

3. Si nosotros traemos la paella, Antonio promete traer bebidas.

   _____

4. Si salimos a las ocho, llegamos a las once.

   _____

5. Si practicamos mucho, podemos ganar.

   _____

6. Si ella está enferma, no puedes aceptar la invitacíon.

   _____

Práctica 3   Complete the following sentences with the **-ndo** form or the infinitive of the verb, as required.

(**ir**) 1. _____ al centro, Uds. pueden comprar ropa mejor.   2. Despúes de _____ al centro, pasearon por el parque.   3. Al _____ al centro, háganme el favor de cobrar este cheque.

(**leer**) 4. Antes de _____ ese libro, yo no sabía nada de la vida española. 5. _____ ese libro, yo creía que me encontraba en España.   6. Al _____ ese libro, yo recordaba mi niñez.

(**saber**) 7. Al _____ la noticia, corrí a decírsela a Luis.   8. Antes de _____ la noticia, no me interesaba el asunto.   9. _____ la noticia, decidí pasar el fin de semana en casa.

(**volver**) 10. Al _____ de la excursión, me lavé el pelo.   11. _____ de la excursión, cruzamos varios ríos.   12. Después de _____ de la excursión, cenamos en la residencia.

Actividades y práctica: B

C. Position of object and reflexive pronouns with the -ndo form
(Posición de los pronombres objeto y reflexivos con la forma en -ndo)

Pagándoles ahora…	*By paying them now . . .*
Levantándonos temprano…	*By getting up early . . .*
Estamos **haciéndolas.** }	
Las estamos **haciendo.** }	*We are making (doing) them.*
Ella está **bañándose.** }	
Ella **se** está **bañando.** }	*She is bathing.*

■ Object pronouns and reflexive pronouns used as objects of the **-ndo** form are attached to the **-ndo** form, except in the progressive forms of tenses, where the pronouns may be placed before **estar**. An accent mark must be written when a pronoun is attached to the **-ndo** form.

Práctica 4   Rewrite each of the following sentences, placing the object and reflexive pronouns in their correct position.

1. (**las**) Yo vendo. Quiero vender. Estoy vendiendo. _____

_____

2. (**lo**) Ramón hizo. Él no quiso hacer. No está haciendo. _____

_____

3. (**me**) Yo acuesto. Voy a acostar. Estoy acostando. _____

_____

4. (**nos**) ¿Dónde registramos? Queremos registrar. Estamos registrando. _____

_____

Actividades y práctica: C

D. **Se** + verb for the English passive voice
(Se + verbo para la voz pasiva del inglés)

Aquí **se habla** español.	*Spanish is spoken here.*
No **se necesitan** reservas.	*Reservations are not needed.*
Se aceptan tarjetas de crédito.	*Credit cards are accepted.*

- In the active voice the subject acts upon an object: *The clerk opens the bank at ten.* In the passive voice the subject is acted upon: *The bank is opened at ten.*

- If the subject of a passive sentence in English is a thing and the agent (person or thing) is not expressed, **se** is normally used with a verb in Spanish to substitute for the English passive voice. In this case the verb is in the third-person singular or plural, depending on whether the subject is singular or plural. **Se** + verb usually precedes the subject in this construction.[1]

Práctica 5   Rewrite each sentence, changing it to the reflexive construction with **se**.

1. Entonces no conocíamos la música cubana.

   _____

2. Enseñan varias lenguas en la universidad.

   _____

3. ¿Dónde compra uno los boletos?

   _____

4. Celebramos su cumpleaños en el mes de enero.

   _____

5. Venden estos zapatos a precio especial.

   _____

E. **Se** used as an indefinite subject
(El uso de se como sujeto indefinido)

Sólo **se** puede pagar con un cheque.	*One (You) can only pay with a check.*
Se come bien en este hotel.	*One eats well in this hotel.*
Viajando **se** conoce a mucha gente.	*One meets a lot of people while traveling.*
¿Cómo **se** dice… en español?	*How do you say . . . in Spanish?*

- Sometimes an action is expressed without indicating definitely who is doing what the verb implies. In such cases English uses subjects like *one, people, they, you,* which do not refer to a definite person, while in Spanish **se** may be used. In this construction (that is, when no specified subject is expressed), the verb is in the third-person singular.

---

1. For a discussion of the true passive voice, which is formed as in English, see **Lección 22.**

- Uno is also used as an indefinite subject, particularly with reflexive verbs.

Cuando **uno** viaja, **uno** se levanta   *When one travels, one gets up early.*
   temprano.
¿Dónde se registra **uno**?   *Where does one register?*

Práctica 6   Rewrite each sentence using a **se** construction.

1. Abren los bancos a las nueve. _____

2. Cierran las tiendas a las ocho. _____

3. En este hotel no aceptamos cheques. _____

4. Aquí sólo hablamos español. _____

5. En este restaurante uno come muy bien. _____

Actividades y práctica: D

F. Forms and uses of prepositional pronouns
(Formas y usos de los pronombres preposicionales)

Prepositional Pronouns			
	Singular		*Plural*
Preposition +	mí	me	nosotros, -as	us
	ti	you (*fam.*)	vosotros, -as	you (*fam.*)
	él	him, it (*m.*)	ellos	them (*m.*)
	ella	her, it (*f.*)	ellas	them (*f.*)
	Ud.	you (*formal*)	Uds.	you

- The pronoun forms used as the object of a preposition are the same as the subject pronouns, except in the first- and second-person singular: **mí, ti.** Note the written accent on **mí** to distinguish it from the possessive adjective **mi.**

- When used with **con,** the first- and second-persons singular have special forms: **conmigo, contigo.**

- Prepositional pronouns are used in Spanish

   1. particularly with the preposition **a** in addition to the direct and indirect object pronouns for emphasis or contrast, and in the third-person for clarity.

Él me llamó **a mí;** no te llamó **a ti.**   *He called me; he didn't call you.*
Yo le di la llave **a ella (a él, a Ud.).**   *I gave the key to her (to him, to you).*
Elena va **conmigo;** no va **contigo.**   *Helen is going with me; she is not*
                                            going with you.

   2. with **de** to clarify the meaning of **su**(s), *his, her, your* (singular), *their, your* (plural).

La habitación **de él (ella, ellos, ellas,**   *His (Her, Their [m. or f.], your [sing.*
Ud., Uds.) tiene aire acondicionado.   *or pl.]) room has air conditioning.*

¡Atención!   The prepositional phrase with **de** is never used with **mí** or **ti,** but rather a possessive form is used: **mi habitación** or **la habitación mía,** *my room;* **tus toallas** or **las toallas tuyas,** *your towels.*

3. to answer a question when the verb is omitted.

—¿Con quién subimos para ver la habitación?	*"With whom do we go up to look at the room?"*
—**Conmigo**, por favor.	*"With me, please."*
—¿A quién le pagamos?	*"Whom do we pay?"*
—**A mí**.	*"(You pay) me."*

Práctica 7   Add the corresponding form of the prepositional pronoun, following the model.

MODEL: Alberto te escribió. → **Alberto te escribió a ti.**

1. Eso nos interesa. _____

2. El cuarto me gustó. _____

3. Esta vez no le conviene. _____

4. El coche les pareció caro. _____

Práctica 8   Rewrite each sentence, substituting the correct prepositional pronoun for each noun object, as in the model.

MODEL: Mario no estudia con Laura. → **Mario no estudia con ella.**

1. Ana está charlando con Ramón. _____

2. Los discos son de Rita. _____

3. Traigo algo para mis padres. _____

4. Elena está al lado de María. _____

Práctica 9   Complete with the corresponding prepositional phrases.

1. (*with them*) Mis tíos hablaron _____.

2. (*with you*, fam.) Margarita charlaba _____.

3. (*with you*, pl.) Antonio va a vivir _____.

4. (*with me*) El profesor cenó _____.

Actividades y práctica: E

G. Cardinal numbers 100–1,000,000
(*Los números cardinales 100–1.000.000*)

100	cien(to)		700	setecientos, -as
102	ciento dos		800	ochocientos, -as
200	doscientos, -as		900	novecientos, -as
300	trescientos, -as		1.000	mil
400	cuatrocientos, -as		2.000	dos mil
500	quinientos, -as		100.000	cien mil
600	seiscientos, -as		1.000.000	un millón (de)

cien (mil) coches	*one hundred (one thousand) cars*
cien mil estudiantes	*a (one) hundred thousand students*
ciento cincuenta y un dólares	*one hundred fifty-one dollars*
quinientas cuarenta y una pesetas	*five hundred forty-one pesetas*
un millón de jóvenes	*a (one) million young people*
dos millones de personas	*two million persons*

- **Ciento** becomes **cien** before nouns and the numerals **mil** and **millones**, but the full form is retained before numerals under a hundred: **cien personas, cien mil, ciento cincuenta.**

- In Spanish, **y** is normally used only between the tens and units: **treinta *y* seis, cincuenta *y* ocho**; but: **ciento dos, ochocientos dos.**

- Numerals in the hundreds, such as **doscientos, trescientos,** etc., end in **-as** when used with feminine nouns: **doscient*as* toallas,** *two hundred towels.*

- Remember that **uno** drops **-o** before masculine nouns, and that **una** is used before feminine nouns: **ciento *un* cuartos,** *one hundred and one rooms;* **ciento *una* llaves,** *one hundred and one keys.*

- **Un** is omitted before **cien(to)** and **mil**, but is used before **millón.**

- **Millón** (*pl.* **millones**) followed immediately by a noun requires the preposition **de: dos millones *de* dólares,** *two million dollars;* but **dos millones cien mil pesos,** *two million, one hundred thousand pesos.*

- The plurals **cientos, miles,** and **millones** followed by **de** mean *hundreds of, thousands of, millions of: cientos de* **hombres,** *hundreds of men.*

- In writing numerals, the English comma is often written as a period in Spanish and the English period as a comma: **1.000,50 pesos** (**mil pesos, cincuenta centavos**). The English system is being used more and more, however.

Práctica 10   Give the Spanish equivalent for the following.

1. 101 reservations _____

2. 115 keys _____

3. 365 days _____

4. 3,000 towels _____

5. 10,500,000 persons _____

6. 750,000 dollars in cash _____

H. Ordinal numbers   *(Los números ordinales)*

first	primero, -a	sixth	sexto, -a
second	segundo, -a	seventh	séptimo, -a
third	tercero, -a	eighth	octavo, -a
fourth	cuarto, -a	ninth	noveno, -a
fifth	quinto, -a	tenth	décimo, -a

la segunda calle	*the second street*
las primeras canciones	*the first songs*
el primer (tercer) viaje	*the first (third) trip*

- Ordinal numbers agree in gender and number with the nouns they modify: **el cuarto año,** *the fourth year;* **la cuarta semana,** *the fourth week.* Note that **primero** and **tercero** drop the final **-o** before a masculine singular noun.

- Ordinal numbers normally precede the noun: **el primer viaje**, *the first trip*.

- Ordinal numbers are normally used only through *tenth*; beyond *tenth*, the cardinal numbers replace the ordinals and they follow the noun: **Carlos** *Quinto*, *Charles V (Charles the Fifth)*; **Durante el siglo** *dieciséis*, *During the sixteenth century*.

- Like cardinal numbers, ordinal numbers may be used as nouns by simply omitting the noun they modify: —**¿En qué piso está el comedor?** —**Está en** *el* **primer** piso (en el *primero*). *"On what floor is the dining room?" "It is on the first floor (on the first one)."*

Práctica 11   Rewrite the following sentences, using the next higher ordinal number.

1. El cuarto está en el séptimo piso. _____

2. ¿Es éste el segundo concierto? _____

3. Creo que es la quinta canción. _____

4. Es la tercera vez que vengo a España. _____

5. ¿Cuál es el octavo mes del año? _____

Actividades y práctica: F

I. Dates   *(Las fechas)*

¿Cuál es la fecha (de hoy)? ¿Qué fecha es (hoy)?	*What is the date (today)?*
(Hoy) es el dos de diciembre.	*(Today) is the second of December.*
Ayer fue el primero de enero.	*Yesterday was the first of January.*
Vine el treinta y uno de mayo.	*I came (on) the thirty-first of May (May 31).*
¿Para qué fechas necesitan las reservas?	*For what dates do you need the reservations?*

- Cardinal numerals are used to express the days of the month, except for **el primero**, *the first*. Remember that with the day of the month, the definite article **el** means *the, on the*.

- In counting and reading dates, use **mil** with numerals of one thousand or more: **el once de diciembre de** *mil* **novecientos noventa y nueve**, *December 11, 1999.*

- Note that calendars in most Spanish-speaking countries show Monday as the first day of the week.

SEPTIEMBRE						
L	M	M	J	V	S	D
		1	2	3	4	5
6	7	8	9	10	11	12
13	14	15	16	17	18	19
20	21	22	23	24	25	26
27	28	29	30			

Práctica 12   Write in Spanish, following the model.

> MODEL: November 11, 1918 → **el once de noviembre de mil novecientos dieciocho**

1. April 1, 1993 _____

_____

2. September 16, 1810 _____

_____

3. July 14, 1789 _____

_____

4. May 13, 1607 _____

_____

5. October 15, 1066 _____

_____

Repaso

A. Circle the item that does not belong in each series of words.

1. la cama / el piso / la manta / la ropa de cama
2. el jabón / la recepcionista / registrarse / hacer reservas
3. el cheque / la tarjeta de crédito / los cheques de viajero / el desayuno completo
4. el estacionamiento / la foto / el coche / el garaje

B. Give the Spanish equivalent, spelling out all numbers.

1. Michael Ramos' parents made their second trip to Spain during the month of May, 1997. _____

_____

2. Going by car to Granada, they decided to spend the night in Córdoba. _____

_____

3. They are very fortunate (lucky), because there is a vacant room with two single beds and a private bathroom on the third floor. _____

_____

4. The price is twelve thousand pesetas per day with full breakfast for two persons, without the parking.

_____

5. Mrs. Ramos wants to see the room. By seeing it, it is easier to decide whether they wish to take it.

_____

_____

6. Mr. and Mrs. Ramos went down to the main floor to register. _____

_____

Expansión

A. Answer the following questions with complete sentences.

1. ¿Hizo Ud. muchos viajes el año pasado? ¿Adónde fue Ud.? _____

_____

2. ¿Piensa Ud. hacer un viaje largo en coche durante el verano? ¿Adónde quiere ir? _____

_____

3. ¿Cómo le gusta a Ud. viajar, en coche o en avión? ¿Por qué? _____

_____

4. ¿Por qué conviene hacer reservas en los hoteles cuando uno viaja? _____

_____

5. ¿Qué cosas son importantes en la habitación de un hotel? _____

_____

6. ¿Cuáles son los hoteles principales de esta ciudad? ¿Cómo son? _____

_____

B. Write in Spanish a brief account of an imaginary trip you took to Spain last summer. Include the following information: the city and date of departure, and the city and time of arrival; the cities you visited; how and with whom you traveled; what the weather was like; your experiences with the food and meal hours; new friends you met; things you bought; what you enjoyed the most; how and when you returned to the United States.

_____

_____

_____

_____

_____

_____

_____

_____

_____

Para comprender y escribir

A. From the three choices offered, select the one that best completes the statement or answers the question you hear and circle it.

1. (a) la vista.
   (b) el ascensor.
   (c) el siglo.

2. (a) una cama.
   (b) una criada.
   (c) un garaje.

3. (a) setecientas pesetas.
   (b) novecientas pesetas.
   (c) mil pesetas.

4. (a) El cuatro de junio de mil
       novecientos sententa y seis.
   (b) El cuatro de julio de mil setecientos
       sententa y seis.
   (c) El cuatro de julio de mil seiscientos
       sententa y seis.

B. Listen to the statement and the question that follows it. Write the response, according to the model.

> MODEL: Ellos fueron a Granada en coche. ¿Cómo fueron Uds.? →
> **Nosotros también fuimos en coche.**

1. _____

2. _____

3. _____

4. _____

5. _____

C. Dictado. You will hear a short paragraph about travel. You will hear the narrative three times. Listen the first time. Write what you hear on the lines provided the second time. Make any necessary corrections the third time.

_____

_____

_____

_____

_____

_____

_____

_____

✿✿ ✿ *VOCABULARIO*

aceptar to accept
amable (*m.* or *f.*) friendly, kind
animado, -a animated, lively
el **ascensor** elevator
bajar to go down, descend
el **baño** bath, bathroom
brillante (*m.* or *f.*) brilliant
la **cama** bed
cambiar to change
la **civilización** (*pl.* **civilizaciones**) civilization
cobrar to cash (*a check*); to charge, collect

completo, -a complete, full
conmigo with me
contigo with you (*fam. sing.*)
convenir (*like* venir) to be advisable
el **crédito** credit
la **criada** maid
la **cuenta** bill; account
desde *prep.* from, since
desocupado, -a unoccupied, vacant
la **esposa** wife
el **esposo** husband

el **estacionamiento** parking
la **fecha** date
la **foto** photo
el **garaje** garage
la **habitación** (*pl.* **habitaciones**)
    room
el **hotel** hotel
  interesar to interest
el **jabón** (*pl.* **jabones**) soap
la **llave** key
la **manta** blanket
  mejor *adj.* and *adv.* better, best
  mil one thousand, a thousand
  musulmán, -ana[1] Mussulman,
    Moslem
  pagar to pay, pay for
  pasear to walk, stroll
  permitir to permit, allow, let
la **persona** person

la **peseta** peseta (*Spanish monetary
    unit*)
el **piso** floor, story
la **plaza** plaza, square
  privado, -a private
el (la) **recepcionista** receptionist
  registrarse to register
las **reservas** reservation(s)
  sacar to take (out)
  sencillo, -a simple; single (*bed*)
  señalar to point at (to, out),
    indicate
el **siglo** century
  subir (**a**) to go up (to), climb up
    (into)
la **tarjeta** card
la **toalla** towel
el **viajero** traveler (*m.*)
la **vista** view

el **aire acondicionado** air conditioning
  al día per day
  aquí tiene(n) Ud(s). (la llave) here is (the key) (lit., here you
    have…)
la **cama doble** double bed
las **camas sencillas** single beds
los **cheques de viajero** traveler's checks
  con (sin) el desayuno completo with (without) a full breakfast
  ¿cuál es la fecha? what's the date?
  dar a to face, open onto
el **desayuno completo** full breakfast
el **dinero en efectivo** cash
  en efectivo cash, in cash
  en este tiempo del año in (at) this time of (the) year
  en seguida at once, immediately
la **habitación para dos** double room (a room for two)
  hacer reservas to make reservations (a reservation)
  ¿nos permite Ud. ver? may we see? (lit., do you permit or
    allow us to see?)
  pagar en efectivo (con tarjeta de crédito) to pay cash (with a
    credit card)
  ¿para qué fecha(s)? for (by) what date(s)?
el **piso principal** first (main) floor
  por primera vez for the first time
la **ropa de cama** bed linens (*sheets, pillowcases, etc.*), bedclothes
    (*blankets, sheets, etc.*)
  sacar fotografías (fotos [*f.*]**)** to take photographs (photos)
los **señores (Ramos)** Mr. and Mrs. (Ramos)
la **tarjeta de crédito** credit card
  tomar el ascensor to take the elevator

---

1. Most adjectives that end in -**án** or -**ón** add -**a** and lose the accent mark to form the feminine:
musulmán, musulmana.

Lección 13

- Irregular verbs having **u**-stem preterits
- Verbs with spelling changes in the preterit and in formal commands
- Direct and indirect object pronouns used together
- Demonstrative pronouns
- Uses of **volver** and **devolver**
- **Acabar de** + infinitive
- Preterit indicative of **traer**

Regalos para todos

Después de su viaje a España, los señores Ramos decidieron volver a México. Esta vez estuvieron un par de semanas y pudieron visitar las ruinas de Yucatán y otros lugares interesantes. Cuando estaban en Mérida[1] tuvieron tiempo para ir de compras. Estando en el centro, preguntaron por una joyería típica y entraron en ella.

DEPENDIENTE	—¿En qué puedo servirles,[2] señores?
SRA. RAMOS	—¿Tienen Uds. joyas yucatecas?
DEPENDIENTE	—Sí, señora. Tenemos collares, pulseras, aretes… Comience Ud. por esta vitrina.[3]
SRA. RAMOS	—A ver esos aretes de oro, por favor. (*El dependiente los saca de la vitrina y se los enseña a la señora Ramos. Ésta, poniéndoselos, se dirige a su esposo.*) ¿Qué te parecen éstos, Antonio?
SR. RAMOS	—Te quedan preciosos. Te los compro, querida.
SRA. RAMOS	—Mira, Antonio. Este prendedor hace juego con los aretes.
SR. RAMOS	—Sí, Marta, pero piénsalo… Aquí no puedes volver si después quieres devolverlo. ¡Y mira los precios bien!
SRA. RAMOS	—Pues, claro. ¡Ay! Me llevo esta pulsera para Clara, y ésa para Luisa.
DEPENDIENTE	—¿Algo más, señora? ¿O algo para el señor?
SR. RAMOS	(*Hablando a su esposa.*) —Para mí, nada, gracias. Yo sólo quiero comprarme un sombrero de paja fina. Quizás unas camisas típicas para Miguel…
SRA. RAMOS	(*Hablando al dependiente.*) —Bueno, envuélvame Ud. esos anillos de plata para mis hermanas. (*El dependiente le entrega el paquete.*)
SR. RAMOS	(*Al poco rato.*) —Pues, ya pagué la cuenta. Anda, Marta, vamos al mercado. Traje una lista de cosas que allí podemos encontrar: objetos de cerámica, artículos de artesanía para regalos…
SRA. RAMOS	—Tienes razón. Y acabo de recordar que quiero unas hamacas para el patio. Las busqué en la ciudad de México, pero no pude encontrar los colores que quería.

Preguntas sobre el diálogo

1. ¿Qué decidieron hacer los señores Ramos después de su viaje a España? _____

_____

2. ¿Cuánto tiempo estuvieron esta vez? ¿Qué pudieron visitar ellos? _____

_____

---

1. Mérida is the capital of the Mexican state of Yucatan, which occupies the northern part of the peninsula.
2. **¿En qué puedo servirles?**, *What can I do for you?* or *How can I help you?* Forms of **servir** (i, i) (*to serve*) are like those of **pedir** (i, i) given in **Lección 16**.
3. **Comience Ud. por esta vitrina**, *Begin* (i.e., *Begin looking*) *with this showcase.*

3. ¿Qué hicieron los señores Ramos cuando estaban en Mérida? _____

_____

4. ¿Qué le compró el señor Ramos a su esposa? ¿Por qué quería la señora Ramos el prendedor? _____

_____

5. ¿Qué compró la señora Ramos para Clara y Luisa? ¿Y qué compró para sus hermanas? _____

_____

6. ¿Por qué quería ir al mercado el señor Ramos? _____

_____

7. ¿Qué quería comprar su esposa para el patio? _____

_____

8. ¿Por qué no las compró ella en la ciudad de México? _____

_____

✪✪ ✪ *Notas gramaticales*

A. Irregular verbs having **u**-stem preterits
*(Verbos irregulares con **u** en la raíz del pretérito)*

	estar	poder	poner	saber	tener
Singular	estuve	pude	puse	supe	tuve
	estuviste	pudiste	pusiste	supiste	tuviste
	estuvo	pudo	puso	supo	tuvo
Plural	estuvimos	pudimos	pusimos	supimos	tuvimos
	estuvisteis	pudisteis	pusisteis	supisteis	tuvisteis
	estuvieron	pudieron	pusieron	supieron	tuvieron

- The preterit tense of these verbs has a **u** in the stem. Note that the endings are the same as for the four verbs in **Lección 12**, which have i-stems in the preterit tense.

- The English equivalents are **estuve**, *I was*; **puse**, *I put, did put, I placed, did place*; **tuve**, *I had, did have*. **Poder** in the preterit means *to succeed in doing something*: **Pudimos** visitar las ruinas mayas, *We were able (managed) to visit the Mayan ruins*. **Saber** in the preterit usually means *to find out, to learn about something*: **Cuando lo supe**, los llamé, *When I found out (learned) about it, I called them*.

Práctica 1   Complete each sentence with the corresponding form of the preterit indicative tense of **estar**, **poder**, **poner**, **saber**, or **tener**.

1. Ayer yo _____ que ir al centro.   2. (Yo) _____ buscando la librería extranjera casi dos horas.   3. Esta mañana nosotros _____ que te interesaban ciertas revistas

españolas.   4. ¿Dónde las _____ (tú)?   5. Creo que (yo) las _____ en una silla de mi cuarto.   6. Ayer (yo) _____ una carta de mis padres.   7. Me dicen que (ellos) _____ dos semanas en México.   8. Durante el viaje (ellos) _____ visitar la antigua ciudad de Teotihuacán.   9. Nosotros _____ en México el año pasado, pero no salimos de la capital.   10. Cuando (nosotros) _____ el precio de la excursión, decidimos que no nos interesaba.   11. ¿_____ Uds. tiempo para ir al teatro anoche?   12. Estábamos ocupados y no _____ ir.   13. Yo tampoco _____ tiempo para ir.   14. Además, esta mañana (yo) _____ que la comedia es muy mala.   15. Elena compró entradas para esta noche, pero no sabe dónde las _____.

Actividades y práctica: A

B. Verbs with spelling changes in the preterit and in formal commands
(Verbos con cambios ortográficos en el pretérito y en los mandatos formales)

| | | First-Person Singular | |
	Stem	*Preterit*	*Formal Commands*
c → qu	busc-	busqué	busque(n) Ud(s).
g → gu	lleg-	llegué	llegue(n) Ud(s).
z → c	comenz-	comencé	comience(n) Ud(s).

- Verbs ending in **-car**, **-gar**, and **-zar** undergo spelling changes in the preterit and in the **Ud.** and **Uds.** commands. In the case of verbs ending in **-car** and **-gar**, the change is made in order to keep the sound of the final consonant of the stem. In the case of verbs ending in **-zar**, the change is merely in spelling, since **z** should not be written before **e** or **i**.

- Recall that **comenzar** is also a stem-changing verb in the present tense: **comienzo**, **comienzas**, **comienza**, **comenzamos**, **comenzáis**, **comienzan**. Therefore, the same stem changes occur in the command forms: **comience(n) Ud(s)**.

- Other verbs with these spelling changes include the following:

-car	practicar, sacar, tocar
-gar	entregar, pagar
-zar	almorzar (ue), cruzar, gozar

Práctica 2   Rewrite the following sentences, changing the present tense forms to the preterit forms.

1. Yo llego al hotel temprano. _____

2. Yo pago la cuenta. _____

3. Busco objetos de cerámica. _____

4. Saco muchas fotografías. _____

5. El viernes comienzo a prepararme para el viaje. _____

6. Yo almuerzo temprano. _____

7. Gozo de las montañas. _____

8. ¿Qué toco para la fiesta? _____

9. No practico esta semana. _____

10. Envuelvo mal el paquete; no lo entrego. _____

Práctica 3   Complete with the correct formal command forms.

1. (buscar) _____ Ud. las llaves, por favor.

2. (llegar) _____ Ud. a tiempo.

3. (practicar) No _____ Uds. esa canción.

4. (entregar) No _____ Uds. el dinero ahora.

5. (cruzar) _____ Uds. la calle ahora.

6. (pagar) _____ Uds. con tarjeta de crédito.

7. (comenzar) _____ Ud. ahora.

8. (gozar) _____ Ud. de la playa este fin de semana.

C. Direct and indirect object pronouns used together
(El uso conjunto de los pronombres directos e indirectos)

El dependiente **nos las** enseñó.	*The clerk showed them to us.*
Te los compro, querida.	*I'll buy them for you, dear.*
El dependiente **se los** trajo a la señora Ramos.	*The clerk brought them to Mrs. Ramos.*

- Indirect object pronouns precede direct object pronouns when both are used with the same verb.

- When both pronouns are in the third person, **se** replaces the indirect **le** or **les**. Never use two pronouns together that begin with l. Since **se** in this context may mean *to him, her, you, it,* or *them,* the prepositional forms **a él, a ella, a Ud.,** etc., are often required for clarity.

Miguel **se lo** entregó $\begin{cases} \text{a él.} \\ \text{a ella.} \\ \text{a Ud.} \\ \text{a ellos.} \\ \text{a ellas.} \\ \text{a Uds.} \end{cases}$ *Michael handed it* $\begin{cases} \textit{to him.} \\ \textit{to her.} \\ \textit{to you} \text{ (formal sing.).} \\ \textit{to them.} \\ \textit{to them} \text{ (f.).} \\ \textit{to you} \text{ (pl.).} \end{cases}$

- Reflexive pronouns precede any other object pronoun.

    La señora Ramos **se los** puso.   *Mrs. Ramos put them on.*

¡Atención!   An accent is written over the final syllable of the verb when two pronouns are added to the infinitive: **él quiere *dármelos*,** *he wants to give them to me.* An accent is written on the next to the last syllable of an affirmative command or an **-ndo** form when either one or two pronouns are added: **en*vuél*vamelo, por**

favor, *wrap it for me, please*; **ella está envolviéndolo**, *she is wrapping it*; **ella está envolviéndomelo**, *she is wrapping it for me.*

Práctica 4   Rewrite each sentence, substituting the correct object pronoun for each noun and article in italics, placing it in the correct position, and making all necessary changes.

1. Ana me vendió *el anillo*. _____

2. Le devolví *las cartas*. _____

3. Me llevé *las camisas*. _____

4. Te compré *la pulsera*. _____

5. Lupe se puso *las joyas*. _____

6. Póngase Ud. *los aretes*. _____

7. No les dé Ud. *los recibos*. _____

8. No pude traerle *el regalo*. _____

9. Están lavándome *el coche*. _____

10. Acabo de decirle *la verdad*. _____

Práctica 5   Answer each question affirmatively, substituting the correct object pronoun for the direct object noun and making any other necessary changes.

> MODELS: —¿Le llevó Ud. a ella los anuncios? → —Sí, se los llevé a ella.
> —¿Vas a mandarle a ella la cuenta? → —Sí, voy a mandársela a ella.

1. ¿Le dio Ud. a ella el cheque? _____

2. ¿Les enseñó Ud. a ellos las compras? _____

3. ¿Le devolvió Ud. a Lupe los regalos? _____

4. ¿Le entregó Ud. a ellas la mercancía? _____

5. ¿Vas a comprarles los boletos a ellos? _____

6. ¿Necesitas llevarle el dinero a Luis? _____

7. ¿Puede darle Ud. las fotos a él? _____

8. ¿Quiere dejarle Ud. la artesanía a Marta? _____

 Actividades y práctica: B, C

D. Demonstrative pronouns   *(Los pronombres demostrativos)*

this (one)	*these (ones)*	*that (one)*	*those (ones)*
éste	éstos	ése, aquél	ésos, aquéllos
ésta	éstas	ésa, aquélla	ésas, aquéllas

- The demonstrative pronouns, **éste, ése, aquél**, etc., are the same in form and use as the demonstrative adjectives[1], except that demonstrative pronouns have a written accent mark and the noun is deleted.

Me gustan estos collares y **ésos**.	*I like these necklaces and those.*
Compra aquella pulsera y **ésta**.	*Buy that bracelet and this one.*

- The demonstratives **éste, ésta** (-os, -as) often express *the latter* in English.

El dependiente se los enseña a la señora Ramos. **Ésta**, poniéndoselos, le pregunta el precio.	*The clerk shows them to Mrs. Ramos. The latter, (while) putting them on, asks him the price.*

- The neuter demonstrative forms **esto, eso, aquello** are used when referring to a general idea, an action, or something that has not been identified.

Esto me parece interesante.	*This seems interesting to me.*
Eso me interesa.	*That interests me.*
¿Qué es **aquello**?	*What's that (over there)?*

Práctica 6   Rewrite each sentence, substituting the corresponding demonstrative pronoun for the demonstrative adjective and noun in italics.

1. Me interesan *estos collares*. _____

2. *Esa cartera* es de cuero. _____

3. ¿Le gustan a ella *aquellas pulseras*? _____

4. ¿Me envuelve Ud. *esos aretes*? _____

5. ¿Nos enseña Ud. *aquel anilo*? _____

6. *Estas hamacas* no son caras. _____

Práctica 7   Respond negatively to each question, using an appropriate demonstrative pronoun.

MODEL: —¿Qué anillo acabas de comprar? ¿Este? →
        —**No, acabo de comprar ése.**

1. ¿Qué pulsera vas a devolver? ¿Ésta? _____

2. ¿Qué collar acabas de ver? ¿Éste? _____

3. ¿Cuál de los prendedores de plata te gusta más? ¿Ése? _____

4. ¿Qué aretes de oro son más caros? ¿Éstos? _____

5. ¿Cuál de las hamacas quieres para el patio? ¿Ésa? _____

6. ¿Qué artesanías te parecen más finas? ¿Ésas? _____

---

1. See *Spanish On Your Own*, Vol. I, **Lección 6**.

Actividades y práctica: D

E. Uses of **volver** and **devolver**   *(Los usos de volver y devolver)*

■ **Volver** means *to return, go back*.

Volvimos a la joyería.	*We returned (went back) to the jewelry shop.*
Volvimos para ver la pulsera.	*We went back in order to see the bracelet.*

■ **Volver a** + infinitive may mean *to do something once more, again*.

Ella **volvió a ver** los aretes.	*She saw the earrings again.*

■ **Devolver** means *to return, give* or *send back something*.

El dependiente les **devolvió** el dinero.	*The clerk returned (gave back) the money to them.*

Práctica 8   Complete each sentence with the appropriate form of **volver** or **devolver**.

Mi madre me compró una pulsera pero no me gustó y queríamos _____la. Yo _____ con ella a la joyería. La dependienta no quiso _____le su dinero a mi madre pero le dijo, "Búsquese otra cosa, si quiere". Miramos todas las joyas sin encontrar nada, pero mi madre _____ a la vitrina una vez más y me señaló unos aretes preciosos. Después de hacer el cambio nosotras _____ a casa contentas.

F. **Acabar de** + infinitive   *(Acabar de + el infinitivo)*

■ The present and imperfect tenses of **acabar de** + infinitive are the equivalent of English *have (had) just* + the English past participle.

Acaban de llegar de México.	*They have just arrived from Mexico.*
Acababan de llegar cuando yo llamé.	*They had just arrived when I called.*

Práctica 9   Create sentences to express that the subjects given *have just done* something. (If the elements suggest that a subject *had just done* something when something else happened, use the imperfect tense of **acabar**.)

1. Ellos / devolver / regalo _____

2. Ana / traerme / llave _____

3. Nosotros / hacer / reserva _____

4. Ud. / leer / artículo _____

5. Tú / pagar / cuenta / llegar tus amigos _____

6. Ellas / llegar / sonar el teléfono _____

Actividades y práctica: E

G. Preterit indicative of **traer**   *(El pretérito del indicativo de **traer**)*

Singular	Plural
traje	trajimos
trajiste	trajisteis
trajo	trajeron

- A few verbs have a **j** in the stem of the preterit. Note that the ending for the third-person plural is **-eron: ellos trajeron. Decir** also follows this pattern.
- The English equivalents of **traje, trajiste,** etc., are *I brought, I did bring, you brought, you did bring,* etc.

Práctica 10   Rewrite the questions in the preterit indicative tense, and then answer the questions affirmatively, using the preterit tense.

1. ¿Traes la ropa en ese paquete? _____

   _____

2. ¿Trae tu padre los regalos? _____

   _____

3. Yo traigo el mapa ¿verdad? _____

   _____

4. ¿Traen ellos las llaves? _____

   _____

5. ¿Trae Ud. suficiente dinero? _____

   _____

6. ¿Lo traen Uds. en cheques de viajero? _____

   _____

Repaso

A. Circle the item that does not belong in each series of words.

1. la joyería / la guayabera / el sombrero / el cinturón
2. el recibo / la cuenta / el precio / la vitrina
3. el anillo / el arete / el collar / la hamaca
4. la pulsera / el prendedor / el mercado / la joya

B. Use the following elements to write sentences, changing the infinitives in the middle column to the corresponding form of the present indicative tense. Use each element only once.

Clara y yo	acabar de	a su esposo.
El señor Ramos	devolver	por la joyería.
La señora Ramos	preguntar	llevarnos los aretes.
Tú	dirigirse	las joyas de fantasía.

1. _____

2. _____

3. _____

4. _____

C. Give the Spanish equivalent.

1. After their trip to Spain, Mr. and Mrs. Ramos decided to go back to Mexico. _____

_____

2. During that trip, they were able to visit the Yucatan ruins and other interesting places. _____

_____

3. While they were in Merida, they had time to go shopping. _____

_____

4. They entered a jewelry store to buy some jewels. _____

_____

5. The clerk (*f.*) took a pair of earrings out of the case and showed them to Mrs. Ramos. _____

_____

6. Turning to her husband, she asked, "What do you (*fam. sing.*) think of these?" _____

_____

7. After looking at some bracelets, Mrs. Ramos told the clerk (*f.*), "I'll take this one (with me) for Clara, and that one, for Louise." _____

_____

Expansión

A. Answer the following questions with complete sentences.

1. ¿Dónde estuvo Ud. durante las vacaciones? ¿Pudo Ud. hacer algún viaje? _____

_____

2. ¿Qué cosas pudo hacer Ud. durante esas vacaciones? _____

_____

3. ¿Estuvo Ud. con muchos amigos? ¿Qué cosas le contaron ellos a Ud.? ¿Supo Ud. alguna noticia importante? _____

_____

4. ¿Tuvo Ud. tiempo para ir de compras? ¿Qué cosas compró? _____

_____

5. ¿Tuvo Ud. que devolver algunos regalos? ¿Le devolvieron el dinero a Ud.? _____

_____

6. ¿Cuándo volvió Ud. de sus vacaciones? ¿Qué cosas trajo Ud. de su viaje? _____

_____

B. Write a short letter in Spanish to a friend about a vacation trip you and a friend took to a state or national park: tell him / her when you left and from where; how you traveled; three activities you engaged in; a purchase you made; friends you met; something that delighted you or your companion; whether you had fun or not; and when you returned.

Querido(-a) _____ :

_____

_____

_____

_____

_____

_____

_____

_____

_____

_____

Para comprender y escribir

A. From the three choices offered, select the one that best completes the statement or answers the question you hear and circle it.

1. (a) A una joyería.
   (b) A una vitrina.
   (c) A una joya.

2. (a) el recibo.
   (b) la paja.
   (c) el par.

3. (a) volverlo.
   (b) envolverlo.
   (c) devolverlo.

4. (a) una hamaca.
   (b) un prendedor.
   (c) un paquete.

5. (a) En un par de semanas.
   (b) En el cinturón.
   (c) En el centro.

B. Listen to the question and write a response, following the model.

> MODEL: ¿Vas a estar en la universidad hoy? → **No, estuve en la universidad ayer.**

1. _____
2. _____
3. _____
4. _____
5. _____
6. _____

C. Answer the questions affirmatively, using an object pronoun, as in the model.

> MODEL: ¿Quién buscó las llaves ayer? → **Yo las busqué ayer.**

1. _____
2. _____
3. _____
4. _____
5. _____
6. _____

D. Dictado. You will hear a short paragraph about the trip that señor and señora Ramos took to Mexico. You will hear the paragraph three times. Listen the first time. Write what you hear on the lines provided the second time. Make any necessary corrections the third time.

_____

_____

_____

_____

_____

_____

_____

_____

_____

_____

✵✵✵ VOCABULARIO

acabar to end, finish	la **artesanía** handicraft
el **anillo** ring	la **cartera** pocketbook, wallet
el **arete** earring	el **cenicero** ashtray

la **cerámica** ceramics, pottery
el **cinturón** (*pl.* **cinturones**) belt
el **collar** necklace
    devolver (**ue**) to return, give *or* send back
    dirigir to direct
    entregar to hand (over)
    envolver (**ue**) to wrap (up)
la **guayabera** *shirt with decorative stitching, worn outside trousers*
la **hamaca** hammock
la **joya** jewel; *pl.* jewels, jewelry
la **joyería** jewelry shop (store)
la **lista** list
el **llavero** key chain, key ring
    llevarse to take (away with oneself)
el **lugar** place
el **mercado** market

el **objeto** object
el **oro** gold
la **paja** straw
el **paquete** package
el **par** pair, couple
el **patio** patio, courtyard
la **plata** silver
el **prendedor** pin, brooch
la **pulsera** bracelet
    quizás perhaps
el **recibo** receipt (invoice)
el **regalo** gift
la **ruina** ruin
    sacar (**de**) to take out (of)
el **sombrero** hat
la **vitrina** showcase
    yucateco, -a of (pertaining to) Yucatan

    a ver let's (let me) see
    acabar de + *inf.* to have just + *p.p.*
    al poco rato after a short while
    algo más something more, anything else
    (**el anillo**) **de plata** silver (ring)
    (**el arete**) **de oro** gold (earring)
los **artículos de artesanía** handiwork, work of craftspeople
 la **ciudad de México** Mexico City
    dirigirse a to turn to, direct oneself to, address (*a person*)
    ¿en qué puedo servirle(s)? what can I do for you? how can I help you?
    (**estar**) **en el centro** (to be) downtown
    hacer juego con to match, go (or make a set) with
las **joyas de fantasía** costume jewelry
los **objetos de cerámica** ceramics, pottery objects, pieces of pottery
    preguntar por to ask (inquire) about
    su viaje por España their (his, her, your [*formal*]) trip around Spain
    (**te**) **quedan preciosos** they look great on (you)
    un par de (**semanas**) a couple of (weeks)

Lección 14

- ❂ The past participle
- ❂ The present perfect and pluperfect indicative
- ❂ The past participle used as an adjective
- ❂ Summary of other uses of **haber**
- ❂ **Hace** meaning *ago*, *since*
- ❂ Forms of **oír**

Unas vacaciones fantásticas

Miguel Ramos y su hermana habían ido a pasar sus vacaciones de primavera a Cozumel. Un grupo de chicos y chicas habían ido con ellos. El último día de sus vacaciones, Miguel había buceado mucho y necesitaba descansar un rato. Sus amigos se quedaron en la playa tomando el sol un par de horas, mientras que las chicas habían ido de compras y luego a la peluquería para arreglarse el pelo.[1] Al entrar Miguel en su habitación, el teléfono estaba sonando.

MIGUEL	*(Contestando el teléfono.)* —¡Bueno!
SR. RAMOS	—¡Hola, hijo! Hace apenas unos minutos que los hemos llamado. ¡No contestaba nadie! ¿Cuánto tiempo hace que volvieron?
MIGUEL	—¡Hemos estado afuera todo el día, papá! Yo acabo de volver a la habitación.
SR. RAMOS	—Bueno, es que tu madre y yo estábamos preocupados porque no habíamos recibido noticias de Uds. ¿Cómo lo han pasado?
MIGUEL	—¡Estupendo, papá! Hemos visto pueblos encantadores y ruinas de antiguas ciudades mayas.
SR. RAMOS	—¿Y cómo les han parecido las playas de Cozumel? ¿No son hermosas?
MIGUEL	—Uds. tenían razón. El mar es verde-azul y la arena es tan blanca… ¡Pero el agua… ! Es tan clara que se puede ver el fondo cubierto de corales.
SR. RAMOS	—¡Qué fantástico bucear allí! ¿No? Nosotros aquí tenemos que conformarnos con nadar en la piscina. En fin… Pero, cuéntame, ¿cómo está tu hermana?
MIGUEL	—No se encuentra en su habitación. Había vuelto del centro con sus amigas, y ahora han ido a la peluquería. Se ha puesto muy bronceada y se ve estupenda.
SR. RAMOS	—Miguel, hay que hablar un poco más alto. Casi no se oye.
MIGUEL	—Yo tampoco puedo oírte bien. Es que la puerta está abierta y hay gente charlando en el corredor.
SR. RAMOS	—¡Me parece que Uds. han disfrutado bastante de estas vacaciones! ¿No has ido de pesca?
MIGUEL	—Pues, sé que la pesca aquí es excelente… ¡Pero papá, ya sabes que a mí me gusta más bucear!
SR. RAMOS	—¡Qué lástima! Bueno, aquí está tu madre que va a saludarte. Quiere saber a qué hora llegan Uds. mañana…

Preguntas sobre el diálogo

1. ¿Por qué habían ido Miguel y su hermana a Cozumel? ¿Quiénes habían ido con ellos? _____

_____

———

1. Remember that the definite article often replaces the possessive adjective with a noun that represents a part of the body or an article of clothing (see *Spanish On Your Own*, Vol I, **Lección 8**).

2. ¿Qué había hecho Miguel el último día de sus vacaciones en Cozumel? _____

_____

3. ¿Qué hicieron ese día sus amigos? ¿Y qué habían hecho las chicas? _____

_____

4. ¿Por qué llamaron por teléfono los padres de Miguel? _____

_____

5. ¿Qué han visto los jóvenes? _____

_____

6. ¿Cómo es el mar y la arena de las playas de Cozumel? ¿Y cómo es el agua? _____

_____

7. ¿Por qué no se encontraba en su habitación la hermana de Miguel cuando llamaron sus padres? _____

_____

8. ¿Por qué le dijo Miguel a su padre que su hermana se veía estupenda? _____

_____

9. ¿Por qué no se podía oír bien cuando Miguel y su padre hablaban por teléfono? _____

_____

10. ¿Por qué no ha ido de pesca Miguel? _____

_____

✿✿✿ Notas gramaticales

A. The past participle (*El participio pasado*)

Formation of Past Participles				
hablar	habl-	+ ado	hablado	spoken
comer	com-	+ ido	comido	eaten
vivir	viv-	+ ido	vivido	lived

- Past participles are regularly formed by adding **-ado** to the stem of **-ar** verbs and **-ido** to the stem of **-er** and **-ir** verbs.
- A written accent over the **í** of **ido** is required when the stem ends in **-a**, **-e**, or **-o**, since no diphthong is formed.

    traer: **traído**, *brought*
    creer: **creído**, *believed*
    leer: **leído**, *read*
    oír: **oído**, *heard*

■ The following verbs have irregular past participles.

Irregular Past Participles						
abrir	**abierto**	opened	hacer	**hecho**	done, made
cubrir	**cubierto**	covered	ir	**ido**	gone
decir	**dicho**	said	poner	**puesto**	put, placed
devolver	**devuelto**	given back	ver	**visto**	seen
envolver	**envuelto**	wrapped (up)	volver	**vuelto**	returned
escribir	**escrito**	written			

B. The present perfect and pluperfect indicative
(El perfecto presente y el pluscuamperfecto del indicativo)

Present Perfect

Singular					
	he			I have	
	has	hablado		you (*fam.*) have	spoken
	ha			he, she has	
Ud.	ha			you (*formal*) have	

Plural					
	hemos			we have	
	habéis	hablado		you (*fam.*) have	spoken
	han			they have	
Uds.	han			you have	

Pluperfect

Singular					
	había			I had	
	habías	comido		you (*fam.*) had	eaten
	había			he, she had	
Ud.	había			you (*formal*) had	

Plural					
	habíamos			we had	
	habíais	comido		you (*fam.*) had	eaten
	habían			they had	
Uds.	habían			you had	

The present perfect tense

■ The present tense of **haber** + the past participle form the present perfect tense.

Ellos **han hecho** un viaje a Yucatán.   *They have taken a trip to Yucatan.*
Han visitado las ruinas mayas.   *They have visited the Mayan ruins.*

■ The present perfect tense is used in Spanish to describe events in the past that are still going on in the present or that have consequences bearing upon the present.

He **estudiado** mucho para esta clase,
    pero el semestre no **ha terminado**
    todavía.

I have studied a lot for this class, but
    the semester hasn't ended yet.

He **estado** de vacaciones y **he**
    regresado muy contento.

I have been on vacation and I have
    come back very happy.

The pluperfect tense

■ The imperfect tense of **haber** + the past participle form the pluperfect tense,
often called the past perfect tense in English.

Yo **había estado** en otras playas
    mexicanas, pero nunca **había ido** a
    Cozumel.

I had been to other Mexican beaches,
    but I had never gone to Cozumel.

■ Spanish, like English, uses the pluperfect tense to describe events that took
place before another event in the past.

Yo **había visitado** la ciudad de
    México y este verano fui a Cozumel.

I had visited Mexico City and this
    summer I went to Cozumel.

¡Atención!   Note the following points: 1. The past participle used with **haber**
always ends in -o: **Ella ha cerrado las ventanas**; *She has closed the windows*;
2. Negative words precede the form of **haber**: **Yo** *nunca* **había ido a Cozumel**; *I*
had never gone to Cozumel; 3. Object pronouns and reflexives precede the form
of **haber**: *Lo* **he hecho**; *I have done it*. If there is a negative word, it comes
between it and the form of **haber**: **Ella nunca** *me* **ha escrito**; *She has never written*
to me.

Práctica I   Complete each sentence with the correct form of the present perfect
indicative tense. Then rewrite it in the corresponding singular or plural form, following
the model.

MODEL: (envolver) ¿_____ _____ vosotros el
            paquete? → ¿**Habéis envuelto** vosotros el paquete?
            ¿**Has envuelto** tú el paquete?

1. (bajar) Nosotros _____ _____ en el ascensor.

_____

2. (vender) ¿_____ _____ Ud. el tocadiscos?

_____

3. (disfrutar) Yo _____ _____ de las vacaciones.

_____

4. (subir) Uds. _____ _____ al cuarto piso.

_____

5. (estar) Yo _____ _____ en el mercado.

_____

6. (escribir) ¿Les _____ _____ tú una tarjeta?

_____

7. (**ver**) Ella _____ _____ las ruinas mayas.

_____

8. (**ponerse**) Yo me _____ _____ muy bronceado.

_____

9. (**ir**) Mis tíos _____ _____ a pescar.

_____

10. (**hacer**) ¿Qué _____ _____ tú durante las vacaciones?

_____

Actividades y práctica: A

Práctica 2   Complete each sentence with the correct form of the pluperfect indicative tense, and then rewrite it in the corresponding singular or plural form, as required.

1. (**traer**) Ellos no _____ _____ sus trajes de baño.

_____

2. (**arreglarse**) Nosotros no nos _____ _____ el pelo.

_____

3. (**creer**) ¿_____ _____ Ud. las palabras del profesor?

_____

4. (**oír**) Nosotros no _____ _____ esos discos.

_____

5. (**volver**) Las jóvenes _____ _____ de la joyería.

_____

6. (**venir**) ¿_____ _____ a tiempo los invitados?

_____

Actividades y práctica: B

Práctica 3   Write an affirmative answer to each question, following the model.

MODEL: ¿Les compró Ud. estampillas? → **Sí, ya se las he comprado.**

1. ¿Les prometió Ud. el dinero? _____

2. ¿Les leyó Ud. los anuncios? _____

3. ¿Les vendió Ud. las joyas? _____

4. ¿Le devolvieron Uds. la pulsera? _____

5. ¿Le dijeron Uds. el precio? _____

6. ¿Les abrieron Ud. las puertas? _____

C. The past participle used as an adjective
(El participio pasado usado como adjetivo)

No se puede estudiar con la puerta **abierta**.	*One cannot study with the door open.*
Hace frío y las ventanas no están **cerradas**.	*It's cold and the windows are not closed.*

■ Past participles may be used as adjectives, in which case they agree with the noun they modify.

■ **Estar** is used with a past participle to describe a state or condition that is the result of a previous action.

—¿Envolviste los regalos? —Sí, ya **están envueltos**.	*"Did you wrap the gifts?" "Yes, they are already wrapped."*
—¿Hicieron Uds. las reservas? —Sí ya **están hechas**.	*"Did you (pl.) make the reservations?" "Yes, they are already made."*

■ Certain verbs like **encontrarse**, **hallarse**, and **verse** are often substituted for **estar** with past participles, although they normally retain in such cases something of their original meaning.

Miguel había nadado mucho y estaba (**se encontraba**, **se hallaba**, **se veía**) cansado.	*Michael had swum a lot and he was (found himself, looked) tired.*

Práctica 4   Write a negative answer to each question, following the model.

MODEL: ¿Pagó Ud. la cuenta? → **No, ya estaba pagada.**

1. ¿Escribió Ud. el anuncio? _____

2. ¿Cubrió Ud. la mesa? _____

3. ¿Puso Ud. la estampilla? _____

4. ¿Preparó Ud. el almuerzo? _____

5. ¿Lavaron Uds. los platos? _____

6. ¿Hicieron Uds. las reservas? _____

7. ¿Envolvieron Uds. los regalos? _____

8. ¿Abrieron Uds. las cartas? _____

9. ¿Pusieon Uds. las estampillas? _____

10. ¿Cobraste los cheques? _____

✪✪✪ Actividades y práctica: C

D. Summary of other uses of **haber**   *(Resumen de otros usos de haber)*

Haber used impersonally

Hay mucha gente en la playa.	*There are a lot of people on the beach.*
No **había** nadie en el hotel.	*There was no one in the hotel.*

Hubo una cena y un baile anoche.	*There was a dinner and a dance last night.*
Ha habido muchas fiestas.	*There have been many parties.*

■ The third-person singular of **haber** is used impersonally, i.e., without a definite personal subject: **hay** (used for **ha**), *there is, there are*; **había**, *there was, there were*; **hubo**, *there was, there were* (meaning *there took place*); **ha habido**, *there has been, there have been.*

Hay que + infinitive

Hay que disfrutar de las vacaciones.	*One must enjoy vacations.*
Hay que descansar de vez en cuando.	*One must (has to) rest once in a while.*
Había que hablar más despacio.	*One (You) had to speak more slowly.*

■ **Hay que** + infinitive means *It is necessary to,* or the indefinite subject *One (You, We, People, etc.) must.* The imperfect **había que** + infinitive is less common.

¡Atención! Remember that when *must* = *to have to,* expressing a personal obligation or necessity, **tener que** + infinitive is used.

Tu madre **ha tenido que ir** a la peluquería.	*Your mother has had to go to the beauty parlor.*
Tienes que verlas, hijo.	*You have to (must) see them, son.*

Práctica 5   Complete with the correct form of **haber**.

1. ¿Cuántos lagos _____ por aquí?

2. _____ un baile ayer en la universidad.

3. ¿Cuántos bailes _____ hasta ahora?

4. Los profesores dicen que _____ que estudiar más.

5. La profesora contestó que _____ que entregar los cuadernos.

6. En aquellos tiempos no _____ residencias en la universidad.

Actividades y práctica: D

E. Hace meaning *ago, since*   (*Hace con el significado de* ago, since)

Los llamé **hace unos minutos.**	*I called you a few minutes ago.*
He vuelto **hace apenas unos días.**	*I returned scarcely a few days ago.*
Hace un rato que llegó.	*It has been a short while since she arrived.*
Hace apenas una hora que hemos salido.	*It's been hardly an hour since we left.*

■ When **hace** is used with an expression of time in a sentence that is in the past tense, it normally means *ago* or *since.*

■ If the **hace** clause comes first in the sentence, **que** usually introduces the main clause.

Práctica 6   Write two answers to each pair of questions, following the model.

MODEL: ¿Cuándo llegó Ud.? ¿Hace una hora? → **Sí, llegué hace una hora. Sí, hace una hora que llegué.**

1. ¿Cuándo volvió Elena? ¿Hace tres días? _____

_____

2. ¿Cuándo sacó Ud. las fotos? ¿Hace un mes? _____

_____

3. ¿Cuándo salieron sus padres de Cuba? ¿Hace quince años? _____

_____

4. ¿Cuándo oyeron Uds. ese disco? ¿Hace una semana? _____

_____

5. ¿Cuándo pagaste la cuenta? ¿Hace seis semanas? _____

_____

6. ¿Cuándo comenzó Ud. a escribir el artículo? ¿Hace dos horas? _____

_____

 Actividades y práctica: E

F. Forms of **oír**   *(Formas del verbo **oír**)*

oír, *to hear*	
Pres. Part.	oyendo
Pres. Ind.	oigo, oyes, oye, oímos, oís, oyen
Pret.	oí, oíste, oyó, oímos, oísteis, oyeron
Sing. Imp.	oye
Past. Part.	oído

- In certain verbs like **oír,** *to hear,* whose stem ends in a vowel, unaccented **i** between vowels is written **y** (note the present participle and the third-person singular and plural preterit forms).
- Note the written accent on **oyó** and on other forms of **oír.**
- **Creer** and **leer** have similar changes in the preterit tense.

Práctica 7   Complete each sentence with the corresponding form of the present indicative tense of **oír**; then rewrite each sentence twice, first in the imperfect tense and then in the preterit indicative tense.

1. ¿_____ ellos la música? _____

_____

2. Rita no _____ mis palabras. _____

_____

3. ¿_____ tú algo? _____

_____

4. Yo no _____ nada. _____

_____

5. ¿Qué _____ Uds.? _____

_____

6. Nosotros _____ la conversación. _____

_____

Práctica 8   Complete each sentence with the appropriate form of **leer** or **creer**.

1. Le dije la verdad a Susana pero ella no me _____. 2. Yo estaba _____ un
libro cuando llamaste.   3. Juan compró el periódico por la mañana y lo _____ por la tarde.
4. Mi madre me ha dicho muchas veces, y siempre la he _____, que es importante viajar.
5. Les escribí una carta a mis primos pero no la _____.

Actividades y práctica: F

Repaso

A. Use the expressions in parentheses in complete sentences.

1. (conformarse con) _____

2. (disfrutar de) _____

3. (encontrarse) _____

4. (la estampilla) _____

5. (hay que) _____

6. (oír) _____

7. (preocuparse por) _____

8. (la tarjeta postal) _____

B. Give the Spanish equivalent.

1. Michael, his sister, and some friends (*m.* and *f.*) have gone to Cozumel to spend their spring vacation.

_____

2. The last day of his vacation, Michael had swum a lot and he needed to rest for a while. _____

_____

3. His friends stayed at the beach sunbathing for a couple of hours. _____

_____

4. Michael had scarcely entered the room when the telephone rang. _____

_____

5. His parents were a bit worried because they had not received news from them. _____

_____

6. It has been scarcely a week since Michael and his sister have been in Cozumel, and they have already

seen charming villages and ancient ruins. _____

_____

7. Michael's sister was not (did not find herself) in her room. She had gone to the beauty parlor. She had

gotten tanned and looked great. _____

_____

Expansión

A. Write answers to these questions, using complete sentences.

1. ¿A qué lugar o lugares le gusta a Ud. ir para pasar las vacaciones? _____

_____

2. ¿A quiénes escribe Ud. tarjetas postales cuando está de vacaciones? _____

_____

3. ¿Hay muchas playas cerca de donde vive Ud.? _____

_____

4. ¿Cuántos años tenía Ud. cuando aprendió a nadar? _____

_____

5. ¿Le gusta a Ud. nadar y correr las olas en el mar? _____

_____

6. ¿Ha oído que es divertido bucear? _____

_____

7. ¿Se pone Ud. bronceado (bronceada) durante el verano? _____

_____

B. Write a short account of a real or imaginary day you spent at the beach. Include the
following: how long ago you made the trip; where you went, and how you traveled;
who your companions were; how long you stayed; whether there were many people
on the beach; what you did there, and how the weather was.

_____

_____

_____

_____

_____

_____

_____

_____

_____

_____

_____

_____

Para comprender y escribir

A. From the three choices offered, select the one that best completes the statement or answers the question you hear and circle it.

1. (a) preocuparse.
   (b) pescar.
   (c) oír.

2. (a) abierta.
   (b) cubierta.
   (c) antigua.

3. (a) Yo tampoco.
   (b) Yo en fin.
   (c) Yo también.

4. (a) peluquería.
   (b) traje de baño.
   (c) piscina.

5. (a) alguna vez?
   (b) hace media hora?
   (c) poco después?

B. Write negative answers to the questions, as in the model. Be sure to use object pronouns where possible.

>   MODEL: ¿Ya les compraste los regalos? → **No, todavía no se los he comprado.**

1. _____
2. _____
3. _____
4. _____
5. _____

C. Answer the questions affirmatively, following the model.

>   MODEL: ¿Has escrito la carta? → **Sí, está escrita.**

1. _____
2. _____
3. _____
4. _____
5. _____
6. _____

D. Dictado. You will hear a short narrative about how the Ramos's spent their vacation in Cozumel. You will hear the narrative three times. Listen the first time. Write what you hear the second time. Make any necessary corrections the third time.

_____

_____

_____

_____

_____

_____

_____

_____

_____

_____

_____

_____

_____

_____

_____

_____

_____

VOCABULARIO

abierto, -a (_p.p. of_ **abrir** _and adj._) open, opened
adentro _adv._ inside, within
afuera _adv._ outside
alto _adv._ loudly
antiguo, -a ancient, old; former (_before a noun_)
apenas _adv._ scarcely, hardly
la **arena** sand
arreglar to arrange, fix
bronceado, -a tanned
cansarse to get tired
claro, -a clear
conformar to adapt, adjust
los **corales** coral
el **corredor** corridor, hall
cubierto, -a (**de**) (_p.p. of_ **cubrir** _and adj._) covered (with)
cubrir to cover
despacio _adv._ slowly
disfrutar (**de** + _obj._) to enjoy
encantador, -ora enchanting, charming

encontrarse (**ue**) to find oneself, be found, be
la **estampilla** stamp
el **fondo** bottom, depth
hallar to find; _reflex._ to find oneself, be found, be
hermoso, -a beautiful, handsome
maya (_m. or f.; also noun_) Maya, Mayan
oír to hear, listen
la **peluquería** beauty parlor (shop), barber shop
la **pesca** fishing
pescar to fish
la **piscina** swimming pool
preocuparse (**por**) to worry, to be or become worried (about)
rápido _adv._ fast
el **traje** suit
último, -a last (in a series)
verde-azul (_m. or f._) greenish blue

alguna vez sometime, ever

arreglarse el pelo to have one's hair done

ayer por la mañana (tarde) yesterday morning (afternoon)

casi no se oye one can hardly (scarcely) hear

¿cómo lo han pasado? how have things gone?

conformarse con to resign oneself to

¿cuánto tiempo hace que Uds. volvieron? how long has it
   been since you returned?

(ella) se ve estupenda (muy bien, mal) (she) looks great (very
   good/well, bad/ill)

en fin in short

es que the fact is (that)

hablar más alto to talk louder, more loudly

hace apenas (unos minutos) que it has been scarcely (a few
   minutes) since

hay que + *inf.* one (you, we, people, etc.) must *or* it is
   necessary to + *verb*

ir de pesca to go fishing

mañana por la mañana (tarde, noche) tomorrow morning
   (afternoon, night *or* evening)

poco después shortly afterward

ponerse + *adj.* to become, get + *adj.*

(yo) tampoco neither can (I), (I) cannot either

la **tarjeta postal** postcard

el **traje de baño** bathing suit

Lección 15

- ❂ The future indicative
- ❂ The conditional indicative
- ❂ Verbs irregular in the future and conditional
- ❂ Uses of the future and the conditional
- ❂ The future and conditional to express probability or conjecture
- ❂ The future perfect and conditional perfect
- ❂ Forms of **jugar**

La Copa Mundial de Fútbol

Jorge y Alberto están en la sala de su apartamento esperando a Luis Sánchez, un estudiante colombiano que acaba de ingresar en la escuela de verano. Lo han invitado a mirar por televisión uno de los partidos de la Copa Mundial de Fútbol. Jorge está hojeando la sección de deportes del periódico.

ALBERTO —¿Habrá algún programa especial antes del partido de fútbol?

JORGE —No lo sé,[1] pero podré decírtelo después de mirar la guía. ¿Qué hora será?

ALBERTO —Es la una y cuarto. Luis dijo que vendría temprano, así que ya debería llegar.

JORGE —Perfecto. El partido no habrá comenzado todavía, pero a la una y media el canal hispano mostrará algunas escenas de la final entre la Argentina y Alemania en la Copa de 1990.

ALBERTO —Este partido de los Estados Unidos contra Colombia será muy emocionante, ¿no te parece?

JORGE —El estadio de la ciudad de Los Ángeles estará completamente lleno.

ALBERTO —¡Cómo me habría gustado a mí estar allí! Así gozaría más del partido y podría participar de la emoción del público.

JORGE —También será un partido difícil. Recuerda que en la Copa Italia 1990 los Estados Unidos no tuvieron mucha suerte.

ALBERTO —Colombia es un equipo importante, pero hoy día este deporte se ha puesto muy popular aquí.

JORGE —¡Ah! Casi que podríamos avanzar a las semifinales… ¡Pronto lo sabremos!

A la una y veinticinco Jorge pone la televisión. Suena el timbre de la puerta. Alberto la abre y él y Luis se saludan. Jorge se acerca y también saluda a Luis.

JORGE —¡Hola, Luis! ¡Pasa! Nos alegramos mucho de verte.

ALBERTO —¿Sabes, Jorge? Luis es muy aficionado a los deportes.

JORGE —¿De veras? ¿Y qué deportes te gustan a ti, Luis?

LUIS —Pues, hombre, en Colombia, cuando estábamos en la escuela secundaria, jugábamos al fútbol siempre. Me encanta este deporte, pero también practicaba el tenis, la natación y me gustaba hacer excursiones en bicicleta.

JORGE —¿Y ahora? ¿Qué deporte practicas en la universidad?

LUIS —Debería jugar más al tenis, pero hasta ahora mis estudios no me han dejado mucho tiempo libre. ¿Te gustaría jugar conmigo, Jorge?

---

1. Remember that **lo** may refer to an action, a statement, or an idea.

JORGE   —Es que siempre hay mucha gente en las canchas. Pero te llamaré uno de estos días para hacer una cita contigo. (*Jorge entra en la cocina y regresa con un plato de maníes y unos refrescos.*)

ALBERTO —Bueno, chicos, ¿nos sentamos? ¡Miren, miren! Ya salen los equipos. ¿Quién ganará?

Preguntas sobre los diálogos

1. ¿Quién es Luis Sánchez? ¿Por qué va él al apartamento de Jorge y Alberto? _____

   _____

2. ¿Cuándo dijo Luis que llegaría? ¿Habrá comenzado el partido a la una y cuarto? _____

   _____

3. ¿Qué mostrará el canal hispano a la una y media? _____

   _____

4. ¿Qué países jugarán en el partido que los jóvenes van a mirar? ¿Cómo será ese partido? _____

   _____

5. ¿Dónde se jugará el partido? ¿Por qué le habría gustado a Alberto estar allí? _____

   _____

6. ¿Qué le recordó Jorge a Alberto? ¿Qué piensa Alberto? _____

   _____

7. ¿Qué deportes practicaba Luis cuando estaba en Colombia? ¿Qué deportes practica él ahora? ____

   _____

8. ¿A qué le gustaría jugar más a Luis? ¿Para qué lo llamará Jorge? _____

   _____

❀❀❀ *Notas gramaticales*

A. The future indicative   *(El futuro del indicativo)*

hablar	leer	escribir
hablaré	leeré	escribiré
hablarás	leerás	escribirás
hablará	leerá	escribirá
hablaremos	leeremos	escribiremos
hablaréis	leeréis	escribiréis
hablarán	leerán	escribirán

- The future indicative tense is regularly formed by adding the endings -é, -ás, -á, -emos, éis, -án to the infinitive of -ar, -er, and -ir verbs.

- Observe that all the endings except the first-person plural have a written accent.

Práctica 1   Combine elements from each column to form five sentences, changing the infinitives to the appropriate forms of the future indicative tense. Use each element only once.

Yo	ganar	la carta	el sábado.
Mis padres	recibir	el paquete	esta noche.
Ud.	ver	la película	el verano que viene.
Nosotras	vender	la bicicleta	pasado mañana.
Tú	contestar	el partido	más tarde.

1. _____

2. _____

3. _____

4. _____

5. _____

Actividades y práctica: A

B. The conditional indicative   *(El condicional del indicativo)*

hablar	*leer*	*escribir*
hablaría	leería	escribiría
hablarías	leerías	escribirías
hablaría	leería	escribiría
hablaríamos	leeríamos	escribiríamos
hablaríais	leeríais	escribiríais
hablarían	leerían	escribirían

- The conditional indicative tense is regularly formed by adding the endings **-ía, -ías, -ía, -íamos, -íais, -ían** to the infinitive of all **-ar, -er,** and **-ir** verbs, except for a few **-er** and **-ir** verbs.

- Observe that all six forms are accented.

Práctica 2   Complete with the corresponding form of the conditional indicative tense of the verb.

1. ¿Te (**gustar**) _____ cenar con nosotros mañana?   2. Nos (**alegrar**) _____ mucho de verte.   3. Luis dijo que él y Alberto (**comer**) _____ con nosotros también.

4. También dijo que nos (**mostrar**) _____ algunos objetos que ha traído de México.   5. Yo creía que Ud. le (**escribir**) _____ de vez en cuando. 6. Uds. no (**deber**) _____ preocuparse por eso.   7. Ellos dijeron que ellos (**subir**) _____ a nuestro cuarto.   8. ¿Qué le (**dar**) _____ nostotros a Alberto para su cumpleaños?   9. ¿No (**deber**) _____ nosotros ir de compras esta tarde?   10. Yo ya sabía que Uds. no (**entender**) _____ mi problema.

Actividades y práctica: B

C. Verbs irregular in the future and conditional
(Verbos irregulares en el futuro y en el condicional)

	Infinitive	Stem	Future	Conditional
Group 1	haber	habr-	**habré**, etc.	**habría**, etc.
	poder	podr-	**podré**, etc.	**podría**, etc.
	querer	querr-	**querré**, etc.	**querría**, etc.
	saber	sabr-	**sabré**, etc.	**sabría**, etc.
Group 2	poner	pondr-	**pondré**, etc.	**pondría**, etc.
	salir	saldr-	**saldré**, etc.	**saldría**, etc.
	tener	tendr-	**tendré**, etc.	**tendría**, etc.
	venir	vendr-	**vendré**, etc.	**vendría**, etc.
Group 3	decir	dir-	**diré**, etc.	**diría**, etc.
	hacer	har-	**haré**, etc.	**haría**, etc.

- The verbs that have an irregular stem in the future have the same irregular stem in the conditional. The endings are the same as those for regular verbs.

- In group (1) the final vowel of the infinitive has been dropped; in (2) the final vowel has been dropped and the glide **d** introduced to facilitate the pronunciation of the consonant groups **lr** and **nr**; and in (3) shortened stems are used.

Práctica 3   Complete the following sentences logically, by using the appropriate forms of the verbs in parentheses in the future indicative tense and supplying the other missing elements.

1. En el año 2010, yo (**tener**) _____ _____ años.

2. El año que viene, mis padres (**poder**) _____ comprar _____.

3. ¿(**querer**) _____ el profesor _____ la excursión mañana?

4. ¿Quién le (**decir**) _____ a Jorge que no _____ quedarnos?

5. ¿Qué (**hacer**) _____ nosotros si _____ el comedor?

6. Mis hermanos (**venir**) _____ mañana para _____ el almuerzo aquí.

7. Estoy seguro de que nadie (**saber**) _____ _____ la paella.

8. Para llegar _____ al estudio, (**haber**) _____ que salir a las doce en punto.

9. Si _____ frío, ¿qué ropa nos (**poner**) _____?

Práctica 4   Complete the following sentences by selecting appropriate words from the list that follows. Use each word only once.

la dirección	hablar	podría	querría
dirían	harías	podríamos	saldríamos
la fiesta	música	pondría	tendría

1. ¿Qué discos _____ nosotros poner durante _____? 2. Yo

_____ discos de _____ cubana. 3. ¿No _____ tú eso

también? 4. ¿Le _____ Uds. eso al profesor? 5. No, nosotros _____ antes

de la clase. 6. ¿_____ Ud. decirme _____ del profesor? 7. Juan me dijo

que (él) no _____ decírmela. 8. Al _____ con él, yo _____

mucho cuidado.

Actividades y práctica: C

D. Uses of the future and the conditional
(Usos del futuro y del condicional)

The future

- The future tense in Spanish is the equivalent of the verb forms with *shall* and *will* in English.

- The impersonal form **habrá** (future of **hay**, *there is, there are*) means *there will be* or, as an interrogative, *will there be*?

Te llamaré mañana.	*I'll call you tomorrow.*
Haremos una cita y **jugaremos** la semana que viene.	*We'll make a date and we shall (we will) play next week.*
Habrá mucha gente en las canchas de tenis esta noche.	*There will be a lot of people at the tennis courts tonight.*
¿**Habrá** una cancha libre esta tarde?	*Will there be a free court this afternoon?*

- Remember that future actions are very frequently expressed in Spanish with the present indicative: **Te** *llamo* **mañana**, *I'll call you tomorrow*; and with **ir a** + infinitive: **Voy a llamarte** **mañana**, *I'm going to call you tomorrow*.

¡Atención!   When *will* means *be willing to*, it is translated by the present tense of **querer**. In the negative, **no querer** may mean *be unwilling to*.

¿**Quieres** jugar al tenis conmigo?	*Will you (Are you willing to) play tennis with me?*

The conditional

- The conditional tense is used in Spanish to express the English equivalent of *would* or *should*.

Me dijo que me **llamaría** uno de estos días. **Haríamos** una cita; **jugaríamos** al tenis.	*He told me that he would call me one of these days. We would make a date; we would play tennis.*

- The conditional is also used to express polite assertions and requests.

Me **gustaría** ganar el partido. ¿**Podrías** practicar conmigo?	*I would like to win the match. Could (Would) you practice with me?*

■ When *should* means *ought to*, *must*, expressing a moral obligation, duty, or customary action, **deber** may be used in all tenses.

Debo jugar más.   *I should (ought to, must) play more.*
Deberías practicar más.   *You should (ought to) practice more.*

¡Atención!   The future and conditional are used after **si** only when it means *whether*; it is never used when **si** means *if*: Él no sabía *si tendría* tempo libre para jugar hoy, *He didn't know whether he would have the free time to play today.*

Práctica 5   Transform the following sentences to express specific plans, using the future tense.

> MODEL: Voy a salir temprano o voy a llegar tarde. → **Saldré temprano; no saldré tarde.**

1. Vamos a ir al cine o vamos a mirar la televisión.

   _____

2. Voy a cenar en un restaurante o voy a comer aquí.

   _____

3. Vas a ir a la fiesta o vas a quedarte en casa.

   _____

4. Ellos van a tomar cerveza o van a tomar refrescos.

   _____

5. Ella va a jugar al béisbol o va a alzar las pesas.

   _____

Práctica 6   Write what the following people would do if they won the lottery, using the conditional tense.

1. Ana y yo / hacer muchos viajes _____

2. tú / no trabajar más _____

3. el equipo de fútbol / comprar un estadio _____

4. mis padres / buscar una casa más grande _____

5. yo / ingresar en la universidad _____

Práctica 7   Complete each sentence with the corresponding form of the future or conditional tense of the verb, as required.

1. ¿Qué programas (**haber**) _____ en la televisión esta tarde?   2. Creo que se (**mostrar**) _____ la final de la Copa Mundial.   3. Jorge dijo que (**jugar**) _____ los equipos de Alemania y de Holanda.   4. ¿Qué equipo (**ganar**) _____?   5. Pronto lo (**saber**) _____ nosotros.   6. Y tú, Alberto, ¿qué equipo (**decir**) _____ tú que va a ganar?   7. No prometió Luis que él (**traer**) _____ maníes y bebidas?   8. No traje nada de comer porque no sabía si (**tener**) _____ (nosotros) tiempo para tomar algo durante el partido.

Actividades y práctica: D, E

E. The future and conditional to express probability or conjecture
(El futuro y el condicional para expresar probabilidad o conjetura)

¿Dónde **estará** Miguel ahora?	*Where do you suppose Michael is now?*
(Probablemente) **mirará** el partido de béisbol.	*He is probably watching the baseball game.*
¿Qué hora **será**?	*What time do you suppose it is?*
(Posiblemente) **serían** las diez cuando el juego terminó.	*It was possibly ten o'clock when the game ended.*
Los Estados Unidos **podrían** ganar el partido.	*The United States could win the game.*

- The future tense is used in Spanish to express probability, supposition, or conjecture concerning an action or state in the present, whereas the conditional expresses the same idea with respect to the past. The adverbs **probablemente**, *probably*, or **posiblemente**, *possibly*, may be added to reinforce the conjecture.

Práctica 8   Rewrite each sentence according to the model and give the English meaning.

> MODEL: Son las cinco. → Serán las cinco. → "It's probably five o'clock."

1. ¿Qué hora es? _____

2. Es la una y media. _____

3. ¿Dónde están las chicas? _____

4. Uds. tienen sed. _____

5. Ellas quieren descansar. _____

6. ¿Qué hace tu compañero? _____

Práctica 9   Rewrite each sentence according to the model and give the English meaning.

> MODEL: Eran las cinco. → Serían las cinco. → "It was probably (must have been, was about) five o'clock."

1. ¿Qué dijeron los alumnos? _____

2. Ellos fueron al cine. _____

3. ¿A qué hora salió Miguel? _____

4. María no sabía la verdad. _____

5. Elena estaba jugando al tenis. _____

6. Los jóvenes miraron el partido por televisión. _____

Actividades y práctica: F

F. The future perfect and conditional perfect

(El futuro perfecto y el condicional perfecto)

	Future Perfect	Conditional Perfect
Singular	habré habrás } hablado habrá	habría habrías } hablado habría
Plural	habremos habréis } hablado habrán	habríamos habríais } hablado habrían

■ These tenses are regularly used as in English and are expressed by *shall* or *will have* + past participle, *must have* + past participle, and *would* or *should have* + past participle.

Hoy para las once **habré comprado** las entradas. Entonces te llamaré.	*By eleven o'clock today, I will (shall) have bought the tickets. I will (shall) call you then.*
Hoy **habría sido** difícil comprar boletos para el juego.	*Today, it would have been difficult to buy tickets for the game.*

Práctica 10   Answer each question, following the model, and give the English meaning.

> MODEL: ¿Ha comprado Luis las entradas? —**Sí, habrá comprado las entradas.** → "Yes, he has probably purchased the tickets."

1. ¿Ha ido María al cine? _____

_____

2. ¿Han llegado tus padres? _____

_____

3. ¿Han salido todos? _____

_____

4. ¿Ha comenzado el partido? _____

_____

Práctica 11   Answer each question and give the English meaning.

> MODEL: ¿Había escrito Carlos la carta? —**Sí, habría escrito la carta.** → "Yes, he had probably written the letter."

1. ¿Habían recibido todas las noticias? _____

_____

2. ¿Había estado enfermo Jorge? _____

_____

3. ¿Había llamado Felipe a Isabel? _____

_____

4. ¿Habían vuelto los estudiantes? _____

_____

G. Forms of **jugar**   (*Formas del verbo jugar*)

Present Indicative Tense	
Singular	*Plural*
juego	jugamos
juegas	jugáis
juega	juegan

¿Dónde **juegan** Uds. al basquetbol?	*Where do you play basketball?*
Ayer **jugué** al voleibol con un grupo de amigos.	*Yesterday I played volleyball with a group of friends.*
Nunca **he jugado** al béisbol.	*I have never played baseball.*
¿Qué equipos **están jugando** ahora?	*What teams are playing now?*

- **Jugar**, *to play* (*a game*), is the only verb in Spanish in which **u** changes to **ue** when the stem is stressed. The first-person singular preterit form is **jugué**. The forms of **jugar** are regular in the other tenses.

- In everyday conversation **jugar** is often used without **a** + article: **jugar tenis** instead of **jugar al tenis**, *to play tennis.*

¡Atención!   Remember that *to play* (*music*) is expressed in Spanish with a different verb, **tocar**: *Tocamos unos discos de salsa y de merengue, We played some salsa and merengue records.*

Práctica 12   Complete with the corresponding forms of **jugar** in the present indicative tense, and then rewrite the sentence in the preterit indicative tense.

1. ¿_____ Uds. al tenis durante las vacaciones?

_____

2. Sí, y nosotros _____ al golf también.

_____

3. Y tú, María, ¿_____ al golf también?

_____

4. Sí, yo _____ al golf todos los días.

_____

5. Tomás no ＿＿＿＿＿＿ al fútbol.

＿＿＿＿＿＿＿＿＿＿＿＿＿＿＿＿＿＿＿＿＿＿＿＿＿＿＿＿＿＿

6. Y sus hermanos no ＿＿＿＿＿＿＿ al fútbol tampoco.

＿＿＿＿＿＿＿＿＿＿＿＿＿＿＿＿＿＿＿＿＿＿＿＿＿＿＿＿＿＿

Repaso

A. Circle the item that does not belong in each series of words.

1. el partido / el juego / la cita / la final
2. el canal / la escena / la televisión / la pesa
3. el aerobismo / la natación / la cancha / el béisbol
4. el deporte / el equipo / el timbre / el jugador

B. Use the expressions in parentheses in complete sentences.

1. (aficionado, -a a) ＿＿＿＿＿＿＿＿＿＿＿＿＿＿＿＿＿＿＿＿＿＿＿

＿＿＿＿＿＿＿＿＿＿＿＿＿＿＿＿＿＿＿＿＿＿＿＿＿＿＿＿＿＿

2. (alegrarse de + *inf.*) ＿＿＿＿＿＿＿＿＿＿＿＿＿＿＿＿＿＿＿＿

＿＿＿＿＿＿＿＿＿＿＿＿＿＿＿＿＿＿＿＿＿＿＿＿＿＿＿＿＿＿

3. (deber) ＿＿＿＿＿＿＿＿＿＿＿＿＿＿＿＿＿＿＿＿＿＿＿＿＿＿＿

＿＿＿＿＿＿＿＿＿＿＿＿＿＿＿＿＿＿＿＿＿＿＿＿＿＿＿＿＿＿

4. (ingresar en) ＿＿＿＿＿＿＿＿＿＿＿＿＿＿＿＿＿＿＿＿＿＿＿＿

＿＿＿＿＿＿＿＿＿＿＿＿＿＿＿＿＿＿＿＿＿＿＿＿＿＿＿＿＿＿

C. Give the Spanish equivalent.

1. George and Albert are waiting for Louis, a Colombian student who has just enrolled in our summer school. ＿＿＿＿＿＿＿＿＿＿＿＿＿＿＿＿＿＿＿＿＿

＿＿＿＿＿＿＿＿＿＿＿＿＿＿＿＿＿＿＿＿＿＿＿＿＿＿＿＿＿＿

2. Albert asks whether there will be some special program before the football match. ＿＿＿＿＿＿＿

＿＿＿＿＿＿＿＿＿＿＿＿＿＿＿＿＿＿＿＿＿＿＿＿＿＿＿＿＿＿

3. Albert doesn't know (it). He'll be able to tell him after looking at the TV guide. ＿＿＿＿＿＿

＿＿＿＿＿＿＿＿＿＿＿＿＿＿＿＿＿＿＿＿＿＿＿＿＿＿＿＿＿＿

4. Louis said he would arrive early; the match will not have started yet. ＿＿＿＿＿＿＿＿＿

＿＿＿＿＿＿＿＿＿＿＿＿＿＿＿＿＿＿＿＿＿＿＿＿＿＿＿＿＿＿

5. George thinks (believes) that the Los Angeles stadium is probably (must be) completely full. ＿＿＿＿＿

＿＿＿＿＿＿＿＿＿＿＿＿＿＿＿＿＿＿＿＿＿＿＿＿＿＿＿＿＿＿

6. Louis and George would like to play tennis; one of these days they will make a date and will play a match. ＿＿＿＿＿＿＿＿＿＿＿＿＿＿＿＿＿＿＿＿＿＿＿＿

＿＿＿＿＿＿＿＿＿＿＿＿＿＿＿＿＿＿＿＿＿＿＿＿＿＿＿＿＿＿

Expansión

A. Write answers to these questions, using complete sentences.

1. ¿Qué deportes le interesan a Ud. más? _____

   _____

2. ¿Qué deportes practica Ud. ahora? _____

   _____

3. ¿Qué deportes practicaba Ud. en la escuela secundaria? _____

   _____

4. ¿Qué harás hoy después de estudiar? _____

   _____

5. ¿Adónde irás este fin de semana? _____

   _____

6. ¿Qué te gustaría hacer en el futuro? _____

   _____

B. Complete the following dialogue. Luis, a student from Colombia, discusses with you a semifinal match of the NCAA tournament held the previous evening.

USTED —¡Hola, Luis! ¿Qué hay de nuevo?
LUIS   —¡Tan ocupado como siempre. A propósito, ¿fuiste a los partidos semifinales de basquetbol anoche?

USTED —_____
LUIS   —Yo no pude ir tampoco. Pero verías algunos minutos de los partidos por televisión, ¿verdad?

USTED —_____
LUIS   —¿No dirías que nuestro equipo jugó muy bien?

USTED —_____
LUIS   —¿Crees que nuestro equipo podrá ganar la final la semana que viene?

USTED —_____
LUIS   —Sí, tendremos que jugar muy bien. El jugador cubano del equipo de ellos es brillante, ¿verdad?

USTED —_____
LUIS   —¡Con mucho gusto! ¿Habrá que salir temprano?

USTED —_____
LUIS   —Pues, estaré preparado para salir a esa hora.

USTED —_____

Para comprender y escribir

A. From the three choices offered, select the one that best completes the statement or answers the question you hear and circle it.

1. (a) maní.
   (b) aficionado.
   (c) guía.

2. (a) la pelota?
   (b) el gimnasio?
   (c) el equipo?

3. (a) los deportes.
   (b) la natación.
   (c) las pesas.

4. (a) basquetbol.
   (b) estadio.
   (c) timbre.

5. (a) ¡Cuánto me alegro!
   (b) ¡No lo sé!
   (c) ¡Me acerco mucho!

B. Answer the questions affirmatively. Then give an alternate negative response, as in the model.

> MODEL: ¿Van a ir Uds. al juego esta noche o van a regresar a la biblioteca?
> → **Nosotros iremos al juego; no regresaremos a la biblioteca.**

1. _____
2. _____
3. _____
4. _____
5. _____

C. Write contradictions to the statements made, using the conditional, as in the model.

> MODEL: Voy a comprar una casa en México. → **¡Yo no compraría una casa en México!**

1. _____
2. _____
3. _____
4. _____
5. _____

D. Dictado. You will hear a short narrative about plans Jorge and Alberto have for going to a basketball game. You will hear the narrative three times. Listen the first time. Write what you hear on the lines provided the second time. Make any necessary corrections the third time.

_____

_____

_____

_____

_____

_____

_____

_____

_____

_____

❁❁ VOCABULARIO

acercarse (a + *obj.*) to approach
el **aeróbic** aerobics
aficionado, -a (a) fond (of); *noun* fan
Alemania Germany
alzar to lift
aún *adv.* even; still, yet
avanzar to advance
el **basquetbol** basketball
el **béisbol** baseball
la **bicicleta** bicycle
el **canal** channel
la **cancha** (tennis) court
la **cita** date, appointment
la **cocina** kitchen
completamente *adv.* completely
contra *prep.* against
la **copa** cup
deber to owe; must, should, ought to
el **deporte** sport
la **emoción** (*pl.* **emociones**) excitement; emotion
emocionante (*m.* or *f.*) exciting, thrilling
el **equipo** team
la **escena** scene
el **estadio** stadium
la **final** final match (game), finals
el **fútbol** soccer, football
el **gimnasio** gym
el **golf** golf
la **guía** guidebook; guide (*f.*)
hispano, -a Spanish, Hispanic

hojear to turn the pages of
ingresar (en + *obj.*) to enter, enroll (in)
Italia Italy
el **juego** game
el **jugador** player (*m.*)
la **jugadora** player (*f.*)
jugar (ue) (a + *obj.*) to play (a game)
libre (*m.* or *f.*) free, available
el **maní** (*pl.* **maníes**) peanut (Am.)
mostrar (ue) to show
mundial (*m.* or *f.*) world (*adj.*)
la **natación** swimming
participar (**de**) to participate (in)
el **partido** game, match
la **pelota** ball
perfecto *adv.* perfectly
la **pesa** weight
poner to turn on (radio, televisión, CD player)
posiblemente *adv.* possibly
probablemente *adv.* probably
la **profesión** (*pl.* **profesiones**) profession
profesional (*m.* or *f.*) professional
el **público** audience, public
la **raqueta** racket
la **sección** (*pl.* **secciones**) section
secundario, -a secondary
la **semifinal** semifinal match
el **tenis** tennis
el **timbre** (door)bell
el **voleibol** volleyball

alegrarse (**mucho**) **de** + *inf.* to be (very) glad to (+ *verb*)
alzar (**las**) **pesas** to lift weights
así que *conj.* so, so that
la **cancha** (**de tenis**) (tennis) court
casi que *adv.* nearly
la **Copa Mundial** World Cup
de veras really, truly
en bicicleta by (on a) bicycle
la **escuela de verano** summer school
la **escuela secundaria** secondary school, high school

el **fútbol americano** football
   hacer (el) aeróbic to do aerobics
   hacer ejercicio to exercise
   hacer una excursión to take (make) an excursion (a trip)
   Los Ángeles Los Angeles
   mirar por televisión to watch on TV
   no lo sé I don't know
   ¡pasa (tú)! come in!
   practicar un deporte to play a sport
   ¿qué hora será? I wonder what time it is?
   se ha puesto (muy) popular it has become (very) popular
la **sección de deportes** sports section
   ser aficionado, -a (a) to be fond (of)
el **tiempo libre** free time
el **timbre de la puerta** doorbell
   tocar a la puerta to knock on the door
   tocar el timbre to ring the doorbell

Repaso, Lecciones 12–15: Appendix C

Lección 16

- ❁ Stem-changing **-ir** verbs
- ❁ More familiar singular (**tú**) command forms
- ❁ Comparisons of inequality: Irregular comparative adjectives
- ❁ Comparisons of inequality: Regular and irregular comparative adverbs
- ❁ Comparisons of equality
- ❁ The absolute superlative

En el hospital de la universidad

Un domingo de primavera, después de asistir a misa en la iglesia de San José,[1] Rita y Jaime fueron al hospital a visitar a una buena amiga suya.

JAIME	(*En el corredor del hospital.*) —Nunca he visto un hospital tan grande como éste… ¡Ah! Ésta será su habitación.
ANA	—¡Ay, pero qué sorpresa tan agradable![2] ¿Uds. aquí?
RITA	—Hemos venido a traerte unas flores. Ayer te llamamos a la residencia y una compañera tuya nos dijo que estabas enferma. Dinos, Ana, ¿qué te pasa?[3]
ANA	—Pesqué un resfriado terrible la semana pasada. Tenía fiebre muy alta, me dolían mucho el pecho y la espalda… Me ha dicho el médico que tengo una pulmonía viral.
JAIME	—¡Qué barbaridad! ¡Por eso estás aquí! ¿Y te sientes algo mejor ahora?
ANA	—No tengo tanta fiebre como ayer, pero todavía me duele muchísimo todo el cuerpo,[4] y tengo dolor de cabeza.
JAIME	—Al menos podrás descansar algo en el hospital.
ANA	—¡Qué va! Aquí me despiertan a cada rato, me toman la temperatura, la presión… Anoche no podía dormirme. Estuve despierta la mayor parte de la noche. (*Ana comienza a toser mucho.*)
RITA	—¡Dios mío! ¡Cómo tose esta mujer! Ya no hables tanto y toma un poco de jugo.
ANA	—Pídele a la enfermera las píldoras[5] para la congestión, por favor.

Rita sale a buscar a la enfermera y las dos regresan al cuarto.

ENFERMERA	—El médico también le ha recetado este jarabe para la tos y unas gotas para la nariz.
ANA	—En la vida he tomado tantas medicinas. Les digo que no me divierte nada estar en cama. ¡Es una gran molestia!
JAIME	—¡Cálmate, mujer! Hazle caso al médico.
RITA	—Con paciencia vas a mejorarte muy pronto. Descansa… y te voy a dar un consejo: de ninguna manera vuelvas a clase si no te sientes bien.
ANA	—Uds. son mis mejores amigos. Gracias por la visita, y por estas flores hermosísimas que me han traído.

---

1. **San José**, *St. Joseph*. **San** is used for **Santo** before masculine names of saints not beginning with **Do-** and **To-**.

2. **¡Qué sorpresa tan agradable!**, *What a pleasant surprise!* In Spanish exclamations, when an adjective follows the noun, **tan** or **más** regularly precedes the adjective.

3. Literally, *what is happening to you?*

4. Note that sentences with **doler**, *to hurt, ache*, are constructed in the same way as those with **gustar**. With some body parts the expression **tener dolor de**, *to have an ache of* or *in the* conveys the meaning of **doler**: **Tengo dolor de cabeza** or **Me duele la cabeza**, *I have a headache (My head hurts)*. Remember that the definite article is used instead of the possessive adjective with a body part.

5. **Pídele a la enfermera las píldoras**, *Ask the nurse for the pills*. Certain verbs, such as **decir**, **pedir**, and others to be given later, require a personal object to be expressed as an indirect object. Remember that the corresponding indirect object pronoun (**le** in this example) is also normally used.

RITA   (*Bajando en el ascensor.*) —Con todos esos síntomas, Ana debería quedarse varios días en el hospital. Una pulmonía viral es algo muy serio.

JAIME   (*Riéndose divertido.*) —¡Cómo se ve que estás preparándote para estudiar medicina!

Preguntas sobre los diálogos

1. ¿Qué hicieron Rita y Jaime un domingo de primavera? _____

_____

2. ¿Qué le llevaron a Ana sus dos amigos? ¿Cómo supieron ellos que Ana estaba enferma? _____

_____

3. ¿Qué le pasó a Ana? ¿Qué le ha dicho el médico? ¿Cómo se siente ella? _____

_____

4. ¿Por qué no puede Ana descansar en el hospital? _____

_____

5. ¿Por qué necesita Ana unas píldoras para la congestión? _____

_____

6. ¿Quién sale a buscar a la enfermera? _____

_____

7. ¿Qué medicinas le ha recetado el médico a Ana? _____

_____

8. ¿Por qué no le divierte a Ana estar en cama? _____

_____

9. ¿Qué le dice Rita a su amiga? _____

_____

10. ¿Por qué debería quedarse Ana varios días en el hospital? _____

_____

Notas gramaticales

A. Stem-changing **-ir** verbs
*(Verbos terminados en **-ir** con cambios en la raíz)*

	sentir, *to feel*	**dormir,** *to sleep*	**pedir,** *to ask* (*for*)
Present Indicative	siento	duermo	pido
	sientes	duermes	pides
	siente	duerme	pide
	sentimos	dormimos	pedimos
	sentís	dormís	pedís
	sienten	duermen	piden

	sentir, *to feel*	dormir, *to sleep*	pedir, *to ask (for)*
Preterit	sentí	dormí	pedí
	sentiste	dormiste	pediste
	sintió	**durmió**	**pidió**
	sentimos	dormimos	pedimos
	sentisteis	dormisteis	pedisteis
	sintieron	**durmieron**	**pidieron**
-ndo *Form*	**sintiendo**	**durmiendo**	**pidiendo**

- Remember that certain -ar and -er verbs have a stem change in the present tense: e becomes ie (**pensar: yo pienso**, etc.), and o becomes ue (**volver: yo vuelvo**, etc.).[1] Certain -ir verbs have similar changes (**sentir: yo siento**, etc.; **dormir, yo duermo**, etc.).

- These -ir verbs like **sentir** and **dormir** also undergo stem changes in the third-person singular and plural of the preterit and in the **-ndo** form: e changes to i, and o changes to u. Such stem-changing verbs are designated in the vocabularies: **sentir (ie, i)**, **dormir (ue, u)**. **Divertir(se)**, *to amuse, enjoy oneself*, follows the same pattern.

- In other -ir verbs, like **pedir**, the stem change in the present, the preterit, and the **-ndo** form is always e to i (never to ie). These verbs are designated **pedir (i, i)**. **Servir**, *to serve*, and **reír(se)**, *to laugh*, follow the same pattern.[2]

Atención!   The verb **pedir** means *to ask for, ask (request) someone to do something, ask a favor*: **Pídele** a la enfermera un jarabe para la tos, *Ask the nurse for a cough syrup*. **Preguntar** means *to ask a question*: **Pregúntale** a la enfermera si el médico recetó algo, *Ask the nurse whether the doctor prescribed anything*.

Práctica 1   Complete with the corresponding form of the present indicative tense of the verb, and then rewrite the sentence in the preterit indicative tense.

(**divertirse**)   1. —¿Te _____ mucho en el baile?

_____

2. —Sí, me _____ muchísimo.

_____

3. Pero nosotros no nos _____ mucho.

_____

---

1. See *Spanish On Your Own*, Vol. I, **Lección 8**.
2. Note that a written accent mark on the i is required for the present tense forms of **reír(se)** so that no diphthong is formed: (**me**) **río**, (**te**) **ríes**, (**se**) **ríe**, (**nos**) **reímos**, (**os**) **reís**, (**se**) **ríen**.

4. Yo los jóvenes no se _____ tampoco.

_____

(**dormir**)   5. Yo no _____ bien en el hospital.

_____

6. ¿_____ tú bien en el campo?

_____

7. Nosotros _____ bien en el campo.

_____

8. Los muchachos _____ mejor en casa.

_____

(**pedir**)   9. —¿Qué _____ tú?

_____

10. —Yo _____ un vaso de agua.

_____

11. —¿Qué _____ Uds.?

_____

12. —Nosotros no _____ nada.

_____

Actividades y práctica: A

B. More familiar singular (**tú**) command forms
*(Más formas para el mandato con **tú**)*

Verbs with irregular **tú** commands
(Verbos con formas irregulares para el mandato con tú)

- The following frequently used verbs have irregular **tú** command forms:

Infinitive	Affirmative Command		Negative Command	
decir	**di** (tú)	say, tell	**no digas** (tú)	don't say (tell)
hacer	**haz** (tú)	do, make	**no hagas** (tú)	don't do (make)
ir	**ve** (tú)	go	**no vayas** (tú)	don't go
poner	**pon** (tú)	put, place	**no pongas** (tú)	don't put (place)
salir	**sal** (tú)	go out, leave	**no salgas** (tú)	don't go out (leave)
ser	**sé** (tú)	be	**no seas** (tú)	don't be
tener	**ten** (tú)	have	**no tengas** (tú)	don't have
venir	**ven** (tú)	come	**no vengas** (tú)	don't come

Verbs with stem changes in **tú** commands
*(Verbos con cambios en la raíz para el mandato con **tú**)*

Infinitive	Present Indicative	Affirmative Command	Negative Command
sentir to feel	**él siente** he feels	**siente** (**tú**) feel	**no sientas** (**tú**) don't feel
dormir to sleep	**él duerme** he sleeps	**duerme** (**tú**) sleep	**no duermas** (**tú**) don't sleep
pedir to ask for	**él pide** he asks for	**pide** (**tú**) ask for	**no pidas** (**tú**) don't ask for

- Verbs with a stem change in the third-person singular of the present indicative (e → ie, o → ue, and e → i) use this form to express the **tú** commands. (See page 60 for other -**ir** verbs that follow this pattern.)
- Remember that the ending for the negative **tú** command is -**as** for the -**ir** verbs.

Verbs with spelling changes in negative **tú** commands
*(Verbos con cambios ortográficos para el mandato negativo con **tú**)*

Infinitive	Preterit	Negative Command
buscar	**yo busqué** I looked for	**no busques** (**tú**) don't look for
llegar	**yo llegué** I arrived	**no llegues** (**tú**) don't arrive
comenzar	**yo comencé** I began	**no comiences** (**tú**) don't begin

- Verbs that have spelling changes in the first-person singular of the preterit tense have the same spelling changes in the negative familiar **tú** command in order to maintain the same sounds of the infinitive endings -**car**, -**gar**, and -**zar**. The **c** changes to **qu**; **g** changes to **gu**; and **z** changes to **c**. (See page 19 for other verbs that follow this pattern.)

¡Atención!   Remember that the appropriate reflexive pronoun must be used with a reflexive verb. In affirmative commands the reflexive pronoun is attached to the verb form; in negative commands it immediately precedes the verb form.

Infinitive	Affirmative Command	Negative Command
levantarse	**levántate** (**tú**) get up	**no te levantes** (**tú**) don't get up
divertirse	**diviértete** (**tú**) enjoy yourself	**no te diviertas** (**tú**) don't enjoy yourself
dormirse	**duérmete** (**tú**) go to sleep, fall asleep	**no te duermas** (**tú**) don't go to sleep, don't fall asleep
reírse	**ríete** (**tú**) laugh	**no te rías** don't laugh

Práctica 2   Complete each sentence with the appropriate **tú** command forms of the verbs given.

1. (**Abrir**) _____ la puerta, pero no (**cerrar**) _____ las ventanas.   2. No lo (**pensar**) _____ tanto, no se lo (**decir**) _____ a ellos y no (**hacer**)

_____ nada todavía.   3. (**Recordar**) _____ que mañana salimos temprano, no (**venir**) _____ muy tarde; (**volver**) _____ pronto.   4. No (**jugar**) _____ al tenis con tus amigos hoy; tenemos invitados, no (**llegar**) _____ tarde; (**ser**) _____ puntual, por favor.   5. (**Tener**) _____ paciencia, no (**cruzar**) _____ la calle todavía.   6. No (**almorzar**) _____ en ese restaurante, (**buscar**) _____ otro menos caro.   7. No (**ir**) _____ al gimnasio esta noche, (**acostarse**) _____ temprano y no (**cansarse**) _____ tanto.   8. No (**quedarse**) _____ en casa el sábado por la noche, (**hacer**) _____ algo, (**salir**) _____ con alguien, (**ir**) _____ a alguna fiesta, (**divertirse**) _____ un poco, no (**estudiar**) _____ siempre.

Práctica 3   Answer first with an affirmative singular **tú** command, and then with a negative one.

1. ¿Pongo las flores en la mesa? _____

2. ¿Salgo en seguida? _____

3. ¿Digo el precio? _____

4. ¿Vuelvo hoy? _____

5. ¿Me siento aquí? _____

6. ¿Entrego las cartas? _____

7. ¿Almuerzo ahora? _____

8. ¿Pago en efectivo? _____

Actividades y práctica: B, C

C. Comparisons of inequality: Irregular comparative adjectives

(La comparación de desigualdad: Adjetivos comparativos irregulares)

Adjective	Regular Comparative	Irregular Comparative
bueno good		(el, la) **mejor** (the) better, best
malo bad		(el, la) **peor** (the) worse, worst
grande[1] large	**más grande** (the) larger, largest	(el, la) **mayor** (the) older, oldest
pequeño small	**más pequeño** (the) smaller, smallest	(el, la) **menor** (the) younger, youngest

- A few adjectives in Spanish have irregular comparative forms: **mejor**, **peor**, **mayor**, and **menor**. **Mejor** and **peor** are normally used to compare qualities or

---

1. The adjective **grande** becomes **gran** before a masculine or feminine singular noun and generally means _great_. The full form is used before plural nouns: **un gran amigo**, _a great friend_; **una gran enfermera**, _a great nurse_; **unos grandes médicos**, _some great doctors_.

abilities; **mayor** and **menor** to compare ages; and **grande** and **pequeño** to compare size.

Ellas son **mejores** (**peores**) estudiantes que Rita.	*They are better (worse) students than Rita.*
Antonio es **mayor** (**menor**) que su hermano.	*Anthony is older (younger) than his brother.*
Estos apartamentos son más **grandes** (**pequeños**) que los que vimos ayer.	*These apartments are bigger (smaller) than the ones we saw yesterday.*

■ To express the superlative degree in a comparison, the corresponding form of the definite article precedes these adjectives.

Ellas son **las mejores** amigas de Rita.	*They are Rita's best friends.*
Antonio es **el menor** (de los tres).	*Anthony is the youngest (of the three).*

Práctica 4   Complete each sentence with a comparative form of the adjective (**más** or **menos** + *adjective* or irregular comparative form, as appropriate).

1. Estas píldoras son muy buenas; son _____ que las de Ud.

2. Este apartamento tiene cinco cuartos y ése tiene tres; éste es _____ que ése.

3. Felipe tiene 40 años y yo tengo 25; él es _____ que yo.

4. María tiene quince años y tú tienes 32; ella es _____ que tú.

5. Ellos perdieron el partido; su equipo es _____ que nuestro equipo.

6. Esta falda es de talla ocho y aquélla es de talla diez; ésta es _____ que aquélla.

Práctica 5   Complete with the superlative form of each adjective, following the models. (Watch for irregular forms.)

> MODELS: Esta tienda es pequeña. → **Es la más pequeña de todas.**
> Estos carros son viejos. → **Son las más viejos de todas.**

1. Estas sillas con cómodas. _____

2. Este camino es bueno. _____

3. Estas jóvenes som amables. _____

4. Este ejercicio es difícil. _____

5. Estos anillos son grandes. _____

6. Este chico es grande (= viejo). _____

7. Estas chicas son pequeñas (= jóvenes). _____

8. Este hotel es malo. _____

Actividades y práctica: D

D. Comparisons of inequality: Regular and irregular comparative adverbs

(Comparaciones de desigualdad: Adverbios comparativos regulares e irregulares)

Regular comparative adverbs   *(Adverbios comparativos regulares)*

$$\left.\begin{matrix} \text{más} \\ \text{menos} \end{matrix}\right\} + adverb + \text{que} \qquad \left.\begin{matrix} \text{-er} \\ or \\ \left.\begin{matrix} \text{more} \\ \text{less} \end{matrix}\right\} + \text{ly} \end{matrix}\right\} + \text{than}$$

- The constructions with **más** (**menos**) plus **que** used to make comparisons of inequality between nouns[1] are also used to compare adverbs. Note that the comparative adverb (**más tarde, menos rápido,** etc.) is invariable in form.

Tomás llegó **más tarde** que Miguel.	*Thomas arrived later than Michael.*
Tú estás hablando **más alto** que Ana.	*You are speaking more loudly (louder) than Ann.*

Irregular comparative adverbs   *(Adverbios comparativos irregulares)*

- The following adverbs in Spanish have irregular comparative forms:

Adverb		Irregular Comparative	
bien	well	mejor	better, best
mal	badly	peor	worse, worst
mucho	a lot	más	more, most
poco	little	menos	less, least

Carolina canta **bien**, pero tú cantas **mejor** que ella.	*Caroline sings well, but you sing better than she.*
Ramón baila **poco**, pero Luis baila **menos** que él.	*Raymond dances little, but Louis dances less than he.*

¡Atención!   Note that the adverbs **mejor** and **peor** are invariable for gender and number, but the comparative adjectives **mejor** and **peor** have a plural form.

Ellos juegan **peor** (**mejor**) que nosotros.	*They play worse (better) than we.*
Ellos son **peores** (**mejores**) jugadores que nosotros.	*They are worse (better) players than we.*

Práctica 6   Rewrite the sentences, using the comparative form of the adverb, following the model.

> MODEL: Elena habla alto. → **Elena habla más alto que su hermano.**

1. Mario se acuesta tarde. _____

2. Luis se prepara rápidamente. _____

---

1. See *Spanish On Your Own*, Vol. I, **Lección 7**.

3. Jaime trabaja poco. _____

4. Carlos llegó temprano. _____

5. Yo corro rápido. _____

6. Inés pronuncia claro. _____

7. Miguel estudia mucho. _____

8. Jorge lee mal. _____

9. Ellas cantan bajo. _____

10. Nosotros jugamos bien. _____

E. Comparisons of equality   (*La comparación de igualdad*)

With adjectives or adverbs   (*Con adjetivos o adverbios*)

$$
\text{tan} + \left\{ \begin{array}{c} adjective \\ or \\ adverb \end{array} \right\} + \textbf{como} \qquad \text{as (so) . . . as}
$$

Nunca he visto un hospital **tan grande como** éste.
I have never seen a hospital as large as this one.

Rita no está **tan enferma como** Ana.
Rita is not as sick as Ann.

Ella no se siente **tan mal** como Ana.
She doesn't feel as bad as Ann.

With nouns or pronouns   (*Con sustantivos o pronombres*)

$$
\left\{ \begin{array}{c} \textbf{tanto, -a} \\ \\ \textbf{tantos, -as} \end{array} \right\} + \left\{ \begin{array}{c} noun \\ or \\ pronoun \end{array} \right\} + \textbf{como} \qquad \text{as (so)} \left\{ \begin{array}{c} much \\ many \\ well \end{array} \right\} \ldots \text{as}
$$

No tengo **tanto dolor de cabeza como** ayer.
I don't have as (so) much of a headache as yesterday

Hay **tantos médicos como** enfermeras.
There are as many doctors as (there are) nurses.

Tanto él como ella son muy buenos amigos de Ana.
Both he and she are very good friends of Ann. (lit., He as well as she . . .)

With verbs   (*Con verbos*)

$$
\text{verb} + \textbf{tanto como} + \left\{ \begin{array}{c} noun \\ or \\ pronoun \end{array} \right\} \qquad \text{as (so) much . . . as}
$$

| Isabel **estudia tanto como Felipe.** | *Elizabeth studies as much as Phillip.* |
| Ella también **se divierte tanto como él.** | *She also enjoys herself as much as he.* |

¡Atención!   Tanto (invariable in form) and **tan** are adverbs meaning *so much* and *so*, respectively. **Tanto, -a (-os, -as)** used as an adjective means *so much (many)*.

No estudies **tanto.**	*Don't study so much.*
¿Por qué vienen Uds. **tan** pronto?	*Why are you coming so soon?*
No bebas **tanta** cerveza.	*Don't drink so much beer.*
¡Él tiene **tantos** amigos!	*He has so many friends!*

Práctica 7   Complete each sentence with **tanto,-a (-os, -as)**, or **tan**, as required.

1. Pocas personas leen _____ claro como el profesor.

2. Ana ha recibido _____ flores como Elena.

3. Hoy no hace _____ calor como ayer.

4. Ana no ha tosido _____ como anoche.

5. Jaime no ha hecho _____ viajes a Europa como Miguel.

6. ¿Es Elena _____ inteligente como su hermana?

7. ¿Habrá _____ gente en el estadio como el sábado pasado?

8. Jorge no se levanta _____ temprano como Alberto.

Actividades y práctica: E

F. The absolute superlative   *(El superlativo absoluto)*

Estas flores son **muy hermosas (hermosísimas).**	*These flowers are very pretty (extremely pretty).*
Jaime es **muy inteligente (inteligentísimo).**	*James is very intelligent (extremely intelligent).*
Ana tiene **muchísimas amigas.**	*Ann has a great many (a lot of) friends.*
Ellas se divierten **muchísimo.**	*They amuse themselves a lot (a great deal).*

- To express a high degree of quality, without any element of comparison, Spanish uses **muy** before the adjective or adverb, or adds the ending **-ísimo, -a (-os, -as)** to the adjective. The form **-ísimo** is very common in Spanish.

- When **-ísimo** is added, the final vowel is dropped: **grande → grandísimo, hermosa → hermosísima, rápido → rapidísimo.** Adjectives ending in **-ble** change to **-bil: amable → amabilísimo; agradable → agradabilísimo.**

- The absolute superlative form of the adjective **mucho, -a (-os, -as)** is **muchísimo, -a (-os, -as),** *very much (many).* The corresponding form of the adverb **mucho** is **muchísimo,** *very much.* The adverb **muy** is never used before forms of **mucho.**

Práctica 8   Write the corresponding superlative with **-ísimo**.

1. una persona muy alegre _____

2. unos jóvenes muy divertidos _____

3. unas enfermeras muy amables _____

4. un médico muy famoso _____

5. una amiga muy buena _____   8. unas revistas muy interesantes _____

6. unos temas muy difíciles _____   9. unos mapas muy viejos _____

7. un artículo muy aburrido _____   10. una canción muy popular _____

Actividades y práctica: F

Repaso

A. Complete the following exchanges by selecting appropriate words or phrases from the list that follows. Use each word or phrase only once.

un antibiótico	la nariz	la rodilla	mi temperatura
el hospital	no te rías	tan alta	la tos
un jarabe	el pecho	te recetó	tosiste
me duelen	peor	te sientes	un resfriado

1. —La enferma dice que _____ mucho anoche, Ana. ¿Cómo _____ esta mañana?

2. —_____ que ayer. _____ muchísimo la garganta y _____.

3. —Has pescado _____ terrible. ¿Qué _____ el médico?

4. —Me recetó _____. Me dice que _____ no es _____ como antes.

5. —¿Qué te han dado para _____?

6. —La enfermera me trajo _____ y además gotas para _____.

7. —¿Sabías que Carlos se ha lastimado _____ jugando al basquetbol?

8. —_____. Varios compañeros nuestros están en _____.

B. Give the Spanish equivalent, using the familiar forms for *you, yours*.

1. One Sunday, Rita and James went to the hospital to visit a friend (*f.*) of theirs. _____

2. Rita handed Ann some flowers that they had brought (to) her. Ann said, "Thanks, you are my best friends." _____

3. "Tell us, Ann, what's the matter with you? How do you feel?" _____

4. Ann feels somewhat better; she doesn't have as much fever as yesterday, but her entire body still aches. She could not sleep most of the night. _____

5. Ann is not enjoying herself in the hospital, but Rita thinks that she ought to stay there several days. _____

6. Rita gave Ann some advice: "Listen to the doctor, and in no way go back to class if you don't feel well."

_____

_____

Expansión

A. Write answers to these questions, using complete sentences.

1. ¿Cómo se siente Ud. hoy? _____

_____

2. ¿Ha tenido Ud. un resfriado este año? _____

_____

3. ¿Tiene Ud. dolores de cabeza a menudo? _____

_____

4. ¿A quién debemos llamar cuando estamos enfermos? _____

_____

5. ¿Qué recetan los médicos para la tos? _____

_____

6. ¿Es Ud. alérgico(-a) a alguna medicina? _____

_____

7. ¿Cuántas veces ha estado Ud. en el hospital? _____

_____

8. ¿Qué nos traen a veces los amigos cuando estamos en el hospital? _____

_____

B. Write a brief essay about a time when you were ill. What were your symptoms? Did you go to the doctor or to the hospital? Were you given medicine? Did any friends come to visit you? How long were you sick?

_____

_____

_____

_____

_____

_____

_____

_____

_____

Para comprender y escribir

A. From the three choices offered, select the one that best completes the statement or answers the question you hear and circle it.

1. (a) el tobillo?
   (b) el cuello?
   (c) la nariz?

2. (a) la rodilla.
   (b) la garganta.
   (c) la oreja.

3. (a) los pulmones.
   (b) las piernas.
   (c) los dedos.

4. (a) enfermera.
   (b) alérgica.
   (c) divertida.

5. (a) tos, fiebre y dolor de cabeza.
   (b) píldoras, paciencia y congestión.
   (c) jarabe, penicilina y sueño.

B. Answer the first question you hear negatively and the second question affirmatively, as in the model.

MODEL: ¿Dormiste bien anoche? → **No, no dormí bien.**
¿Y tu compañero de cuarto? → **Él sí durmió bien.**

1. _____
   _____
2. _____
   _____
3. _____
   _____
4. _____
   _____
5. _____
   _____
6. _____
   _____

C. Answer each question first with an affirmative command and then with a negative command, as in the model.

MODEL: ¿Busco a Carolina más tarde o la busco ahora? → **Búscala más tarde; no la busques ahora.**

1. _____
2. _____
3. _____
4. _____
5. _____
6. _____

D. Dictado. You will hear a short narrative about a visit Rita and Jaime made to a friend in the hospital. You will hear the narrative three times. Listen the first time. Write what you hear on the lines provided the second time. Make any necessary corrections the third time.

_____

_____

_____

_____

_____

_____

_____

_____

_____

_____

_____

_____

❀❀❀ VOCABULARIO

algo _adv._ somewhat
alto, -a high; tall
el **antibiótico** antibiotic
asistir (a) to attend
la **aspirina** aspirin
el **brazo** arm
la **cabeza** head
calmar to calm; _reflex._ to calm oneself, become calm, calm down
la **congestión** congestion
el **consejo** (piece of) advice
el **cuello** neck
el **cuerpo** body
el **dedo** finger
despierto, -a awake
divertir (ie, i) to divert, amuse; _reflex._ to amuse _or_ enjoy oneself, have a good time
doler (ue) to ache, pain, hurt
el **dolor** ache, pain
dormir (ue, u) to sleep; _reflex._ to fall asleep, go to sleep
enfermarse to get sick (ill)
la **enfermera** nurse (_f._)
el **enfermero** nurse (_m._)

la **espalda** back
el **estómago** stomach
la **fiebre** fever
la **flor** flower
la **garganta** throat
la **gota** drop
gran _adj._ large, great (_before sing. noun_)
el **hospital** hospital
la **iglesia** church
el **jarabe** syrup
el **jugo** juice
lastimarse to get hurt, hurt oneself
el **médico** doctor, physician
mejorarse to get better
la **misa** Mass
la **molestia** bother, annoyance
muchísimo _adv._ very much
muchísimo, -a (-os, -as) very much (many)
la **nariz** (_pl._ **narices**) nose
la **oreja** (outer) ear
la **paciencia** patience
el **pecho** chest
pedir (i, i) to ask, ask for, request

la **penicilina** penicillin
  peor *adv.* worse, worst
el **pie** foot
la **pierna** leg
la **píldora** pill
la **presión** (blood) pressure
el **pulmón** (*pl.* **pulmones**) lung
la **pulmonía** pneumonia
  rápidamente *adv.* fast, rapidly
  recetar to prescribe
  reír (**i, i**) (*also reflex.*) to laugh
el **resfriado** cold (illness)

la **rodilla** knee
  San(**to**) Saint, St.
  sentir (**ie, i**) to feel; to regret, be
    sorry; *reflex.* to feel (*well, ill,*
    happy, etc.)
el **síntoma** (*note gender*) symptom
la **sorpresa** surprise
  terrible (*m.* or *f.*) terrible
el **tobillo** ankle
la **tos** cough
  toser to cough
  viral (*m.* or *f.*) viral

a cada rato every short while (moment)
al menos at least
¿cómo te sientes? how do you (*fam. sing.*) feel?
dar un consejo to give (a piece of, some) advice
de ninguna manera (in) no way
dinos = **di** (*fam. sing. command of* **decir**) + **nos** tell us
en la vida never in my life
hacer caso a to notice, listen to, pay attention to
hazle = **haz** (*fam. sing. command of* **hacer**) + **le** do
  (something) for him or her
el **jarabe para la tos** cough syrup
la **mayor parte de** most (of), the greater part of
me lastimé el (*or* **la**)… I hurt (injured) my . . .
pescar una pulmonía (**un virus, un resfriado**) to catch (*or*
  come down with) pneumonia (a virus, a cold)
por eso because of that, for that reason, that's why
¡qué barbaridad! how awful!
¡qué sorpresa tan agradable! what a pleasant surprise!
¿qué te pasa? what's the matter with you?, what's wrong with
  you?
¡qué va! of course not!
ser alérgico, -a a to be allergic to
tener dolor de cabeza to have a headache
tener (**muchísima**) **fiebre** to have a (very high) fever
tener un resfriado (**una pulmonía viral**) to have a cold (viral
  pneumonia)
tomarle la temperatura (**presión**) (**a uno**) to take (one's)
  temperature (blood pressure)

Lección 17

- The present subjunctive of regular verbs
- The present subjunctive of stem-changing verbs
- The present subjunctive of irregular verbs and of verbs with special stem forms
- Indicative vs. subjunctive mood
- The subjunctive used with verbs expressing wish or volition, preference, advice, permission, request, or implied command
- Indicative or subjunctive in noun clauses: Reporting information or implied command

Silvia y Alberto se casan

Silvia y su novio Alberto han decidido casarse este verano y necesitan encontrar un apartamento. Ellos quieren que sea un apartamento pequeño y barato y prefieren que esté amueblado.

SILVIA —¡Mira, Alberto! Aquí tengo la lista de aparatos eléctricos que necesitamos: tostadora, cafetera, mezcladora, batidora, plancha…

ALBERTO —¡Dios mío! ¡Cuántas cosas quieres… ! Te sugiero que le pidas a tu madre que ponga esos aparatos en la lista de regalos que tenemos en los almacenes.

SILVIA —No te preocupes, Alberto. Le diré que les avise también a mis tías y primas. Ellas quieren que les demos algunas ideas para el regalo de boda…

ALBERTO —A propósito, Silvia, hay un apartamento muy bonito en la Calle 24. Me parece ideal para nosotros. Es cómodo y, para esta ciudad, el alquiler es una ganga; sólo cuesta 700 dólares al mes.

SILVIA —Sí, sí… Ana me llamó esta mañana. Insiste en que lo veamos. Dice que tiene una cocina muy moderna con refrigerador, lavadora de platos… ¡y con horno microondas!

ALBERTO —Pues ya hice la cita para verlo. El gerente del edificio me ha aconsejado que vayamos lo más pronto posible porque pueden alquilarlo en cualquier momento.

SILVIA —¡Fantástico! Iremos esta misma tarde. Pero, Alberto, ¿no deseas que prepare algo y que almorcemos antes?

ALBERTO —No, no. Prefiero que salgamos en seguida y que demos un paseo por el barrio. Quiero que lo conozcas porque es muy agradable. Es un barrio tranquilo y tendremos todo cerca.

SILVIA —Alberto, quiero que sepas que sólo deseo que tú estés contento y que seamos felices.

ALBERTO —¡Eres un encanto, mujer!

Preguntas sobre el diálogo

1. ¿Por qué necesitan Silvia y Alberto encontrar un apartamento? _____

_____

2. ¿Cómo quieren ellos que sea el apartamento? _____

_____

3. ¿Qué aparatos eléctricos necesitan ellos? _____

_____

4. ¿Qué le sugiere Alberto a Silvia? _____

_____

5. ¿Qué quieren las tías y las primas de Silvia? _____

_____

6. ¿Por qué a Alberto le parece ideal el apartamento de la Calle 24? _____

_____

7. ¿Cómo es la cocina del apartamento? ¿Qué aparatos tiene? _____

_____

8. ¿Qué le ha aconsejado el gerente del edificio a Alberto? ¿Por qué? _____

_____

9. ¿Por qué quiere Alberto dar un paseo por el barrio con Silvia? ¿Cómo es el barrio? _____

_____

10. ¿Cómo desea Silvia que esté Alberto? _____

_____

Notas gramaticales

A. The present subjunctive of regular verbs
(El presente del subjuntivo de los verbos regulares)

	hablar	**comer**	**vivir**
Singular	hable	coma	viva
	hables	comas	vivas
	hable	coma	viva
Plural	hablemos	comamos	vivamos
	habléis	comáis	viváis
	hablen	coman	vivan

- The stem used to form the present subjunctive is the same as that of the first-person singular of the present indicative. The endings are: **-e, -es, -e, -emos, -éis,** and **-en** for all **-ar** verbs, and **-a, -as, -a, -amos, -áis,** and **-an** for all **-er** and **-ir** verbs.

- The forms of the present subjunctive are used in negative familiar singular commands: **no** *hables* **tú**[1]; and in affirmative and negative formal commands: (**no**) *hable* **Ud.**; (**no**) *hablen* **Uds.**[2]

Práctica I   Complete the following sentences by using the corresponding form of the present subjunctive of one of the verbs listed below. Use each verb only once.

abrir	asistir a	correr	hablar
aceptar	beber	escribir	vender
alquilar	comer	estudiar	vivir

_____

1. See *Spanish On Your Own*, Vol. I, **Lección 4**.
2. See *Spanish On Your Own*, Vol. I, **Lección 11**.

1. Deseamos que Alberto y Silvia _____ el apartamento. 2. ¿Quieres tú que Mario _____ con nosotros esta noche? 3. No quieren que los estudiantes _____ cerveza en el estadio. 4. Mis padres no desean que yo _____ en esa residencia. 5. No quiero que Jaime _____ su carro. 6. ¿Prefiere Ud. que nosotros no _____ la invitación? 7. Preferimos que Uds. no _____ las olas hoy. 8. Ellos desean que nosotros _____ misa el domingo que viene. 9. Todos quieren que tú _____ más alto. 10. El profesor desea que yo _____ francés. 11. Ella desea que tú _____ las ventanas. 12. La profesora quiere que Uds. _____ las frases.

B. The present subjunctive of stem-changing verbs

(*El presente del subjuntivo de los verbos con cambios en la raíz*)

	pensar	**querer**	**volver**	**poder**
Singular	piense	quiera	vuelva	pueda
	pienses	quieras	vuelvas	puedas
	piense	quiera	vuelva	pueda
Plural	pensemos	queramos	volvamos	podamos
	penséis	queráis	volváis	podáis
	piensen	quieran	vuelvan	puedan

■ Verbs ending in **-ar** and **-er** that have a stem change e → ie and o → ue have the same changes in the present subjunctive.

	sentir	**dormir**	**pedir**
Singular	sienta	duerma	pida
	sientas	duermas	pidas
	sienta	duerma	pida
Plural	sintamos	durmamos	pidamos
	sintáis	durmáis	pidáis
	sientan	duerman	pidan

■ Remember that in the present indicative, verbs ending in **-ir** like **sentir** and **dormir** have a stem change e → ie and o → ue, except in the first- and second-person plural forms. These same changes occur in the present subjunctive; in addition, the first- and second-person plural forms change e → i and o → u: que nosotros **sintamos**; que vosotros **sintáis**; que nosotros **durmamos**, que vosotros **durmáis**.

- Similarly, remember that in the present indicative verbs ending in -ir like **pedir** have a stem change e → i except in the first- and second-person plural forms. In the present subjunctive this change occurs in all forms: **pidamos, pidáis**.

Práctica 2   Complete the following sentences by using the corresponding form of the present subjunctive of one of the verbs listed below. Use each verb only once.

contar	divertirse	llover	recomendar
costar	dormir	pedir	sentarse
devolver	encontrar	preferir	sentir(se)

1. Ella quiere que yo _____ el aparato.   2. Recomendamos que (tú) _____ el dinero que llevas en la billetera.   3. Sugieren que Uds. _____ aquí esta noche.   4. No estoy seguro de que _____ durante la excursión.   5. Deseo que Uds. me _____ un hotel más barato.   6. No estamos seguros de que ella _____ mejor esta mañana.   7. Ellos quieren que Ud. _____ junto a la chimenea.   8. Deseo que Luisa _____ un compañero más inteligente.   9. Desean que nosotros _____ durante nuestra visita.   10. No estoy seguro de que ellos _____ ir al concierto.   11. Nos recomiendan que (nosotros) no _____ cosas imposibles.   12. Ella no está segura de que estos muebles _____ más que aquéllos.

C. The present subjunctive of irregular verbs and of verbs with special stem forms

(El presente del subjuntivo de los verbos irregulares y de verbos con formas especiales en la raíz)

Infinitive	1st Person Sing. Pres. Ind.	Present Subjunctive
conocer	conozco	conozca, conozcas, conozca, etc.
decir	digo	diga, digas, diga, etc.
hacer	hago	haga, etc.
oír	oigo	oiga, etc.
poner	pongo	ponga, etc.
salir	salgo	salga, etc.
tener	tengo	tenga, etc.
traer	traigo	traiga, etc.
venir	vengo	venga, etc.
ver	veo	vea, etc.

- With the exception of **dar, estar, haber, ir, saber,** and **ser,** the present subjunctive of irregular verbs is formed in the same manner as the present subjunctive of regular verbs: drop the **-o** of the first-person present indicative and add to this stem the subjunctive endings for the corresponding conjugation.

	dar	estar	haber	ir	saber	ser
Singular	dé	esté	haya	vaya	sepa	sea
	des	estés	hayas	vayas	sepas	seas
	dé	esté	haya	vaya	sepa	sea
Plural	demos	estemos	hayamos	vayamos	sepamos	seamos
	deis	estéis	hayáis	vayáis	sepáis	seáis
	den	estén	hayan	vayan	sepan	sean

Práctica 3   Rearrange the following items to form sentences, changing the infinitive to the corresponding form of the present subjunctive.

1. nos / la verdad / queremos / que él / decir _____

2. hacer / ellos quieren / el viaje / que nosotros / con ellos _____

3. que ellos / el refrigerador / aquí / poner / él recomienda _____

4. para Madrid / salir / que Ud. / en seguida / queremos _____

5. cuidado / yo recomiendo / tener / que tú / mucho _____

6. Uds. / que él / su grabadora / traer / pídanle _____

7. a las tres / ellos / que nosotros / venir / piden _____

8. puntuales / que ellos / Uds. / ser / díganles _____

9. al profesor / que Uds. / quiero / conocer / yo _____

10. un regalo / que yo / ellos sugieren / le / dar _____

11. a las ocho / estar / quieren / en el hospital / que yo _____

12. conmigo / ir / a la agencia / que Uds. / yo quiero _____

13. ella / la noticia / que tú / saber / quiere _____

D. Indicative vs. subjunctive mood

(El indicativo en contraste con el subjuntivo)

- Up to this point, the indicative mood, which indicates facts, has been used almost exclusively. The present, the preterit, the imperfect, and the future tenses, for example, are all tenses of the indicative mood. Spanish uses the subjunctive mood more than English, particularly in certain dependent clauses.

- Certain English verbal constructions, in which the infinitive or the *-ing* form has a subject different from that of the main verb, must be expressed in Spanish through dependent clauses. Compare the following:

Her family doesn't want her to go out (going out) with Michael.	Su familia no quiere que ella salga con Miguel.

- In the Spanish sentence, **su familia no quiere** is the main clause; **que ella salga con Miguel** is the dependent clause. Note that each clause has a different subject, and that **que**, *that*, connects the two clauses.

- In Spanish, the dependent clause takes a verb in either the indicative or the subjunctive, depending on the meaning of the verb in the main clause. If the verb in the main clause expresses a fact, the verb in the dependent clause is in the indicative.

Main Clause (Verb Expresses a Fact)	Connector	Dependent Clause (Verb in Indicative)
Sus padres saben *Her parents know*	que *that*	ella sale con Miguel. *she is going out with Michael.*
Yo estoy seguro de *I'm sure*	que *that*	ellos van a casarse. *they are going to get married.*

If the verb in the main clause expresses an indirect command, volition, doubt, uncertainty, or reflects feelings and attitudes of the speaker, the verb in the dependent clause is in the subjunctive.

Main Clause (Verb expresses indirect command, volition, doubt, uncertainty; reflects speaker's feelings, attitudes)	Connector	Dependent Clause (Verb in subjunctive)
Por favor, yo te pido *Please, I ask you*	que	avises a tus padres. *to inform your parents.*
Su familia quiere (prefiere) *Her family wants (prefers)*	que	ella **salga** con Miguel. *her to go out with Michael.*
No estoy seguro de *I'm not sure*	que *(that)*	ellos **vayan** a casarse. *they will get married.*
No estoy seguro de *I'm not sure*	que *(that)*	la **quieras.** *you love her.*

■ Note that in Spanish, **que** must be used to introduce the dependent clause, while its English equivalent *that* is sometimes omitted.

■ As you will see in section E and in later lessons, the Spanish present subjunctive, as it is used in various clauses, is expressed in English in several ways: by the infinitive, by the present indicative or subjunctive, by the future tense, and by the auxiliary *may*, which conveys the idea of something uncertain or not yet accomplished.

Práctica 4   Complete the following sentences with the corresponding form of the verb in the present indicative or present subjunctive mood.

1. No estoy seguro de que Jorge (**poder**) _____ asistir a la fiesta.   2. Deseamos que Ana (**aceptar**) _____ el dinero.   3. Creo que Marta (**quedarse**) _____ aquí hasta el viernes.   4. Sabemos que Luis (**salir**) _____ de excursión mañana.   5. Deseo que Uds. (**estar**) _____ contentos con el apartamento.   6. Recomiendo que Luis (**volver**) _____ pronto.   7. Ella desea que tú (**ir**) _____ al teatro con ella.   8. Dígale Ud. a Jorge que (él) (**hacer**) _____ el mueble.   9. Nosotros deseamos que ellos (**ser**) _____ felices.   10. Recomendamos que Elena (**acostarse**) _____ temprano. 11. Recuerdo que Uds. (**levantarse**) _____ generalmente antes de las seis. 12. Estoy seguro de que ella (**tener**) _____ suficiente dinero.

E. The subjunctive used with verbs expressing wish or volition, preference, advice, permission, request, or implied command

(El subjuntivo con verbos que expresan deseo, preferencia, consejo, permiso, pedido o mandato implícito)

Ellos **prefieren** (**quieren**) que el apartamento **esté** amueblado.	*They prefer (want) the apartment to be furnished.*
Yo les **aconsejo** (**sugiero**) que Uds. lo **vean** pronto.	*I advise (suggest) that you see it soon.*
¿Me **permiten** Uds. que yo los **lleve**?	*Will you allow me to take you?*
Nosotros les **pedimos** (**pediremos**) que Uds. **tengan** paciencia.	*We ask (will ask) you to be patient.*
Dile a Silvia que me **dé** la lista de sus regalos.	*Tell Sylvia to give me the list of her gifts.*

■ In Spanish, when the verb in the main clause expresses ideas or feelings of the subject such as those of wish or volition, preference, advice or suggestion, permission, request, or an indirect command, the verb in the dependent clause—the noun clause—must be in the subjunctive.

■ The present subjunctive can be used in the dependent clause when the verb in the main clause is in the present indicative, or the future tense, or is an **ir a** + infinitive construction: **Nosotros les pedimos (les pediremos, vamos a pedirles) a Uds.** que *tengan* paciencia, *We ask (will ask, are going to ask) you to be patient.*

¡Atención!   In Spanish, a clause, usually introduced by **que**, is normally used if the subject of the dependent clause is different from that of the main verb. In English, however, an infinitive is most commonly used. Note that when there is no change in subject, Spanish, like English, also uses the infinitive.

Same subject: Infinitive	*Different subject: Subjunctive*
Ellos quieren **casarse** ahora.	Sus padres no quieren que ellos **se casen** ahora.
They want to get married now.	*Their parents do not want them to get married now.*
Ellos prefieren **comprar** una casa.	Sus padres prefieren que ellos **alquilen** un apartamento.
They prefer to buy a house.	*Their parents prefer that they rent an apartment.*

Práctica 5   Write complete sentences, using the verb in parentheses and adding any information needed to make a logical statement, as in the model.

MODEL: Deseo que tú (cobrar) → **Deseo que tú cobres este cheque.**

1. Quiero que Uds. (**asistir a**) _____

2. Sugiero que Ud. (**pensar**) _____

3. Deseamos que tú (**poner**) _____

4. Recomiendo que Uds. (**oír**) _____

5. Desean que nosotros (**volver**) _____

6. Permitimos que ella (**ver**) _____

7. Recomiendan que Uds. (**pedir**) _____

8. Aconsejo que tú (**aprender**) _____

9. Dígales Ud. a todos que (**esperar**) _____

10. Pídale Ud. a Margarita que (**arreglarse**) _____

Práctica 6   Answer each question with both a negative and an affirmative statement expressing wish or volition. Provide a logical conclusion for each affirmative statement.

MODEL: ¿Hablo ahora? → **No, no quiero que Ud. hable ahora; quiero que hable más tarde.**

1. ¿Salgo ahora? _____

2. ¿Voy hoy? _____

3. ¿Me acuesto a las diez? _____

4. ¿Me arreglo ahora? _____

5. ¿Se lo doy esta mañana? _____

6. ¿Se lo pido mañana? _____

Práctica 7   Change each affirmative familiar command to an affirmative implied command, following the model.

MODEL: Carmen, lee la carta. → **Carmen, te pido que leas la carta.**

1. Luis, ponte los zapatos. _____

2. Lupe, ven a la oficina. _____

3. Jaime, haz el viaje. _____

4. Rita, envuelve las compras. _____

5. Laura, trae los platos. _____

6. Ana, llévate el libro. _____

✪✪✪ Actividades y práctica: A, B, C, D 🎧

F. Indicative or subjunctive in noun clauses: Reporting information or implied command

(Indicativo o subjuntivo en cláusulas sustantivas: Información expresa o mandato implícito)

Verbs such as **decir**, **escribir**, **avisar**, and **informar** may either report information or express an implied command. When these verbs are used in the main clause, the verb in the dependent clause is in the indicative if it is used merely to report information. If a command is implied, the verb in the dependent clause must be in the subjunctive.

Reporting information: Indicative	*Implied command: Subjunctive*
Escríbele a Silvia que Lupe **viene** a vernos.	Escríbele a Silvia que **venga** a vernos.
Write to Sylvia that Lupe is coming to see us.	*Write to Sylvia that she come to see us.*
Dile (Avísale) a Rita que los invitados **llegan** a las siete.	Dile (Avísale) a Rita que **llegue** a las siete.
Tell (Inform) Rita that the guests are arriving at seven.	*Tell (Inform) Rita to arrive at seven.*

Práctica 8   Fill in the blanks with the appropriate form of the verb in the future indicative or the present subjunctive.

1. Dile a Tomás que yo (**estar**) ____ en casa a las ocho; dile que (**venir**) ____ él a buscarme.

2. Escríbele a Carolina que Alberto y Silvia (**casarse**) ____ este verano. Escríbeles también a Tomás y a Juan que (**venir**) ____ a la boda.

3. Avísele a Jorge que (**traer**) ____ las bebidas; avísele que Ud. (**comprar**) ____ los vasos.

✪✪✪ Actividades y práctica: E 🎧

Repaso

A.   Circle the item that does not belong in each series of words.

1. la mesa / el gerente / el sofá-cama / el aparador
2. la tostadora / la mezcladora / el barrio / la batidora

3. la aspiradora / la lavadora de platos / el refrigerador / la dueña
4. el dormitorio / los muebles / el sofá / el sillón
5. el estéreo / la grabadora / el ordenador / el almacén
6. la cocina / la sartén / el horno / el alquiler
7. la almohada / el paseo / la funda / la sábana
8. el plato / el cubierto / la boda / el mantel

B. Give the Spanish equivalent.

1. Sylvia and Albert have decided to get married this summer. _____

2. They are looking for an apartment; they want it to be small and inexpensive. _____

3. Sylvia shows her boyfriend a list of appliances that they need for their home: a mixer, a percolator, a toaster, and a blender. _____

4. Albert tells Sylvia that there is a comfortable apartment on 24th Street. He wants Sylvia to see it because it only costs 700 dollars a month. _____

5. The manager of the building has suggested to them that they go and see it as soon as possible. _____

6. Albert wants Sylvia to get acquainted with the neighborhood, which is very pleasant and quiet. _____

Expansión

A. Write answers to the following questions, using complete sentences.

1. Cuando dos personas se casan, ¿qué buscan generalmente? _____

2. ¿Hay muchos apartamentos amueblados en esta ciudad? _____

3. ¿Cuánto cuesta el alquiler de un apartamento de dos dormitorios en esta ciudad? _____

4. ¿Qué muebles tiene Ud. en su casa o apartamento? _____

5. ¿Cuáles son algunos de los aparatos que se necesitan en la cocina? _____

6. ¿Cómo sería su casa (o apartamento) ideal? _____

B. Write a letter in Spanish to some friends to tell them that you will soon have a new address. You have found a two-bedroom apartment in a quiet neighborhood. The building is modern, and the apartment has all the necessary appliances. Provide as much description as possible, and invite them to visit you soon.

Queridos amigos:

_____
_____
_____
_____
_____
_____
_____
_____
_____
_____
_____

Para comprender y escribir

A. From the three choices offered, select the one that best completes the statement or answers the question you hear and circle it.

1. (a) un gerente.
   (b) un apartamento.
   (c) una batidora.

2. (a) la ganga?
   (b) el alquiler?
   (c) la almohada?

3. (a) un paseo?
   (b) un mantel?
   (c) una plancha?

4. (a) ¡Cuántas cosas quieres... !
   (b) ¡Eres un encanto!
   (c) ¡Qué barbaridad!

5. (a) un dueño.
   (b) una tostadora.
   (c) un sillón.

B. Write an answer to the question, saying you don't want it to happen yet, as in the model.

MODEL: ¿Puedo regresar ahora? → **No, no quiero que regreses todavía.**

1. _____
2. _____
3. _____
4. _____
5. _____
6. _____

C. Answer each question negatively and then affirmatively, following the models.

> MODELS: ¿Quieres verlo tú? → **No, no quiero verlo; quiero que tú lo veas.**
>
> ¿Quieren verlo Uds.? → **No, no queremos verlo; queremos que Uds. lo vean.**

1. _____
2. _____
3. _____
4. _____
5. _____
6. _____

D. Dictado. You will hear a paragraph about Silvia and Alberto's marriage plans. You will hear the narrative three times. Listen the first time. Write what you hear on the lines provided the second time. Make any necessary corrections the third time.

_____
_____
_____
_____
_____
_____
_____
_____
_____
_____
_____

✸✸✸ VOCABULARIO

aconsejar to advise
el almacén (*pl.* almacenes)
   department store
la almohada pillow
  alquilar to rent
el alquiler rent; rental (property)
  amueblar to furnish
el aparador buffet
el aparato (eléctrico) (electrical)
   appliance, gadget
la aspiradora vacuum cleaner
el barrio quarter, district,
   neighborhood

la batidora mixer, beater, blender
la boda wedding
la cafetera coffee pot, percolator
  casarse to get married
la cocina kitchen; stove
los cubiertos place setting (knife,
   fork, and spoon)
el dormitorio bedroom, dormitory
la dueña owner (*f.*)
el dueño owner (*m.*)
  eléctrico, -a electric
el estéreo stereo
  feliz (*m. or f.; pl.* felices) happy

la **funda** pillowcase
la **ganga** bargain
el (la) **gerente** manager
la **grabadora** (tape) recorder
el **horno** oven
   ideal (*m.* or *f.*) ideal
   insistir en to insist upon
el **mantel** tablecloth
la **mezcladora** mixer
   moderno, -a modern
los **muebles** furniture
la **novia** girlfriend (steady), fiancée, bride
el **novio** boyfriend (steady), fiancé, groom
la **opinión** (*pl.* **opiniones**) opinion
el **ordenador** word processor, computer (*Spain*)

el **paseo** walk, stroll, ride
la **plancha** (**eléctrica**) (electric) iron
   preferir (**ie, i**) to prefer
   recomendar (**ie**) to recommend
el **refrigerador** refrigerator
   rogar (**ue**) to ask, beg
la **sábana** sheet
la **sartén** (*pl.* **sartenes**) skillet
el **sillón** (*pl.* **sillones**) armchair
el **sofá** (*pl.* **sofás**) sofa
el **sofá-cama** sofabed
   sugerir (**ie, i**) to suggest
la **tostadora** toaster
   tranquilo, -a quiet
la **videograbadora** video recorder (VCR)

al mes a (per) month, monthly
¡cuántas cosas quieres… ! how many things you want!
dar un paseo to take a walk (ride)
en cualquier momento (at) any moment
¡eres un encanto! you're a dear!
esta misma tarde this very afternoon
el **horno microondas** microwave oven
la **lavadora de platos** dishwasher
la **lista de regalos** gift registry, gift list
lo más pronto posible as soon as possible
el **regalo de boda** wedding gift
la **sartén eléctrica** electric skillet
sin amueblar unfurnished

Lección 18

- ☸ The present subjunctive of verbs with spelling changes
- ☸ The subjunctive in noun clauses after verbs expressing emotion
- ☸ The subjunctive in noun clauses after verbs expressing doubt or uncertainty
- ☸ The infinitive or subjunctive after some verbs of persuasion
- ☸ Indirect commands and **nosotros** commands
- ☸ The present perfect subjunctive

Un accidente de tráfico

El profesor de economía les ha pedido a sus estudiantes que asistan a la conferencia que un economista famoso dará en la universidad de una ciudad cercana. Quiere que hagan un resumen de la conferencia y que le entreguen sus comentarios escritos. Cuatro compañeros van en el carro de Juan, camino del lugar donde se dará la conferencia.

JUAN —¡Me parece raro que haya tanto tráfico a esta hora! Temo que haya habido un accidente. Tal vez haya sido un choque.

ROBERTO —Miren, me parece que ese carro no paró a tiempo. Quizás hayan fallado los frenos.

INÉS —¡Caramba! ¡Qué mala suerte tenemos hoy! Ya son las tres y media… No estoy segura de que vayamos a llegar a tiempo.

JUAN —Tengan paciencia, chicos. No creo que tengamos que esperar mucho. Allí viene la policía.

ISABEL —¡Cuánto me alegro de que ya esté aquí! Juan, te sugiero que dejes pasar el carro patrulla por la izquierda. (*Se oyen las sirenas. Llega el carro patrulla y un policía empieza a organizar el tráfico.*)

JUAN —Me extraña que no haya heridos ni ambulancias. No creo que haya sido un accidente muy grave.

ROBERTO —¡Mira ese taxista entremetido! No le permitas que siga adelante. ¡Anda, pásalo!

ISABEL —Pero, ¿cuál es el apuro? Déjalo seguir…

JUAN —Por favor, chicos, les pido que se calmen todos. Me molesta que no me dejen conducir.

ROBERTO —¡Hombre! Creo que tú eres un genio en el volante, pero bueno…

INÉS —Chicos, yo estoy segura de que no hay mejor conductor que Juan.

JUAN —Gracias, Inés. ¡Me gusta mucho que hayas dicho eso!

ISABEL —Sigue manejando,[1] Juan, y salgamos rápidamente de aquí. Te aconsejo que no le hagas caso a Roberto.

ROBERTO —Bueno, bueno… ¡Quizás tengamos suerte, y espero que la conferencia no empiece a las cuatro en punto!

Preguntas sobre el diálogo

1. ¿Qué les ha pedido el profesor de economía a sus estudiantes? ¿Qué quiere él que ellos hagan después?

_____

_____

---

1. **Seguir** may be followed by the **-ndo** form to express the idea of *to continue* or *to keep on* (*doing something*).

2. ¿Por qué teme Juan que haya habido un accidente? _____

_____

3. ¿Qué piensa Roberto del accidente? _____

_____

4. ¿Por qué no cree Juan que tengan que esperar mucho? ¿Qué les pide él a sus compañeros? _____

_____

5. ¿Qué le sugiere Isabel a Juan? _____

_____

6. ¿Qué le extraña a Juan? ¿Qué cree él del accidente? _____

_____

7. Cuando Roberto ve al taxista entremetido, ¿qué le dice él a Juan? _____

_____

8. ¿Qué les pide Juan a sus compañeros? _____

_____

9. ¿Qué les dice Inés a ellos? ¿Y qué le pide Isabel a Juan? _____

_____

10. ¿Qué espera Roberto? _____

_____

Notas gramaticales

A. The present subjunctive of verbs with spelling changes
(El presente del subjuntivo de verbos con cambios ortográficos)

Verbs ending in -car, -gar, and -zar   *(Verbos que terminan en -car, -gar y -zar)*

busque	llegue	empiece
busques	llegues	empieces
busque	llegue	empiece
busquemos	lleguemos	empecemos
busquéis	lleguéis	empecéis
busquen	lleguen	empiecen

■ Remember from **Lección 13** that in the preterit and in formal commands, before the ending -e, all verbs ending in -car change c to qu, those ending in -gar change g to gu, and those ending in -zar change z to c. This spelling change also occurs in the present subjunctive. The verb **empezar**, *to start, begin*, also has the stem change e to ie.

Verbs ending in -guir   (*Verbos que terminan en -guir*)

seguir, *to follow, continue*	
Pres. Part.	siguiendo
Pres. Ind.	sigo, sigues, sigue, seguimos, seguís, siguen
Pres. Subj.	siga, sigas, siga, sigamos, sigáis, sigan
Preterit	seguí, seguiste, siguió, seguimos, seguisteis, siguieron
Sing. Imper.	sigue

■ In verbs ending in **-guir**, the **u** is dropped after **g** before the endings **-o** and **-a**, that is, in the first-person singular present indicative and in all six forms of the present subjunctive. **Seguir** and **conseguir** also have the stem change of **e** to **i**, as in **pedir** (see **Lección 16**).

Práctica 1   Complete each sentence with the corresponding form of the present subjunctive tense of the verb.

1. Queremos que Juan (**llegar**) _____ a tiempo.

2. Sugiero que Elena (**acercarse**) _____ a la mesa.

3. Preferimos que Inés (**almorzar**) _____ con Juan.

4. No creo que Ana me (**entregar**) _____ el dinero.

5. Recomiendo que Mario (**seguir**) _____ adelante.

6. Dudamos que Luis (**jugar**) _____ al fútbol.

Práctica 2   Answer first with an affirmative formal command, and then with a statement expressing wish or volition, substituting object pronouns for noun objects, following the model.

MODEL: ¿Empiezo el resumen? → **Sí, empiécelo Ud. Sí, deseo que lo empiece.**

1. ¿Comienzo la clase? _____

2. ¿Saco las fotos? _____

3. ¿Pago la cuenta? _____

4. ¿Organizamos la fiesta? _____

5. ¿Buscamos las llaves? _____

6. ¿Entregamos los ejercicios? _____

B. The subjunctive in noun clauses after verbs expressing emotion
(*El subjuntivo en cláusulas sustantivas después de verbos que expresan emoción*)

■ In Spanish, when the verb in the main clause expresses emotion or feelings such as joy, surprise, hope, pity, or sorrow, the verb in the dependent clause—the noun clause—must be in the subjunctive, provided that the subjects of the two clauses are different. Remember that in Spanish the noun clause is regularly introduced by **que**, while its English equivalent *that* is sometimes omitted.

Me alegro de que no **sea** un accidente grave.	*I'm glad that it's not a serious accident.*
Me extraña que no **haya** heridos.	*I'm surprised (that) there are no injured persons.*
Esperamos que la conferencia no **empiece** a las cuatro.	*We hope that the lecture doesn't (won't) begin at four.*
Temo que Uds. no **puedan** llegar a tiempo.	*I'm afraid you (pl.) won't be able to arrive on time.*
Siento que **tengas** tan mala suerte.	*I'm sorry (I regret) that you have such bad luck.*

■ Emotions or feelings are also conveyed by expressions such as **estar contento, -a (de) que**, *to be happy (glad) that*; **me (no me) gusta que**, *I (don't) like it that*; **me encanta que**, *I'm delighted that*; **me (no me) duele que**, *it hurts (doesn't hurt) me that*; **me (no me) molesta que**, *it bothers (doesn't bother) me that*.

Estoy contento de que **podamos** ir.	*I'm happy (glad) that we can go.*
No me gusta que Uds. me **hablen** cuando estoy manejando.	*I don't like it that you (pl.) talk to me while I'm driving.*
Me duele que Uds. **piensen** que yo soy mal conductor.	*It hurts me that you think that I am a bad driver.*

¡Atención!   Remember that in Spanish, the subjunctive is used in the dependent clause if the subject is different from that of the main clause. When there is no change in subject, however, Spanish, like English, uses the infinitive.

Same subject: Infinitive	*Different subjects: Subjunctive*
Yo **me alegro** de (**Espero**) poder asistir a la conferencia.	Yo **me alegro** de (**Espero**) que Uds. **puedan** asistir a la conferencia.
I'm glad (I hope) to be able to attend the lecture.	*I'm glad (I hope) that you (pl.) can attend the lecture.*

Práctica 3   Complete with the corresponding form of the present indicative or present subjunctive, as required.

1. Tememos que ella no (**conseguir**) _____ la licencia de manejar.   2. Me alegro de que Mario (**querer**) _____ asistir a esta universidad.   3. Me dicen que ellos (**saber**) _____ mi dirección.   4. Estamos contentos de que ellos (**casarse**) _____ en junio.   5. Estoy seguro de que ellos (**pensar**) _____ invitar al profesor.   6. Me encanta que tus padres (**poder**) _____ visitarnos.   7. Estoy seguro de que ellos (**preferir**) _____ hacer el viaje en avión.   8. Me duele que él no (**pagar**) _____ sus cuentas.   9. Se dice que Roberto (**tener**) _____ dolor de cabeza.   10. Sabemos que Luis no (**contestar**) _____ sus cartas.   11. Me molesta que (**haber**) _____ tanto tráfico en esta calle.   12. Es lástima que tú (**ser**) _____ alérgico(-a) a la penicilina.

Práctica 4 Write a logical response to each statement, beginning with expressions such as **¡Cuánto me alegro de que... !**, **Me extraña que...**, **Siento mucho que...**, or **Me molesta que.**

> MODEL: ¡Sabes tú que ya tenemos el apartamento! → ¡Cuánto me alegro
> de que ya tengan el apartamento!

1. ¡Sabes tú que Silvia se casa con Alberto!

   _____

2. ¡Saben tú que Ana está en el hospital!

   _____

3. ¡Sabes tú que mi novio (novia) llega mañana!

   _____

4. ¡Sabes tú que Juan ya no me escribe!

   _____

5. ¡Sabes tú que Marta no me llama!

   _____

 Actividades y práctica: A

C. The subjunctive in noun clauses after verbs expressing doubt or uncertainty

(El subjuntivo en cláusulas sustantivas después de verbos que expresan duda o incertidumbre)

When the verb in the main clause conveys doubt or uncertainty, the verb in the dependent clause must be in the subjunctive, provided that the subjects of the two clauses are different. Note that verbs and expressions of belief such as **creer** or **estar seguro, -a,** convey certainty when used in the affirmative; in such cases they are followed by the indicative. When used in the negative, however, such verbs convey doubt or uncertainty; they then require the subjunctive. **Dudar** in the negative also implies certainty.

Certainty implied: Indicative	*Uncertainty implied: Subjunctive*
¡Yo creo que tú **eres** un genio en el volante! *I believe you are a genius at the steering wheel!*	**¡No creo** que tú **seas** un genio en el volante! *I don't believe (that) you are a genius at the steering wheel!*
Estoy seguro de que **llegaremos** a tiempo. *I'm sure we'll arrive on time.*	**No estoy seguro de** que **lleguemos** a tiempo. *I'm not sure (that) we will arrive on time.*
Nuestro profesor **no duda** que nosotros **podemos** comprender la conferencia. *Our professor doesn't doubt that we can (indeed) understand the lecture.*	Nuestro profesor **duda** que nosotros **podamos** comprender la conferencia. *Our professor doubts that we will be able to understand the lecture.*

■ **Creer** used in questions may or may not imply uncertainty, depending on the attitude of the speaker. If doubt is implied, the subjunctive is used. If no implication of doubt is made, the indicative is used. **No creer que** in a question implies certainty.

Certainty implied: Indicative   *Uncertainty implied: Subjunctive*

¿**Crées** tú que ellos **asistirán** a la   ¿**Crees** tú que ellos **asistan** a la
   conferencia?   conferencia?
Do you believe (that) they will   *Do you believe (that) they might*
   attend the lecture?   *attend the lecture?*

¿**No creen** Uds. que ya es muy tarde
   para ir?
Don't you believe (think) it's already
   too late to go?

■ **Decir** used in the negative implies uncertainty. Therefore, the verb in the dependent clause is in the subjunctive mood.

No digo que tú no **sepas** manejar   *I'm not saying that you don't know*
   bien.   *how to drive well.*

¡Atención!   Other expressions that may be used in a main clause are **tal vez** and **quizá(s)**, *perhaps*. When certainty is implied, the indicative mood is used. When doubt, uncertainty, or conjecture is implied, the subjunctive mood is used.

Certainty implied: Indicative   *Uncertainty implied: Subjunctive*

Tal vez es un accidente de tráfico.   **Tal vez sea** un accidente de tráfico.
Perhaps it is a traffic accident.   *It may be a traffic accident. (Perhaps*
                                                       it's . . .)

Quizá(s) han fallado los frenos.   **Quizá(s) hayan fallado** los frenos.
Perhaps the brakes have failed.   *Perhaps the brakes have failed. (It may*
                                                       be the brakes have failed.)

Práctica 5   Complete each sentence with the corresponding form of the present indicative or present subjunctive, as required.

1. Yo no digo que Carmen (**leer**) _____ mis cartas.   2. No creo que Elena (**saber**) _____ esquiar.   3. Laura dice que (**ir**) _____ al centro.   4. ¿No cree Ud. que el alquiler del cuarto (**ser**) _____ caro?   5. No estamos seguros de que ellos (**traer**) _____ sus trajes de baño.   6. No dudo que ella (**tocar**) _____ bien.   7. ¿No crees que ella (**deber**) _____ llamar al médico?   8. No, no creemos que ella (**tener**) _____ fiebre.   9. No estoy seguro de que ellos nos (**permitir**) _____ entrar.   10. Dudo que mis compañeros (**conocer**) _____ al gerente.   11. Estoy seguro de que ellos (**tener**) _____ una grabadora.   12. No dudo que Ana (**estar**) _____ enferma.

   Actividades y práctica: B

D. The infinitive or subjunctive after some verbs of persuasion
(El infinitivo o el subjuntivo después de algunos verbos de persuasión)

As stated before, Spanish requires a clause in the subjunctive after certain verbs when there is a change in subject. A few verbs of persuasion, however, such as **aconsejar**, *to advise*; **dejar**, *to let, allow*; **permitir**, *to permit, allow*; **recomendar** (**ie**), *to recommend*; **sugerir** (**ie, i**), *to suggest*, may take an infinitive when the subject is different from that of the main verb. But for emphasis or clarity, a clause with the subjunctive may be used with these verbs.

Déjenme Uds. **conducir.** **Déjenme** Uds. que yo **conduzca.**	*Let me (Allow me to) drive.*
No le permitas al taxista **seguir** adelante. **No le permitas** al taxista que **siga** adelante.	*Don't let the taxi driver go on ahead.*
Yo te **aconsejo** (**recomiendo, sugiero**) **no hacerle** caso a Roberto. Yo te **aconsejo** (**recomiendo, sugiero**) que **no le hagas** caso a Roberto.	*I advise (recommend, suggest) you not to (that you do not) pay attention to Robert.*

Práctica 6   Rewrite the following sentences, changing the infinitive constructions or noun clauses with **que**, as in the models.

> MODELS: Me aconseja que asista a sus clases. → **Me aconseja asistir a sus clases.**
> No le permitas a Isabel hablar en inglés. → **No le permitas a Isabel que hable inglés.**

1. Te aconsejo que moderes la marcha.

   _____

2. Dejen Uds. que yo conduzca.

   _____

3. El médico me recomienda tomar estas píldoras.

   _____

4. El gerente no permite que nosotros veamos el apartamento.

   _____

5. Les sugiero a Uds. volver más tarde.

   _____

6. No le permitas al taxista pasar por la izquierda.

   _____

  Actividades y práctica: C

E. Indirect commands and **nosotros** commands
*(Mandatos indirectos y mandatos con **nosotros**)*

Indirect commands   *(Mandatos indirectos)*

¡Que espere él un momento!	*Have him wait a moment!*
¡Que lleguen Uds. bien!	*May (I hope, I wish) you arrive safely!*

¡**Que tengas** un feliz cumpleaños!   *I wish you (I hope you have) a happy*
                                        birthday!

- **Que**, equivalent to English *have*, *let*, *may*, *I wish*, or *I hope*, introduces indirect commands in the second and third persons.[1] Object and reflexive pronouns always precede the verb. If a subject is expressed, it usually follows the verb.

  ¡**Que te diviertas!**   *May (I hope) you have a good time!*

- The negative **no** precedes any pronouns.

  ¡**Que no te pase** ese taxi!   *Don't let that taxi pass you!*

Nosotros commands   *(Mandatos con nosotros)*

Sigamos manejando.   *Let's keep on driving.*
Salgamos de aquí.   *Let's get out of here.*

- The Spanish equivalent of the English *let's* or *let us* + a verb is expressed by the first-person plural forms of the present subjunctive. **No** precedes object pronouns and the verb in negative commands.

  No le hagamos caso.   *Let's not pay attention to him (her).*

- When the reflexive pronoun **nos** is added to the **nosotros** command, the final **-s** is dropped from the verb and an accent mark is written over the stressed syllable.

  Sentémonos aquí.   *Let's sit down here.*
  Casémonos ahora.   *Let's get married now.*

- **Vamos** is used for the affirmative *let's (let us) go*. In the negative, the subjunctive form must be used.

  Vamos a casa ahora.   *Let's go home now.*
  No vayamos a casa todavía.   *Let's not go home yet.*

- **Vamos a** + an infinitive, in addition to meaning *we are going to*, may be used for *let's* or *let us* + a verb if the intention is to perform the action at once.

  Vamos a salir ahora.   *We are going to (Let's) leave now.*

¡**Atención!**   The expression **a ver**, *let's see* (**Lección 13**), is often used without **vamos**.

A ver esos aretes de oro, por favor.   *Let's see those gold earrings, please.*

Práctica 7   Change to an indirect command with **él**, preceded by **Yo no puedo**, following the model.

     MODEL: Ciérrela Ud. → **Yo no puedo; que la cierre él.**

1. Envuélvalo Ud. _____
2. Entréguelo Ud. _____

---

1. An indirect command is really a clause dependent upon a verb that expresses wish, hope, permission, and the like, with the main verb understood: (**Yo quiero**) **que tú tengas un feliz cumpleaños**, (*I want*) *you to have a happy birthday.*

3. Búsquelos Ud. _____

4. Cuéntelas Ud. _____

5. Empiécelo Ud. _____

6. Léalo Ud. _____

Práctica 8   Write two affirmative replies and one negative reply, substituting object pronouns for noun objects, following the model.

> MODEL: ¿Vendemos el carro? → **Sí, vendámoslo. Sí, vamos a venderlo.**
> **No, no lo vendamos.**

1. ¿Devolvemos el dinero? _____

_____

2. ¿Hacemos el resumen? _____

_____

3. ¿Pagamos la cuenta? _____

_____

4. ¿Mostramos las fotos? _____

_____

5. ¿Abrimos las ventanas? _____

_____

6. ¿Ponemos la televisión? _____

_____

Actividades y práctica: D, E

F. The present perfect subjunctive   *(El perfecto presente del subjuntivo)*

Present Perfect Subjunctive			
Singular		*Plural*	
haya		hayamos	
hayas	hablado, comido, vivido	hayáis	hablado, comido, vivido
haya		hayan	

- The present perfect subjunctive tense is formed by the present subjunctive tense of **haber** with the past participle. After verbs in the main clause in the present or future tense that require the subjunctive in the dependent clause, Spanish uses the present perfect subjunctive to describe events that have ended prior to the time indicated by the verb in the main clause. The English equivalents of the present perfect subjunctive are *have* or *has* + the past participle. The word *may* is sometimes part of the English meaning.

Temo que **haya habido** un accidente.	*I fear there has (may have) been an accident.*
Yo espero que él no **haya manejado** muy rápido.	*I hope he didn't drive very fast.*
¡Cuánto me alegro de que no **hayas vuelto** con ellos!	*How glad I am that you didn't come back with them!*

Práctica 9   Complete the noun clause, using the corresponding form of the verb in the present perfect subjunctive tense, following the model.

MODEL: Dudamos que ella (sugerir) _____ eso. → **Dudamos que ella haya sugerido eso.**

1. Dudamos que ella (**sacar**) _____ buenas fotos.   2. Temen que Isabel (**ver**) _____ la película.   3. Es lástima que Ud. no (**poder**) _____ ir conmigo. 4. No creo que ellos (**traer**) _____ los discos.   5. Ellos sienten que nosotros (**saber**) _____ la noticia.   6. No estoy seguro de que él (**volver**) _____ todavía.

✪✪
✪   **Actividades y práctica: F**   🎧

Repaso

A. Use the words given in complete sentences. You may use the words in any order; be sure to conjugate verbs and add additional elements as necessary.

1. apuro, chocar, carro patrulla _____

_____

2. carro, freno, avería _____

_____

3. temer, hacerse daño, accidente _____

_____

4. oír, sirena, ambulancia _____

_____

5. me extraña, dejar, manejar _____

_____

B. Give the Spanish equivalent.

1. The economics professor has asked his students to go to a nearby university to attend a lecture. _____

_____

2. Four classmates are going in John's car to the place where the lecture will be given. _____

_____

3. It seems strange to John that there is so much traffic; he fears that there has been a collision. _____

_____

4. Agnes thinks that they are having (have) bad luck and she is not sure that they'll be able to arrive on time. _____

_____

5. John asks his friends to be patient. He doesn't think (believe) that they will have to wait too long. _____

_____

Expansión

A. Write answers to these questions, using complete sentences.

1. ¿Cuántos años tenía Ud. cuando consiguió la licencia de manejar? _____

_____

2. ¿Le gusta a Ud. manejar un carro? ¿Por qué? _____

3. ¿Modera Ud. la marcha cuando ve un carro patrulla? ¿Por qué? _____

_____

4. ¿Ha tenido Ud. un accidente grave manejando un carro? (¿Cuándo?) _____

_____

5. ¿A quiénes hay que avisar cuando uno tiene un accidente? _____

_____

6. ¿A qué horas del día hay mucho tráfico en el centro? _____

_____

B. You and some Spanish-speaking friends are relating embarrassing moments that you have experienced. Your story is as follows: You took driving lessons (**lecciones de manejar**) in high school, and the day you turned (use **cumplir**) sixteen, you went to the office where driver's licenses are issued (use **expedir**, conjugated like **pedir**). The examiner (**examinador**) sat down in the car, and you started (use **poner en marcha**) it. When you entered the street, the wind carried away some of the examiner's papers. Looking for other papers that were on the floor, you collided with a car that was passing on the right; you didn't get your driver's license that day.

_____

_____

_____

_____

_____

_____

_____

_____

_____

Para comprender y escribir

A. From the three choices offered, select the one that best completes the statement or answers the question you hear and circle it.

1. (a) Buscar un taxista.
   (b) Seguir adelante.
   (c) Avisar a la policía.

2. (a) un herido.
   (b) un conductor.
   (c) un carro.

3. (a) ¡Cuánto me alegro!
   (b) ¡Cuánto me canso!
   (c) ¡Cuánto me preocupa!

4. (a) Le fallarían los frenos.
   (b) Seguramente moderó la marcha.
   (c) Tendría que esperar mucho.

5. (a) un volante.
   (b) un apuro.
   (c) una avería.

B. Write a new sentence using the subjunctive in the dependent clause, as in the model.

> MODEL: Juan va a la conferencia. (Me alegro de que) → **Me alegro de que Juan vaya a la conferencia.**

1. _____
2. _____
3. _____
4. _____
5. _____
6. _____
7. _____
8. _____

C. Respond in writing to the question you hear, using a logical statement such as ¡Cuánto me alegro de que... ! Me extraña que... , Siento mucho que... , or Me molesta que...

1. _____
2. _____
3. _____
4. _____
5. _____
6. _____
7. _____
8. _____

D. Dictado. You will hear a short description of Silvia and Alberto's problems. You will hear the passage three times. Listen the first time. Write what you hear the second time. Make any necessary corrections the third time.

_____

_____

_____

_____

_____

_____

_____

_____

_____

_____

_____

_____

_____

VOCABULARIO

el **accidente** accident
adelante _adv._ ahead, forward
la **ambulancia** ambulance
el **apuro** hurry, rush
la **avería** breakdown, failure (_of a motor vehicle_)
el **carro** car (_Am._)
cercano, -a nearby, neighboring
chocar (con) to hit, collide (with)
el **choque** collision
el **comentario** commentary, comment
conducir to drive (_Spain_)
el **conductor** driver (_m._)
la **conductora** driver (_f._)
la **conferencia** lecture
conseguir (i, i) to get, obtain
¡cuánto + _verb!_ how . . . !
dejar to let, allow, permit
dudar to doubt
empezar (ie) (a + _inf._**)** to begin to (+ _verb_)

entremetido, -a meddlesome
extrañar to surprise
fallar to fail
el **freno** brake (_of a car_)
grave _adj._ (_m._ or _f._) grave, serious
el **herido** wounded (injured) person
irse to go (away), leave
manejar to drive (_Am._)
organizar to organize
parar to stop
el **policía** police officer (_m._)
la **policía** police (force)
raro, -a strange
el **resumen** (_pl._ **resúmenes**) summary
seguir (i, i) to follow, continue, go on
la **sirena** siren
el (la) **taxista** taxi driver
temer to fear, suspect
el **tráfico** traffic
el **volante** steering wheel

el **accidente de tráfico** traffic accident
alegrarse de que to be glad that
el **carro patrulla** patrol (police) car
¿cuál es el apuro? what's the hurry (rush)?
¡cuánto me alegro de que… ! how glad I am that . . . !
(tú) eres un genio en el volante you are a genius at the wheel
esperar mucho to wait long (a long time)

hacerse daño to hurt oneself, get hurt

la **licencia de manejar (conducir)** driver's license

me extraña I am surprised, it surprises me

me gusta que... I like it that . . .

me parece raro... it seems strange to me . . .

moderar la marcha to slow down

la **mujer policía** police officer (*f.*)

no hay heridos ni ambulancias there aren't any injured
   persons or ambulances (there are no . . . nor . . .)

por la derecha (izquierda) on (to) the right (left)

¡qué mala suerte! what bad luck!

seguir adelante to continue (go on) ahead

tal vez perhaps

tener paciencia to be patient

tener una avería to have a breakdown, failure (*in the car*)

Lección 19

- Forms of verbs ending in **-ducir**
- The subjunctive in noun clauses after impersonal expressions
- Adjective clauses and relative pronouns
- Subjunctive or indicative in adjective clauses
- **Hacer** in time clauses
- Spanish equivalents for *to become* or *to get*
- The infinitive after verbs of perception

Miguel se gradúa[1] y busca trabajo

El director de la Escuela de Ingeniería Agrícola[2] acaba de recibir una carta del señor Antonio Ruiz, gerente[3] de una importante empresa norteamericana, la cual tiene una sucursal en Puerto Rico. El señor Ruiz se dirige al director de la Escuela para preguntarle si conoce a algún joven que pueda trabajar como agente de su compañía en la Isla. El director le dice a su secretaria, la señorita White, que Miguel Ramos, estudiante de la Escuela, sería un candidato excelente para el puesto y le pide que hable con Miguel acerca del asunto. Poco después la señorita White ve pasar a Miguel y lo llama.

SRTA. WHITE —¡Miguel! ¡Miguel! (*Miguel entra en la oficina.*) Oí decir que buscas trabajo. ¿Es verdad?

MIGUEL —Como Ud. sabe, ¡este trimestre me gradúo de ingeniero! Y claro, es urgente que consiga un trabajo pronto.

SRTA. WHITE —Pues precisamente hoy el director de la Escuela ha recibido una carta de un conocido hombre de negocios, el señor Antonio Ruiz, acerca de un puesto vacante que tiene en su compañía. Es posible que te interese.

MIGUEL —Me alegro que Uds. hayan pensado en mí. Me he vuelto loco buscando trabajo en esta ciudad, pero no encuentro ninguno.

SRTA. WHITE —El señor Ruiz busca una persona que entienda de asuntos de maquinaria agrícola y que quiera residir en San Juan.

MIGUEL —¡Caramba! Hace mucho tiempo que deseo conocer esa isla.

SRTA. WHITE —Dice además que como el puesto es en Puerto Rico, es necesario que el candidato sea bilingüe, lo cual no sería ningún problema para ti, ya que hablas muy bien el inglés y el español.

MIGUEL —Señorita White, por favor le pido que me ayude a obtener ese puesto. ¿Sería posible que el director de la Escuela me escribiera una carta de recomendación?

SRTA. WHITE —¡Por supuesto, Miguel! Según me indicó, va a escribirle al señor Ruiz que no hay nadie que esté mejor preparado que tú.

MIGUEL —¡No se imagina cuánto se lo agradezco, señorita White! ¡A veces me preocupo tanto!

SRTA. WHITE —No te pongas nervioso, Miguel. Nosotros te ayudaremos. Pero ahora, quiero perdirte un favor. Oí decir que hablas muy bien el francés. Necesito que me traduzcas estos versos; me los mandó un amigo mío, pero no los entiendo muy bien.

MIGUEL —Con mucho gusto trataré de hacerlo. Déjeme ver. (*Leyendo los versos.*) Bueno, pero no se ponga roja... ¡Dudo que encuentre Ud. otro amigo tan romántico!

---

1. See **Lección 20**, Section A, for the conjugation of **graduarse** and other verbs ending in -**uar**.
2. This institution is also known as la **Escuela de Ingenieros Agrónomos**.
3. The article is usually omitted before a noun in apposition when the speaker is supplying information the audience does not know: **del señor Antonio Ruiz, gerente...**, *from Mr. Anthony Ruiz, the manager . . .* ; **Miguel Ramos, estudiante de la Escuela,** *a student of the School.* The use of the definite article, however, implies that the fact is well known; **Buenos Aires, la capital de la Argentina,** *Buenos Aires, the capital of Argentina.*

Preguntas sobre el diálogo

1. ¿Quién es el señor Antonio Ruiz? ¿Quién es la señorita White? _____

_____

2. ¿Por qué le escribe el señor Ruiz una carta al director de la Escuela de Ingeniería Agrícola? _____

_____

3. ¿Por qué es urgente que Miguel consiga un trabajo? _____

_____

4. ¿Qué busca el señor Ruiz? _____

_____

5. ¿Por qué es necesario que el candidato sea bilingüe? ¿Por qué no sería esto un problema para Miguel?

_____

_____

6. ¿Qué le pregunta Miguel a la señorita White? _____

_____

7. ¿Qué le dirá el director en su carta al señor Ruiz sobre Miguel? _____

_____

8. ¿Qué favor le pide la señorita White a Miguel? _____

_____

Notas gramaticales

A. Forms of verbs ending in **-ducir**
(Formas de verbos que terminan en -ducir)

traducir, *to translate*	
Pres. Ind.	traduzco, traduces, traduce, traducimos, traducís, traducen
Pres. Subj.	traduzca, traduzcas, traduzca, traduzcamos, traduzcáis, traduzcan
Preterit	traduje, tradujiste, tradujo, tradujimos, tradujisteis, tradujeron

- Verbs ending in -ducir, such as **traducir**, **conducir**, and **producir**, are irregular in the first-person singular of the present indicative and in all forms of the preterit and the present subjunctive. These verbs are regular in the imperfect indicative, the future, the conditional, and the past participle.

Práctica I   Complete with the corresponding form of **conducir**, **producir**, or **traducir** in the present indicative, present subjunctive, or preterit tense.

1. No creo que la joyería _____ artículos de plata.   2. Yo _____ la solicitud

para la agencia de empleo ayer.   3. El taxista _____ desde hace muchos años.   4. ¿Ha visto

Ud. los hermosos edificios que la civilización musulmana _____ en España? 5. Por lo común yo _____ el carro. 6. Hoy día esos pueblos _____ objetos de cerámica. 7. Es lástima que tu padre no _____ de noche. 8. Queremos que Uds. _____ estos versos al francés. 9. ¿Qué tipo de artículo quieren Uds. que nosotros _____? 10. Me dicen que Jorge y Roberto _____ la carta ayer.

Actividades y práctica: A

B. The subjunctive in noun clauses after impersonal expressions

(El subjuntivo en cláusulas sustantivas después de expresiones impersonales)

- In Spanish, the subjunctive is used after impersonal expressions of possibility, necessity, uncertainty or conjecture, pity, and the like, provided that the verb of the dependent clause has a subject expressed.

Es posible (Es probable) que él consiga ese trabajo.	*It's possible (probable) that he'll get that job.*
Es dudoso que haya mejor candidato que Miguel.	*It's doubtful that there is a better candidate than Michael.*

- The verb in the dependent clause is in the present subjunctive if the impersonal expression is in the present, the future, or the **ir a** + infinitive construction: **es necesario que**, *it is necessary that*; **será necesario que**, *it will be necessary that*; **va a ser necesario que**, *it's going to be necessary that*.

- Impersonal expressions of certainty, such as **es cierto** and **es verdad**, require the indicative in the dependent clause. When these expressions are negative, however, they imply uncertainty and require the subjunctive.

Es cierto (verdad) que Miguel se gradúa este trimestre.	*It's certain (true) that Michael graduates (is graduating) this trimester.*
No es cierto que él tenga trabajo.	*It's not certain that he has a job.*

- Some commonly used impersonal expressions, most of which you have already seen, are:

es bueno *it's good*	**es (una) lástima** *it's a pity (too bad)*
es difícil *it's difficult, unlikely*	**es mejor** *it's better*
es dudoso *it's doubtful*	**es necesario** *it's necessary*
es extraño *it's strange*	**es posible** *it's possible*
es fácil *it's easy*	**es preciso** *it's necessary*
es importante *it's important*	**es probable** *it's probable*
es imposible *it's impossible*	**es urgente** *it's urgent*

¡Atención! Most of these impersonal expressions may take an infinitive as their object rather than a dependent clause in the subjunctive.

Indefinite subject: Infinitive	*Definite subject: Subjunctive clause*
Es bueno trabajar.	**Es bueno que tú trabajes.**
It's good to work.	*It's good that you work.*
Es difícil conseguir trabajo.	**Es difícil que yo consiga trabajo.**
It's difficult to obtain a job.	*It's difficult for me to obtain a job.*

Práctica 2 Complete with the infinitive, or with the corresponding form of the verb in the present indicative or present subjunctive tense, as required.

1. Es importante que Juan (**obtener**) _____ el puesto. 2. Es cierto que ella (**jugar**) _____ muy bien al tenis. 3. ¿Es difícil (**aprender**) _____ japonés? 4. Es urgente que yo (**encontrar**) _____ trabajo. 5. Es lástima que tú no (**saber**) _____ manejar. 6. No es cierto que él (**poder**) _____ ingresar en la universidad. 7. Será mejor (**traducir**) _____ la palabra. 8. Es necesario que tú (**comprar**) _____ los boletos. 9. Es verdad que ella (**pensar**) _____ siempre en Uds. 10. ¿Es posible que ella (**llegar**) _____ mañana? 11. Es dudoso que Elena (**manejar**) _____ el carro. 12. Será preciso que Ud. (**hacer**) _____ las reservas.

Actividades y práctica: B

C. Adjective clauses and relative pronouns
(Cláusulas adjetivales y pronombres relativos)

Adjective clauses *(Cláusulas adjetivales)*

■ An adjective clause modifies a noun or pronoun and is introduced by a relative pronoun, usually **que**, *who, which, that,* or **quien,** *who.* Relative pronouns relate or link additional information to an antecedent; the noun or pronoun to which the relative pronoun refers is the antecedent of the adjective clause.

Antecedent	Relative Pronoun	Continuation of Adjective Clause	
Mi amigo Miguel,	**quien**	es estudiante de ingeniería,	se gradúa este otoño.
My friend Michael,	*who*	*is an engineering student,*	*is graduating this fall.*
Él,	**que**	es muy inteligente,	encontrará un trabajo pronto.
He,	*who*	*is very intelligent,*	*will find a job soon.*

Relative pronouns *(Pronombres relativos)*

Que, *that, which, who, whom*

Los estudiantes **que** recibieron las becas son muy inteligentes.	*The students who received the scholarships are very intelligent.*
El puesto **que** Miguel consiguió es excelente.	*The job (that) Michael got is excellent.*
Las empresas de **que** me hablaste no tienen sucursales en Suramérica.	*The corporations (that) you talked to me about do not have branches in South America.*

■ **Que,** which is invariable in form, is the most frequently used relative pronoun. The noun antecedent to which **que** refers may be either a person or a thing.

- **Que** may be used with a preposition only when the noun antecedent refers to a non-living thing.

- Unlike its English equivalent, the relative pronoun **que** cannot be omitted.

Quien (*pl.* quienes), *who, whom*[1]

El agente con **quien** hablé ayer me enseñó la maquinaria.	*The agent with whom I talked yesterday showed me the machinery.*
Se lo diré al señor Ruiz, a **quien** conocí hace unos meses.	*I'll tell Mr. Ruiz, whom I met a few months ago.*
Miguel, **quien** (**que**) es estudiante de ingeniería, es bilingüe.	*Michael, who is an engineering student, is bilingual.*

- **Quien** and **quienes** refer only to persons and are used mainly after prepositions.

- The personal **a** is required when **quien**, **quienes** is the direct object of the verb.

- When the adjective clause is set off by commas and does not require a preposition or personal **a**, either **que** or **quien**(**es**) may introduce the adjective clause (as in the last example).

El cual and el que, *that, which, who, whom*

El señor Ruiz es el gerente de una empresa norteamericana, **la cual** (**que**) tiene una sucursal en Puerto Rico.	*Mr. Ruiz is the manager of a North American company, which has a branch in Puerto Rico.*
La señorita White es la secretaria del director, **el cual** (**quien**) escribirá la carta.	*Miss White is the secretary of the director, (the one) who will write the letter.*

- The longer forms of the relative pronouns, **el cual** (**la cual, los cuales, las cuales**) and **el que** (**la que, los que, las que**) may be used in more formal speech and writing instead of **que** or **quien** (**quienes**) to clarify which one of the two possible antecedents the adjective clause modifies. The form of the relative pronoun is determined by the antecedent.

El puesto **acerca del cual** (**de que**) te hablé es excelente.	*The position about which I spoke to you is excellent.*
Allí están las oficinas **cerca de las cuales** (**las que**) querían construir una fábrica.	*Over there are the offices near (to) which they wanted to build a factory.*

- These forms are also used after compound prepositions such as **acerca de**, **cerca de**, **antes de**, **después de**.

Es necesario que el candidato sea bilingüe, **lo cual** (**lo que**) no sería ningún problema para ti.	*It is necessary that the candidate be bilingual, which (fact) would not be a problem for you.*

- The neuter form **lo cual** or **lo que**, *which (fact)*, is used to refer to a preceding idea, statement, or situation.

---

1. **Quien**(**-es**) may also correspond to English *he (those) who, the one(s) who*, particularly in proverbs: **Quien** busca, encuentra: *He (The one) who seeks, finds.*

Práctica 3   Supply the relative pronouns (in some cases, there is more than one correct answer).

1. Las ingenieras con _____ hablamos ayer son de Chile.   2. El problema de la maquinaria, de _____ me escribieron Uds., es muy grave.   3. El gerente de la empresa, _____ reside en Puerto Rico, acaba de llamarme por teléfono.   4. El profesor no devolvió los ejercicios, _____ nos pareció raro.   5. La secretaria _____ tradujo la carta se llama Carmen.   6. Los empleados _____ nos escribieron no están contentos con el horario de las comidas.   7. Agradecemos mucho las tarjetas _____ nos han mandado.   8. Los primos de Diana, _____ residen en Buenos Aires, pasarán las vacaciones con nosotros.

✪✪✪ Actividades y práctica: C

D. Subjunctive or indicative in adjective clauses
(El subjuntivo o el indicativo en cláusulas adjetivales)

■ When the antecedent of an adjective clause refers to an indefinite, non-existent, or negative person or thing, the verb in the adjective clause is in the subjunctive. If the antecedent refers to a definite, specific person or thing, the verb in the dependent clause is in the indicative.

Indefinite, non-specific antecedent: *Subjunctive*	*Definite, specific antecedent:* *Indicative*
Buscan un ingeniero que entienda de maquinaria agrícola. *They are looking for an engineer who understands agricultural machinery.*	**Buscan al ingeniero** que entiende de maquinaria agrícola. *They are looking for the engineer who understands agricultural machinery.*
¿Conoce Ud. a alguien que sea ingeniero? *Do you know anyone who is an engineer?*	**¿Conoce Ud. al joven** que es ingeniero? *Do you know the young man who is an engineer?*
No hay nadie que esté mejor preparado que tú. *There is no one who is better prepared than you.*	**Hay alguien** que está mejor preparado que tú. *There is someone who is better prepared than you.*

¡Atención!   Remember that the personal **a** is omitted when the noun does not refer to a specific person.[1] However, the pronouns **alguien, nadie** (also **alguno** and **ninguno** when referring to a person), and **quien** require the personal **a** when used as direct objects.

---

1. See *Spanish On Your Own*, Vol. I, **Lección 5**.

Práctica 4   Complete each sentence with the corresponding form of the present indicative or present subjunctive tense, as required.

1. Buscamos un médico que (**hablar**) _____ alemán.   2. No conozco a nadie que (**ser**) _____ tan competente como él.   3. ¿Conoce Ud. a los señores que (**pensar**) _____ comprar este edificio?   4. Buscan una persona que (**querer**) _____ residir allí.   5. Preferimos un empleo que (**pagar**) _____ bien.   6. En esta tienda siempre hallamos algo que nos (**gustar**) _____.   7. Busco a la enfermera que (**trabajar**) _____ los domingos.   8. ¿Conocen Uds. a alguien a quien yo (**poder**) _____ recomendar?   9. Nos interesa la secretaria que (**saber**) _____ varias lenguas.   10. No encuentro a nadie que (**recordar**) _____ las palabras de la canción.   11. No hay ninguna joven que (**conocer**) _____ a la señora Ortega.   12. Necesitamos una persona que (**haber**) _____ vivido allí.

Actividades y práctica: D

E. **Hacer** in time clauses   *(Hacer en cláusulas de tiempo)*

Hace... que or desde hace...

To express an action begun in the past and still in progress at the present time, Spanish uses either of two constructions with the verb **hacer**. Note that English usually uses the present perfect progressive: *have been* + *-ing* form of the verb.

- **hacer** + time expression + **que** + present tense verb

  Hace mucho tiempo **que** quiero visitar la isla.

  I have been wanting to visit the island for a long time.

- present tense verb + **desde hace** + time expression

  Quiero visitar la isla **desde hace** mucho tiempo.

  I have been wanting to visit the island for a long time.

Hacía... que or desde hacía...

To indicate how long an action had been going on when something else (expressed or understood) occurred, the same two constructions with **hacer** are used, but both **hacer** and the main verb of the sentence are in the imperfect. Note that in contrast with Spanish, English usually uses the pluperfect progressive.

Hacía un año **que** ellos buscaban trabajo.	*They had been looking for a job for a year.*
Ellos buscaban trabajo **desde hacía** un año.	*They had been looking for a job for a year.*

¡Atención!   The following constructions are used when asking questions with **hacer** in time expressions:

¿Cuánto tiempo **hace que** quieres visitar la isla?	*(For) how long have you been wanting (wanted) to visit the island?*

¿Cuánto tiempo **hacía que** ellos   *(For) how long had they been looking*
  buscaban trabajo?   *for work (a job)?*

¡Atención!   Remember from **Lección 14** that **hace** + verb in the past tense corresponds to the English *ago* or *since*: Lo conocí *hace* unos años, (*Hace* unos años *que* lo conocí), *I met him a few years ago*.

Práctica 5   Answer the questions, using the information given in parentheses to express an action that started in the past and is still going on, following the model.

> MODEL: ¿Desde cuándo conoces a María? (**dos años**) → Conozco a María
> desde hace dos años, *or* Hace dos años que conozco a María.

1. ¿Desde cuándo asiste Miguel a la Escuela de Ingeniería? (**cuatro años**)

_____

2. ¿Cuánto tiempo hace que tú piensas estudiar medicina? (**dos semestres**)

_____

3. ¿Cuánto tiempo hace que tus tíos viven en México? (**seis meses**)

_____

4. ¿Desde cuándo estudia Ud. el español? (**siete meses**)

_____

5. ¿Desde cuándo conduce Ud. el mismo carro? (**unos cinco años**)

_____

Práctica 6   Answer the questions, using the information given in parentheses to express how long an action has been going on, following the model.

> MODEL: ¿Cuánto tiempo hacía que conocías a María? (**seis meses**) → Yo
> conocía a María desde hacía seis meses. *or* Hacía seis meses que
> yo conocía a María.

1. ¿Cuánto tiempo hacía que Roberto se sentía mal? (**dos días**)

_____

2. ¿Desde cuándo trabajaba Jaime en esa tienda? (**dos semanas**)

_____

3. ¿Cuánto tiempo hacía que Ana no asistía a clase? (**ocho días**)

_____

4. ¿Cuánto tiempo hacía que Uds. recibían esa revista? (**un año**)

_____

5. ¿Desde cuándo jugaba Ud. al fútbol? (**unos cinco años**)

_____

Actividades y práctica: E

F. Spanish equivalents for *to become* or *to get*
(*Los equivalentes de* to become *o* to get *en español*)

- The most common construction used in Spanish to express the idea of *becoming* or *getting to be* is a reflexive verb.

Me alegré mucho.	*I became very happy.*
Su madre **se enfermó** mucho.	*His (Her) mother got very ill.*

- **Ponerse** followed by an adjective or a past participle that expresses a mental, emotional, or physical change may also be used to convey the idea of *becoming*.

Me puse muy alegre.	*I became very happy.*
¡A veces **me pongo** tan preocupado!	*At times I get so worried!*

- **Hacerse** followed by some adjectives such as **rico** denotes a conscious effort on the part of the subject. **Hacerse** is also often followed by nouns of profession.

Miguel **se hizo** ingeniero.	*Michael became an engineer.*
Se hará rico con esa profesión.	*He will become rich with that profession.*

- **Llegar a ser** expresses a final result due to the natural development of time and circumstances.

Miguel **llegó a ser** muy buen ingeniero.	*Michael became (turned out to be) a very good engineer.*

Práctica 7   Complete the following sentences by using the corresponding form of the preterit indicative tense of one of the verbs listed below; in the case of certain sentences, there is more than one correct answer.

hacerse   llegar a ser   ponerse

1. Al ver al médico, ella _____ muy nerviosa.

2. Como ella es muy inteligente, pronto _____ profesora.

3. El día _____ muy nublado.

4. Al saber la noticia, Roberto _____ rojo.

5. Trabajando día y noche, ese hombre de negocios _____ rico.

G. The infinitive after verbs of perception
(*El infinitivo después de verbos de percepción*)

La señorita White **vio pasar** a Miguel por el corredor.	*Miss White saw Michael passing through the hall.*
Oigo salir a Inés con sus amigas.	*I hear Agnes leaving with her friends.*
Anoche **escuché cantar** a las chicas.	*Last night I listened to the girls singing.*
Oí decir que Miguel se gradúa este trimestre.	*I heard people saying that Michael is graduating this trimester.*

- After a few verbs of perception such as **ver**, **oír**, and **escuchar**, the infinitive is often used in Spanish, while the present participle (*-ing* form) is used in English.

Práctica 8   Rewrite the following sentences, changing the clauses with **cuando** to
the infinitive construction, as in the model.

> MODEL: Vimos al taxista cuando pasaba por la izquierda. → **Vimos al
> taxista pasar por la izquierda.**

1. Miguel vio a Inés cuando ella salía de la residencia.

   _____

2. Mirábamos a los jóvenes cuando jugaban al fútbol.

   _____

3. Yo oí el teléfono cuando sonó.

   _____

4. Escuchábamos al profesor cuando pronunciaba las palabras nuevas.

   _____

5. Vimos a Miguel cuando entraba en la agencia de empleo.

   _____

6. ¿Oíste a Isabel cuando tocó anoche?

   _____

Actividades y práctica: F

Repaso

A. Circle the item that does not belong in each series of words.

1. la empresa / la fábrica / la isla / la compañía
2. el trimestre / la entrevista / el candidato / la vacante
3. la solicitud / la beca / la recomendación / la maquinaria
4. la jefe / la sucursal / el secretario / el empleado

B. Use the expressions in parentheses in complete sentences.

1. (ponerse nervioso, -a) _____   _____
2. (trabajador, -ora) _____
3. (oír decir que) _____

C. Give the Spanish equivalent.

1. The director of the School of Agricultural Engineering has just received a letter from the manager of a

   firm that has a branch in Puerto Rico. _____

   _____

2. Mr. Ruiz wants to know if the director knows someone who can work as an agent of his company on the

   island. _____

   _____

3. When Miss White, who is the director's secretary, sees Michael Ramos pass, she calls him and informs him about the job opening. _____

_____

4. Michael tells Miss White that since he is graduating as an engineer, it is urgent for him to find work soon. _____

_____

5. Mr. Ruiz needs a competent person who would want to reside in San Juan. It is also necessary that the candidate be bilingual, which would not be a problem for Michael. _____

_____

Expansión

A. Write answers to these questions, using complete sentences.

1. ¿Qué profesión le interesa a Ud.? _____

2. ¿Qué carrera profesional recomendaría Ud. a un joven que va a empezar sus estudios universitarios?

_____

_____

3. ¿Qué es necesario que una persona haga para conseguir un trabajo? _____

_____

4. ¿Es fácil o difícil encontrar trabajo hoy día? ¿Por qué? _____

_____

5. Si Ud. necesita un puesto, ¿a quién pedirá que lo (la) recomiende? _____

_____

B. Write a brief account of a job-hunting experience you have had. Describe how you found out about the job, the application process, and any interviews you participated in. Were you nervous or confident? Did you get the job, and if so, how did it turn out? Say also what you learned from the experience.

_____

_____

_____

_____

_____

_____

_____

_____

_____

Para comprender y escribir

A. From the three choices offered, select the one that best completes the statement or answers the question you hear.

1. (a) un asunto.
   (b) un ascenso.
   (c) un agente.

2. (a) una beca.
   (b) un empleado.
   (c) una sucursal.

3. (a) hace una recomendación.
   (b) se gradúa de ingeniero.
   (c) se pone nervioso.

4. (a) una empresa.
   (b) un ingeniero.
   (c) un negocio.

B. Write a new sentence using the cues you hear, as in the model.

> MODEL: Es bueno trabajar. (que Uds.) → **Es bueno que Uds. trabajen.**

1. _____
2. _____
3. _____
4. _____
5. _____
6. _____
7. _____
8. _____

C. Combine the two sentences you hear, using **a quien** or **a quienes**, as in the model.

> MODEL: Vimos a la joven. Es española. → **La joven a quien vimos es española.**

1. _____
2. _____
3. _____
4. _____

D. Dictado. You will hear a short narrative about a letter the director of the School of Agricultural Engineering received and what he plans on doing with it. You will hear the passage three times. Listen the first time. Write what you hear the second time. Make any necessary corrections the third time.

_____
_____
_____
_____
_____

_____

_____

_____

_____

✿✿ ✿ *VOCABULARIO*

el (la) **agente** agent
agradecer to be grateful (thankful) for
agrícola (*m. or f.*) agricultural, farm (*adj.*)
el **ascenso** promotion
el **asunto** matter, affair
ayudar (a + *inf.*) to help *or* aid (to + *verb*)
la **beca** scholarship
la **candidata** candidate (applicant for a job, position) (*f.*)
el **candidato** candidate (applicant for a job, position) (*m.*)
la **compañía** company
competente (*m. or f.*) competent, qualified
el **director** director (*m.*)
la **directora** director (*f.*)
la **empleada** employee (*f.*)
el **empleado** employee (*m.*)
la **empresa** company, firm, house (business)
entender (ie) to understand
la **entrevista** interview
la **fábrica** factory
graduarse (**de**) to graduate (as *or* from)
imaginarse to imagine
la **isla** island
el (la) **jefe** boss
loco, -a crazy, wild, mad

la **maquinaria** machinery
obtener (*like* **tener**) to obtain, get
precisamente *adv.* precisely
producir to produce
el **puerto** port (*shipping*)
el **puesto** position, place, job
quien (*pl.* **quienes**) who, whom (*after prep.*)
la **recomendación** (*pl.* **recomendaciones**) recommendation
la **referencia** reference
residir to reside
rico, -a rich, wealthy
romántico, -a romantic
la **secretaria** secretary (*f.*)
el **secretario** secretary (*m.*)
la **solicitud** application
la **sucursal** branch (*of a company*)
el **sueldo** salary
trabajador, -ora industrious, hard-working
el **trabajo** work, employment, position, job
traducir to translate
el **trimestre** trimester, quarter
unos, -as about (*quantity*)
urgente (*m. or f.*) urgent
vacante (*m. and f.*) unfilled; unoccupied
la **vacante** job opening
el **verso** verse

a partir de beginning with
la **agencia de empleo** employment agency
la **carta de recomendación** letter of recommendation
como agente as an agent
¡cuánto se lo agradezco! how grateful I am to you for it (that)!
¿cuánto tiempo hace? how long is it (has it been)?
entender (ie) **de** (**asuntos de maquinaria agrícola**) to understand *or* have experience in (matters of agricultural machinery)
hacer la solicitud to apply, submit the application

hacer una recomendación to give a recommendation
el **hombre de negocios** businessman
la **ingeniería agrícola** agricultural engineering
   me preocupo tanto I get so worried
la **mujer de negocios** businesswoman
   oír decir que to hear (it said) that
   ponerse nervioso, -a to get (become) nervous
   ponerse rojo, -a to blush, become (get) red
el **puesto vacante** available position (job), job opening
el **viaje de negocios** business trip
   volverse (ue) loco, -a to become *or* go crazy (wild, mad)

Repaso, Lecciones 16–19: Appendix C

Lección 20

- ⚙ Forms of verbs ending in **-ger**, **-gir** and **-iar**, **-uar**
- ⚙ Subjunctive or indicative in adverbial clauses
- ⚙ Possessive pronouns
- ⚙ The definite article as a demonstrative pronoun
- ⚙ The use of **pero** and **sino**

Luna de miel en Suramérica

Alberto y Silvia, que se habían casado en la primavera, decidieron pasar su luna de miel en Suramérica. Lo que siempre habían deseado conocer era Machu Picchu, la gran ciudad de piedra cerca de Cuzco. Buscaron una agencia de viajes y escogieron la del padre de un amigo, que está cerca del parque.

ALBERTO —Buenas tardes, señor Ponce. Le presento a mi esposa Silvia.

SR. PONCE —Mucho gusto en conocerla, Silvia.

SILVIA —El gusto es mío, señor Ponce.

ALBERTO —Deseamos hacer reservas para viajar al Perú. ¿Puede informarnos sobre los vuelos a Cuzco?

SR. PONCE —Hay varios vuelos diarios. Pero no son directos a Cuzco, sino a Lima. Desde allí se continúa el viaje en una línea interna hasta Cuzco.

ALBERTO (*Mirando a Silvia.*) —Lo cual quiere decir que no podremos llevar muchas maletas, a menos que queramos tener problemas..., ¿comprendes?

SILVIA —Solamente dos, mi amor: la tuya y la mía.

SR. PONCE —¿En qué fecha desean Uds. salir de viaje?

ALBERTO —Nos gustaría salir el quince de agosto, en un vuelo de día.

El agente de viajes se excusa y va a consultar la computadora. Luego regresa con la información.

SR. PONCE —Lo siento mucho, pero no quedan asientos en el de la mañana, a menos que alguien cancele.

SILVIA —¿Podría Ud. ponernos en la lista de espera?

SR. PONCE —Con mucho gusto. ¿Boletos sencillos o de ida y vuelta?

ALBERTO —De ida y vuelta. Tenemos que regresar el día treinta, antes de que comiencen las clases en la universidad.

SR. PONCE —Es posible que tengan que partir el día dieciséis. De todos modos les enviaré los boletos a casa. Podrán pagar con tarjeta de crédito o cheque personal.

ALBERTO —Muchas gracias, señor Ponce.

SR. PONCE —No hay de qué. ¡Adiós! ¡Hasta la vista!

Preguntas sobre los diálogos

1. ¿Qué decidieron hacer Alberto y Silvia? _____

_____

2. ¿Qué habían deseado conocer ellos siempre? _____

_____

3. ¿Qué agencia de viajes escogieron para hacer sus reservas? _____

_____

4. ¿Hay vuelos directos a Cuzco? ¿Cómo van a llegar a Cuzco? _____

_____

5. ¿Cuándo les gustaría salir? _____

_____

6. ¿Por qué no pueden salir en el vuelo de la mañana? _____

_____

7. ¿Cuándo tienen que regresar? ¿Por qué tienen que regresar para esa fecha? ___

_____

8. ¿Cómo podrán pagar ellos? _____

_____

Notas gramaticales

A. Forms of verbs ending in **-ger, -gir** and **-iar, -uar**
(Formas de los verbos terminados en -ger, -gir y en -iar, -uar)

Forms of verbs ending in **-ger, -gir**

escoger, *to choose, select*	
Pres. Ind.	escojo, escoges, escoge, escogemos, escogéis, escogen
Pres. Subj.	escoja, escojas, escoja, escojamos, escojáis, escojan

- In verbs ending in -ger like **escoger**, *to choose, select,* and -gir like **dirigir**, *to direct, address,* the **g** of the stem changes to **j** before verb endings beginning with -o or -a, that is, in the first-person singular form of the present indicative and in all six forms of the present subjunctive.

Forms of verbs ending in **-iar, -uar**

enviar, *to send*	
Pres. Ind.	envío, envías, envía, enviamos, enviáis, envían
Pres. Subj.	envíe, envíes, envíe, enviemos, enviéis, envíen
Sing. Imper.	envía

continuar, *to continue*	
Pres. Ind.	continúo, continúas, continúa, continuamos, continuáis, continúan
Pres. Subj.	continúe, continúes, continúe, continuemos, continuéis, continúen
Sing. Imper.	continúa

- A few verbs ending in **-iar**, such as **enviar** and **esquiar**, and **-uar**, such as **continuar** and **graduarse**, require an accent mark on the final stem vowels **i** and **u** in the singular and third-person plural forms of the present indicative tense, in the same forms as in the present subjunctive tense, and in the singular familiar commands.

Práctica 1   Complete the following sentences by using the corresponding form of the present indicative or present subjunctive tense of one of the four verbs listed below.

escoger   dirigirse a   enviar   continuar

1. Si yo _____ el paquete por avión, llegará mañana.

2. Insistimos en que Uds. _____ sus estudios en esta universidad.

3. ¿A quién _____ (yo) para cambiar los boletos?

4. Queremos que los jóvenes _____ la fecha para la fiesta.

5. Estando en Montevideo, ¿por qué no _____ tú el viaje hasta Buenos Aires?

6. Ellos _____ el dinero mañana, ¿verdad?

7. Tus amigos siempre _____ los peores asientos.

8. Oí decir que los problemas de Ana _____.

9. Recomiendo que Uds. _____ al gerente sobre ese asunto.

10. ¿Es necesario que nosotros _____ viviendo en la residencia?

11. Es mejor que él me _____ la revista a casa.

12. ¿Cuál de los discos _____ nosotros para Isabel?

Actividades y práctica: A

B. Subjunctive or indicative in adverbial clauses
(El subjuntivo o el indicativo en cláusulas adverbiales)

Subjunctive vs. indicative in time clauses

- The indicative mood is used in time clauses when the time indicated is present or past, that is, the action is expressed as customary or as an accomplished fact.

- The subjunctive mood is used in time clauses when the time indicated is indefinite or future with respect to that of the main verb.

- By its very meaning, **antes (de) que**, *before*, indicates that the action has not yet happened. Therefore the verb that follows must always be in the subjunctive (last example).

Customary or accomplished event: Indicative

Cuando **veo** a Juan, **charlo** con él.
When (every time) I see John, I chat with him.

Siempre **espero** hasta que mi novia **sale** de clase.
I always wait until my girlfriend gets out of class.

La conferencia **comenzó** en cuanto **sonó** el timbre.

The lecture began as soon as the bell rang.

Event unfulfilled, yet to be accomplished: Subjunctive

Cuando **vea** a Juan, **charlaré** con él.
When I see John (whenever that may be), I'll chat with him.

Esperaré (**Voy a esperar**) hasta que mi novia **salga** de clase.
I'll wait (I am going to wait) until my girlfriend gets out of class (whenever that may be).

La conferencia **comenzará** (**va a comenzar**) en cuanto **suene** el timbre.
The lecture will start (is going to start) as soon as the bell rings.

Voy a escribir el resumen antes (de) que **lleguen** mis amigas.
I'm going to write the summary before my friends arrive.

■ The following are common conjunctions that introduce time clauses:

antes (de) que *before*
así que *as soon as*
cuando *when*
después (de) que *after*

en cuanto *as soon as*
hasta que *until*
luego que *as soon as*
mientras (que) *while, as long as*

Subjunctive vs. indicative in clauses expressing concession

■ Clauses introduced by **aunque**, *although, even though, even if,* describe conditions in spite of which a given result is (was) or is not (was not) accomplished. When the adverbial clause refers to a factual condition or situation, the verb is in the indicative mood. When the adverbial clause refers to a hypothetical condition or situation, the verb is in the subjunctive mood.

Factual condition or situation: Indicative

Aunque **hace** frío, saldré.
Even though it is cold, I shall leave.

Aunque **trabajan** mucho, no reciben buen sueldo.
Although they work hard, they don't receive a good salary.

Hypothetical condition or situation: Subjunctive

Aunque **haga** frío mañana, saldré.
Even though it may be cold tomorrow, I shall leave.

Aunque **trabajen** mucho, no recibirán (van a recibir) buen sueldo.
Although they may work hard, they will not (are not going to) receive a good salary.

The subjunctive mood in other adverbial clauses

■ Conjunctions that denote purpose, condition, exception, negation, and the like always require the adverbial clause to be in the subjunctive mood, since these conjunctions cannot introduce a statement of fact.

Mi familia me enviará dinero para
que yo **compre** el boleto de avión.

*My family will send me money in order
(so) that I may buy the plane ticket.*

No quedan asientos a menos que
alguien **cancele**.

*There are no seats left unless someone
cancels.*

No pagaré sin que **confirmen** las
reservas.

*I will not pay without their confirming
the reservations.*

Tomaré un vuelo directo con tal (de)
que no **salga** demasiado temprano.

*I'll take a nonstop flight provided
(that) it doesn't leave too early.*

- The following are common conjunctions that introduce clauses expressing
  condition:

a menos que *unless*
con tal (de) que *provided (that)*
en caso de que *in case (the
    event) that*

para que *in order (so) that*
sin que *without*

¡Atención!   When there is no change in subject, the prepositions **para** and **sin** +
infinitive are normally used instead of a clause with the subjunctive.

No partirán **sin decírnoslo**.

They won't leave without telling us.

Traerán el dinero **para comprar**
unas maletas.

*They will bring the money in order to
buy some suitcases.*

Práctica 2   After reading the two statements, combine them in one sentence by
means of the conjunction in parentheses, following the model.

> MODEL: Ana no partirá. Su padre le enviará el dinero. (**hasta que**) → **Ana
> no partirá hasta que su padre le envíe el dinero.**

1. Entraremos en la sala. Empezará la conferencia. (**cuando**)

   _____

2. Cerraremos los libros. El profesor llegará. (**en cuanto**)

   _____

3. Haremos la excursión. Continuará lloviendo. (**aunque**)

   _____

4. Iremos a la boda. Ana se enfermará. (**a menos que**)

   _____

5. Lo visitaré. Él volverá de clase. (**después de que**)

   _____

6. Veremos a Laura. Ella se graduará en junio. (**luego que**)

   _____

7. Dígaselo. Ella no escogerá otra universidad. (**para que**)

   _____

8. Le mandaré flores. Ella regresará del hospital. (**antes de que**)

   _____

Práctica 3   Complete each sentence with the corresponding form of the present indicative or present subjunctive tense, as required.

1. No le dé Ud. nada hasta que él (**acercarse**) _____. 2. En cuanto llego a Puerto Rico, (**asistir**) _____ a las fiestas. 3. Déjémosle las maletas para que él las (**facturar**) _____. 4. Ellos no podrán llevarse el carro sin que nosotros los (**oír**) _____.

5. El partido comienza ahora, aunque se (**decir**) _____ que va a llover. 6. Saldremos por la mañana a menos que se (**cancelar**) _____ el vuelo. 7. Después de que Rita te (**traer**) _____ las fotos, quiero que me las enseñes. 8. Hable Ud. más despacio para que nosotros (**poder**) _____ comprenderlo. 9. Ese chico siempre me pide algo cuando me (**ver**) _____. 10. A Elena le gusta escuchar la radio mientras (**manejar**) _____ su carro.

Actividades y práctica: B

C. Possessive pronouns   *(Pronombres posesivos)*

| Singular | | Plural | | |
Masculine	Feminine	Masculine	Feminine	
el mío	la mía	los míos	las mías	mine
el tuyo	la tuya	los tuyos	las tuyas	yours (*fam.*)
el nuestro	la nuestra	los nuestros	las nuestras	ours
el vuestro	la vuestra	los vuestros	las vuestras	yours (*fam.*)
el suyo	la suya	los suyos	las suyas	his, hers, its, yours (*formal and pl.*), theirs

Aquí está mi carro; ¿dónde está **el tuyo**?   *Here is my car; where is yours?*
Las maletas de Diana no llegaron; éstas   *Diane's suitcases didn't arrive;*
   son **las nuestras**.   *these are ours.*
Este paquete es **el mío**; **el suyo**   *This package is mine; hers is that*
   (**el de ella**) es aquél.   *one.*
Éste es el asiento de Ud.; **el suyo**   *This is your seat; his is that one.*
   (**el de él**) es aquél.

- In **Lección 11**, you learned about the long forms of the possessive adjectives. Possessive pronouns are formed by using the definite article **el** (**la, los, las**) with the long forms of the possessive adjectives.

- Since **el suyo** (**la suya, los suyos, las suyas**) may mean *his, hers, its, yours* (formal), and *theirs*, these pronouns may be clarified by substituting **el de él, el de ella, el de Ud., el de ellos (ellas), el de Uds.** The article agrees with the thing possessed (last two examples).

Práctica 4   Answer the questions affirmatively, using a possessive pronoun for the words in italics, following the model.

MODEL: ¿Confirmó Ud. *su boleto*? → **Sí, confirmé el mío.**

1. ¿Compró Ud. *el carro de Juan?* _____

2. ¿Viene Ud. a *nuestro cuarto?* _____

3. ¿Traen Uds. *sus pasaportes?* _____

4. ¿Hallaron Uds. *mis llaves?* _____

5. ¿Facturó Ud. *mi maleta?* _____

6. ¿Envolvió Ud. *mis paquetes?* _____

7. ¿Vieron Uds. *mi bicicleta?* _____

8. ¿Es de oro *el anillo de Ana?* _____

D. The definite article as a demonstrative pronoun
(El artículo definido como pronombre demostrativo)

- Before a phrase beginning with **de**, Spanish uses the definite article instead of the demonstrative pronoun. **El (la, los, las) de** is translated *that (those) of (with, in)*, and occasionally by an English possessive (first example).

El vuelo de hoy sale a las diez; **el de mañana** sale a las ocho.	*Today's flight leaves at ten; tomorrow's (that of tomorrow) leaves at eight.*
Tengo tus boletos y **los de Silvia.**	*I have your tickets and Sylvia's (those of Sylvia).*

- Spanish also uses the definite article instead of the demonstrative (or personal) pronoun before a relative clause introduced by **que**. **El (la, los, las) que** corresponds to *the one(s) who (that, which), those who (that, which).*[1] These forms, which may refer to persons or things, are often called compound relatives. This construction is often used instead of **quien(-es)** to refer to persons.

¡Atención!   Do not use **el cual** in this construction.

Ésta es mi maleta; **la que** está allá es la tuya.	*This is my suitcase; the one that is over there is yours.*
Éstos son los asientos que escogimos, pero **los que** ellos tienen son mejores.	*These are the seats we chose, but the ones (that) they have are better.*

Práctica 5   Rewrite each sentence, substituting the corresponding definite article for the noun before **de** and **que**, as in the models.

> MODELS: Queremos esa foto y la foto de Ana. → Queremos esa foto y la **de Ana.**
> Esta tarjeta y la tarjeta que tú mandaste son bonitas. → Esta **tarjeta y la que** tú mandaste son bonitas.

1. Este carro y el carro del profesor no son caros.

   _____

2. Me llevo este anillo y el anillo que Isabel escogió.

   _____

---

1. **Lo que** is the neuter form of **el que** and means *that which, what:* **Siempre creo lo que la gente me dice,** *I always believe what people tell me.*

3. Vamos a enviarle este mapa y el mapa de Inés.

_____

4. Me gustan esta clase y la clase de francés.

_____

5. Estas maletas y las maletas de Carolina son muy caras.

_____

6. Me interesan esas comedias y las comedias que recomendó Ud.

_____

 Actividades y práctica: C

E. The use of **pero** and **sino**   *(El uso de pero y sino)*

■ **Pero** usually corresponds to the English conjunction *but*.

Lo siento mucho, **pero** no quedan asientos.	*I'm very sorry, but there are no seats left.*

■ **Sino** is used in an affirmative statement that is in direct contrast to a preceding negative statement. **Sino** corresponds to the English *but* when it means *on the contrary*, *but instead*, *but rather*. No other verb form except an infinitive may be used after **sino** (last example).

No hay vuelos directos a Cuzco, **sino** a Lima.	*There are no direct flights to Cuzco, but (there are) to Lima.*
Yo no quiero estudiar, **sino** ir al cine.	*I don't want to study, but (rather) go to a movie.*

■ **Sino que** is used if clauses containing different verbs are contrasted: **No mirábamos la televisión *sino que* escuchábamos unos discos**, *We weren't watching television but (instead) we were listening to some records.* (This construction is not used in the **Prácticas** or **Actividades**.)

Práctica 6   Complete with **pero** or **sino**, as required.

1. No fuimos al cine, _____ a la discoteca.

2. La profesora no es rica, _____ es muy inteligente.

3. Me gustó la chaqueta, _____ no quise comprarla.

4. Ese vuelo no va a San Antonio, _____ a Los Ángeles.

5. Busqué a Laura, _____ no la encontré.

6. Parece que Jorge no va en carro, _____ en avión.

 Actividades y práctica: D

Repaso

A. Find among the following words and phrases the ones you associate with the words and phrases listed below. Use each word or phrase only once.

el asiento	de la salida	interna	el parque
el boleto	de piedra	la luna de miel	el pasajero
la computadora	de viajes	la maleta	el pasaporte
confirmar	directo	la parada	personal

1. la agencia _____
2. casarse _____
3. consultar _____
4. el cheque _____
5. sencillo _____

6. facturar _____
7. la fecha _____
8. presentar _____
9. la línea _____
10. el vuelo _____

B. Give the Spanish equivalent.

1. Albert and Sylvia have decided to spend their honeymoon in Peru. _____
_____

2. They learn that there are several daily flights; but they are not direct to Cuzco, (but) rather to Lima.
_____
_____

3. They hope to leave on August 15, provided that there is a morning flight. _____
_____

4. The travel agent consults the computer and finds that there are no seats left on that flight; Sylvia asks him to put them on the waiting list. _____
_____

5. They bought round-trip tickets, because they have to return on August 30. _____
_____

Expansión

A. Write answers to these questions, using complete sentences.

1. Cuando Ud. tiene que hacer un viaje en avión, ¿dónde puede comprar los boletos? _____
_____

2. ¿Paga Ud. sus cuentas con tarjeta de crédito o con cheque personal? _____
_____

3. Cuando Ud. viaja en avión, ¿prefiere facturar sus maletas o llevarlas consigo? _____
_____

4. ¿Adónde piensa Ud. ir en su próximo viaje en avión? ¿Por qué? _____
_____

5. Para poder entrar en muchos países, ¿qué necesita uno llevar? _____
_____

6. ¿Le gustaría a Ud. poder estudiar español en algún país extranjero? ¿En cuál, y por qué? _____

_____

B. The Business School has invited Mr Campos, a Mexican economist, to give a lecture. You are the secretary of the school. Write a brief report in Spanish informing the faculty about the arrangements being made. Include the following information: The date of the lecture, and when Mr. Campos will arrive; what kind of travel and hotel accommodations he has requested, and whether the school will pay for it; who will meet his plane and take him to his hotel; and the time of the lecture. Note also that the lecture should be of interest not only to the students and professors of the School, but also the general public.

_____

_____

_____

_____

_____

_____

_____

_____

_____

Para comprender y escribir

A. From the three choices offered, select the one that best completes the statement or answers the question you hear and circle it.

1. (a) parada.
   (b) azafata.
   (c) vuelo.

2. (a) el asiento.
   (b) el pasajero.
   (c) el pasaporte.

3. (a) un boleto de ida y vuelta.
   (b) una lista de espera.
   (c) una línea interna.

4. (a) despedirse.
   (b) partir.
   (c) salir.

5. (a) no salen de viaje.
   (b) no hacen la maleta.
   (c) no quedan asientos.

B. Combine the two sentences you hear, using the conjunction suggested. Follow the model.

> MODEL: Ana no partirá. Su familia le envía el dinero. (hasta que) → **Ana no partirá hasta que su familia le envíe el dinero.**

1. _____

2. _____

3. _____

4. _____

5. _____

6. _____

C. Write an alternate form for the sentence you hear, using a possessive pronoun. Follow the model.

MODEL: Tengo el libro de Ana. → **Tengo el suyo.**

1. _____

2. _____

3. _____

4. _____

5. _____

6. _____

7. _____

8. _____

D. Dictado. You will hear a short passage about Silvia and Alberto's honeymoon plans. You will hear the passage three times. Listen the first time. Write what you hear the second time. Make any necessary corrections the third time.

_____

_____

_____

_____

_____

_____

_____

_____

_____

_____

_____

_____

_____

✿✿ ✿ *VOCABULARIO*

el **aeromozo** flight attendant (*m.*)
el **aeropuerto** airport
el **asiento** seat
la **azafata** flight attendant (*f.*)
  cancelar to cancel

confirmar to confirm
consultar to consult
continuar to continue, go on
despedirse (**i, i**) (**de** + *obj.*) to say
  good-bye (to), take leave (of)

diario, -a daily
directo, -a direct
enviar to send
escoger to choose, select
excusar to excuse; *reflex.* to excuse
    oneself
facturar to check (*baggage*)
la **ida** departure
la **información** information
informar to inform
interna internal, domestic
la **maleta** suitcase, bag
la **parada** stop
el **parque** park
la **partida** departure
partir (de) to depart, leave
    (from)

partir (para) to depart, leave
    (for)
la **pasajera** passenger (*f.*)
el **pasajero** passenger (*m.*)
el **pasaporte** passport
    personal (*m.* or *f.*) personal
el **Perú** Peru
la **piedra** stone
el **plan** plan
    presentar to present, introduce
    sino *conj.* but, but rather
    solamente *adv.* only
el (la) **turista** tourist
el **vuelo** flight
la **vuelta** return

la **agencia de viajes** travel agency
el (la) **agente de viajes** travel agent
el **boleto sencillo (de ida y vuelta)** one-way
        (round-trip) ticket
la **(ciudad) de piedra** stone (city)
la **clase turista** tourist (economy) class
    de todos modos in any case
    el gusto es mío the pleasure is mine
    hacer la maleta to pack one's bag
la **línea interna** domestic airline
la **lista de espera** waiting list
la **luna de miel** honeymoon
    mucho gusto en conocerla (I am)
        pleased (glad) to know *or* nice meeting (to
        meet) you (*formal f. sing.*)
    no hay de qué you're welcome, don't mention it
    no quedan asientos no seats are left
        (remain), there aren't any seats left
la **primera clase** first class
    querer decir to mean
    salir de viaje to leave on the (one's) trip
    tenemos que regresar el día (treinta)
        we have to return on the (thirtieth)
el **vuelo de día** daytime flight, flight by day (in the daytime)
el **vuelo de la mañana** morning flight
el **vuelo directo** non-stop (direct) flight

Lección 21

✿✿✿

- ✿ The imperfect subjunctive
- ✿ The pluperfect subjunctive
- ✿ Uses of the subjunctive tenses
- ✿ **Si**-clauses
- ✿ Forms of **valer**

Hacen planes para un viaje

Al salir de la casa de correos una tarde, Alberto y Silvia se encuentran con José Soto, un ingeniero cubano muy simpático que ha viajado varias veces por Suramérica. Se detienen para saludarlo y hacerle algunas preguntas.

SILVIA —¡Hola, José! ¡Qué casualidad! Pensábamos llamarte esta noche.

ALBERTO —Salimos para Chile la semana que viene y queremos pedirte algunos consejos.

JOSÉ —¡Hombre! Si yo lo hubiera sabido antes, los habría invitado a casa para ver las transparencias de mi último viaje.

ALBERTO —No te preocupes por eso, José. Pero, ¡oye! Como sabes, las líneas aéreas no le permiten a uno llevar mucho equipaje.

SILVIA —¿Llevarías abrigo si fueras allá en esta estación del año?

JOSÉ —¡Cómo no! No olviden que es invierno ahora al sur del ecuador. Si yo volviera por allí ahora, llevaría ropa de lana, un abrigo ligero y unos guantes.

SILVIA —Yo pienso llevar un suéter y sin duda necesitaremos impermeables y un paraguas. Lloverá allí a veces, ¿no?

JOSÉ —¡Ya lo creo! Y también llevaría una cámara vídeo.

SILVIA —Sí, mi padre nos aconsejó que además de la cámara fotográfica compráramos una vídeo.

JOSÉ —¡Es una idea magnífica! Valdría la pena llevar las dos.

SILVIA —Nos dijo que le gustaría que tomáramos algunas películas de los Andes.

JOSÉ —Es lástima que no me llamaran antes; los habría ayudado a escogerla. Si tuvieran una cámara vídeo, traerían recuerdos inolvidables del viaje.

ALBERTO —Pues, todavía no hemos tenido la oportunidad de buscarla.

SILVIA —Si no tienes nada que hacer mañana por la mañana, nos gustaría que nos acompañaras a varias tiendas para comparar las diferentes marcas y precios.

JOSÉ —Con mucho gusto. Estaré listo a cualquier hora.[1]

SILVIA —Entonces, ¿por qué no nos encontramos aquí enfrente de la casa de correos a las once en punto?

JOSÉ —De acuerdo. Estaré aquí sin falta. Hasta mañana, entonces.

SILVIA —Hasta la vista, José.

ALBERTO —Óyeme, y si después tuvieses[2] tiempo, nos gustaría invitarte a almorzar.

Preguntas sobre el diálogo

1. ¿Con quién se encuentran Alberto y Silvia? _____

_____

---

1. **Cualquier(a)** (*pl.* **cualesquier[a]**), which may drop the final -a before a noun, means *any* or *anyone* (*at all*), *just any* (*one at all*).
2. The **-se** form of the imperfect subjunctive is used by speakers from Spain.

2. ¿Por qué pensaban Silvia y Alberto llamar a José? _____

3. ¿Qué llevaría José si volviera por Chile durante el invierno? _____

_____

4. ¿Qué piensa llevar Silvia? ¿Y qué otras cosas necesitarán? _____

_____

5. ¿Por qué les aconsejó el padre de Silvia que compraran una cámara vídeo? _____

_____

6. ¿Por qué es lástima que no hubieran llamado a José antes? _____

_____

7. ¿Dónde van a encontrarse los tres mañana por la mañana? ¿Qué piensan hacer? _____

_____

✿✿
✿ *Notas gramaticales*

A. The imperfect subjunctive   *(El imperfecto del subjuntivo)*

Regular verbs   *(Verbos regulares)*

	hablar	**comer**	**vivir**
Singular	hablara	comiera	viviera
	hablaras	comieras	vivieras
	hablara	comiera	viviera
Plural	habláramos	comiéramos	viviéramos
	hablarais	comierais	vivierais
	hablaran	comieran	vivieran

- To form the imperfect subjunctive tense of all verbs, regular and irregular, drop **-ron** of the third-person plural preterit indicative and add **-ra, -ras, -ra, -ramos, -rais,** or **-ran**.[1] Only the first-person plural forms have a written accent.

- Just as the present subjunctive is often expressed in English with *may* as a part of its meaning, so the imperfect subjunctive is expressed with *might*: **Espero que él hable,** *I hope that he may talk;* **Yo esperaba que él hablara** (or **hablase**), *I hoped that he might talk.*

---

1. A second form of the imperfect subjunctive ends in **-se** rather than **-ra**: **hablase, hablases, hablase, hablásemos, hablaseis, hablasen.** The two forms are interchangeable, but the **-ra** form is more commonly used.

Stem-changing verbs   *(Verbos con cambios en la raíz)*

Infinitive	3rd Pl. Preterit	Imperfect Subjunctive
pensar	pensaron	pensara, -ras, etc.
volver	volvieron	volviera, -ras, etc.
sentir	sintieron	sintiera, -ras, etc.
pedir	pidieron	pidiera, -ras, etc.
seguir	siguieron	siguiera, -ras, etc.
dormir	durmieron	durmiera, -ras, etc.

- Remember that verbs like **pensar** and **volver** (which have a stem change e → ie, o → ue in the present indicative) do not have a stem change in the preterit indicative. Therefore, this class of verbs, like regular verbs, does not undergo a stem change in the imperfect subjunctive.

- Verbs ending in -ir that have a stem change e → i or o → u in the third-person singular and plural of the preterit indicative do have this change throughout the imperfect subjunctive.

Irregular verbs   *(Verbos irregulares)*

Inf.	3rd Pl. Pret.	Imp. Subj.	Inf.	3rd Pl. Pret.	Imp. Subj.
creer	creyeron	creyera	poder	pudieron	pudiera
dar	dieron	diera	poner	pusieron	pusiera
decir	dijeron	dijera	querer	quisieron	quisiera
estar	estuvieron	estuviera	saber	supieron	supiera
haber	hubieron[1]	hubiera	ser	fueron	fuera
hacer	hicieron	hiciera	tener	tuvieron	tuviera
ir	fueron	fuera	traducir	tradujeron	tradujera
leer	leyeron	leyera	traer	trajeron	trajera
oír	oyeron	oyera	venir	vinieron	viniera

- Note that the imperfect subjunctive forms for **ser** and **ir** are identical.

Práctica 1   Complete the sentences by using one of the verbs listed below in the corresponding form of the imperfect subjunctive. Certain verbs may be used more than once.

comprar	llamar	recibir
comprender	llevar	vivir
escribir	prometer	

1. Él me aconsejó que (yo) no _____ el artículo.

2. Sería bueno que Uds. _____ una lavadora de platos de otra marca.

---

1. See Appendix B for the preterit form of **haber**.

3. Yo les aconsejé que _____ suficiente dinero.

4. Sería mejor que Uds. _____ boletos de ida y vuelta.

5. Temíamos que ellos no _____ el paquete a tiempo.

6. Fue lástima que Uds. no me _____ antes de la conferencia.

7. Yo dudaba que él _____ comprarle un anillo.

8. Querían que nosotros _____ a los padres de Juan.

9. Fue necesario que nosotros _____ lejos del centro.

10. Temíamos que los estudiantes no _____ al profesor.

Práctica 2   Form sentences by rearranging the elements and changing the infinitives of the stem-changing verbs to the corresponding form of the imperfect subjunctive.

1. aquéllos / que estos boletos / ella no creía / costar / más que

   _____

2. pedir / que la policía / el carnet / me / yo temía

   _____

3. la cámara / yo le / cinematográfica / devolver / dije que

   _____

4. divertirse / de que / en la fiesta / Uds. / nos alegramos

   _____

5. la casa de correos / encontrar / querían / enfrente de / que nos

   _____

6. recomendar / me pidió / un buen hotel / que le / Alberto

   _____

7. en la residencia / dormir / fue mejor / anoche / que ellos

   _____

8. anoche / que / durante la fiesta / llover / fue lástima

   _____

Práctica 3   Complete the sentences with the corresponding form of the imperfect subjunctive of one of the irregular verbs listed below. Use each verb only once.

creer   leer   querer   traer
estar   oír   saber
ir   poner   ser

1. Fue imposible que nosotros _____ nuestras bicicletas.

2. Queríamos que ella _____ la novela.

3. Nos pidieron que (nosotros) _____ los abrigos sobre el sofá.

4. No podían creer que Elena _____ nuestra profesora.

5. Sería mejor que Ud. _____ a consultar al médico.

6. No creíamos que ella _____ nuestra dirección.

7. Nos pareció extraño que nadie _____ mirar las transparencias.

8. Temíamos que ellos no _____ las noticias.

9. Fue lástima que Uds. _____ enfermos.

10. Fue lástima que nosotros no _____ el teléfono.

✪✪
✪   **Actividades y práctica: A**   🎧

B. The pluperfect subjunctive   *(El pluscuamperfecto del subjuntivo)*

hablar, comer, vivir
hubiera hubieras hubiera hubiéramos hubierais hubieran } hablado, comido, vivido

- The pluperfect subjunctive is formed by using either form of the imperfect subjunctive of **haber** with the past participle. Its meaning is similar to that of the pluperfect indicative.

| Alberto temía que José ya lo **hubiera** (hubiese) sabido. | *Albert was afraid that Joseph had already known about it.* |
| José sentía que Alberto no lo **hubiera** llamado la semana pasada. | *Joseph was sorry that Albert hadn't called him last week.* |

Práctica 4   Form sentences by rearranging the elements and changing the infinitives to the corresponding form of the pluperfect subjunctive.

1. comprar / no creía / la cámara / que Alberto / yo

_____

2. esa película / no / es extraño / ver / que ellas

_____

3. al profesor / se lo / no parecía posible / decir / que Ana

_____

4. traducir / que él / todavía / no lo / me molestó

_____

5. el dinero / le / todos dudaban / dar / que nosotros

_____

6. escribir / que Uds. / algunas líneas / no nos / sentíamos

_____

Actividades y práctica: B

C. Use of the subjunctive tenses _(Uso de los tiempos del subjuntivo)_

■ When the main verb in a sentence requiring the subjunctive mood in the dependent clause is in the present, future, present of **ir a** + infinitive, present perfect tense, or is a command, the verb in the dependent clause is regularly in the present or present perfect subjunctive.

Main clause: Present, future, present   Dependent clause: Present or
    of **ir a** + infinitive, present perfect,   present perfect subjunctive
    or command

Main Clause		_Dependent Clause_
Yo **espero**	que	José **esté** listo a la una.
I hope	_that_	_Joseph will be ready at one._
José **querrá**	que	nosotros lo **llamemos** primero.
Joseph will want		_us to call him first._
Marta **va a pedirte**	que	la **lleves** a la fiesta.
Martha is going to ask (you)	_that_	_you take her to the party._
Ella te **ha llamado**	para que	la **invites.**
She has called you	_so_	_you will invite her._
Dile a Miguel	que	la **traiga.**
Tell Michael		_to bring her._
Temo	que	ella no te **haya encontrado.**
I'm afraid	_that_	_she has not found you._

■ When the main verb is in the imperfect, preterit, imperfect of **ir a** + infinitive, conditional, or pluperfect indicative, the verb in the dependent clause is normally in the imperfect subjunctive. The pluperfect subjunctive, however, is used in Spanish to express the English past perfect subjunctive in the dependent clause (last example).

Main clause: Imperfect, preterit,   Dependent clause: Imperfect or
    imperfect of **ir a** + infinitive,   pluperfect subjunctive
    conditional, or pluperfect
    indicative

Main Clause		*Dependent Clause*
Luis **esperaba**	que	lo **invitáramos** a la fiesta.
Louis hoped	*that*	*we would invite him to the party.*
Su novia me **aconsejó**	que	te **hablara**.
His girlfriend advised me		*to talk to you.*
Ella **iba a pedirte**	que	lo **llamaras**.
She was going to ask you		*to call him.*
Nos **gustaría**	que	tú lo **hicieras**.
We would like		*you to do it.*
Ella te **había llamado**	para que	lo **invitaras**.
She had called you	*so*	*you would invite him.*
Sentí	que	no lo **hubieras hecho**.
I was sorry	*that*	*you had not done it.*

¡Atención!   Note, however, that the imperfect subjunctive tense may follow the present or present perfect tense when, as in English, the action of the dependent verb took place in the past.

Es (una) lástima que Uds. **llegaran** tarde.

It's a pity that you (pl.) arrived late.

No **has querido** que yo los **llamara** antes.

You have not wanted me to call them before.

Práctica 5   Rewrite each sentence, using the initial phrase given in parentheses, following the model.

> MODEL: Es mejor que Ud. se vaya. (**Fue mejor**) → **Fue mejor que Ud. se fuera.**

1. No hay nadie que comprenda eso. (**No había**) _____

   _____

2. Alberto busca una cámara que le guste. (**Alberto buscaba**) _____

   _____

3. No es ceirto que Jaime conozca la ciudad. (**No fue cierto**) _____
   .
   _____

4. Quieren que nos encontremos enfrente de la casa de correos. (**Querían**) ___

   _____

5. Será posible que ella escoja otra marca. (**Sería posible**) _____

   _____

6. Les traigo las fotos para que Uds. las vean. (**Les traje**) _____

_____

7. Yo le aconsejo a Luis que les muestre la carta. (**Yo le aconsejé**) _____

_____

8. José recomienda que nosotros vayamos a otra tienda. (**José recomendó**) _____

_____

Práctica 6   Complete with the corresponding form of the present or imperfect subjunctive of the verb in parentheses.

1. Fue lástima que el novio de Silvia (**tener**) _____ que salir de viaje.   2. Ellos se alegran de que nosotros no (**hacer**) _____ la excursión mañana.   3. Los novios buscaban un apartamento que (**estar**) _____ cerca de la universidad.   4. Queríamos visitar a Isabel antes de que ella (**partir**) _____ para España.   5. No había nadie que (**querer**) _____ asistir a la conferencia.   6. Es necesario que Alberto (**buscar**) _____ otra maleta.   7. ¿Les aconsejó a Uds. que (**escoger**) _____ otra agencia?   8. Fue preciso que ellos (**volver**) _____ pronto.

D. **Si**-clauses   *(Cláusulas con si)*

Si-clauses describe a hypothetical condition upon which a subsequent event depends. To express contrary-to-fact conditions or future hypothetical events unlikely to happen, the subjunctive mood is used in the **si**-clause and the verb in the main clause is in the conditional or conditional perfect tense.

Contrary-to-fact conditions: Subjunctive

■ To express something that is contrary to fact (i.e., not true) at the present time, Spanish uses the imperfect subjunctive in the **si**-clause and the conditional in the main or result clause.

Si él **tuviera** (*or* **tuviese**) dinero, me lo **daría**.	*If he had money* (but he doesn't), *he would give it to me.*
Si él **fuera** (*or* **fuese**) simpático, yo lo **invitaría** a casa.	*If he were likable* (but he isn't), *I would invite him to my house.*

■ To express something that was contrary to fact in the past, Spanish uses the pluperfect subjunctive in the **si**-clause and the conditional perfect in the main or result clause.

Si él **hubiera** (*or* **hubiese**) **tenido** dinero, me lo **habría dado**.	*If he had had money* (but he didn't), *he would have given it to me.*
Si él **hubiera** (*or* **hubiese**) **sido** simpático, yo lo **habría invitado** a casa.	*If he had been likable* (but he wasn't), *I would have invited him to my house.*

¡Atención!   Como si, *as if*, also expresses a contrary-to-fact condition.

Estamos charlando **como si no tuviéramos** (*or* **tuviésemos**) nada más que hacer.	*We are chatting as if we had nothing else to do* (but we do have).

| Estábamos charlando **como si no hubiéramos** (*or* **hubiésemos**) **tenido** nada más que hacer. | *We were chatting as if we hadn't had anything else to do* (but we did have). |

Hypothetical future events: Subjunctive

The imperfect subjunctive tense is used in the **si**-clause to express something that is not expected to happen, but that *might* happen in the future. The verb in the result or main clause is in the conditional.

| Si ellos **vinieran** (*or* **viniesen**) mañana, yo los **vería**. | *If they should (were to) come tomorrow, I would see them.* |
| ¿**Necesitaría** yo abrigo si **viajara** (*or* **viajase**) por los Andes? | *Would I need a coat if I should (were to) travel in the Andes?* |

¡Atención!

- If the condition established in the **si**-clause is likely to be met and the result is, therefore, likely to be achieved, then both clauses are in the indicative.

| Si ellos **vienen** mañana, yo los **veré**. | *If they come tomorrow, I'll see them.* |
| ¿**Necesitaré** abrigo si **viajo** por los Andes? | *Will I need a coat if I travel in the Andes?* |

- The future indicative, the conditional, and the present subjunctive tenses are not used after **si** meaning *if* in conditional sentences. These tenses can only be used when **si** means *whether*: **No sé *si* él irá o *si* se quede aquí**, *I don't know whether he'll go or whether he'll stay here.*

Práctica 7 Complete with the corresponding form of the verb. When the imperfect subjunctive tense is required, use the **-ra** form.

1. Si Ud. (**poder**) _____ enviarme las entradas, se lo agradecería mucho.

2. Si yo (**haber**) _____ sabido que Uds. estaban aquí, los habría invitado.

3. Si Uds. (**hacer**) _____ las reservas hoy, no tendrán problemas.

4. Si tú (**haber**) _____ traído un abrigo, no habrías pescado un resfriado.

5. Podremos sacar muchas fotos si (**llevar**) _____ una cámara.

6. Si me lo (**permitir**) _____ mis padres, yo haría el viaje con Uds.

7. Yo le haré a José algunas preguntas si (yo) (**encontrarse**) _____ con él.

8. Yo le daría a él algunos consejos si (yo) (**ser**) _____ profesor suyo.

Práctica 8 Form new conditional sentences, following the model.

> MODEL: Yo lo haría, pero no tengo tiempo. → **Si yo tuviera tiempo, lo haría.**

1. Yo compraría el libro, pero el profesor no lo recomienda.

_____

2. Le enviaríamos una tarjeta, pero no tenemos estampillas.

_____

3. Te acompañaríamos, pero no quedan asientos en ese vuelo.

_____

4. Ellos alquilarían el apartamento, pero no está amueblado.

_____

5. Luis llevaría un paraguas, pero no está lloviendo ahora.

_____

6. Yo le daría algunos consejos, pero él no me consulta.

_____

 Actividades y práctica: C, D

E. Forms of **valer**   _(Formas de valer)_

valer, _to be worth_	
Pres. Ind.	valgo, vales, vale, valemos, valéis, valen
Pres. Subj.	valga, valgas, valga, valgamos, valgáis, valgan
Familiar (tú) Command	val (vale)
Future	valdré, valdrás, etc.
Cond.	valdría, valdrías, etc.

- All other forms of **valer,** t_o be worth_, are regular.

- The impersonal expression **vale más (la pena)**, _it is better (worthwhile)_, is followed by the subjunctive mood when the dependent clause has a specific subject: **Vale (Valdrá) la pena** _que Uds._ **lleven** una cámara, _It is (will be) better (worthwhile) for you_ (pl.) _to take a camera._ When the sentence makes a general observation or when the subject is clear to both the speaker and listener, the infinitive is used: **Vale (Valdrá) la pena** **llevar** una cámara, _It is (will be) better (worthwhile) to take a camera._

Práctica 9   Complete with the corresponding form of **valer** in the present indicative, present subjunctive, future, or conditional. (In certain cases, two or more answers may be correct.)

1. ¿Creen Uds. que _____ la pena estudiar español?

2. Nosotros creemos que _____ la pena estudiarlo.

3. ¿Cuánto _____ estos aretes de oro?

4. Es posible que _____ mucho.

5. _____ la pena que Uds. estudiaran un poco más.

6. No creo que yo _____ mucho como cantante.

Repaso

A. Find among the following words and phrases the ones you associate with the words and phrases listed below. Use each word or phrase only once.

aérea	el impermeable
de película	la lana
falta	mañana
fotográfica	la pena

1. valer _____

2. el suéter _____

3. el rollo _____

4. pasado _____

5. el paraguas _____

6. la cámara _____

7. la línea _____

8. sin _____

B. Give the Spanish equivalent.

1. Upon leaving the post office, Albert and Sylvia run across Joseph Soto. _____
   _____

2. The latter is a very likable Cuban engineer who has traveled in (**por**) South America three or four
   times. _____
   _____

3. They want to ask him for some advice because they are leaving for Chile next week. _____
   _____

4. If Joseph had known it before, he would have invited them to his home to see the slides of his last trip.
   _____
   _____

5. Sylvia's father advised them that, besides the camera, they should take a video camera. _____
   _____

6. If they had a video camera, they would bring unforgettable memories. _____
   _____

Expansión

A. Write answers to these questions, using complete sentences.

1. Si Ud. pudiera hacer un viaje por los Estados Unidos este verano, ¿qué estados visitaría? ¿Por qué?
   _____
   _____

2. ¿Qué ropa tendría Ud. que comprar si tuviera que salir pasado mañana? _____
   _____

3. Si Ud. necesitara dinero durante su viaje, ¿a quién se lo pediría? _____
   _____

4. ¿A quiénes escribiría Ud. cartas o tarjetas durante su viaje? _____

_____

5. ¿Saca Ud. muchas fotografías cuando viaja? _____

_____

6. Si Ud. hubiera viajado por Hispanoamérica el año pasado, ¿habrías tenido problemas con la lengua?

_____

_____

B. Write a letter to some friends with the following information: the School of Business has selected you to attend a program in Japan (**el Japón**). You speak Japanese quite well, but if you had known that you would have this opportunity, you would have studied much harder. You will visit several factories and firms. You have received your passport and are almost ready for the trip. You hope that your friends will let you use their camera during the trip. Mention some other things you hope to do there.

Queridos amigos:

_____

_____

_____

_____

_____

_____

_____

_____

_____

_____

_____

_____

_____

Para comprender y escribir

A. From the three choices offered, select the one that best completes the statement or answers the question you hear and circle it.

1. (a) unos guantes.
   (b) unas marcas.
   (c) una transparencia.

2. (a) Hasta mañana.
   (b) Todavía no.
   (c) Pasado mañana.

3. (a) la cámara?
   (b) el paraguas?
   (c) el equipaje?

4. (a) la casa de correos.
   (b) una línea aérea.
   (c) un impermeable bueno.

5. (a) viajan por carro.
   (b) vale la pena.
   (c) se preocupan mucho.

B. Change the sentences from the present to the past, as in the model.

> MODEL: Quieren que yo lleve un abrigo ligero. → **Querían que yo llevara un abrigo ligero.**

1. _____
2. _____
3. _____
4. _____
5. _____
6. _____
7. _____
8. _____

C. Respond affirmatively to the questions you are asked, as in the model.

> MODEL: ¿Qué harías si consiguieras trabajo en España? ¿Vivir allí? → **Sí, si yo consiguiera trabajo en España, viviría allí.**

1. _____
2. _____
3. _____
4. _____
5. _____
6. _____

D. Dictado. You will hear a short narrative about Silvia and Alberto's encounter with José Soto. You will hear the narrative three times. Listen the first time. Write what you hear the second time. Make any necessary corrections the third time.

_____
_____
_____
_____
_____
_____
_____
_____
_____
_____
_____

✿✿ ✿ VOCABULARIO

el **abrigo** topcoat, overcoat, coat
   acompañar to accompany, go with
   aéreo, -a air (adj.)
la **cámara** camera
   comparar to compare
   cualquier(a) (pl. **cualesquier[a]**)
      any (one) (at all), just any (one)
      (at all)
   detener (like **tener**) to detain,
      stop; reflex. to stop (oneself)
   diferente (m. and f.) different
la **duda** doubt
el **ecuador** equator
   encontrarse (ue) (con) to meet,
      run across
el **equipaje** baggage, luggage
la **falta** lack, want
el **guante** glove
el **impermeable** raincoat
   inolvidable (m. and f.)
      unforgettable
la **lana** wool

ligero, -a light(weight)
listo, -a ready
llevar to wear; to take
magnífico, -a magnificent, fine
la **marca** brand, kind, make
la **oportunidad** opportunity,
   chance
el (los) **paraguas** umbrella(s)
   pesado, -a heavy (weight)
   preocuparse (por) to worry
      (about)
   revelar to develop (film)
el **rollo** roll (film)
   simpático, -a charming,
      likeable, nice
el **suéter** sweater
el **sur** south
la **transparencia** transparency,
      slide
   valer to be worth
el **vídeo** video

a cualquier hora at any time (hour)
al sur de(l) south of
la **cámara fotográfica** camera
la **(cámara) vídeo** video camera
la **casa de correos** post office
   como si as if
   hacer una pregunta (a) to ask a question (of)
   hasta mañana until (see you) tomorrow
   invitar a casa to invite to one's house
la **línea aérea** airline
   no tener nada que hacer not to have anything (to have
      nothing) to do
   pasado mañana day after tomorrow
el **rollo de película** roll of film
la **ropa de lana** wool clothes, woolen clothing
   sin duda doubtless, no doubt
   sin falta without fail
   tener la oportunidad de + inf. to have the opportunity of
      (to) + verb
   todavía no not yet
   tomar una película to film (a movie)
   valer la pena to be worthwhile
   valer más to be better
   viajar por to travel in (through)
   ¡ya lo creo! of course! certainly!

Lección 22

✦✦✦

- ✿ Familiar plural (**vosotros**) commands
- ✿ The passive voice
- ✿ Reflexives as reciprocal pronouns
- ✿ Other uses of the subjunctive mood
- ✿ Forms of **reunirse** and of verbs ending in **-uir**
- ✿ Summary of uses of **para** and **por**

No digamos adiós, sino hasta luego

Al terminar sus exámenes y antes de marcharse de la universidad, varios compañeros se reúnen para almorzar en un restaurante que les ha sido recomendado por Miguel Ramos. Desgraciadamente, Miguel no ha podido asistir a la reunión. Después de una deliciosa comida, charlan de sus planes. Jorge, uno de los muchachos, es español y emplea formas peninsulares.

CARLOS —¡Es lástima que Miguel tuviera otro compromiso hoy!

JORGE —Si no hubiese[1] estado muy ocupado preparando su partida a Puerto Rico, habría venido a almorzar con nosotros. Ya sabéis que consiguió un buen puesto allí.

BEATRIZ —¡Cuánto me alegro! Hay que felicitarlo. Y a propósito, ¿por qué no hablamos un poco de nuestros planes para el futuro?

JORGE —Entonces, empezad, guapas.[2] ¿Qué piensas hacer tú, Isabel?

ISABEL —¡Tú siempre echando piropos! Pues de momento, voy a pasar el verano en la costa… ¡en la casa construida por mis abuelos hace casi cien años!

JORGE —Y después, ¿en el otoño?

ISABEL —En el otoño regresaré para continuar mis estudios de arquitectura. ¿Y tú?

JORGE —Pues, ¡asombraos, amigos! Mi padre me sugirió que volviese a Madrid.

CARLOS —Pero, ¿no decías que pensabas buscar un puesto en este país?

JORGE —Con mi maestría en administración de negocios, él quisiera que yo llegase a ser el gerente de su compañía. Por ahora es una oportunidad muy buena para mí.

BEATRIZ —¡Ojalá que tengas mucho éxito! ¡Ya es hora de que te hagas rico! Así podrás volver a los Estados Unidos cuando quieras…

JORGE —Y vosotros, no dejéis de visitarme en Madrid. Yo quisiera que todos mis buenos amigos vinieseis pronto a verme.

BEATRIZ —¡Cuánto me gustaría viajar por España si tuviera el dinero! Si consigo la beca que he solicitado para estudiar arte, nos veremos en septiembre.

Mientras toman café, el camarero les trae un pastel en que está escrita la frase: «No digamos adiós, sino hasta luego». Está firmada por Miguel. Continúan charlando animadamente como si no tuvieran nada que hacer. Por fin Jorge anuncia que es hora de despedirse.

JORGE —Bueno, amigos, ya es tarde. Levantaos y despidámonos. ¡Ojalá que nos veamos otra vez antes de marcharnos!

BEATRIZ —¡Cuánto vamos a echarte de menos, Jorge!

---

1. The **-se** form of the imperfect subjunctive is used primarily in Spain.
2. The adjectives **guapo**, *handsome*, and **guapa**, *beautiful*, are used quite frequently as nouns in Spain when addressing friends.

Preguntas sobre los diálogos

1. ¿Qué hacen Jorge y sus compañeros antes de marcharse de la universidad? _____

_____

2. ¿Por quién les ha sido recomendado el restaurante a los amigos? _____

_____

3. ¿Por qué no pudo asistir Miguel a la reunión? _____

_____

4. ¿Dónde piensa pasar el verano Isabel? _____

_____

5. ¿Por quiénes fue construida la casa? _____

_____

6. ¿Qué le sugirió a Jorge su padre? _____

_____

7. ¿Qué quisiera él que llegara a ser Jorge? _____

_____

8. ¿Qué frase está escrita en el pastel que Miguel ha enviado? _____

_____

✿✿✿ *Notas gramaticales*

A. Familiar plural (**vosotros**) commands
(Formas familiares del mandato con vosotros)

Familiar plural commands

Inf.	Affirmative	Negative	Inf.	Affirmative	Negative
hablar	hablad	no habléis	dormir	dormid	no durmáis
comer	comed	no comáis	pedir	pedid	no pidáis
escribir	escribid	no escribáis	venir	venid	no vengáis

- To form the affirmative familiar vosotros commands[1] of all verbs, drop -**r** of the infinitive and add -**d**.
- For the negative familiar **vosotros** commands, use the second-person plural of the present subjunctive.

_____

1. In this text we have followed the practice, which is common in Spanish America, of using the third-person plural present subjunctive for all plural commands: **Hablen Uds.; Vengan Uds.** The familiar plural forms used in this lesson will, however, be needed for recognition in reading.

■ The subject pronoun **vosotros, -as** is usually omitted with these commands.

Familiar commands of reflexive verbs

	Singular		Plural	
Infinitive	*Affirmative*	*Negative*	*Affirmative*	*Negative*
levantarse	levántate	no te levantes	levantaos	no os levantéis
sentarse	siéntate	no te sientes	sentaos	no os sentéis
ponerse	ponte	no te pongas	poneos	no os pongáis
reunirse	reúnete	no te reúnas	reuníos	no os reunáis
irse	vete	no te vayas	idos	no os vayáis

■ In forming the affirmative familiar **vosotros** commands of reflexive verbs, final **-d** is dropped before adding **os**, except for **idos** (**vosotros**), (*you*) *go.*

■ An accent mark must be written when **te** is added to a singular command form of more than one syllable. When **os** is added to an **-ir** reflexive verb, except for **idos**, an accent mark must be written on the **i: reuníos**.

Práctica 1 Answer each question with a negative and an affirmative familiar **vosotros** command, following the model.

> MODEL: ¿Contestamos ahora? → No, no contestéis ahora. Contestad más tarde.

1. ¿Volvemos ahora? _____

2. ¿Salimos ahora? _____

3. ¿Almorzamos ahora? _____

4. ¿Nos levantamos ahora? _____

5. ¿Nos lavamos ahora? _____

6. ¿Se lo damos ahora? _____

   Actividades y práctica: A

B. The passive voice   *(La voz pasiva)*

La casa **fue construida** por mis abuelos.	*The house was built by my grandparents.*
El restaurante les **ha sido recomendado** por Miguel.	*The restaurant has been recommended to them by Michael.*
Las dos cartas **fueron firmadas** por el gerente.	*The two letters were signed by the manager.*

■ The true passive voice in Spanish is formed as in English. When an action is performed by an agent, Spanish uses **ser** and the past participle. The past participle agrees with the subject in gender and number, and the agent is usually expressed by **por**, where English uses *by.*

- In the spoken language the passive voice is often avoided, in Spanish as in English, by changing the sentence to the active voice: **La casa fue construida por mis abuelos** → **Mis abuelos construyeron la casa**, *The house was built by my grandparents* → *My grandparents built the house.*

- Remember from **Lección 12** that when an action is expressed without indicating who is doing it (i.e., with no agent expressed), and the subject is a thing, Spanish uses the reflexive **se**: **Aquí** *se habla* **español**, *Spanish is spoken here.*

¡Atención!   Do not confuse the true passive voice, which expresses action, with the use of **estar** + a past participle to express the state or condition that results from the action of a verb (**Lección 14**).

Las cartas **fueron traducidas** por la secretaria.	Las cartas ya **están traducidas**.
The letters were translated by the secretary.	*The letters are already translated.*

Práctica 2   Answer the questions in the affirmative, changing the active verb to the passive voice, as in the model.

> MODEL: ¿Envió Miguel el pastel? → **Sí, el pastel fue enviado por Miguel.**

1. ¿Recibió Alberto el pasaporte?

   _____

2. ¿Solicitaron las becas muchos estudiantes?

   _____

3. ¿Sacaron los estudiantes esas fotos?

   _____

4. ¿Facturará José las maletas mañana?

   _____

5. ¿Anunciará el profesor la fecha del examen?

   _____

Práctica 3   Complete the sentences with either **ser** or **estar**. Pay attention to the use of **ser** + past participle to express the passive voice and **estar** + past participle to express a resultant state or condition.

1. El resumen ____ escrito por Miguel; ____ muy bien escrito.

2. Las fotografías ya ____ reveladas; ____ reveladas mientras esperábamos.

3. Todos los boletos para clase turista ____ vendidos; ____ vendidos hace meses.

4. Ya podemos irnos porque la cuenta ____ pagada; ____ pagada por mi amigo José.

5. Las fechas del viaje ____ decididas después que hablamos con la agencia. ¿____ nosotros decididos a salir pasado mañana?

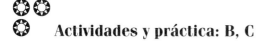

Actividades y práctica: B, C

C. Reflexives as reciprocal pronouns
(Formas reflexivas como pronombres recíprocos)

Nos veremos en septiembre.	*We'll see one another (each other) in September.*
Nos conocemos muy poco.	*We know each other very little.*
¿**Se escribían** Uds. a menudo?	*Did you used to write to one another (each other) often?*

The plural forms of the reflexive pronouns, **nos**, **os**, **se**, may be used with verbs to express reciprocal action. The English equivalents are *each other*, *one another*.

Práctica 4 Complete the sentences by using the corresponding form of one of the verbs listed below in the reciprocal construction, in the present indicative or present subjunctive tense. Use each verb only once, following the model.

> MODEL: Desde el accidente Juan y Luis no _____ (hablar). →
> **Desde el accidente Juan y Luis no se hablan.**

conocer	escribir	ver
entender	querer	visitar

1. Como tenemos las mismas clases, Ana y yo _____ casi todos los días.

2. Aunque Luis y José son muy diferentes, parece que _____ muy bien.

3. Como mis padres y yo preferimos hablar por teléfono, ya no _____.

4. Como Mario y yo fuimos a la misma escuela, _____ desde hace mucho tiempo.

5. Aunque Clara almuerza con Marta casi todos los días, ellas no _____ a menudo.

6. Aunque Roberto sale mucho con Laura, no creo que _____ mucho.

D. Other uses of the subjunctive mood
(Otros usos del modo subjuntivo)

The subjunctive mood in a polite or softened statement

- It is considered polite to soften statements by using the -ra forms of the imperfect subjunctive of **querer**.

Yo quiero verte pronto.	*I want to see you soon.*
Yo **quisiera** verte pronto.	*I should like to see you soon.*

- The -ra forms of **deber**, and occasionally of **poder**, are also used to form a polite or softened statement or question.

Ella debe solicitar una beca.	*She must apply for a scholarship.*
Ella **debiera** solicitar una beca.	*She should (ought to) apply for a scholarship.*
¿Puede Ud. llamarme?	*Can you call me?*
¿**Pudiera** Ud. llamarme?	*Would you be able to call me?*

¡Atención!   Remember from **Lección 15** that the conditional tense may also be used with **deber** and **poder** to express a polite or softened statement or question. The two previous examples of the use of the imperfect subjunctive may be expressed, perhaps more commonly, as: **Ella debería solicitar una beca; ¿Podría Ud. llamarme?**

■ In the case of other verbs, softened statements or questions are expressed with the conditional tense, as in English (**Lección 15**).

Yo **diría** que Juan tiene razón.	*I would say that John is right.*
¿Te **gustaría** salir conmigo?	*Would you like to go out with me?*

The subjunctive mood with ¡ojalá (que)!   *(I wish [hope] that! Would that!)*

■ In exclamatory wishes **¡ojalá!**, with or without **que**, is followed by the subjunctive. The present subjunctive is used in an exclamatory wish that refers to something that may happen in the future (first example). The imperfect subjunctive is used to express a wish concerning something that is contrary to fact (that is, not true) in the present (second example). The pluperfect subjunctive is used to express a wish concerning something that was contrary to fact in the past (third example).

¡Ojalá (que) **puedas** venir mañana!	*I hope (that) you can come tomorrow!*
¡Ojalá (que) él **estuviera** aquí!	*I wish (that) he were here!*
¡Ojalá (que) él **hubiera estado** aquí!	*I wish (that) he had been here!*

Práctica 5   Complete with the corresponding subjunctive form of the verb.

1. Yo (**querer**) _____ solicitar la beca.

2. Nosotros (**querer**) _____ reunirnos de vez en cuando.

3. ¿(**deber**) _____ yo usar las formas peninsulares?

4. Uds. (**deber**) _____ invitar a la profesora también.

5. ¿No (**poder**) _____ tú buscar otro empleo?

6. ¿(**poder**) _____ Ud. visitar a José en el hospital?

Práctica 6   Write responses in support of the following statements, beginning with **ojalá que** and using the appropriate form of the verb appearing in the infinitive form in the original statement, as in the model. Use the present subjunctive form of the verb in responses 1 and 2, the imperfect subjunctive in 3 and 4, and the pluperfect subjunctive in 5 and 6.

> MODEL: Juan y María quieren ir a Puerto Rico. → **¡Ojalá que Juan y María vayan a Puerto Rico.**

1. Beatriz piense estudiar arte en España.

   ¡Ojalá (que) _____!

2. Los estudiantes desean llegar a tiempo al concierto.

   ¡Ojalá (que) _____!

3. Nosotros quisiéramos pasar el verano en la costa.

   ¡Ojalá (que) _____!

4. Uds. esperaban graduarse en junio.

¡Ojalá (que) _____!

5. Yo no pude visitar la fábrica con Uds.

¡Ojalá (que) _____!

6. El profesor no pudo darle una buena recomendación.

¡Ojalá (que) _____!

✪✪
✪   Actividades y práctica: D

E. Forms of **reunirse** and of verbs ending in **-uir**
*(Formas de **reunirse** y de los verbos que terminan en **-uir**)*

reunirse, *to meet, gather*		
Pres. Ind.	me **reúno**, te **reúnes**, se **reúne**, nos reunimos, os reunís, se **reúnen**	
Pres. Subj.	me **reúna**, te **reúnas**, se **reúna**, nos reunamos, os reunáis, se **reúnan**	
Imper. (Commands)	**reúnete**, **reúnase**	reuníos, **reúnanse**

- All other forms of **reunirse** are regular.
- A written accent is needed on the **u** in the same forms as in **continuar**.

construir, *to construct, build*		
-ndo Form	construyendo	
Pres. Ind.	construyo, construyes, construye, construimos, construís, construyen	
Pres. Subj.	construya, construyas, construya, construyamos, construyáis, construyan	
Preterit	construí, construiste, **construyó**, construimos, construisteis, **construyeron**	
Imp. Subj.	construyera, etc.; construyese, etc.	
Imper. (Commands)	construye, construya	construid, construyan

- All other forms of **construir** are regular.
- Verbs ending in **-uir** add **y** except before the endings beginning with **i**, and change the unaccented **i** of the endings **ieron**, **ió** to **y**.

Práctica 7   Complete with the corresponding form of **reunirse** in the present indicative, present subjunctive, or imperative, as required.

1. ¿_____ ellos con los estudiantes mexicanos?   2. Sí, y nosotros _____ con ellos también.   3. Quiero que tú _____ con los estudiantes de primer año.   4. Y queremos que Ud. _____ con los estudiantes de primer año.   5. Pero yo _____ con ellos a menudo.   6. _____ tú con ellos también, Juan.

Práctica 8   Complete with the corresponding form of **construir**, as required by the context.

1. Se _____ los edificios de la universidad hace muchos años.   2. Ahora quieren que se _____ algunos edificios nuevos.   3. Yo _____ la casa en que vivimos hace cinco años.   4. Una casa al lado de la mía fue _____ por un amigo mío.

5. _____ (tú) otra casa en la playa —me dice mi padre.

F. Summary of uses of **para** and **por**   (*Resumen de los usos de para y por*)

Para and **por** are not interchangeable, even though both often mean *for*.

Para is used

- to express the purpose, use, or destination for which something is intended.

Esta raqueta es **para** jugar al tenis.	*This racket is for playing tennis.*
Se marcharon **para** España.	*They left for Spain.*
Los regalos son **para** la novia.	*The gifts are for the bride.*

- to express a point or farthest limit of time in the future, often meaning *by*.

El resumen es **para** mañana.	*The summary is for tomorrow.*
Estén Uds. aquí **para** las siete.	*Be here by seven o'clock.*

- with an infinitive to express purpose, meaning *to, in order to*.

Regresaré **para** continuar mis estudios.	*I shall return (in order) to continue my studies.*

- to express *for* in comparisons that are understood.

Para norteamericano, Ud. habla muy bien el español.	*For a North American, you speak Spanish very well.*

Por is used

- to express *for* in the sense of *because of, on account of, for the sake of, on behalf of, in exchange for, as*, etc.

Por eso te llamé.	*Because of that (Therefore, That's why) I called you.*
Lo hicieron **por** mí.	*They did it for me (for my sake).*
Lo vendimos **por** veinte dólares.	*We sold it for twenty dollars.*
Lo tomamos **por** español.	*We took him for a Spaniard.*

- to express the space of time during which an action continues, *for, during*.

Se reúnen **por** la noche.	*They get together in the evening.*
Jorge estuvo allí **por** una semana.	*George was there for a week.*

- to express the place *through, in, along,* or *around* which motion takes place.

Me gustaría viajar **por** España.	*I should like to travel in (through) Spain.*
por aquí	*this way, around here*

- to express the agent by which something is done, *by*.

El edificio fue construido **por** esa compañía.	*The building was built by that company.*

Luis la llamó **por** teléfono.	*Louis called her by telephone.*
¿Se puede llegar a Cuzco **por** avión?	*Can you get to Cuzco by plane?*

- to express *for* (the object of an errand or search) after verbs such as **ir, mandar, enviar, venir, preguntar.**

Hemos enviado (ido) **por** José.	*We have sent (gone) for Joseph.*
Pregunten Uds. **por** Rita.	*Ask for (about) Rita.*

- to form certain idiomatic expressions.

por ahora *for the present, for now*	**por fin** *finally, at last*
por casualidad *by chance*	**por lo común** *commonly,*
por cierto *certainly, surely, for*	*generally, usually*
certain (sure), by the way	**por supuesto** *of course, certainly*
por ejemplo *for example*	**por todas partes** *everywhere*
por favor *please*	

Práctica 9   Complete with **para** or **por**, as required.

1. ¿Tienes tiempo _____ dar un paseo conmigo? 2. Es agradable pasearse _____ aquí. 3. _____ ejemplo, podríamos ir al parque. 4. Vamos a prepararnos _____ salir en seguida. 5. ¿Qué planes tienen Uds. _____ las vacaciones? 6. Pensamos viajar _____ Centroamérica. 7. Estaremos allí _____ cuatro semanas. 8. Tenemos que volver _____ el día primero de septiembre. 9. Mi abuelo nos dará el dinero _____ el viaje. 10. Él pagó doscientos dólares _____ la cámara. 11. Tengo que preparar este ejercicio _____ mañana. 12. No me gusta estudiar _____ la tarde. 13. Espero poder terminar _____ las once. 14. Me han preguntado _____ la novia de Miguel. 15. _____ fin Miguel anuncia que se casan en junio. 16. Se celebra la boda mañana _____ la mañana. 17. Muchas gracias _____ la carta de recomendación. 18. Veo que la carta fue firmada _____ el jefe. 19. No te preocupes _____ lo que digan. 20. Ana ha venido _____ su pasaporte.

Repaso

A. A group of friends have vacationed together and now they are saying good-bye to one another. Complete the following exchanges by selecting appropriate words or phrases from the list below. Use each word or phrase only once.

antes de	despedirnos	podamos	se haría
consiguiera	para	por casualidad	sepan
de menos	pasado	se alegrarán	

1. —Es lástima que no _____ cenar juntos otra vez _____ marcharnos.

2. —Marta se marchó el sábado _____ y ya le echamos _____.

3. —¡Cuánto _____ los hijos de Julia y Enrique cuando _____ que van a regresar hoy!

4. —Juan _____ famoso si _____ un puesto en este lugar.

5. —¿Han visto _____ a Isabel? Queremos que ella vaya con nosotros a _____ de los otros.

6. —Yo tengo que salir _____ la estación en seguida. ¡Hasta la próxima!

B. Give the Spanish equivalent, using the familiar forms of the verbs in sentence 6.

1. Upon finishing their exams and before leaving the university, several companions gather to have lunch.

_____

_____

2. The restaurant was recommended to them by Michael Ramos, who wasn't able to attend the gathering.

_____

_____

3. George, who is Spanish, says that if Michael hadn't been so busy preparing his departure for Puerto Rico, he would have had lunch with them. _____

_____

4. Elizabeth is going to spend two months on the coast in the house that was built by her grandfather almost a hundred years ago. _____

_____

5. George is going to receive a master's degree in business administration, and his father would like him to become the manager of his company. _____

_____

6. Finally George announces, "Friends, it is late now. Get up (*fam. pl. command*) and let's take leave of one another. I hope that we will see one another again soon!" _____

_____

Expansión

A. Write answers to these questions, using complete sentences.

1. ¿Se reúne Ud. con algunos compañeros para almorzar o cenar de vez en cuando? ¿Adónde van Uds.?

_____

2. ¿Le gusta a Ud. ir de vacaciones solo(-a), con amigos o con miembros de su familia? ¿Por qué?

_____

3. ¿Piensa Ud. continuar sus estudios de español?

_____

4. ¿Qué tipo de puesto espera Ud. conseguir?

_____

5. ¿Piensa Ud. que saber hablar español le podría ayudar en el trabajo? ¿Cómo?

_____

B. Complete the dialogue by writing the missing exchanges in Spanish. While checking your mail at a travel agency in Seville, you run across a former classmate, Louise.

USTED —Pero, ¿quién se imaginaría que nos encontraríamos en Sevilla? ¿Cuánto tiempo hace que estás aquí, Luisa?

LUISA —_____

USTED —¿Estás sola o estás viajando con un grupo?

LUISA —_____

USTED —Yo estoy en el Hotel Alfonso XIII. Pero, vamos a tomar algo en un café.

(Entran en un café y charlan mientras toman unas bebidas.)

USTED —Pues, empieza a contar. ¿Dónde has estado?

LUISA —_____

USTED —Si hubieras llegado unos días antes, nos hubiéramos encontrado allí.

LUISA —_____

USTED —No, no he tenido muchas noticias de nuestros compañeros.

LUISA —_____

USTED —¡Qué interesante! Si yo pudiera, me gustaría pasar más tiempo por aquí. Pero ya tengo que regresar.

LUISA —_____

USTED —Salgo mañana por la mañana, en un vuelo de la línea Iberia.

LUISA —_____

USTED —Gracias, Luisa. ¡Que te diviertas mucho! Nos veremos en el otoño.

Para comprender y escribir

A. From the three choices offered, select the one that best completes the statement or answers the question you hear and circle it.

1. (a) ¡Cuánto me alegro!
   (b) ¡Espero que no tengas éxito!
   (c) ¡Ojalá que consigas empleo!

2. (a) Firmen aquí, por favor.
   (b) Ojalá que soliciten el puesto.
   (c) No digamos adiós, sino hasta luego.

3. (a) ¡Échenos piropos!
   (b) ¡Es hora de hacerse rico!
   (c) ¡No dejes de escribirnos!

4. (a) Un pastel.
   (b) Una costa.
   (c) Unas formas.

5. (a) En la reunión.
   (b) Por la noche.
   (c) Es hora de estudiar.

B. Make each of the commands you hear negative, as in the model.

MODEL: Solicitad las becas. → **No solicitéis las becas.**

1. _____

2. _____

3. _____

4. _____

5. _____

6. _____

C. Write a new sentence with the cue you hear.

1. _____

2. _____

3. _____

4. _____

5. _____

6. _____

7. _____

8. _____

D. Dictado. You will hear a short narrative about a group of students gathering for lunch before leaving the university for the summer. You will hear the narrative three times. Listen the first time. Write what you hear the second time. Make any necessary corrections the third time.

_____

_____

_____

_____

_____

_____

_____

_____

_____

_____

_____

_____

✸✸ ✸ *VOCABULARIO*

animadamente *adv.* animatedly
anunciar to announce
asombrarse (de) to be amazed, be surprised (at)
la **camarera** waitress
el **camarero** waiter
el **compromiso** engagement, commitment

construir to construct, build
la **costa** coast
delicioso, -a delicious
echar to throw, cast
emplear to employ, use
felicitar to congratulate
firmar to sign
la **forma** form

el **futuro** future

la **maestría** master's degree (M.A., M.B.A., M.S., etc.)

marcharse (**de** + *obj.*) to leave (from)

¡ojalá (**que**)! I wish that! I hope that!

el **pastel** cake

peninsular (*m.* or *f.*) peninsular (*of Spain*)

el **piropo** compliment

primero *adv.* first

la **reunión** (*pl.* **reuniones**) meeting, gathering

reunirse to gather, get together, meet

solicitar to apply for, ask for

¡cuánto me alegro! how glad I am!

¡cuánto me gustaría viajar… ! how I should (would) like to travel . . . !

de momento for the time being, moment

despidámonos let's say good-bye to each other

echar de menos to miss (someone or something)

echar piropos to pay compliments

no dejar de + *inf.* not to fail to + *verb*

por ahora for the present, for now

ser hora de to be time to

tener (**mucho**) **éxito** to be (very) successful

Repaso, Lecciones 20–22: Appendix C

✠✠✠ Appendix A

The Spanish alphabet   (El alfabeto español)

Letter	Name	Letter	Name	Letter	Name
a	a	j	jota	r	ere
b	be	k	ka	rr	erre
c	ce	l	ele	s	ese
(ch)	che	(ll)	elle	t	te
d	de	m	eme	u	u
e	e	n	ene	v	ve, uve
f	efe	ñ	eñe	w	doble ve
g	ge	o	o	x	equis
h	hache	p	pe	y	i griega
i	i	q	cu	z	zeta

The Spanish alphabet is divided into vowels (a, e, i, o, u) and consonants. The letter **y** represents the vowel sound **i** in the conjunction y, *and*, or when final in a word: **hoy**, *today*; **muy**, *very*; **hay**, *there is, there are*.

In 1994, the **Real Academia Española** made a new ruling on the alphabetization of the Spanish consonants **ch, ll, ñ,** and **rr. Ch, ll,** and **rr** are no longer alphabetized as compound letters; the letter **ñ** continues to follow the letter **n**. Accordingly, Spanish **cancha**, *court*, precedes **canción**, *song*; **bollo**, *roll*, precedes **bolsa**, *purse*; **canela**, *cinnamon*, precedes **caña**, *cane*; **carro**, *car*, precedes **carta**, *letter*, etc. The Academia's revision of the Spanish alphabet has been followed in *Spanish On Your Own*. One should note, however, that dictionaries and vocabularies published before or shortly after this recent decision may use the older system in which Spanish words or syllables beginning with **ch** and **ll** are ordered after words or syllables beginning with **c** and **l**, respectively.

The sounds of Spanish vowels

In general, Spanish pronunciation is much clearer and more uniform than the English. The vowel sounds are clipped short and are not followed by the diphthongal glide that is commonly heard in English, as in *no* (*no^u*), *came* (*ca^ime*), *why* (*why^e*). Even unstressed vowels are pronounced clearly and distinctly; the slurred sound of English *a* in *firearm*, for example, never occurs in Spanish.

Spanish has five vowels, which are pronounced as follows:

- **a** is pronounced between the *a* of English *ask* and the *a* of *father*: **ac-*tual*, *cá*-ma-ra, *ca*-sa, ma-*má*, ma-*ña*-na, *Mar*-ta.**

- **e** is pronounced like *e* in *café*, but without the glide sound that follows the *e* in English: ***de*-be, de-fen-*der*, E-*le*-na, *le*-che, mo-*der*-no, *tres*.**

- **i** (**y** in the conjunction *and*) is pronounced like *i* in *machine*: ***dí*-a, di-vi-*dir*, do-*min*-go, *sí*, *vis*-ta, *y*.**

- **o** is pronounced like *o* in *tone*, but without the glide sound that follows the *o* in English: **ca-*ñón*, co-*lor*, *ho*-la, *no*, *o*-cho, *po*-co.**

- u is pronounced like *oo* in *cool*: *lu*-nes, *mú*-si-ca, oc-*tu*-bre, *plu*-ma, sa-*lu*-dos, us-*ted*.

The Spanish consonants   *(Las consonantes del español)*[1]

- b and v are pronounced exactly alike. At the beginning of a breath group or after m and n, the sound is that of a weakly pronounced English *b*: *bien*, *bue*-nas, *ver*-de, *vi*-da. In other places, particularly between vowels, the sound is much weaker than the English *b*. The lips touch very lightly, leaving a narrow opening in the center, and the breath continues to pass between them. Avoid the English *v* sound. Examples: *li*-bro, es-*cri*-bo, *la*-vo, *Cu*-ba.

- c before e and i, and z in all positions, are pronounced like the English hissed *s* in *sent* in Spanish America and in southern Spain. In northern and central Spain this sound is like *th* in *thin*. Examples: cen-*ta*-vo, *ci*-ne, *gra*-cias, *lá*-piz.

- c before all other letters, k, and qu are like English *c* in *cat*, but without the *h* sound that often follows the c in English: *ca*-sa, *cla*-se, ki-*ló*-me-tro, *qué*, *par*-que. Note both sounds of c in *cin*-co, lec-*ción*.

- ch is pronounced like English *ch* in *church*: *mu*-cho, *le*-che, cho-co-*la*-te.

- d has two sounds. At the beginning of a breath group or following l or n, it is pronounced like a weak English *d*, but with the tongue touching the back of the upper front teeth rather than the ridge above the teeth, as in English: *dos*, *dón*-de, sal-*dré*. In other places, particularly between vowels and at the end of a word, the sound is like a weakly articulated English *th* in *this*: *ca*-da, *to*-do, us-*ted*, Ma-*drid*.

- f is pronounced like English *f*: ca-*fé*, Fe-*li*-pe.

- g before e and i, and j in all positions, have no English equivalent. They are pronounced approximately like a strongly exaggerated *h* in *halt* (rather like the rasping German *ch* in *Buch*): *gen*-te, *hi*-jo, *Jor*-ge, re-*gión*. (The letter x in the words **México, mexicano, Texas, texano,** and **Xavier,** spelled **Méjico, mejicano, Tejas, tejano,** and **Javier** in Spain, is pronounced like Spanish j.)

- g in other positions and gu before e or i are pronounced like a weak English *g* in *go* at the beginning of a breath group or after n. In other cases, especially between vowels, the sound is much weaker, and the breath continues to pass between the back of the tongue and the palate. Examples: *gra*-cias, gui-*ta*-rra, *ten*-go; but *ha*-go, *lue*-go, por-tu-*gués*. (In the combinations gua and guo, the u is pronounced like English *w* in *wet*: *len*-gua, *a*-gua, an-*ti*-guo; when the diaeresis is used over u in the combinations güe and güi, the u has the same sound: ni-ca-ra-*güen*-se.)

- h is always silent: ha-*blar*, her-*ma*-no, *hoy*.

- l is pronounced *l* in *leap*, with the tip and front part of the tongue well forward in the mouth: *la*-do, pa-*pel*.

- ll is pronounced like *y* in *yes* in most of Spanish America and in some sections of Spain; in other parts of Spain it is somewhat like *lli* in *million*: e-*lla*, *ca*-lle, lla-*mar*.

- m is pronounced like English *m*: *to*-ma, *me*-sa.

---

1. The stressed syllable in these examples is indicated by italics. The stressed syllable may or may not contain the targeted sound.

- n is pronounced like English *n*: *no*, ***Car***-men. Before b, v, m, and p, however, it is pronounced like *m*: ***un***-po-co, con-***Bár***-ba-ra. Before c, qu, g, and j it is pronounced like English *n* in *sing*: ***blan***-co, ***ten***-go, ***án***-gel.

- ñ is pronounced somewhat like the English *ny* in *canyon*: se-***ñor***, ma-***ña***-na, es-pa-***ñol***.

- p is pronounced like English *p*, but without the *h* sound that often follows the *p* in English: ***pe***-lo, pa-***pel***.

- q (always written with u): see above under c, k, and qu.

- r and rr represent two different sounds. Single r, except at the beginning of a word, or after l, n, or s, is pronounced with a single tap produced by the tip of the tongue against the gums of the upper teeth. The sound is much like *dd* in *eddy* pronounced rapidly: *ca*-ra, *to*-ro, ha-*blar*. Initial r, r after l, n, or s, and rr are strongly trilled: ***ri***-co, ***ro***-jo, Ro-***ber***-to, pi-***za***-rra, ***co***-rre, En-***ri***-que.

- s is pronounced somewhat like the English hissed *s* in *sent*: *ca*-sa, *es*-tos. Before b, d, g, l, ll, m, n, r, v, and y, however, the sound is like the English *s* in *rose*: los-***bai***-les, los-***li***-bros, ***mis***-mo, *es*-ver-dad.

- t is pronounced with the tip of the tongue touching the back of the upper front teeth (rather than the ridge above the teeth, as in English); it is never followed by the *h* sound that is often heard in English: *to*-do, *tar*-des, *tiem*-po.

- v: see under b.

- x is pronounced as follows: (1) Before a consonant it is pronounced like English hissed *s* in *sent*: ex-plo-*rar*, ex-tran-*je*-ro; (2) between vowels it is usually a double sound, consisting of a weak English *g* in *go* followed by a hissed *s*: e-xa-men, *ć*-xi-to; (3) in a few words, x, even between vowels, is pronounced like English *s* in *sent*: e-*xac*-to, au-*xi*-lio, au-xi-*liar*.

- y is pronounced like a strong English *y* in *you*: ***ya***, ***yo***, ***ma***-yo. The conjunction y, *and*, when combined with the initial vowel of a following word is similarly pronounced: ***Car***-los-*y* A-na; ***és***-te-y a-***quél***.

Diphthongs[1]

The Spanish vowels are divided into two groups: strong vowels (a, e, o) and weak vowels (i, u). The vowels i and u are called weak vowels because they become semivowels or semiconsonants—like the sounds of English *y* or *w*—when they combine with the strong vowels a, e, o, or with each other, to form single syllables. Such combinations of two vowels are called diphthongs. In diphthongs, the strong vowel retains its full vocalic value, while the weak vowel, or the first vowel if both are weak, loses part of its vocalic nature.

As the first element of a diphthong, unstressed i is pronounced like a weak English *y* in *yes*, and unstressed u is pronounced like *w* in *wet*. The following Spanish diphthongs begin with unstressed i or u.

ia: his-to-*ria*, gra-*cias*, es-tu-*dian*-te
ie: *vier*-nes, *sie*-te, sep-*tiem*-bre
io: e-di-fi-*cio*, An-to-*nio*, ju-*lio*
iu: *ciu*-dad, *viu*-da, *triun*-fo
ua: ¿*cuán*-do?, *cua*-tro, a-*gua*
ue: *jue*-ves, *nue*-ve, *bue*-no

---

1. See also *Spanish On Your Own*, Vol. I, **Lecciones** 6, 7, 8, and 9.

uo: an-ti-*guo*, ar-*duo*, mu-*tuo*
ui: *cui*-da-do, L*uis*, R*uiz*

Remember that two adjacent strong vowels within a word form separate sylla-bles: **le-o**, **tra-en**. Likewise, when a weak vowel adjacent to a strong vowel has a written accent, it retains it syllabic value and forms a separate syllable: **dí-as**, **pa-ís**. An accent mark on a strong vowel merely indicates stress: **tam-bién**, **diá-lo-go**, **fá-cil**.

Division of words into syllables

Spanish words are hyphenated at the end of a line and are divided into syllables according to the following principles:

- A single consonant (including **ch, ll, rr**) is placed with the vowel that follows: **me-sa**, **no-che**, **si-lla**, **pi-za-rra**.

- Two consonants are usually divided: **tar-des**, **es-pa-ñol**, **bas-tan-te**. Consonants followed by l or r, however, are generally pronounced with the l or r, and the two together go with the following vowel: **ha-blan**, **li-bro**, **ma-dre**, **a-pren-do**. By exception to the last principle, the groups **nl, rl, sl, tl, nr**, and **sr** are divided: **Car-los**, **En-ri-que**.

- In combinations of three or more consonants, only the last consonant or the two consonants of the inseparable groups just mentioned (consonant plus l or r, with the exceptions listed) begin a syllable: **in-glés**, **en-tra**, **siem-pre**, **cons-tru-ye**.

- Two adjacent strong vowels (**a, e, o**) are in separate syllables: **cre-o**, **ca-en**, **le-a**.

- Combinations of a strong and weak vowel (**i, u**) or of two weak vowels normally form single syllables: **An-to-nio**, **bue-nos**, **bien**, **gra-cias**, **ciu-dad**, **Luis**. Such combinations are called diphthongs.

- In combinations of a strong and weak vowel, a written accent mark on the weak vowel divides the two vowels into separate syllables: **dí-as**, **pa-ís**, **tí-o**. An accent on the strong vowel of such combinations does not result in two syllables: **a-diós**, **lec-ción**, **tam-bién**.

Word stress and use of the written accent

- Most words that end in a vowel, or in **n** or **s**, are stressed on the next to the last syllable. The stressed syllable or syllables are shown here in italics: *cla*-se, *to*-mo, *en*-tran, *Car*-men.

- Most words that end in a consonant, except **n** or **s**, are stressed on the last sylla-ble: us-*ted*, re-gu-*lar*, ha-*blar*, se-*ñor*, ciu-*dad*, es-pa-*ñol*.

- Words not pronounced according to these two rules have a written accent on the stressed syllable: a-*diós*, es-*tás*, lec-*ción*, tam-*bién*, *lá*-piz.

Intonation *(La entonación)*

The term *intonation* refers to the variations in pitch that occur in speech. Every language has its characteristic patterns of intonation. The intonation of Spanish is quite different from that of English.

The alternate rise and fall of pitch depends upon the particular meaning of the sentence, the position of stressed syllables, and whether the sentence expresses command, affirmation, interrogation, exclamation, request, or other factors. In general, three meaningful levels of pitch can be distinguished in Spanish: one below the speaker's normal pitch (level 1), the speaker's normal tone (level 2), and a tone higher than the normal one (level 3). Study carefully these examples.

Declarative Statement

level 3
level 2
level 1

Estudiamos español.

Es-tu-dia-mo-ses-pa-ñol. |

Interrogative Sentences

3
2
1

¿Estudiamos español?

¿Es-tu-dia-mo-ses-pa-ñol? |

3
2
1

¿Cómo está usted?

¿Có-mo es-tá us-ted? |

(Or, more politely)

3
2
1

¿Có-mo es-tá us-ted? |

Exclamatory Sentence

3
2
1

¡Qué muchacha más bonita!

¡Qué-mu-cha-cha más-bo-ni-ta! |

(Or, with special interest)

3
2
1

¡Qué-mu-cha-cha-más-bo-ni-ta! |

Command

3
2
1

¡Escuche usted!

¡Es-cu-che us-ted! |

Request

3
2
1

Escuche usted.

Es-cu-che us-ted. |

With respect to the use of these levels, the following basic principles should be observed:

- At the beginning of a breath group, the voice begins and continues in a relatively low pitch (level 1) as long as the first accented syllable is not reached.

- When the first accented syllable of a breath group is reached, the voice rises to the speaker's normal tone (level 2) and continues in the same pitch as long as the last accented syllable is not reached.

- When the last accented syllable of the breath group is reached, the voice falls or rises, depending on the following circumstances:

1. At the end of a declarative statement, the voice falls to a pitch even lower than that of the initial unaccented syllable or syllables.

2. At the end of an interrogative sentence, or of an incomplete sentence interrupted by a pause, the voice rises to a pitch above the normal tone (level 3).

- In exclamations, and in questions that begin with an interrogative word, the voice begins in a pitch above the normal tone (level 3) and gradually falls in the following syllables as long as the final accented syllable is not reached; when the last accented syllable is reached, the voice falls to a pitch even lower than that of the initial unaccented syllable or syllables, as in the case of the end of a simple affirmative sentence, unless special interest or courtesy is intended, in which case the voice rises to the normal tone or even higher.

- The pattern observed in an exclamatory sentence is also typical of commands and requests. In commands, the voice begins on a relatively low tone (level 1) as long as the first stressed syllable is not reached. When the first stressed syllable is reached, it is pronounced on a tone above the normal one (level 3), and then the voice descends notably in the following syllables; the last syllable (stressed or unstressed) is uttered on a tone below that of the initial unstressed syllable or syllables. Requests differ from commands in that the entire breath group is usually uttered on a somewhat higher tone.

Punctuation marks   *(Signos de puntuación)*

,	coma	( )	(los) paréntesis
;	punto y coma	« »	comillas
:	dos puntos	´	acento escrito
.	punto final	¨	(la) diéresis
...	puntos suspensivos	~	(la) tilde
¿ ?	signo(s) de interrogación	-	(el) guión
¡ !	signo(s) de admiración	—	raya

Spanish punctuation is much the same as in English. The most important differences are as follows:

- Inverted question marks and exclamation points precede questions and exclamations. They are placed at the actual beginning of the question or exclamation, not necessarily at the beginning of the sentence.

¿Cómo se llama Ud.?	*What is your name?*
El señor Ruiz es el profesor de español, ¿verdad?	*Mr. Ruiz is the Spanish teacher, isn't he?*
¡Buenos días, estudiantes!	*Good morning, students!*

- In Spanish a comma is not used between the last two words of a series, while in English it often is.

Tenemos libros, cuadernos y lápices.	*We have books, notebooks, and pencils.*

- A dash is generally used instead of the quotation marks of English and to denote a change of speaker in dialogue. It appears at the beginning of each speech, but is omitted at the end.

—¿Eres tú estudiante?	*"Are you a student?"*
—Sí, soy estudiante de español.	*"Yes, I am a student of Spanish."*

If Spanish quotation marks are used, the statement is placed on the same line:

Pablo contestó: «Buenos días».	*Paul answered, "Good morning."*

Capitalization *(Mayúsculas)*

Only proper names and the first word of a sentence begin with a capital letter in Spanish. The subject pronoun **yo** (*I* in English), names of months and days of the week, adjectives of nationality and nouns formed from them, and titles (unless abbreviated) are not capitalized. In titles of books and works of art, only the first word is capitalized. By exception, sometimes short titles are capitalized.

Carmen y yo hablamos.	*Carmen and I are talking.*
Hoy es lunes.	*Today is Monday.*
Buenos días, señorita (Srta.) Martí.	*Good morning, Miss Martí.*
Son españoles.	*They are Spanish (Spaniards).*
Las meninas	The Little Ladies in Waiting
Don Quijote de la Mancha	Don Quixote of La Mancha

Grammatical terms *(Términos gramaticales)*

el **adjetivo** adjective
   demostrativo demonstrative
   posesivo possessive
el **adverbio** adverb
el **artículo** article
   definido definite
   indefinido indefinite
el **cambio ortográfico** change in
   spelling
la **capitalización** capitalization
la **cláusula** clause
la **comparación** comparison
el **comparativo** comparative
el **complemento** object
   directo direct
   indirecto indirect
la **composición** composition
la **concordancia** agreement
la **conjugación** conjugation
la **conjunción** conjunction
la **consonante** consonant
el **diptongo** diphthong
el **género** gender
   masculino masculine
   femenino feminine
el **gerundio** gerund, present
   participle
el **infinitivo** infinitive
la **interjección** interjection
la **interrogación** interrogation,
   question (mark)
la **letra** letter (*of the alphabet*)
   mayúscula capital
   minúscula small, lowercase
el **modo indicativo (subjuntivo)**
   indicative (subjunctive) mood
el **nombre (sustantivo)** noun,
   substantive

el **nombre propio** proper noun
el **número** number, numeral
   cardinal (ordinal) cardinal
   (ordinal)
el **objeto** object
la **palabra (negativa)** (negative) word
las **partes de la oración** parts of
   speech
el **participio pasado (presente)** past
   (present) participle
la **persona** person
   primera first
   segunda second
   tercera third
el **plural** plural
la **posición** position
el **predicado** predicate
la **preposición** preposition
el **pronombre** pronoun
   interrogativo interrogative
   personal personal
   reflexivo reflexive
   relativo relative
la **puntuación** punctuation
el **radical (la raíz)** stem
el **significado** meaning
la **sílaba** syllable
   última last
   penúltima next to the last
el **singular** singular
el **subjuntivo** subjunctive
el **sujeto** subject
el **superlativo (absoluto)** (absolute)
   superlative
la **terminación** ending
el **tiempo** tense
   compuesto compound
   simple simple

presente present
imperfecto imperfect
pretérito preterit
futuro future
condicional conditional
perfecto presente present
  perfect
pluscuamperfecto pluperfect
futuro perfecto future perfect
condicional perfecto
  conditional perfect
el **triptongo** triphthong

el **verbo** verb
  auxiliar auxiliary
  impersonal impersonal
  irregular irregular
  reflexivo reflexive
  regular regular
  (in)transitivo (in)transitive
la **vocal** vowel
la **voz** voice
  activa active
  pasiva passive

✦✦✦ *Appendix B*

Regular verbs

Infinitive	hablar, *to speak*	comer, *to eat*	vivir, *to live*
Spanish Gerund (-ndo form)	hablando, *speaking*	comiendo, *eating*	viviendo, *living*
Past Participle	hablado, *spoken*	comido, *eaten*	vivido, *lived*

The simple tenses

Indicative mood

Present	*I speak, do speak, am speaking, etc.*	*I eat, do eat, am eating, etc.*	*I live, do live, am living, etc.*
	hablo	como	vivo
	hablas	comes	vives
	habla	come	vive
	hablamos	comemos	vivimos
	habláis	coméis	vivís
	hablan	comen	viven
Imperfect	*I was speaking, used to speak, spoke, etc.*	*I was eating, used to eat, ate, etc.*	*I was living, used to live, lived, etc.*
	hablaba	comía	vivía
	hablabas	comías	vivías
	hablaba	comía	vivía
	hablábamos	comíamos	vivíamos
	hablabais	comíais	vivíais
	hablaban	comían	vivían
Preterit	*I spoke, did speak, etc.*	*I ate, did eat, etc.*	*I lived, did live, etc.*
	hablé	comí	viví
	hablaste	comiste	viviste
	habló	comió	vivió
	hablamos	comimos	vivimos
	hablasteis	comisteis	vivisteis
	hablaron	comieron	vivieron
Future	*I shall (will) speak, etc.*	*I shall (will) eat, etc.*	*I shall (will) live, etc.*
	hablaré	comeré	viviré
	hablarás	comerás	vivirás
	hablará	comerá	vivirá
	hablaremos	comeremos	viviremos
	hablaréis	comeréis	viviréis
	hablarán	comerán	vivirán

Conditional	*I should (would) speak, etc.*	*I should (would) eat, etc.*	*I should (would) live, etc.*
	hablaría	comería	viviría
	hablarías	comerías	vivirías
	hablaría	comería	viviría
	hablaríamos	comeríamos	viviríamos
	hablaríais	comeríais	viviríais
	hablarían	comerían	vivirían

Subjunctive mood

Present	*(that) I may speak, etc.*	*(that) I may eat, etc.*	*(that) I may live, etc.*
	hable	coma	viva
	hables	comas	vivas
	hable	coma	viva
	hablemos	comamos	vivamos
	habléis	comáis	viváis
	hablen	coman	vivan

Imperfect (-ra)	*(that) I might speak, etc.*	*(that) I might eat, etc.*	*(that) I might live, etc.*
	hablara	comiera	viviera
	hablaras	comieras	vivieras
	hablara	comiera	viviera
	habláramos	comiéramos	viviéramos
	hablarais	comierais	vivierais
	hablaran	comieran	vivieran

Imperfect (-se)	*(that) I might speak, etc.*	*(that) I might eat, etc.*	*(that) I might live, etc.*
	hablase	comiese	viviese
	hablases	comieses	vivieses
	hablase	comiese	viviese
	hablásemos	comiésemos	viviésemos
	hablaseis	comieseis	vivieseis
	hablasen	comiesen	viviesen

Imperative

	speak	*eat*	*live*
	habla (tú)	come (tú)	vive (tú)
	hablad (vosotros)	comed (vosotros)	vivid (vosotros)

The compound tenses

Perfect Infinitive	*to have spoken*	*to have eaten*	*to have lived*
	haber hablado	haber comido	haber vivido

Perfect Participle	*having spoken*	*having eaten*	*having lived*
	habiendo hablado	habiendo comido	habiendo vivido

Indicative mood

Present Perfect	Pluperfect	Preterit Perfect[1]
I have spoken, eaten, lived, etc.	*I had spoken, eaten, lived, etc.*	*I had spoken, eaten, lived, etc.*

he		había		hube	
has		habías		hubiste	
ha	hablado	había	hablado	hubo	hablado
hemos	comido	habíamos	comido	hubimos	comido
habéis	vivido	habíais	vivido	hubisteis	vivido
han		habían		hubieron	

Future Perfect	Conditional Perfect
I shall (will) have spoken, eaten, lived, etc.	*I should (would) have spoken, eaten, lived, etc.*

habré		habría	
habrás		habrías	
habrá	hablado	habría	hablado
habremos	comido	habríamos	comido
habréis	vivido	habríais	vivido
habrán		habrían	

Subjunctive mood

Present Perfect	Pluperfect
(that) I may have spoken, eaten, lived, etc	*(that) I might have spoken, eaten, lived, etc.*

haya		hubiera *or* hubiese	
hayas		hubieras *or* hubieses	
haya	hablado	hubiera *or* hubiese	hablado
hayamos	comido	hubiéramos *or* hubiésemos	comido
hayáis	vivido	hubierais *or* hubieseis	vivido
hayan		hubieran *or* hubiesen	

Irregular past participles of regular and stem-changing verbs

abrir: **abierto**	devolver: **devuelto**	escribir: **escrito**
cubrir: **cubierto**	envolver: **envuelto**	volver: **vuelto**
descubrir: **descubierto**		

Comments concerning forms of verbs

■ From five forms (infinitive, Spanish gerund [**-ndo** form], past participle, first-person singular present indicative, and third-person plural preterit) all other forms may be derived.

Infinitive *decir*	Span. Ger. *diciendo*	Past. Part. *dicho*	Pres. Ind. *digo*	Preterit *dijeron*
Imp. Ind. decía	*Progressive Tenses* estoy, etc. diciendo	*Compound Tenses* he, etc. dicho	*Pres. Subj.* diga *Imperative* di decid	*Imp. Subj.* dijera dijese
Future diré				
Conditional diría				

---

1. The preterit perfect tense is used only after conjunctions such as **cuando, en cuanto, después que, apenas**. In spoken Spanish the pluperfect or the simple preterit often replaces the preterit perfect.

- The first- and second-persons plural of the present indicative tense of all verbs are regular, except in the cases of **haber**, **ir**, and **ser**.

- The third-person plural is formed by adding **-n** to the third-person singular in all tenses, except the preterit (of all verbs) and the present indicative tense of **ser**.

- All familiar forms (second-person singular and plural) end in **-s**, except the second-person singular preterit tense and the imperative.

- The imperfect indicative tense is regular in all verbs, except **ir** (**iba**), **ser** (**era**), and **ver** (**veía**).

- If the first-person singular preterit tense ends in unaccented **-e**, the third-person singular ends in unaccented **-o**; the other endings are regular, except that after **j** the ending for the third-person plural is **-eron**. Eight verbs of this group, in addition to those that end in **-ducir**, have a u-stem preterit (**andar**, **caber**, **estar**, **haber**, **poder**, **poner**, **saber**, **tener**); four have an i-stem (**decir**, **hacer**, **querer**, **venir**); **traer** has a regular stem with the above endings. (The third-person plural preterit forms of **decir** and **traer** are **dijeron** and **trajeron**, respectively. The third-person singular form of **hacer** is **hizo**). **Ir** and **ser** have the same preterit, while **dar** has second-conjugation endings in this tense.

- The conditional tense always has the same stem as the future. Only twelve verbs have irregular stems in these tenses. Five drop **e** of the infinitive ending (**caber**, **haber**, **poder**, **querer**, **saber**); five drop **e** or **i** and insert **d** (**poner**, **salir**, **tener**, **valer**, **venir**); and two (**decir**, **hacer**) retain the Old Spanish stems **dir-**, **har-**.

- The stem of the present subjunctive tense of all verbs is the same as that of the first-person singular present indicative, except for **dar**, **estar**, **haber**, **ir**, **saber**, and **ser**.

- The imperfect subjunctive tense of all verbs is formed by dropping **-ron** of the third-person plural preterit and adding the **-ra** or **-se** endings.

- The singular imperative is the same in form as the third-person singular present indicative tense, except in the case of ten verbs (**decir**, **di**; **haber**, **he**; **hacer**, **haz**; **ir**, **ve**; **poner**, **pon**; **salir**, **sal**; **ser**, **sé**; **tener**, **ten**; **valer**, **val** *or* **vale**; **venir**, **ven**). The plural imperative is always formed by dropping the final **-r** of the infinitive and adding **-d**. (Remember that the imperative is used only for familiar affirmative commands.)

- The compound tenses of all verbs are formed by using the various tenses of the auxiliary verb **haber** with the past participle.

Irregular verbs

Participles are given with the infinitive; tenses not listed are regular.

1. **andar**, andando, andado, *to go*, *walk*

Preterit	anduve	anduviste	anduvo	anduvimos	anduvisteis	anduvieron
Imp. Subj.	anduviera, etc.		anduviese, etc.			

2. **caber**, cabiendo, cabido, *to fit*, *be contained in*

Pres. Ind.	quepo	cabes	cabe	cabemos	cabéis	caben
Pres. Subj.	quepa	quepas	quepa	quepamos	quepáis	quepan
Future	cabré	cabrás, etc.				
Cond.	cabría	cabrías, etc.				
Preterit	cupe	cupiste	cupo	cupimos	cupisteis	cupieron
Imp. Subj.	cupiera, etc.		cupiese, etc.			

3. caer, cayendo, caído, *to fall*

Pres. Ind.	caigo	caes	cae	caemos	caéis	caen
Pres. Subj.	caiga	caigas	caiga	caigamos	caigáis	caigan
Preterit	caí	caíste	cayó	caímos	caísteis	cayeron
Imp. Subj.	cayera, etc.		cayese, etc.			

4. dar, dando, dado, *to give*

Pres. Ind.	doy	das	da	damos	dais	dan
Pres. Subj.	dé	des	dé	demos	deis	den
Preterit	di	diste	dio	dimos	disteis	dieron
Imp. Subj.	diera, etc.		diese, etc.			

5. decir, diciendo, dicho, *to say, tell*

Pres. Ind.	digo	dices	dice	decimos	decís	dicen
Pres. Subj.	diga	digas	diga	digamos	digáis	digan
Imperative		di			decid	
Future	diré	dirás, etc.				
Cond.	diría	dirías, etc.				
Preterit	dije	dijiste	dijo	dijimos	dijisteis	dijeron
Imp. Subj.	dijera, etc.		dijese, etc.			

6. estar, estando, estado, *to be*

Pres. Ind.	estoy	estás	está	estamos	estáis	están
Pres. Subj.	esté	estés	esté	estemos	estéis	estén
Preterit	estuve	estuviste	estuvo	estuvimos	estuvisteis	estuvieron
Imp. Subj.	estuviera, etc.		estuviese, etc.			

7. haber, habiendo, habido, *to have* (auxiliary)

Pres. Ind.	he	has	ha	hemos	habéis	han
Pres. Subj.	haya	hayas	haya	hayamos	hayáis	hayan
Imperative		he			habed	
Future	habré	habrás, etc.				
Cond.	habría	habrías, etc.				
Preterit	hube	hubiste	hubo	hubimos	hubisteis	hubieron
Imp. Subj.	hubiera, etc.		hubiese, etc.			

8. hacer, haciendo, hecho, *to do, make*

Pres. Ind.	hago	haces	hace	hacemos	hacéis	hacen
Pres. Subj.	haga	hagas	haga	hagamos	hagáis	hagan
Imperative		haz			haced	
Future	haré	harás, etc.				
Cond.	haría	harías, etc.				
Preterit	hice	hiciste	hizo	hicimos	hicisteis	hicieron
Imp. Subj.	hiciera, etc.		hiciese, etc.			

Like hacer: **satisfacer**, *to satisfy*

9. ir, yendo, ido, *to go*

Pres. Ind.	voy	vas	va	vamos	vais	van
Pres. Subj.	vaya	vayas	vaya	vayamos	vayáis	vayan
Imperative		ve			id	
Imp. Ind.	iba	ibas	iba	íbamos	ibais	iban
Preterit	fui	fuiste	fue	fuimos	fuisteis	fueron
Imp. Subj.	fuera, etc.		fuese, etc.			

10. oír, oyendo, oído, *to hear*

Pres. Ind.	oigo	oyes	oye	oímos	oís	oyen
Pres. Subj.	oiga	oigas	oiga	oigamos	oigáis	oigan
Imperative		oye			oíd	
Preterit	oí	oíste	oyó	oímos	oísteis	oyeron
Imp. Subj.	oyera, etc.		oyese, etc.			

11. poder, pudiendo, podido, *to be able*

Pres. Ind.	puedo	puedes	puede	podemos	podéis	pueden
Pres. Subj.	pueda	puedas	pueda	podamos	podáis	puedan
Future	podré	podrás, etc.				
Cond.	podría	podrías, etc.				
Preterit	pude	pudiste	pudo	pudimos	pudisteis	pudieron
Imp. Subj.	pudiera, etc.		pudiese, etc.			

12. poner, poniendo, **puesto**, *to put, place*

Pres. Ind.	pongo	pones	pone	ponemos	ponéis	ponen
Pres. Subj.	ponga	pongas	ponga	pongamos	pongáis	pongan
Imperative		pon			poned	
Future	pondré	pondrás, etc.				
Cond.	pondría	pondrías, etc.				
Preterit	puse	pusiste	puso	pusimos	pusisteis	pusieron
Imp. Subj.	pusiera, etc.		pusiese, etc.			

13. querer, queriendo, querido, *to wish, want*

Pres. Ind.	quiero	quieres	quiere	queremos	queréis	quieren
Pres. Subj.	quiera	quieras	quiera	queramos	queráis	quieran
Future	querré	querrás, etc.				
Cond.	querría	querrías, etc.				
Preterit	quise	quisiste	quiso	quisimos	quisisteis	quisieron
Imp. Subj.	quisiera, etc.		quisiese, etc.			

14. saber, sabiendo, sabido, *to know*

Pres. Ind.	sé	sabes	sabe	sabemos	sabéis	saben
Pres. Subj.	sepa	sepas	sepa	sepamos	sepáis	sepan
Future	sabré	sabrás, etc.				
Cond.	sabría	sabrías, etc.				
Preterit	supe	supiste	supo	supimos	supisteis	supieron
Imp. Subj.	supiera, etc.		supiese, etc.			

15. salir, saliendo, salido, *to go out, leave*

Pres. Ind.	salgo	sales	sale	salimos	salís	salen
Pres. Subj.	salga	salgas	salga	salgamos	salgáis	salgan
Imperative		sal			salid	
Future	saldré	saldrás, etc.				
Cond.	saldría	saldrías, etc.				

16. ser, siendo, sido, *to be*

Pres. Ind.	soy	eres	es	somos	sois	son
Pres. Subj.	sea	seas	sea	seamos	seáis	sean
Imperative		sé			sed	
Imp. Ind.	era	eras	era	éramos	erais	eran
Preterit	fui	fuiste	fue	fuimos	fuisteis	fueron
Imp. Subj.	fuera, etc.		fuese, etc.			

17. tener, teniendo, tenido, *to have*

Pres. Ind.	tengo	tienes	tiene	tenemos	tenéis	tienen
Pres. Subj.	tenga	tengas	tenga	tengamos	tengáis	tengan
Imperative		ten			tened	
Future	tendré	tendrás, etc.				
Cond.	tendría	tendrías, etc.				
Preterit	tuve	tuviste	tuvo	tuvimos	tuvisteis	tuvieron
Imp. Subj.	tuviera, etc.		tuviese, etc.			

Like **tener**: **contener**, *to contain*; **detener**, *to stop*; **entretener**, *to entertain*; **mantener**, *to maintain*; **obtener**, *to obtain*.

18. traer, trayendo, traído, *to bring*

Pres. Ind.	traigo	traes	trae	traemos	traéis	traen
Pres. Subj.	traiga	traigas	traiga	traigamos	traigáis	traigan
Preterit	traje	trajiste	trajo	trajimos.	trajisteis	trajeron
Imp. Subj.	trajera, etc.		trajese, etc.			

19. valer, valiendo, valido, *to be worth*

Pres. Ind.	valgo	vales	vale	valemos	valéis	valen
Pres. Subj.	valga	valgas	valga	valgamos	valgáis	valgan
Imperative		val (vale)			valed	
Future	valdré	valdrás, etc.				
Cond.	valdría	valdrías, etc.				

20. venir, viniendo, venido, *to come*

Pres. Ind.	vengo	vienes	viene	venimos	venís	vienen
Pres. Subj.	venga	vengas	venga	vengamos	vengáis	vengan
Imperative		ven			venid	
Future	vendré	vendrás, etc.				
Cond.	vendría	vendrías, etc.				
Preterit	vine	viniste	vino	vinimos	vinisteis	vinieron
Imp. Subj.	viniera, etc.		viniese, etc.			

21. **ver**, viendo, **visto**, *to see*

Pres. Ind.	veo	ves	ve	vemos	veis	ven
Pres. Subj.	vea	veas	vea	veamos	veáis	vean
Preterit	vi	viste	vio	vimos	visteis	vieron
Imp. Ind.	veía	veías	veía	veíamos	veíais	veían

Verbs with changes in spelling

Changes in spelling are required in certain verbs as explained on pages 18–19 and 90–91. The changes occur in only seven forms: in the first four types given below and on page 176, the change is in the first-person singular of the preterit tense, and in the remaining types in the first-person singular of the present indicative tense, while all types change throughout the present subjunctive tense.

Spanish sounds	before *a*	before *o*	before *u*	before *e*	before *i*
Sound of *k*	ca	co	cu	que	qui
Sound of *g*	ga	go	gu	gue	gui
Sound of *th* (*s*)	za	zo	zu	ce	ci
Sound of *j*	ja	jo	ju	ge, je	gi , ji
Sound of *gw*	gua	guo		güe	güi

1. Verbs ending in **-car** change **c** to **qu** before **e**: **buscar**, *to look for.*

| Preterit | busqué | buscaste | buscó, etc. | | | |
| Pres. Subj. | busque | busques | busque | busquemos | busquéis | busquen |

Like **buscar**: **acercarse**, *to approach*; **comunicar**, *to communicate*; **dedicar**, *to dedicate*; **desembocar**, *to empty*; **destacarse**, *to stand out*; **indicar**, *to indicate*; **intensificar**, *to intensify*; **mascar**, *to chew*; **pescar**, *to fish*; **practicar**, *to practice*; **sacar**, *to take out*; **significar**, *to mean*; **simplificar**, *to simplify*; **tocar**, *to play* (music).

2. Verbs ending in **-gar** change **g** to **gu** before **e**: **llegar**, *to arrive.*

| Preterit | llegué | llegaste | llegó, etc. | | | |
| Pres. Subj. | llegue | llegues | llegue | lleguemos | lleguéis | lleguen |

Like **llegar**: **cargar**, *to load*; **entregar**, *to hand* (*over*); **jugar** (**ue**),[1] *to play* (a game); **navegar**, *to sail*; **pagar**, *to pay*; **rogar** (**ue**), *to beg, ask.*

3. Verbs ending in **-zar** change **z** to **c** before **e**: **cruzar**, *to cross.*

| Preterit | crucé | cruzaste | cruzó, etc. | | | |
| Pres. Subj. | cruce | cruces | cruce | crucemos | crucéis | crucen |

Like **cruzar**: **alcanzar**, *to reach*; **almorzar** (**ue**), *to have lunch*; **caracterizar**, *to characterize*; **comenzar** (**ie**), *to commence, begin*; **empezar** (**ie**), *to begin*; **organizar**, *to organize*; **realizar**, *to realize, carry out*; **utilizar**, *to utilize.*

---

1. See pages 178–180 for stem changes.

4. Verbs ending in **-guar** change **gu** to **gü** before **e**: **averiguar**, *to find out*.

Preterit	averigüé	averiguaste	averiguó, etc.			
Pres. Subj.	averigüe	averigües	averigüe	averigüemos	averigüéis	averigüen

5. Verbs ending in **-ger** or **-gir** change **g** to **j** before **a** or **o**: **escoger**, *to choose*.

Preterit	escojo	escoges	escoge, etc.			
Pres. Subj.	escoja	escojas	escoja	escojamos	escojáis	escojan

Like **escoger**: **dirigir**, *to direct*; **proteger**, *to protect*; **recoger**, *to pick up*.

6. Verbs ending in **-guir** change **gu** to **g** before **a** or **o**: **distinguir**, *to distinguish*.

Pres. Ind.	distingo	distingues	distingue, etc.			
Pres. Subj.	distinga	distingas	distinga	distingamos	distingáis	distingan

Like **distinguir**: **conseguir** (i, i), *to get*; **seguir** (i, i), *to follow*.

7. Verbs ending in **-cer** or **-cir** preceded by a consonant change **c** to **z** before **a** or **o**: **vencer**, *to overcome*.

Pres. Ind.	venzo	vences	vence, etc.			
Pres. Subj.	venza	venzas	venza	venzamos	venzáis	venzan

Like **vencer**: **ejercer**, *to exert*.

8. Verbs ending in **-quir** change **qu** to **c** before **a** and **o**: **delinquir**, *to commit a crime*.

Pres. Ind.	delinco	delinques	delinque, etc.			
Pres. Subj.	delinca	delincas	delinca	delincamos	delincáis	delincan

Verbs with special changes

1. Verbs ending in **-cer** or **-cir** following a vowel insert **z** before **c** in the first-person singular present indicative tense and throughout the present subjunctive tense: **conocer**, *to know, be acquainted with*.

Pres. Ind.	conozco	conoces	conoce, etc.			
Pres. Subj.	conozca	conozcas	conozca	conozcamos	conozcáis	conozcan

Like **conocer**: **aparecer**, *to appear*; **establecer**, *to establish*; **merecer**, *to deserve*; **nacer**, *to be born*; **parecer**, *to seem*; **pertenecer**, *to belong*; **prevalecer**, *to prevail*; **reconocer**, *to recognize*.

2. Verbs ending in **-ducir** have the same changes as **conocer**, with additional changes in the preterit indicative and imperfect subjunctive tenses: **traducir**, *to translate*.

Pres. Ind.	traduzco	traduces	traduce, etc.			
Pres. Subj.	traduzca	traduzcas	traduzca	traduzcamos	traduzcáis	traduzcan
Preterit	traduje	tradujiste	tradujo	tradujimos	tradujisteis	tradujeron
Imp. Subj.	tradujera, etc.		tradujese, etc.			

Like **traducir**: **conducir**, *to lead, drive* (Spain); **introducir**, *to introduce*; **producir**, *to produce*.

3. Verbs ending in **-uir** (except **-guir**) insert **y** except before **i**, and change unaccented **i** between vowels to **y**: **construir**, *to construct*.

Span. Ger.	construyendo					
Pres. Ind.	construyo	construyes	construye	construimos	construís	construyen
Pres. Subj.	construya	construyas	construya	construyamos	construyáis	construyan
Imperative		construye			construid	
Preterit	construí	construiste	construyó	construimos	construisteis	construyeron
Imp. Subj.	construyera, etc.		construyese, etc.			

Like **construir**: **constituir**, *to constitute*; **destruir**, *to destroy*.

4. Certain verbs ending in -er preceded by a vowel replace unaccented **i** of the ending by **y**: **creer**, *to believe*.

Span. Ger.	creyendo					
Past Part.	creído					
Preterit	creí	creíste	creyó	creímos	creísteis	creyeron
Imp. Subj.	creyera, etc.		creyese, etc.			

Like **creer**: **leer**, *to read*; **poseer**, *to possess*.

5. Some verbs ending in **-iar** require a written accent on the **i** in all singular and in the third-person plural in the present indicative and present subjunctive tenses and in the singular imperative: **enviar**, *to send*.

Pres. Ind.	envío	envías	envía	enviamos	enviáis	envían
Pres. Subj.	envíe	envíes	envíe	enviemos	enviéis	envíen
Imperative		envía			enviad	

Like **enviar**: **criar**, *to grow*; **variar**, *to vary*.

However, verbs such as **ampliar**, *to enlarge*; **anunciar**, *to announce*; **apreciar**, *to appreciate*; **cambiar**, *to change*; **estudiar**, *to study*; **iniciar**, *to initiate*; **limpiar**, *to clean*; **pronunciar**, *to pronounce*, do not have the accented **i**.

6. Verbs ending in **-uar** have a written accent on the **u** in the same forms as verbs in section 5:[1] **continuar**, *to continue*.

Pres. Ind.	continúo	continúas	continúa	continuamos	continuáis	continúan
Pres. Subj.	continúe	continúes	continúe	continuemos	continuéis	continúen
Imperative		continúa			continuad	

---

1. **Reunir**(se), *to gather*, has a written accent on the **u** in the same forms as **continuar**.

Pres. Ind.	reúno, reúnes, reúne...reúnen
Pres. Subj.	reúna, reúnas, reúna...reúnan
Imperative	reúne

Stem-changing verbs

Class I (-ar, -er)

Many verbs of the first and second conjugations change the stem vowel **e** to **ie** and **o** to **ue** when the vowels **e** and **o** are stressed, i.e., in the singular and third-person plural of the present indicative and present subjunctive tenses and in the singular imperative. Class I verbs are designated: **cerrar** (**ie**), **volver** (**ue**).

cerrar, *to close*					
Pres. Ind.	cierro	cierras	cierra	cerramos	cerráis	cierran
Pres. Subj.	cierre	cierres	cierre	cerremos	cerréis	cierren
Imperative		cierra			cerrad	

Like **cerrar**: **atravesar**, *to cross*; **comenzar**, *to commence*; **empezar**, *to begin*; **pensar**, *to think*; **recomendar**, *to recommend*; **sentarse**, *to sit down*.

perder, *to lose*					
Pres. Ind.	pierdo	pierdes	pierde	perdemos	perdéis	pierden
Pres. Subj.	pierda	pierdas	pierda	perdamos	perdáis	pierdan
Imperative		pierde			perded	

Like **perder**: **defender**, *to defend*; **entender**, *to understand*; **extenderse**, *to extend*.

contar, *to count*					
Pres. Ind.	cuento	cuentas	cuenta	contamos	contáis	cuentan
Pres. Subj.	cuente	cuentes	cuente	contemos	contéis	cuenten
Imperative		cuenta			contad	

Like **contar**: **acostarse**, *to go to bed*; **almorzar**, *to have lunch*; **costar**, *to cost*; **encontrar**, *to find*; **mostrar**, *to show*; **probar**, *to try*; **recordar**, *to remember, remind*; **rogar**, *to beg, ask*; **sonar**, *to sound, ring*.

volver,[1] *to return*					
Pres. Ind.	vuelvo	vuelves	vuelve	volvemos	volvéis	vuelven
Pres. Subj.	vuelva	vuelvas	vuelva	volvamos	volváis	vuelvan
Imperative		vuelve			volved	

---

1. The past participles of **volver**, **devolver**, **envolver**, **resolver** are: **vuelto**, **devuelto**, **envuelto**, **resuelto**.

Like **volver**: devolver, *to give back*; doler, *to ache*; envolver, *to wrap up*; llover, *to rain*; mover, *to move*; resolver, *to resolve*.

jugar, *to play* (a game)					
Pres. Ind.	juego	juegas	juega	jugamos	jugáis	juegan
Pres. Subj.	juegue	juegues	juegue	juguemos	juguéis	jueguen
Imperative		juega			jugad	

Class II (*-ir*)

Certain verbs of the third conjugation have the changes in the stem indicated below. Class II verbs are designated: **sentir (ie, i) dormir (ue, u)**.

Pres. Ind. 1st, 2nd, 3rd sing.; 3rd plural
Pres. Subj. 1st, 2nd, 3rd sing.; 3rd plural } e > ie
Imperative *Sing.* o > ue

Span. Ger.
Preterit 3rd sing.; 3rd pl.
Pres. Subj. 1st, 2nd pl. } e > i
Imp. Subj. 1st, 2nd, 3rd sing.; o > u
1st, 2nd, 3rd pl.

sentir, *to feel*	singular			plural		
	1st person	2nd person	3rd person	1st person	2nd person	3rd person
Pres. Ind.	siento	sientes	siente	sentimos	sentís	sienten
Pres. Subj.	sienta	sientas	sienta	sintamos	sintáis	sientan
Imperative		siente			sentid	
Preterit	sentí	sentiste	sintió	sentimos	sentisteis	sintieron
Imp. Subj.	sintiera, etc.		sintiese, etc.			
Span. Ger.	sintiendo					

Like **sentir**: advertir, *to advise*; convertir, *to convert*; divertirse, *to amuse oneself*; preferir, *to prefer*; sugerir, *to suggest*.

dormir, *to sleep*					
Pres. Ind.	duermo	duermes	duerme	dormimos	dormís	duermen
Pres. Subj.	duerma	duermas	duerma	durmamos	durmáis	duerman
Imperative		duerme			dormid	
Preterit	dormí	dormiste	durmió	dormimos	dormisteis	durmieron
Imp. Subj.	durmiera, etc.		durmiese, etc.			
Span. Ger.	durmiendo					

Class III (-*ir*)

Certain verbs of the third conjugation change **e** to **i** in all forms in which changes occur in Class II verbs. These verbs are designated: **pedir** (i, i).

pedir, *to ask*					
Pres. Ind.	pido	pides	pide	pedimos	pedís	piden
Pres. Subj.	pida	pidas	pida	pidamos	pidáis	pidan
Imperative		pide			pedid	
Preterit	pedí	pediste	pidió	pedimos	pedisteis	pidieron
Imp. Subj.	pidiera, etc.		pidiese, etc.			
Span. Ger.	pidiendo					

Like **pedir**: **competir**, *to compete*; **conseguir**, *to get*; **despedirse**, *to say good-bye*; **repetir**, *to repeat*; **seguir**, *to follow*; **servir**, *to serve*.

reír, *to laugh*					
Past Part.	reído					
Pres. Ind.	río	ríes	ríe	reímos	reís	ríen
Pres. Subj.	ría	rías	ría	riamos	riáis	rían
Imperative		ríe			reíd	
Preterit	reí	reíste	rió	reímos	reísteis	rieron
Imp. Subj.	riera, etc.		riese, etc.			
Span. Ger.	riendo					

Appendix C

The **Repaso** sections that follow, including written exercises that correspond to the audio program, should be completed on separate sheets of paper. Answers to the **Repaso** are found in Appendix E.

REPASO 3: *Lecciones 12–15*

A. Read each statement and respond negatively to the follow-up question, using the same tense and the subject pronoun for emphasis.

1. Ellos vuelven al centro hoy. ¿Y Uds.?
2. Pablo y Lupe juegan al tenis los sábados. ¿Y Uds.?
3. Nosotras les devolvimos la sección de deportes. ¿Y tú?
4. Ellos oyen muy bien. ¿Y tú?
5. Mis amigos pagaron la cuenta. ¿Y Ud.?
6. Marta comenzó a trabajar ayer. ¿Y Ud.?
7. Ellos pudieron esperar hasta las seis. ¿Y Uds.?
8. Ellos vinieron sin dinero. ¿Y Uds.?
9. Miguel y yo les trajimos regalos. ¿Y tú?
10. Yo estuve el año pasado en Cozumel. ¿Y Ud.?
11. Yo he visto esas playas. ¿Y tus amigos?
12. Nosotros hemos hecho esa excursión. ¿Y Ud.?
13. Lola les ha escrito a menudo. ¿Y tú?
14. Ella se había puesto muy bronceada. ¿Y Uds.?
15. Luis había abierto las ventanas. ¿Y Ud.?
16. Nosotros habíamos hecho las reservas. ¿Y Uds.?
17. Uds. tendrán que cambiarlas. ¿Y yo?
18. Ella se pondrá el vestido nuevo. ¿Y tú?
19. Uds. podrían sacar las fotos ahora. ¿Y yo?
20. Luisa haría el viaje en coche. ¿Y sus amigos?

B. Answer each question affirmatively, substituting the appropriate direct object pronoun for the noun and making any other necessary changes.

1. ¿Le diste tú a ella la pulsera?
2. ¿Le trajiste a Luis el reloj?
3. ¿Les devolviste a ellos los anillos?
4. ¿Se puso Ud. los aretes de oro?
5. ¿Estaba ella arreglándose el pelo?
6. ¿Pudiste entregarle a él las gafas?

C. Answer each question, following the model.

MODEL: —¿Llegará Ud. para las once?
—Sin duda, para las once ya habré llegado.

1. ¿Regresarán Uds. para la Navidad?
2. ¿Volverás para la fiesta de Año Nuevo?
3. ¿Recibirán ellos la solicitud para mañana?
4. ¿Llamará el gerente para el viernes?

5. ¿Tendrá Miguel la entrevista para la semana próxima?

MODEL: —¿Vieron Uds. la película sobre Yucatán?
—No, pero la **habríamos visto con gusto.**

6. ¿Escucharon Uds. la conferencia sobre los mayas?
7. ¿Vio Ud. las fotografías de las ruinas?
8. ¿Leyeron Uds. el artículo sobre Cozumel?
9. ¿Hiciste el viaje a la isla?
10. ¿Trajeron Uds. algunas artesanías?

D. Rewrite each sentence, substituting the new subject in parentheses and making any other necessary changes.

1. Me gusta este ritmo. (estos bailes)
2. A ella le encantan esas canciones. (esa música)
3. ¿Qué te parecen estos trajes? (esta blusa)
4. Nos gustan esos zapatos blancos. (esa cartera)
5. Se ve mucha mercancía en las vitrinas. (artículos finos)
6. Se abren las tiendas a las nueve. (la peluquería)

E. Complete each sentence with the necessary preposition.

1. Jorge se acerca _____ nuestra mesa y nos saluda.

2. Mil gracias _____ los aretes.

3. El sábado _____ la tarde fuimos _____ un partido de fútbol.

4. Él se conforma _____ nadar en la piscina.

5. Nosotros hemos disfrutado _____ las vacaciones.

6. Luis acaba _____ ingresar _____ la escuela de verano.

7. ¿La has invitado _____ hacer una excursión _____ bicicleta?

8. Yo comencé _____ trabajar _____ un gimnasio.

9. Nos alegramos mucho _____ conocerte.

10. Yo quería ver el juego _____ Colombia y los Estados Unidos.

11. En el centro pregunté _____ una joyería típica.

12. ¿Eres tú muy aficionado _____ los deportes?

13. Ellos están pensando _____ hacer una excursión _____ las ruinas.

14. Acaban _____ salir _____ hotel.

15. Hágame Ud. el favor _____ hablar despacio.

16. Ellas no tienen tiempo _____ cocinar nada.

F. Answer each question with a complete sentence, using vocabulary from previous lessons.

1. ¿Dónde pasó Ud. sus últimas vacaciones? ¿Qué cosas pudo hacer Ud. allí? ¿Qué cosas tenemos que hacer antes de hacer un viaje?
2. ¿Le gustan a Ud. las joyas? ¿Qué joyas usan las chicas hoy día? ¿Dónde se pueden comprar joyas típicas mexicanas en esta ciudad?

3. ¿Qué deportes ha practicado Ud.? ¿Practica Ud. algún deporte ahora? ¿Mira Ud. los deportes por la televisión? ¿Qué partidos le interesan? ¿Hace Ud. ejercicio todos los días? ¿Qué ejercicio le gusta a Ud. hacer?

G. Give the Spanish equivalent.

1. The girls are probably going to the movie.
2. We saw them (*f.*) an hour ago.
3. They went to Spain in the summer of 1996 and they bought many gifts.
4. My friends (*m.* and *f.*) gave me a gift.
5. Of course! They (*m.* and *f.*) had invited you (*m. pl.*).
6. It was very cold and the windows were open.
7. I wonder what time it is?
8. I'll come back on Sunday evening.
9. We're very glad to see you (*fam. sing.*).
10. Shall we stay inside?
11. One eats very well here.
12. Did Thomas make an excursion with you (*pl.*)?
13. Going by plane one arrives fast; by five o'clock in the afternoon he will have arrived.
14. "What can I do for you (*formal sing.*)?" "Nothing, thank you."
15. It is necessary to decide that today.
16. Mr. and Mrs. Sierra have just entered the jewelry store.
17. That bracelet (*over there*) and this one are beautiful.
18. The boys would have liked to attend the World Cup.
19. I should like to visit many interesting places.
20. He hasn't put on his bathing suit yet.
21. Michael became very tired. He is tired of diving.
22. We got up shortly afterward.

Verbs, Pronouns, Demonstrative Pronouns, *Para comprender y escribir*

REPASO 4: *Lecciones 16–19*

A. Confirm each statement, following the model.

> MODEL: —Este (Ese) apartamento es cómodo.
> —**Sí, es más cómodo que aquél. Es el más cómodo de todos.**

1. Este edificio es nuevo.
2. Estas calles son hermosas.
3. Ese equipo es bueno.
4. Esos jugadores son altos.
5. Esta empresa es importante.
6. Estos empleados son trabajadores.
7. Esa secretaria es competente.
8. Este jefe es amable.

B. Answer each question, following the model.

> MODEL: —La hija de él es muy bonita. ¿Y las hijas de Ud.?
> —**Mis hijas son bonitísimas.**

1. El sobrino de Miguel es muy alto. ¿Y los sobrinos de Ud.?
2. Los padres de él son muy felices. ¿Y los padres de ella?

3. El hijo de los señores Ruiz es muy inteligente. ¿Y las hijas de ellos?
4. El novio de Marta es muy bueno. ¿Y el novio de Silvia?
5. La esposa del señor Ramos es muy guapa. ¿Y la esposa de Ud.?

C. Answer the questions, following the model.

MODEL: —¿Envuelvo el regalo o busco otra cosa? ¿Qué prefiere Ud.?
  —**Prefiero que Ud. envuelva el regalo; no busque otra cosa.**

1. ¿Alquilo un apartamento o compro una casa? ¿Qué sugiere Ud.?
2. ¿Hablo con el gerente o llamo a la dueña? ¿Qué recomienda Ud.?
3. ¿Sirvo las bebidas ahora o comienzo a cocinar? ¿Qué desea Ud.?
4. ¿Voy a la conferencia o me quedo en la biblioteca? ¿Qué recomienda Ud.?
5. ¿Escribo el resumen ahora o pago las cuentas? ¿Qué me dice Ud.?
6. ¿Pongo este disco o busco otro? ¿Qué prefiere Ud.?

D. Rewrite each sentence, using the cue given. Follow the model.

MODEL: Alberto los ha invitado a su boda.   (Dudo mucho que)
  Dudo mucho que Alberto los haya invitado a su boda.

1. Alberto y Silvia quieren casarse.   (Me alegro de que)
2. Ellos son muy felices.   (Yo sé que)
3. Ellos no han dicho nada todavía.   (Me extraña que)
4. Silvia ya ha vuelto de la Argentina.   (Es posible que)
5. Sus amigas no lo han visto todavía.   (Temo que)
6. Alberto se ha puesto muy contento.   (Estoy seguro de que)
7. Nosotros les daremos una gran fiesta.   (No dudo que)
8. Ellos recibirán muchos regalos.   (Espero que)

E. Respond to each question, following the model.

MODEL: —Hace tiempo que no llamo a Lupe. Te extraña, ¿verdad?
  —Sí, me extraña que no la hayas llamado.

1. Hace tiempo que no vuelvo a casa. Te extraña, ¿verdad?
2. Hace tiempo que no veo a Miguel. Lo sientes, ¿verdad?
3. Hace un año que no le escribo. Lo dudas, ¿verdad?
4. Hace meses que no le digo nada. Es importante, ¿verdad?
5. Hace semanas que no voy al cine. Es posible, ¿verdad?
6. Hace días que no vengo a clases. Te preocupa, ¿verdad?
7. Hace tiempo que no me enfermo. Es extraño, ¿verdad?
8. Hace meses que no hago nada interesante. Es lástima, ¿verdad?

F. Complete each sentence, using the present indicative or the present subjunctive tense, as required.

1. Tengo una secretaria que (escribir) bien en español.
2. Necesitamos a alguien que (saber) traducir del inglés.
3. Conozco a una persona que (ser) bilingüe.
4. ¿Hay alguien que (poder) recomendar bien a Miguel?

5. Buscan un joven que (tener) dos años de experiencia.
6. No conozco a nadie que (estar) sin trabajo ahora.

G. The following is a brief letter that you are writing to a friend. Complete the letter by selecting the appropriate missing item(s).

Querido Antonio:

Te extraña que no te haya escrito (1) _____ _____ tiempo, ¿verdad? Pues hace meses que estoy (2) _____. Como sabes, el verano que viene pienso (3) _____ _____ ingeniero. Es posible también que me (4) _____ y que vayamos a vivir (5) _____ _____ a la Argentina. Mi novia, (6) _____ es de Buenos Aires, prefiere que (7) _____ allá. Oigo (8) _____ que allí no es (9) _____ conseguir un (10) _____ de ingeniero, pero (11) _____ _____ que paguen muy bien y necesitaríamos (12) _____ un apartamento y comprar un carro (13) _____. (14) _____ ella pueda trabajar (15) _____ al español artículos sobre economía, pero no es seguro que decidamos (16) _____. Espero que tú puedas venir para (17) _____ _____ y que conozcas a Silvia. Es una chica estupenda, y además es (18) _____. Te encantará conocerla. (19) _____ y hasta pronto. (20) _____ amigo de siempre,

amueblar
case
decir
Escríbeme
graduarme de
irnos
no creo
traduciendo
volvamos

nuestra boda
puesto
un tiempo

difícil
guapísima
nuevo
ocupadísimo
Tu
desde hace
quien
Quizás

Miguel

H. Give the Spanish equivalent.

1. Let's wash our hands.
2. Let's go now.
3. Let's not sit down yet.
4. Have George do it.
5. May they continue ahead.
6. John has been here a week.
7. How long have they been working here?
8. They became very rich some years ago.
9. Maybe Robert may not come. I doubt it.
10. How do you (*fam. sing.*) feel today?
11. Most of the students went to the lecture.
12. John has a headache.
13. Richard's arm hurts.
14. By the way, what's the matter with Thomas?
15. Why don't you (*pl.*) take a walk with me?
16. Anthony became a good doctor.
17. Is there anyone here who knows her?
18. We have heard that he got the position.
19. We are sorry that John's sister has been ill.
20. Let (*pl.*) me drive this afternoon.

Verbs, Adjectives, Time Expressions, *Para comprender y escribir*

REPASO 5: *lecciones 20–22*

A. Answer the first question negatively and the second one affirmatively. Use object pronouns in your answers. Follow the model.

> MODEL: —¿Quién escoge las lecciones diarias? ¿Uds.?
> —**No, nosotros no las escogemos.**
> —¿Las escojo yo?
> —**Sí, Ud. las escoge.**

1. ¿Quién escoge los libros para esta clase? ¿Uds.? ¿Los escojo yo?
2. ¿Quién dirige esta clase? ¿Uds.? ¿La dirijo yo?
3. ¿Quién continúa la clase hoy? ¿Ud.? ¿La continúo yo?
4. ¿Quién le envía los exámenes al profesor? ¿Ud.? ¿Se los envía la oficina del departamento de español?
5. ¿Quiénes se reúnen aquí? ¿Los estudiantes de francés? ¿Se reúnen Uds. aquí?
6. ¿Quién construye los edificios de la universidad? ¿Ud.? ¿Un grupo de ingenieros?

B. Confirm the following statements with either **Sí, quiero que**; **Sí, espero que**; or **Es posible que**, according to the meaning you wish to convey.

> MODEL: —Ana pedirá permiso para salir temprano.
> —**Sí, quiero que** (*or* **espero que** *or* **es posible que**) **Ana pida permiso para salir temprano.**

1. José conseguirá un puesto de ingeniero.
2. Beatriz escogerá la carrera de medicina.
3. Lupe enviará una solicitud a la Escuela de Arquitectura.
4. Ese carro no continuará por esa calle.
5. Ese carro se detendrá a tiempo.
6. El policía dirigirá el tráfico mejor.
7. El policía le pedirá el carnet a ese conductor.
8. La gente se irá pronto.
9. La ciudad construirá mejores avenidas.
10. Eso valdrá la pena.

C. Respond negatively to each question, using the appropriate possessive pronoun.

> MODEL: —¿Tienes mi pasaporte?
> —**No, no tengo el tuyo.**

1. ¿Traes las maletas de Rita?
2. ¿Llevas el equipaje de Miguel?
3. ¿Necesita Ud. los boletos míos?
4. ¿Quiere Ud. el asiento mío?
5. ¿Hace Ud. las reservas nuestras?
6. ¿Conduces el carro nuestro?

D. Confirm each statement, following the model.

> MODEL: —Miguel quiere que tú vayas al concierto.
> —**Sí, él quería que yo fuera al concierto.**

1. El profesor quiere que tú escuches la conferencia.
2. Antonio prefiere que tú traduzcas los versos.

3. Carmen prefiere que Uds. hagan la solicitud.
4. Sus padres esperan que Uds. sean buenos amigos.
5. Ellos no creen que Ud. pueda ser mal empleado.
6. Ellos esperan que yo construya un futuro mejor para Uds.
7. El jefe espera que su secretaria escriba mejores resúmenes.
8. La profesora espera que Uds. lean más artículos.

E. Rewrite each sentence, using the imperfect subjunctive tense in the dependent clauses.

> MODEL: Es preciso que Uds. se sienten.   **Es preciso que Uds. se sienten.**
> (Fue preciso)   **Fue preciso que Uds. se sentaran.**

1. Te traigo los suéteres para que tú escojas uno.   (Te traje)
2. Les aconsejo que duerman un rato.   (Les aconsejé)
3. No hay nadie aquí que nos haga el favor.   (No había nadie)
4. Esperamos que Lola consiga la beca.   (Esperábamos)
5. Me alegro de que Ana salga de viaje con Uds.   (Me alegraba)
6. Será mejor que ellos lleven una cámara vídeo.   (Sería mejor)

F. Complete each sentence with a **si**-clause, according to the models. Observe the appropriate tense agreement.

> MODELS: No solicito el puesto porque no quiero mudarme, pero si
> **quisiera mudarme, solicitaría el puesto.**
>
> No solicité el puesto porque no quería mudarme, pero si **hubiera querido mudarme, habría solicitado el puesto.**

1. No partimos el sábado porque no hay asientos libres en ese vuelo, pero si _____.
2. No te avisé de la reunión porque no te había visto antes, pero si _____.
3. Carolina no sabe traducir; por eso no puede conseguir un buen puesto en Suramérica, pero si ella _____.
4. Como ellos no me invitaron a su fiesta de bodas, no fui; pero si ellos _____.
5. Uds. no tuvieron paciencia, por eso no sacaron mejores fotos; pero si Uds. _____.
6. No te doy más dinero porque no tengo suficiente para mí, pero si yo _____.

G. Supply the correct form of the infinitive in parentheses.

1. Ellos me llamaron en cuanto yo (volver) _____ de mi viaje.
2. Yo sentía que ellos no (tener) _____ nada que hacer.
3. Les aconsejé a ellos que (buscar) _____ otros amigos.
4. No creo que mis compañeros (servir) _____ mucha comida anoche.
5. Aunque (llover) _____ mucho ayer, hicimos la excursión.
6. Si nosotros (tener) _____ el tiempo, iríamos al aeropuerto con Uds.
7. Yo no pude encontrar un impermeable que me (gustar) _____.
8. ¡Ojalá que Miguel (llegar) _____ a ser el gerente de la compañía!

9. No había nadie que (construir) _____ edificios como el señor Morales.

10. Me alegré de que ellos se (haber) _____ marchado ya.

11. Si la película (ser) _____ buena, nos gustaría verla.

12. Si nosotros (estar) _____ libres, saldremos con los chicos.

H. Give the Spanish equivalent.

1. We didn't intend to go to a movie, but to a concert.
2. You are welcome.
3. We used to see each other often, but we never met.
4. It is worthwhile to spend some time in a foreign country.
5. I ran into George an hour ago.
6. The gifts are for Betty.
7. James left for Spain last night.
8. Send (*fam. pl.*) for Rita tomorrow morning.
9. They are very successful.
10. Did he buy a round-trip ticket?
11. This one (*m.*) is for you (*formal sing.*).
12. The verses were translated by Michael.
13. The cards were written by my sister.
14. If I had seen John, I would have given him the photos.
15. If I had the money, I would buy a video camera.
16. I should like to travel through this country.
17. I wish that the boys were here now!
18. Robert has applied for a scholarship in order to study engineering.
19. I paid twenty dollars for the gloves.
20. They should (ought to) be in front of the restaurant by six o'clock.

Verbs, Pronouns, Passive Voice, *Para comprender y escribir*

Appendix D

Answer Keys

Lección 12

Preguntas sobre los diálogos, page 3: **1.** (Los padres de Miguel *or* Ellos) Hicieron un viaje a España en el mes de mayo de 1997. **2.** (Los señores Ramos *or* Ellos) Viajaban a Granada en coche. (Ellos) Decidieron pasar la noche en (un hotel de) Córdoba. **3.** (Los señores Ramos *or* Ellos) No hicieron reservas porque les dijeron que, viniendo en ese tiempo del año, no se necesita hacerlas (*or* hacer las reservas). **4.** (La recepcionista) Les dice que en Córdoba, siempre hay mucha gente de visita. (Ellos) Tienen mucha suerte porque (en el segundo piso) hay una habitación desocupada (con dos camas sencillas y baño privado). **5.** (La habitación con el desayuno completo) Cuesta doce mil pesetas al día (para dos personas) y diez mil pesetas al día sin desayuno. **6.** (La recepcionista *or* Ella) Lleva a los señores Ramos (*or* Los lleva) al segundo piso. Los lleva allí porque ellos (*or* los señores Ramos) quieren ver la habitación (antes de decidir). **7.** No se necesita (aire acondicionado) en la habitación porque en mayo todavía no hace mucho calor. **8.** (En la habitación) Hay dos ventanas grandes que dan a la plaza. (La vista a la plaza) Es agradable porque se ve mucha gente animada paseando y charlando. **9.** (A los señores Ramos *or* A ellos) Les gusta viajar en coche porque así se conoce mejor el país. No, no es la primera vez (que ellos visitan Córdoba. Es la segunda). **10.** (El señor Ramos *or* Él) Quiere saber si hay un comedor (en el hotel) porque (ya es bastante tarde y) tiene un poco de hambre.

Práctica 1, page 4: **1.** dijo **2.** dije **3.** dijeron **4.** dijimos **5.** hizo **6.** hicieron **7.** hicimos **8.** hice **9.** quise **10.** Quisieron **11.** quisimos **12.** quisiste **13.** vine **14.** Vinieron **15.** vinimos **16.** vino

Práctica 2, page 5: **1.** Haciendo reservas, tienes cuartos en los hoteles. **2.** Viniendo temprano, no necesitas boleto. **3.** Trayendo nosotros la paella, Antonio promete traer bebidas. **4.** Saliendo a las ocho, llegamos a las once. **5.** Practicando mucho, podemos ganar. **6.** Estando ella enferma, no puedes aceptar la invitación.

Práctica 3, page 6: **1.** Yendo **2.** ir **3.** ir **4.** leer **5.** Leyendo **6.** leer **7.** saber **8.** saber **9.** Sabiendo **10.** volver **11.** Volviendo **12.** volver

Práctica 4, page 6: **1.** Yo las vendo. Quiero venderlas. Estoy vendiéndolas (Las estoy vendiendo). **2.** Ramón lo hizo. Él no quiso hacerlo. No está haciéndolo (No lo está haciendo). **3.** Yo me acuesto. Voy a acostarme. Estoy acostándome (No me estoy acostando). **4.** ¿Dónde nos registramos? Queremos registrarnos. Estamos registrándonos (Nos estamos registrando).

Práctica 5, page 7: **1.** Entonces no se conocía la música cubana. **2.** Se enseñan varias lenguas en la universidad.

3. ¿Dónde se compran los boletos? **4.** Se celebra su cumpleaños en el mes de enero. **5.** Se venden estos zapatos a precio especial.

Práctica 6, page 8: **1.** Se abren los bancos a las nueve. **2.** Se cierran las tiendas a las ocho. **3.** En este hotel no se aceptan cheques. **4.** Aquí sólo se habla español. **5.** En este restaurante se come muy bien.

Práctica 7, page 9: **1.** Eso nos interesa a nosotros. **2.** El cuarto me gustó a mí. **3.** Esta vez no le conviene a él/a ella/a usted. **4.** El coche les pareció caro a ellos/a ellas/a ustedes.

Práctica 8, page 9: **1.** Ana está charlando con él. **2.** Los discos son de ella. **3.** Traigo algo para ellos. **4.** Elena está al lado de ella.

Práctica 9, page 9: **1.** con ellos/ellas **2.** contigo **3.** con ustedes **4.** conmigo

Práctica 10, page 10: **1.** ciento una reservas **2.** ciento quince llaves **3.** trescientos sesenta y cinco días **4.** tres mil toallas **5.** diez millones quinientas mil personas **6.** setecientos cincuenta mil dólares en efectivo

Práctica 11, page 11: **1.** El cuarto está en el octavo piso. **2.** ¿Es éste el tercer concierto? **3.** Creo que es la sexta canción. **4.** Es la cuarta vez que vengo a España. **5.** ¿Cuál es el noveno mes del año?

Práctica 12, page 12: **1.** el primero de abril de mil novecientos noventa y tres **2.** el dieciséis de septiembre de mil ochocientos diez **3.** el catorce de julio de mil setecientos ochenta y nueve **4.** el trece de mayo de mil seiscientos siete **5.** el quince de octubre de mil sesenta y seis

Repaso

A, *page 12:* **1.** el piso **2.** el jabón **3.** el desayuno completo **4.** la foto

B, *page 12:* **1.** Los padres de Miguel Ramos hicieron su segundo viaje a España durante el mes de mayo de mil novecientos noventa y siete. **2.** Yendo en coche a Granada, (ellos) decidieron pasar la noche en Córdoba. **3.** Ellos tienen mucha suerte porque hay una habitación desocupada con dos camas sencillas y (un) baño privado en el segundo piso. **4.** El precio es (de) doce mil pesetas al día con (el) desayuno completo para dos personas, sin el estacionamiento. **5.** La señora Ramos quiere ver la habitación. Viéndola es más fácil decidir si la quieren tomar (*or* si quieren tomarla). **6.** Los señores Ramos (*or* El señor y la señora Ramos) bajaron al piso principal a registrarse.

Expansión

A, *page 13:* (*Answers will vary.*) **1.** Sí, hice muchos viajes el año pasado. Fui a... y a... **2.** No, no pienso hacer un viaje largo en coche durante el verano.   **3.** Me gusta viajar en avión porque es más rápido.   **4.** Conviene hacer reservas porque hay muchos turistas.   **5.** Son importantes las camas y los baños.   **6.** *Answers will vary.*

B, page 13:   *(Answers will vary.)*

Para comprender y escribir

A, page 13:   **1.** (b) el ascensor.   **2.** (c) un garaje.
3. (b) novecientas pesetas.   **4.** (b) El cuatro de julio de mil setecientos setenta y seis.

B, page 14:   **1.** Nosotros también quisimos descansar.
2. Nosotros también vinimos en una excursión.   **3.** Yo también hice las reservas.   **4.** Yo también decidí tomar la habitación.   **5.** Yo también dije que era cómoda.

C, page 14:   La hermana de Alicia Martí hizo un viaje a Granada el año pasado. Fue con dos amigas de la universidad. Una de las muchachas, Isabel, tenía familia en España. El avión las llevó a Madrid y entonces decidieron ir hasta Granada en tren. Fueron a un hotel muy agradable cerca de una plaza. Allí conocieron a muchas personas de todo el mundo que también estaban de viaje por el país.

Lección 13

Preguntas sobre el diálogo, page 17:   **1.** (Los señores Ramos *or* Ellos) Decidieron volver a México (después de su viaje por España).   **2.** (Esta vez) Estuvieron un par de semanas. (Ellos) Pudieron visitar las ruinas de Yucatán y otros lugares interesantes.   **3.** (Los señores Ramos *or* Ellos) Fueron (*or* tuvieron tiempo para ir) de compras (cuando estaban en Mérida).   **4.** (El señor Ramos *or* Él) Le compró unos aretes de oro (a su esposa). (La señora Ramos *or* Ella) Quería el prendedor porque (el prendedor) hacía juego con los aretes.   **5.** (La señora Ramos *or* Ella) Compró (unas) pulseras para Clara y (para) Luisa. Compró unos anillos de plata para sus hermanas.
6. (El señor Ramos *or* Él) Quería ir al mercado para encontrar objetos de cerámica y artículos de artesanía para regalos.   **7.** Quería comprar unas hamacas.   **8.** No las compró en la ciudad de México porque no pudo encontrar los colores que quería.

Práctica 1, page 18:   **1.** tuve   **2.** estuve   **3.** supimos
4. pusiste   **5.** puse   **6.** tuve   **7.** estuvieron
8. pudieron   **9.** estuvimos   **10.** supimos   **11.** Tuvieron
12. pudimos   **13.** tuve   **14.** supe   **15.** puso

Práctica 2, page 19:   **1.** Yo llegué al hotel temprano.
2. Yo pagué la cuenta.   **3.** Busqué objetos de cerámica.
4. Saqué muchas fotografías.   **5.** El viernes comencé a prepararme para el viaje.   **6.** Yo almorcé temprano.
7. Gocé de las montañas.   **8.** ¿Qué toqué para la fiesta?
9. No practiqué esta semana.   **10.** Envolví mal el paquete; no lo entregué.

Práctica 3, page 20:   **1.** Busque   **2.** Llegue
3. Practiquen   **4.** entreguen   **5.** Crucen   **6.** Paguen
7. Comience   **8.** Goce

Práctica 4, page 21:   **1.** Ana me lo vendió.   **2.** Se las devolví.   **3.** Me las llevé.   **4.** Te la compré.   **5.** Lupe se las puso.   **6.** Póngaselos.   **7.** No se los dé.   **8.** No pude traérselo.   **9.** Están lavándomelo.   **10.** Acabo de decírsela.

Práctica 5, page 21:   **1.** Sí, se lo di a ella.   **2.** Sí, se las enseñé a ellos.   **3.** Sí, se los devolví a Lupe.   **4.** Sí, se la entregué a ellas.   **5.** Sí, voy a comprárselos a ellos.   **6.** Sí, necesito llevárselo a Luis.   **7.** Sí, puedo dárselas a él.
8. Sí, quiero dejársela a Marta.

Práctica 6, page 22:   **1.** Me interesan éstos.   **2.** Ésa es de cuero.   **3.** ¿Le gustan a ella aquéllas?   **4.** ¿Me envuelve Ud. ésos?   **5.** ¿Nos enseña Ud. aquél?   **6.** Éstas no son caras.

Práctica 7, page 22:   **1.** No, acabo de devolver ésa (*or* aquélla).   **2.** No, acabo de ver ése (*or* aquél).   **3.** No, me gusta más éste (*or* aquél).   **4.** No, ésos (*or* aquéllos) son más caros.   **5.** No, quiero ésta (*or* aquélla) para el patio.
6. No, éstas (*or* aquéllas) me parecen más finas.

Práctica 8, page 23:   devolver, volví, devolver, volvió, volvimos

Práctica 9, page 23:   **1.** Ellos acaban de devolver el regalo.   **2.** Ana acaba de traerme la llave.   **3.** Nosotros acabamos de hacer la reserva.   **4.** Ud. acaba de leer el artículo.   **5.** Tú acababas de pagar la cuenta cuando llegaron tus amigos.   **6.** Ellas acababan de llegar cuando sonó el teléfono.

Práctica 10, page 24:   **1.** ¿Trajiste la ropa en ese paquete? Sí, traje la ropa en ese paquete.   **2.** ¿Trajo tu padre los regalos? Sí, mi padre trajo los regalos.   **3.** Yo traje el mapa, ¿verdad? Sí, Ud. trajo (tú trajiste) el mapa.
4. ¿Trajeron ellos las llaves? Sí, ellos trajeron las llaves.
5. ¿Trajo Ud. suficiente dinero? Sí, traje suficiente dinero.
6. ¿Lo trajeron Uds. en cheques de viajero? Sí, lo trajimos en cheques de viajero.

Repaso

A, page 24:   **1.** la joyería   **2.** la vitrina   **3.** la hamaca
4. el mercado

B, page 25:   **1.** Clara y yo acabamos de llevarnos los aretes.   **2.** El señor Ramos preguntó por la joyería.   **3.** La señora Ramos se dirige a su esposo.   **4.** Tú devolviste las joyas de fantasía.

C, page 25:   **1.** Después de su viaje a España, el señor y la señora (*or* los señores) Ramos decidieron volver a México.
2. Durante ese viaje, (ellos) pudieron visitar las ruinas de Yucatán y otros lugares interesantes.   **3.** Mientras estaban (*or* Estando) en Mérida, tuvieron tiempo para ir de compras.
4. Entraron en una joyería para comprar algunas joyas.
5. La dependienta sacó de la vitrina un par de aretes y se los enseñó a la señora Ramos.   **6.** Dirigiéndose a su esposo, ella (le) preguntó: —¿Qué te parecen éstos?   **7.** Después de mirar unas (*or* algunas) pulseras, la señora Ramos le dijo a la dependienta: —Me llevo ésta para Clara, y ésa (aquélla) para Luisa.

Expansión

A, *page 25:* *(Answers will vary.)*   **1.** Estuve en... Hice un viaje a...   **2.** Pude hacer...   **3.** Sí, estuve con muchos amigos. Me contaron que... Supe que...   **4.** Sí, tuve tiempo para ir de compras. Compré...   **5.** Sí, tuve que devolver algunos regalos. Me devolvieron el dinero.   **6.** Volví de mis vacaciones en agosto. Traje muchas cosas.

B, *page 26:* *(Answers will vary.)*

Para comprender y escribir

A, *page 26:*   **1.** (a) A una joyería.   **2.** (a) el recibo.   **3.** (c) devolverlo.   **4.** (b) un prendedor.   **5.** (c) En el centro.

B, *page 27:*   **1.** No, lo hice ayer.   **2.** No, tuve tiempo ayer.   **3.** No, busqué a Diana ayer. (No, la busqué ayer.)   **4.** No, almorcé con ella ayer.   **5.** No, comencé a trabajar ayer.   **6.** No, nos llevamos los paquetes ayer. (No, nos los llevamos ayer.)

C, *page 27:*   **1.** Yo las saqué ayer.   **2.** Yo lo practiqué ayer.   **3.** Yo lo toqué ayer.   **4.** Yo las entregué ayer.   **5.** Yo la pagué ayer.   **6.** Yo lo crucé ayer.

D, *page 27:*   El año pasado los señores Ramos estuvieron en México un par de semanas. Durante ese viaje pudieron visitar las ruinas de Yucatán y otros lugares interesantes. Un día encontraron una joyería típica. El dependiente les mostró muchos artículos de oro y de plata. La señora Ramos quería comprar algo especial para sus dos hijas. El señor Ramos vio unas pulseras de plata que le gustaron mucho. Cuando regresaron a los Estados Unidos, les encantaron los regalos a sus hijas.

Lección 14

Preguntas sobre el diálogo, p. 30:   **1.** (Miguel y su hermana *or* Ellos) Habían ido a Cozumel a pasar sus (*or* las) vacaciones de primavera. Un grupo de chicos y chicas habían ido con ellos.   **2.** (Miguel) Había buceado mucho (el último día de sus vacaciones en Cozumel).   **3.** Sus amigos se quedaron en la playa tomando el sol un par de horas. Las chicas habían ido de compras y (luego a la peluquería) a arreglarse el pelo.   **4.** (Los padres de Miguel *or* Ellos) Llamaron por teléfono porque no habían recibido noticias de ellos (*or* de Miguel y su hermana) y estaban preocupados.   **5.** (Los jóvenes *or* Ellos) Han visto pueblos encantadores y ruinas de antiguas ciudades mayas.   **6.** El mar (de Cozumel) es verde-azul y la arena es (muy) blanca. El agua es tan clara que se puede ver el fondo cubierto de corales.   **7.** (La hermana de Miguel *or* Ella) No se encontraba en su habitación (cuando llamaron sus padres) porque había ido a la peluquería.   **8.** (Miguel) Le dijo (a su padre) que su hermana se veía estupenda porque (ella) se había puesto muy bronceada.   **9.** (Cuando Miguel y su padre hablaban por teléfono) No se podía oír bien porque la puerta del cuarto estaba abierta y había mucha gente charlando en el corredor.   **10.** (Miguel) No ha ido de pesca porque (a él) le gusta más bucear.

Práctica 1, page 33:   **1.** hemos bajado/Yo he bajado en el ascensor.   **2.** Ha vendido/¿Han vendido Uds. el tocadiscos?   **3.** he disfrutado/Nosotros hemos disfrutado de las vacaciones.   **4.** han subido/Ud. ha subido al cuarto piso.   **5.** he estado/Nosotros hemos estado en el mercado.   **6.** ¿Has escrito/¿Les han escrito Uds. una tarjeta?   **7.** ha visto/Ellas han visto las ruinas mayas.   **8.** he puesto/Nosotros nos hemos puesto muy bronceados.   **9.** han ido/Mi tío ha ido a pescar.   **10.** has hecho/¿Qué han hecho Uds. durante las vacaciones?

Práctica 2, page 34:   **1.** habían traído/Él no había traído su traje de baño.   **2.** habíamos arreglado/Yo no me había arreglado el pelo.   **3.** Había creído/¿Habían creído Uds. las palabras del profesor?   **4.** habíamos oído/Yo no había oído esos discos.   **5.** habían vuelto/La joven había vuelto de la joyería.   **6.** Habían venido/¿Había venido a tiempo el invitado?

Práctica 3, page 34:   **1.** Sí, ya se lo he prometido.   **2.** Sí, ya se los he leído.   **3.** Sí, ya se las he vendido.   **4.** Sí, ya se la hemos devuelto.   **5.** Sí, ya se lo hemos dicho.   **6.** Sí, ya se las hemos abierto.

Práctica 4, page 35:   **1.** No, ya estaba escrito.   **2.** No, ya estaba cubierta.   **3.** No, ya estaba puesta.   **4.** No, ya estaba preparado.   **5.** No, ya estaban lavados.   **6.** No, ya estaban hechas.   **7.** No, ya estaban envueltos.   **8.** No, ya estaban abiertas.   **9.** No, ya estaban puestas.   **10.** No, ya estaban cobrados.

Práctica 5, page 36:   **1.** hay   **2.** Hubo   **3.** ha habido   **4.** hay   **5.** había   **6.** había

Práctica 6, page 37:   **1.** Sí, volvió hace tres días. Sí, hace tres días que volvió.   **2.** Sí, saqué las fotos hace un mes. Sí, hace un mes que saqué las fotos.   **3.** Sí, salieron de Cuba hace quince años. Sí, hace quince años que salieron de Cuba.   **4.** Sí, oímos ese disco hace una semana. Sí, hace una semana que oímos ese disco.   **5.** Sí, pagué la cuenta hace seis semanas. Sí, hace seis semanas que pagué la cuenta.   **6.** Sí, comencé a escribir el artículo hace dos horas. Sí, hace dos horas que comencé a escribir el artículo.

Práctica 7, page 37:   **1.** Oyen/¿Oían ellos la música?/¿Oyeron ellos la música?   **2.** oye/Rita no oía mis palabras./Rita no oyó mis palabras.   **3.** Oyes/¿Oías tú algo?/¿Oíste tú algo?   **4.** oigo/Yo no oía nada./Yo no oí nada.   **5.** oyen/¿Qué oían Uds.?/¿Qué oyeron Uds.?   **6.** oímos/Nosotros oíamos la conversación./Nosotros oímos la conversación.

Práctica 8, page 38:   **1.** creyó   **2.** leyendo   **3.** leyó   **4.** creído   **5.** leyeron

Repaso

A, *page 38:*   *(Answers will vary.)*

B, *page 38:*   **1.** Miguel, su hermana y algunos amigos (y amigas) han ido a Cozumel a pasar sus vacaciones de primavera.   **2.** El último día de sus vacaciones, Miguel había nadado mucho y necesitaba descansar un rato.   **3.** Sus amigos se quedaron en la playa tomando el sol un par de horas.   **4.** Miguel apenas acababa de entrar (*or* había entrado) en la habitación cuando el teléfono sonó (*or* sonó el teléfono).   **5.** Sus padres estaban un poco preocupados porque no habían recibido noticias de ellos.   **6.** Hace apenas una semana que Miguel y su hermana están en Cozumel, y (ellos) ya han visto pueblos encantadores y ruinas antiguas.   **7.** La hermana de Miguel no se encontraba en su habitación. (Ella) Había ido a la peluquería. (Ella) Se había puesto bronceada y se veía estupenda.

Expansión

A, page 39: (*Answers will vary.*)   **1.** Me gusta ir a la playa para pasar las vacaciones.   **2.** Les escribo tarjetas postales a todos mis amigos.   **3.** Sí, hay muchas cerca de donde vivo yo.   **4.** Yo tenía diez años cuando aprendí a nadar.   **5.** Sí, me gusta nadar y correr las olas en el mar.   **6.** Sí, he oído que es divertido bucear.   **7.** Sí, durante el verano me pongo bronceado (bronceada).

B, page 39: (*Answers will vary.*)

Para comprender y escribir

A, page 40:   **1.** (b) pescar.   **2.** (b) antigua.   **3.** (c) Yo tampoco.   **4.** (b) traje de baño.   **5.** (a) alguna vez?

B, page 40:   **1.** No, todavía no se las he hecho.   **2.** No, todavía no se los he entregado.   **3.** No, todavía no se las he enseñado.   **4.** No, todavía no se lo he dicho.   **5.** No, todavía no se la he devuelto.

C, page 40:   **1.** Sí, están cobrados.   **2.** Sí, está pagada.   **3.** Sí, está abierto.   **4.** Sí, está envuelto.   **5.** Sí, están escritas.   **6.** Sí, están puestas.

D, page 41:   El año pasado los señores Ramos hicieron un viaje a México. Ellos fueron a Yucatán y pasaron una semana en la isla de Cozumel. Todas las mañanas ellos se levantaban temprano y bajaban a la playa; nadaban un rato, y luego se desayunaban. Después del desayuno, les gustaba sentarse en la arena y tomar el sol. Como se encontraban muy cansados, pasaban muchas horas en la playa, leyendo y descansando.

Lección 15

Preguntas sobre los diálogos, page 45:   **1.** (Luis Sánchez) Es un estudiante colombiano que acaba de ingresar en la escuela de verano. (Él) Va al apartamento de Jorge y Alberto porque ellos lo han invitado a mirar por televisión uno de los partidos de la Copa Mundial de Fútbol.   **2.** (Luis) Dijo que llegaría temprano. No, el partido no habrá comenzado (a la una y cuarto).   **3.** (El canal hispano) Mostrará (a la una y media) algunas escenas de la final entre Argentina y Alemania en la Copa de 1990.   **4.** Los Estados Unidos y Colombia jugarán (en el partido que los jóvenes van a mirar). (Ese partido) Será muy emocionante.   **5.** (El partido) Se jugará en Los Ángeles. (A Alberto) Le habría gustado estar allí porque así gozaría más del partido y podría participar de la emoción del público.   **6.** (Jorge) Le recordó (a Alberto) que en la Copa Italia 1990 los Estados Unidos no tuvieron mucha suerte. Alberto piensa que Colombia es un

equipo muy importante pero que hoy día este deporte (el fútbol) se ha puesto muy popular aquí (en los Estados Unidos).   **7.** (Luis) Practicaba el fútbol, el tenis, la natación y le gustaba hacer excursiones en bicicleta (cuando estaba en Colombia). Ahora él practica el tenis.   **8.** (A Luis) Le gustaría jugar más al tenis. Jorge lo llamará para hacer una cita con él (para jugar al tenis).

Práctica 1, page 46: (*Answers will vary.*)   **1.** Yo ganaré el partido el sábado.   **2.** Mis padres recibirán el paquete pasado mañana.   **3.** Ud. verá la película más tarde.   **4.** Nosotras venderemos la bicicleta el verano que viene.   **5.** Tú contestarás la carta el sábado.

Práctica 2, page 46:   **1.** gustaría   **2.** alegraríamos   **3.** comerían   **4.** mostraría   **5.** escribiría   **6.** deberían   **7.** subirían   **8.** daríamos   **9.** deberíamos   **10.** entenderían

Práctica 3, page 47:   **1.** tendré/treinta   **2.** podrán/un coche   **3.** Querrá/ hacer   **4.** dirá/podemos   **5.** haremos/cierran   **6.** vendrán/tomar   **7.** sabrá/cocinar   **8.** a tiempo/habrá   **9.** hace/pondremos

Práctica 4, page 47:   **1.** podríamos/la fiesta   **2.** pondría/música   **3.** harías   **4.** dirían   **5.** saldríamos   **6.** Querría/la dirección   **7.** sabría   **8.** hablar/tendría

Práctica 5, page 49:   **1.** Iremos al cine; no miraremos la televisión.   **2.** Cenaré en un restaurante; no comeré aquí.   **3.** Irás a la fiesta; no te quedarás en casa.   **4.** Tomarán cerveza; no tomarán refrescos.   **5.** Jugará al béisbol; no alzará las pesas.

Práctica 6, page 49:   **1.** Ana y yo haríamos muchos viajes.   **2.** Tú no trabajarías más.   **3.** El equipo de fútbol compraría un estadio.   **4.** Mis padres buscarían una casa más grande.   **5.** Yo ingresaría en la universidad.

Práctica 7, page 49:   **1.** habrán   **2.** mostrará   **3.** jugarían   **4.** ganará   **5.** sabremos   **6.** dirías   **7.** traería   **8.** tendríamos

Práctica 8, page 50:   **1.** ¿Qué hora será? What time can it be? (I wonder what time it is.)   **2.** Será la una y media. It's probably one thirty.   **3.** ¿Dónde estarán las chicas? Where can the girls be? (I wonder where the girls are.)   **4.** Uds. tendrán sed. You are probably (must be) thirsty.   **5.** Ellas querrán descansar. They probably want to rest.   **6.** ¿Qué hará tu compañero? I wonder what your companion is doing. (What can your companion be doing?)

Práctica 9, page 50:   **1.** ¿Qué dirían los alumnos? I wonder what the students said.   **2.** Ellos irían al cine. They probably went to the movies.   **3.** ¿A qué hora saldría Miguel? I wonder at what time Michael left.   **4.** María no sabría la verdad. Mary probably didn't know the truth.   **5.** Elena estaría jugando al tenis. Helen was probably playing tennis.   **6.** Los jóvenes mirarían el partido por televisión. The young men (people) probably watched the match on television.

Práctica 10, page 51:   **1.** Sí, María habrá ido al cine. Yes, Mary has probably (must have) gone to the movies.

2. Sí, mis padres habrán llegado. Yes, my parents have probably (must have) arrived. **3.** Sí, todos habrán salido. Yes, all have probably (must have) left. **4.** Sí, el partido habrá comenzado. Yes, the game has probably (must have) started.

Práctica 11, page 51: **1.** Sí, todos habrían recibido las noticias. Yes, all had probably received the news. **2.** Sí, Jorge habría estado enfermo. Yes, George had probably been ill. **3.** Sí, Felipe habría llamado a Isabel. Yes, Philip had probably called Isabel. **4.** Sí, habrían vuelto los estudiantes. Yes, the students had probably returned.

Práctica 12, page 52: **1.** Juegan/¿Jugaron Uds. al tenis durante las vacaciones? **2.** jugamos/Sí, y nosotros jugamos al golf también. **3.** juegas/Y tú, María, ¿jugaste al golf también? **4.** juego/Sí, yo jugué al golf todos los días. **5.** juega/Tomás no jugó al fútbol. **6.** juegan/Y sus hermanos no jugaron al fútbol tampoco.

Repaso

A, page 53: **1.** la cita **2.** la pesa **3.** la cancha **4.** el timbre

B, page 53: *(Answers will vary.)*

C, page 53: **1.** Jorge y Alberto están esperando (*or* esperan) a Luis, un estudiante colombiano que acaba de ingresar en nuestra escuela de verano. **2.** Alberto pregunta si habrá algún programa especial antes del partido de fútbol. **3.** Alberto no lo sabe. Él podrá decírselo (*or* decirle) después de mirar la guía (de la televisión). **4.** Luis dijo que llegaría temprano; el partido no habrá comenzado todavía. **5.** Jorge piensa (cree) que el estadio de Los Ángeles estará (debe estar) completamente lleno. **6.** A Luis y a Jorge les gustaría jugar (al) tenis; uno de estos días (ellos) harán una cita y jugarán un partido.

Expansión

A, page 54: *(Answers will vary.)* **1.** A mí me interesan más... **2.** Ahora practico el fútbol y la natación. **3.** En la escuela secundaria yo practicaba... **4.** Hoy después de estudiar iré/haré... **5.** Este fin de semana iré... **6.** En el futuro me gustaría...

B, page 54: *(Answers will vary.)*

Para comprender y escribir

A, page 55: **1.** (b) aficionado. **2.** (c) el equipo? **3.** (c) las pesas. **4.** (a) basquetbol. **5.** (a) ¡Cuánto me alegro!

B, page 55: **1.** Nosotros iremos al cine; no miraremos la televisión. **2.** Nosotros cenaremos en un restaurante; no comeremos aquí. **3.** Iré a la fiesta; no estudiaré. **4.** Saldré temprano; no llegaré tarde. **5.** Ellos harán ejercicio; no alzarán las pesas.

C, page 55: **1.** ¡Yo no ingresaría en la escuela de verano! **2.** ¡Yo no pondría la televisión antes de comenzar el partido! **3.** ¡Yo no diría los nombres de los jugadores! **4.** ¡Yo no iría al estadio en bicicleta! **5.** ¡Yo no le mostraría las canchas de tenis!

D, page 55: El sábado que viene, Jorge y yo iremos al partido de basquetbol. Yo compraré los boletos mañana por la mañana. Jorge y yo saldremos de casa a las doce menos cuarto. Tomaremos el almuerzo en la cafetería. Creo que varios amigos estarán allí también. Será necesario llegar al estadio antes de la una y media porque habrá mucha gente allí para el juego. Luis dijo que él vendría a nuestro apartamento a las once. Yo sabía que él haría eso. Algunos de los jugadores me dijeron anoche que sería un partido muy emocionante. Yo diría eso también.

Lección 16

Preguntas sobre los diálogos, page 60: **1.** Fueron al hospital a visitar a una buena amiga suya. **2.** Le llevaron unas flores. La llamaron a la residencia y una compañera de Ana les dijo que estaba enferma. **3.** Pescó un resfriado terrible la semana pasada. Le ha dicho que tiene una pulmonía viral. Se siente algo mejor. **4.** No puede descansar en el hospital porque la despiertan a cada rato. **5.** Necesita unas píldoras para la congestión porque tose mucho. **6.** Rita sale a buscar a la enfermera. **7.** Le ha recetado un jarabe para la tos y unas gotas para la nariz. **8.** No le divierte porque es una gran molestia. **9.** Le dice que con paciencia va a mejorarse muy pronto. **10.** Debería quedarse varios días en el hospital porque una pulmonía viral es algo muy serio.

Práctica 1, page 61: **1.** diviertes/¿Te divertiste mucho en el baile? **2.** divierto/Sí, me divertí muchísimo. **3.** divertimos/Pero nosotros no nos divertimos mucho. **4.** divierten/Y los jóvenes no se divirtieron tampoco. **5.** duermo/Yo no dormí bien en el hospital. **6.** Duermes/¿Dormiste tú bien en el campo? **7.** dormimos/Nosotros dormimos bien en el campo. **8.** duermen/Los muchachos durmieron mejor en casa. **9.** pides/¿Qué pediste tú? **10.** pido/Yo pedí un vaso de agua. **11.** piden/¿Qué pidieron Uds.? **12.** pedimos/Nosotros no pedimos nada.

Práctica 2, page 63: **1.** Abre /cierra **2.** pienses / digas / hagas **3.** Recuerda / vengas / vuelve **4.** juegues / llegues / sé **5.** Ten / cruces **6.** almuerces / busca **7.** vayas / acuéstate / te canses **8.** te quedes / haz / sal / ve / diviértete / estudies

Práctica 3, page 64: **1.** Sí, ponlas en la mesa. / No, no las pongas en la mesa. **2.** Sí, sal en seguida. / No, no salgas en seguida. **3.** Sí, dilo. / No, no lo digas. **4.** Sí, vuelve hoy. / No, no vuelvas hoy. **5.** Sí, siéntate aquí. / No, no te sientes aquí. **6.** Sí, entrégalas. / No, no las entregues. **7.** Sí, almuerza ahora. / No, no almuerces ahora. **8.** Sí, paga en efectivo. / No, no pagues en efectivo.

Práctica 4, page 65: **1.** mejores **2.** más grande **3.** mayor **4.** menor **5.** peor **6.** más pequeña

Práctica 5, page 65: **1.** Son las más cómodas de todas. **2.** Es el mejor de todos. **3.** Son las más amables de todas. **4.** Es el más difícil de todos. **5.** Son los más grandes de todos.   **6.** Es el mayor de todos.   **7.** Son las menores de todas.   **8.** Es el peor de todos.

Práctica 6, page 66:   **1.** Mario se acuesta más tarde que su hermano.   **2.** Luis se prepara más rápidamente que su hermano.   **3.** Jaime trabaja menos que su hermano.   **4.** Carlos llegó más temprano que su hermano.   **5.** Yo corro más rápido que su hermano.   **6.** Inés pronuncia más claro que su hermano.   **7.** Miguel estudia más que su hermano.   **8.** Jorge lee peor que su hermano.   **9.** Ellas cantan más bajo que su hermano.   **10.** Nosotros jugamos mejor que nuestro hermano.

Práctica 7, page 68:   **1.** tan   **2.** tantas   **3.** tanto   **4.** tanto   **5.** tantos   **6.** tan   **7.** tanta   **8.** tan

Práctica 8, page 68:   **1.** alegrísima   **2.** divertidísimos   **3.** amabilísimas   **4.** famosísimo   **5.** buenísima   **6.** dificilísimos   **7.** aburridísimo   **8.** interesantísimas   **9.** viejísimos   **10.** popularísima

Repaso

A, page 69:   **1.** tosiste/te sientes   **2.** Peor/Me duelen/el pecho   **3.** un resfriado/te recetó   **4.** un antibiótico/mi temperatura/tan alta   **5.** la tos   **6.** un jarabe/la nariz   **7.** la rodilla   **8.** No te rías/el hospital

B, page 69:   **1.** Un domingo, Rita y Jamie fueron al hospital a (*or* para) visitar a una amiga suya (*or* de ellos).   **2.** Rita le entregó a Ana unas flores que (ellos) le habían traído (*or* trajeron). Ana dijo —Gracias, Uds. son mis mejores amigos.   **3.** —Dinos (*or* Cuéntanos) Ana, ¿qué te pasa? ¿Cómo te sientes?   **4.** Ana se siente algo mejor; no tiene tanta fiebre como ayer pero todavía le duele todo el cuerpo. (Ella) No pudo dormir la mayor parte de la noche.   **5.** Ana no se divierte en el hospital, pero Rita piensa (*or* cree) que ella debe quedarse allí varios días.   **6.** Rita le dio a Ana un consejo: —Hazle caso (*or* Escucha) al médico, y de ninguna manera vuelvas a clase si no te sientes bien.

Expansión

A, page 70:   (*Answers will vary.*)   **1.** Me siento bien (mal).   **2.** Sí, (No, no) he tenido un resfriado este año.   **3.** Sí, (No, no) tengo dolores de cabeza a menudo.   **4.** Debemos llamar al médico.   **5.** Recetan jarabe.   **6.** Sí, soy alérgico(-a) a...   **7.** He estado en el hospital... veces. (Nunca he estado en el hospital.)   **8.** Nos traen flores y regalos.

B, page 70:   (*Answers will vary.*)

Para comprender y escribir

A, page 71:   **1.** (a) el tobillo?   **2.** (b) la garganta.   **3.** (c) los dedos.   **4.** (b) alérgica.   **5.** (a) tos, fiebre y dolor de cabeza.

B, page 71:   **1.** No, no sentí frío. Ella sí sintió frío.   **2.** No, no pedí otra manta. Él sí pidió otra manta.   **3.** No, no sentimos calor. Ellos sí sintieron calor.   **4.** No, no pedimos una habitación con aire acondicionado. Jaime sí pidió una habitación con aire acondicionado.   **5.** No, no nos

divertimos en el cine. Ella sí se divirtió en el cine.   **6.** No, no nos reímos mucho con la película. Él sí se rió mucho con la película.

C, page 71:   **1.** Sácalas más tarde; no las saques ahora.   **2.** Págala después; no la pagues ahora.   **3.** Tócalo más tarde; no lo toques ahora.   **4.** Crúzala después de ese coche; no la cruces ahora.   **5.** Juega al tenis más tarde; no juegues ahora.   **6.** Almuerza en un restaurante; no almuerces en la cafetería.

D, page 72:   Un domingo, después de asistir a misa, Rita y Jaime fueron al hospital a visitar a una amiga suya. Ana se puso muy contenta cuando vio a sus amigos. Rita le dio a Ana unas flores que le habían traído. Ana les dijo a Rita y a Jaime que le dolía todo el cuerpo: la espalda, la garganta y el pecho. También tenía mucha fiebre y mucha tos. El médico le había recetado un jarabe y unas gotas para le nariz. A Ana no le divierte estar en el hospital y espera mejorarse pronto.

Lección 17

Preguntas sobre el diálogo, page 75:   **1.** (Silvia y Alberto) Necesitan encontrar un apartamento porque han decidido casarse (este verano).   **2.** (Ellos) Quieren que (el apartamento) sea pequeño y barato (y prefieren que esté amueblado).   **3.** (Ellos) Necesitan una tostadora, cafetera, mezcladora, batidora y plancha.   **4.** (Alberto) Le sugiere (a Silvia) que le pida a su madre que ponga esos aparatos en la lista de regalos (que ellos tienen en los almacenes).   **5.** (Las tías y las primas de Silvia) Quieren que (Silvia y Alberto *or* ellos) les den algunas ideas para el regalo de boda.   **6.** (A Alberto) Le parece ideal (él apartamento de la Calle 24) porque es cómodo y el alquiler es una ganga.   **7.** (La cocina del apartamento) Es muy moderna. Tiene refrigerador, lavadora de platos y un horno microondas.   **8.** (El gerente del edificio) Le ha aconsejado que vayan lo más pronto posible, porque pueden alquilar el apartamento en cualquier momento.   **9.** (Alberto) Quiere dar un paseo por el barrio con Silvia porque él quiere que ella conozca el barrio (*or* lo conozca). El barrio es muy agradable; es tranquilo (y tienen todo cerca).   **10.** (Silvia) Desea que Alberto esté contento (y que los dos sean felices).

Práctica 1, page 77:   **1.** alquilen   **2.** coma   **3.** beban   **4.** viva   **5.** venda   **6.** aceptemos   **7.** corran   **8.** asistamos a   **9.** hables   **10.** estudie   **11.** abras   **12.** escriban

Práctica 2, page 78:   **1.** devuelva   **2.** cuentes   **3.** duerman   **4.** llueva   **5.** encuentre   **6.** se sienta   **7.** se siente   **8.** recomienden   **9.** nos divirtamos   **10.** prefieran   **11.** pidamos   **12.** cuesten

Práctica 3, page 79:   **1.** Queremos que él nos diga la verdad.   **2.** Ellos quieren que nosotros hagamos el viaje con ellos.   **3.** Él recomienda que ellos pongan el refrigerador aquí.   **4.** Queremos que Ud. salga para Madrid en seguida.   **5.** Yo recomiendo que tú tengas mucho cuidado.   **6.** Pídanle Uds. que él traiga su grabadora.   **7.** Ellos piden que nosotros vengamos a las tres.   **8.** Díganles Uds. que ellos sean puntuales.   **9.** Yo quiero que Uds. conozcan al

profesor. **10.** Ellos sugieren que yo le dé un regalo.
11. Quieren que yo esté en el hospital a las ocho. **12.** Yo quiero que Uds. vayan conmigo a la agencia. **13.** Ella quiere que tú sepas la noticia.

Práctica 4, page 81: **1.** pueda **2.** acepte **3.** se queda **4.** sale **5.** estén **6.** vuelva **7.** vayas **8.** haga **9.** sean **10.** se acueste **11.** se levantan **12.** tiene

Práctica 5, page 82: *(Sentence endings will vary.)*
1. Quiero que Uds. asistan a la clase. **2.** Sugiero que Ud. piense en los problemas. **3.** Deseamos que tú pongas el dinero en el banco. **4.** Recomiendo que Uds. oigan lo que dice el profesor. **5.** Desean que nosotros volvamos a casa. **6.** Permitimos que ella vea la película de terror.
7. Recomiendan que Uds. pidan algo de postre.
8. Aconsejo que tú aprendas a hablar español. **9.** Dígales Ud. a todos que esperen a sus amigos. **10.** Pídale a Margarita que se arregle rápidamente.

Práctica 6, page 82: *(Sentence endings will vary.)*
1. No, no salga Ud. ahora; salga más tarde. **2.** No, no vaya Ud. hoy; vaya mañana. **3.** No, no se acueste Ud. a las diez; acuéstese a las once. **4.** No, no se arregle Ud. ahora; arréglese más tarde. **5.** No, no se lo dé Ud. esta mañana; déselo esta tarde. **6.** No, no se lo pida Ud. mañana; pídaselo hoy.

Práctica 7, page 83: **1.** Luis, te pido que te pongas los zapatos. **2.** Lupe, te pido que vengas a la oficina.
3. Jaime, te pido que hagas el viaje. **4.** Rita, te pido que envuelvas las compras. **5.** Laura, te pido que traigas los platos. **6.** Ana, te pido que te lleves el libro.

Práctica 8, page 83: **1.** estaré; venga **2.** se casarán; vengan **3.** traiga; comprará

Repaso

A, page 83: **1.** el gerente **2.** el barrio **3.** la dueña **4.** el dormitorio **5.** el almacén **6.** el alquiler **7.** el paseo **8.** la boda

B, page 84: **1.** Silvia y Alberto han decidido casarse este verano. **2.** (Ellos) Están buscando (*or* Buscan) un apartamento; (ellos) quieren que sea pequeño y barato.
3. Silvia le enseña a su novio la lista de aparatos eléctricos que (ellos) necesitan para su casa: una mezcladora, una cafetera, una tostadora y una batidora. **4.** Alberto le dice a Silvia que hay un apartamento cómodo en la Calle 24. Él quiere que Silvia lo vea porque sólo cuesta setecientos dólares al mes. **5.** El gerente del edificio les ha sugerido que vayan y lo vean (*or* vayan a verlo) lo más pronto posible.
6. Alberto quiere que Silvia conozca el barrio, que es muy agradable y tranquilo.

Expansión

A, page 84: *(Answers will vary.)* **1.** Generalmente se buscan un apartamento o una casa. **2.** No, no hay muchos apartamentos amueblados en esta ciudad. **3.** Cuesta... dólares. **4.** Tengo un sofá, una mesa y cuatro sillas.
5. Se necesitan un lavaplatos, una tostadora y una batidora. **6.** Sería grande, bonito(a) y barato(a).

B, page 85: *(Answers will vary.)*

Para comprender y escribir

A, page 85: **1.** (c) una batidora. **2.** (b) el alquiler?
3. (a) un paseo? **4.** (b) ¡Eres un encanto! **5.** (c) un sillón.

B, page 85: **1.** No, no quiero que salgas todavía.
2. No, no quiero que vayas todavía. **3.** No, no quiero que llames todavía. **4.** No, no quiero que Uds. entren todavía.
5. No, no quiero que Uds. jueguen al tenis todavía. **6.** No, no quiero que Uds. vengan todavía.

C, page 86: **1.** No, no quiero conocerlo; quiero que tú lo conozcas. **2.** No, no queremos saberlo; queremos que Uds. lo sepan. **3.** No, no deseo invitarlas; deseo que tú las invites. **4.** No, no deseamos traerlos; deseamos que Uds. los traigan. **5.** No, no prefiero hacerlo; prefiero que tú lo hagas. **6.** No, no preferimos tenerla; preferimos que Uds. la tengan.

D, page 86: Silvia y Alberto han decidido casarse este verano. Están buscando un apartamento; quieren que esté amueblado y que sea pequeño y barato. Silvia le muestra a su novio la lista de aparatos que necesitan para su casa. Algunos de los artículos son una batidora, una cafetera y una tostadora. También necesitan sábanas y mantas para la cama. Alberto le sugiere a Silvia que ponga los artículos en la lista de regalos que tienen en los almacenes.

Lección 18

Preguntas sobre el diálogo, page 89: **1.** (El profesor de economía) Les ha pedido (a sus estudiantes) que asistan a la conferencia que un economista famoso dará (en la universidad de una ciudad cercana). (Él) Quiere que hagan un resumen de la conferencia (y que le entreguen sus comentarios escritos). **2.** (Juan) Teme que haya habido un accidente porque le parece raro que haya tanto tráfico a esta (*or* esa) hora. **3.** (Roberto) Piensa que el (*or* ese) carro no paró a tiempo (y que quizás hayan fallado los frenos).
4. (Juan) No cree que tengan que esperar mucho porque allí viene la policía. (Él) Les pide a sus compañeros que tengan paciencia. **5.** (Isabel) Le sugiere (a Juan) que deje pasar el carro patrulla por la izquierda. **6.** (A Juan) Le extraña que no haya heridos ni ambulancias. (Él) No cree que haya sido un accidente muy grave. **7.** (Cuando Roberto ve al taxista entremetido,) Él le dice a Juan: —No le permitas que siga adelante. ¡Anda, pásalo! **8.** (Juan) Les pide (a sus compañeros) que se calmen. **9.** (Inés) Les dice que ella está segura de que no hay mejor conductor que Juan. (Isabel) Le pide a Juan que siga manejando (y que salgan rápido de allí) (*or* que no le haga caso a Roberto). **10.** (Roberto) Espera que (quizás tengan suerte y que) la conferencia no empiece a las cuatro en punto.

Práctica 1, page 91: **1.** llegue **2.** se acerque **3.** almuerce **4.** entregue **5.** siga **6.** juegue

Práctica 2, page 91: **1.** Sí, comiéncela Ud. No, no la comience Ud. **2.** Sí, sáquelas Ud. No, no las saque Ud.
3. Sí, páguela Ud. No, no la pague Ud. **4.** Sí, organícela

Uds. No, no la organicen Uds.   **5.** Sí, búsquenlas Uds. No, no las busquen Uds.   **6.** Sí, entréguenlos Uds. No, no los entreguen Uds.

Práctica 3, page 92:   **1.** consiga   **2.** quiera   **3.** saben   **4.** se casen   **5.** piensan   **6.** puedan   **7.** prefieran   **8.** pague   **9.** tiene   **10.** contesta   **11.** haya   **12.** seas

Práctica 4, page 93:   **1.** que Silvia se case   **2.** que Ana esté   **3.** que tu novio (novia) llegue   **4.** que Juan no te escriba   **5.** que Marta no te llame

Práctica 5, page 94:   **1.** lea   **2.** sepa   **3.** va   **4.** es   **5.** traigan   **6.** toca   **7.** debe   **8.** tenga   **9.** permitan   **10.** conozcan   **11.** tienen   **12.** está

Práctica 6, page 95:   **1.** Te aconsejo moderar la marcha.   **2.** Dejen Uds. conducir yo.   **3.** El médico me recomienda que tome estas píldoras.   **4.** El gerente no permite a nosotros ver el apartamento.   **5.** Les sugiero a Uds. que vuelvan más tarde.   **6.** No le permitas al taxista que pase por la izquierda.

Práctica 7, page 96:   **1.** Yo no puedo, que lo envuelva él.   **2.** Yo no puedo, que lo entregue él.   **3.** Yo no puedo, que los busque él.   **4.** Yo no puedo, que las cuente él.   **5.** Yo no puedo, que lo empiece él.   **6.** Yo no puedo, que lo lea él.

Práctica 8, page 97:   **1.** Sí, devolvámoslo./Sí, vamos a devolverlo./No, no lo devolvamos.   **2.** Sí, hagámoslo./Sí, vamos a hacerlo./No, no lo hagamos.   **3.** Sí, paguémosla /Sí, vamos a pagarla./No, no la paguemos.   **4.** Sí, mostrémoslas./Sí, vamos a mostrarlas./No, no las mostremos.   **5.** Sí, abrámoslas./Sí, vamos a abrirlas./No, no las abramos.   **6.** Sí, pongámosla./Sí, vamos a ponerla./No, no la pongamos.

Práctica 9, page 98:   **1.** haya sacado   **2.** haya visto   **3.** haya podido   **4.** hayan traído   **5.** hayamos sabido   **6.** haya vuelto

Repaso

A, page 98:   *(Answers will vary.)*

B, page 98:   **1.** El profesor de economía les ha pedido a sus estudiantes que vayan a una universidad cercana para asistir a una conferencia.   **2.** Cuatro compañeros van en el carro de Juan al lugar donde se dará la conferencia.   **3.** A Juan le parece raro que haya tanto tráfico; él teme que haya habido un choque.   **4.** Inés piensa que ellos tienen mala suerte y ella no está segura de que (ellos) puedan llegar a tiempo.   **5.** Juan les pide a sus amigos que tengan paciencia. Él no cree que ellos tengan que esperar mucho (tiempo).

Expansión

A, page 99:   *(Answers will vary.)*   **1.** Yo tenía 16 años cuando conseguí mi licencia de manejar.   **2.** Sí, me gusta mucho manejar un carro.   **3.** Sí, yo modero la marcha cuando veo un carro patrulla.   **4.** No, yo no he tenido un accidente grave manejando un carro.   **5.** Hay que avisar a la

policía cuando uno tiene un accidente.   **6.** Hay mucho tráfico en el centro a las seis de la tarde.

B, page 99:   *(Answers will vary.)*

Para comprender y escribir

A, page 100:   **1.** (c) Avisar a la policía.   **2.** (b) un conductor.   **3.** (a) ¡Cuánto me alegro!   **4.** (a) Le fallarían los frenos.   **5.** (c) una avería.

B, page 100:   **1.** Nos alegramos de que el profesor Ramos nos dé un conferencia.   **2.** Me gusta que Inés venga a la conferencia con nosotros.   **3.** Estamos contentos de que Juan llegue temprano.   **4.** No me extraña que Roberto almuerce en la cafetería.   **5.** Sentimos que ellos no hablen en español.   **6.** Temo que los señores Soto no se diviertan.   **7.** Nos molesta que Alberto nunca diga la verdad.   **8.** Espero que tú tengas unas vacaciones magníficas.

C, page 100:   **1.** ¡Cuánto me alegro de que Silvia se case con Alberto!   **2.** Sentimos mucho que Ana esté en el hospital.   **3.** ¡Cuánto me alegro de que tu novia llegue mañana!   **4.** Nos extraña que Juan ya no te escriba.   **5.** Me molesta que Marta no te haya llamado.   **6.** ¡Cuánto nos alegramos de que Uds. hayan conseguido el apartamento!   **7.** Siento mucho que tus amigos hayan tenido un choque.   **8.** Nos extraña que tu familia no te haya dicho nada.

D, page 101:   Silvia y Alberto quizás se casen el verano próximo, pero yo lo dudo. Ella necesita volver a su país y los padres de Alberto esperan que él siga sus estudios de medicina. Me extraña mucho que ellos tengan tantos problemas, porque creo que ellos son muy felices. A Alberto no le gusta que Silvia vuelva a su país. También le molesta que sus padres no lo comprendan. Yo espero ver a Silvia mañana y le diré que se quede. No creo que ella me haga mucho caso, pero dudo que Alberto la deje ir. ¡Yo creo que sólo ellos deben decidir sus vidas!

Lección 19

Preguntas sobre el diálogo, page 105:   **1.** (El señor Antonio Ruiz) Es el gerente de una (importante) empresa norteamericana (la cual tiene una sucursal en Puerto Rico). (La señorita White) Es la secretaria del director de la Escuela de Ingeniería Agrícola.   **2.** (El señor Ruiz) Le escribe una carta (al director de la Escuela de Ingeniería Agrícola) para preguntarle si conoce a algún joven que pueda trabajar como agente de su compañía en la Isla (*or* Puerto Rico).   **3.** Es urgente que (Miguel) consiga un trabajo porque este trimestre se gradúa (de ingeniero).   **4.** (El señor Ruiz) Busca una persona que entienda de asuntos de maquinaria agrícola y que quiera residir en San Juan.   **5.** Es necesario (que el candidato sea bilingüe) porque el puesto es en Puerto Rico. Esto no sería un problema para Miguel porque él habla muy bien el inglés y el español.   **6.** (Miguel) Le pregunta (a la señorita White) si sería posible que el director de la Escuela le escribiera una carta de recomendación.   **7.** (El director) Le dirá (en su carta al señor Ruiz) que no hay nadie mejor preparado que Miguel.   **8.** La señorita White le pide a Miguel que le traduzca unos versos (que le mandó un amigo suyo).

Práctica 1, page 105:   **1.** produzca   **2.** traduje   **3.** conduce   **4.** produjo   **5.** conduzco   **6.** producen   **7.** conduzca   **8.** traduzcan   **9.** traduzcamos   **10.** tradujeron

Práctica 2, page 107:   **1.** obtenga   **2.** juega   **3.** aprender   **4.** encuentre   **5.** sepas   **6.** pueda   **7.** traducir   **8.** compres   **9.** piensa   **10.** llegue   **11.** maneje   **12.** haga

Práctica 3, page 109:   **1.** quienes   **2.** que   **3.** quien (el cual)   **4.** lo que   **5.** que   **6.** que   **7.** que   **8.** quienes (los cuales)

Práctica 4, page 110:   **1.** hable   **2.** sea   **3.** piensan   **4.** quiera   **5.** pague   **6.** gusta   **7.** trabaja   **8.** pueda   **9.** sabe   **10.** recuerde   **11.** conozca   **12.** haya

Práctica 5, page 111:   **1.** Miguel asiste a la Escuela de Ingeniería Agrícola hace cuatro años./Hace cuatro años que Miguel asiste a la Escuela de Ingeniería Agrícola.   **2.** Pienso estudiar medicina desde hace dos semestres./Hace dos semestres que pienso estudiar medicina.   **3.** Mis tíos viven en México desde hace seis meses./Hace seis meses que mis tíos viven en México.   **4.** Estudio español desde hace siete meses./Hace siete meses que estudio español.   **5.** Conduzco el mismo carro desde hace cinco años./Hace cinco años que conduzco el mismo carro.

Práctica 6, page 111:   **1.** Roberto se sentía mal desde hacía dos días./Hacía dos días que Roberto se sentía mal.   **2.** Jaime trabajaba en esa tienda desde hacía dos semanas./Hacía dos semanas que Jaime trabajaba en esa tienda.   **3.** Ana no asistía a clase desde hacía ocho días./Hacía ocho días que Ana no asistía a clase.   **4.** Nosotros recibíamos esa revista desde hacía un año./Hacía un año que recibíamos esa revista.   **5.** Yo jugaba al fútbol desde hacía unos cinco años./Hacía unos cinco años que yo jugaba al fútbol.

Práctica 7, page 112:   **1.** se puso   **2.** llegó a ser   **3.** se puso   **4.** se puso   **5.** se hizo (llegó a ser)

Práctica 8, page 113:   **1.** Miguel vio a Inés salir de la residencia.   **2.** Mirábamos a los jóvenes jugar al fútbol.   **3.** Yo oí sonar el teléfono.   **4.** Escuchábamos al profesor pronunciar las palabras nuevas.   **5.** Vimos a Miguel entrar en la agencia de empleo.   **6.** ¿Oíste a Isabel tocar anoche?

Repaso

A, page 113:   **1.** la isla   **2.** el trimestre   **3.** la maquinaria   **4.** la sucursal

B, page 113:   *(Answers will vary.)*

C, page 113:   **1.** El director de la Escuela de Ingeniería Agrícola acaba de recibir una carta del gerente de una empresa que (*or* la cual) tiene una sucursal en Puerto Rico.   **2.** El señor Ruiz quiere saber si el director conoce a alguien que pueda trabajar como agente de su compañía en la isla.

3. Cuando la señorita White, quien (*or* la cual) es la secretaria del director, ve pasar a Miguel Ramos, (ella) lo llama y le informa sobre la vacante (*or* el puesto vacante).   **4.** Miguel le dice a la señorita White que como se gradúa de ingeniero, es urgente que él consiga trabajo pronto.   **5.** El señor Ruiz necesita una persona competente que quiera residir en San Juan. También es necesario (*or* Es necesario también) que el candidato sea bilingüe, lo cual no sería problema para Miguel.

Expansión

A, page 114:   *(Answers will vary.)*   **1.** Me interesa la medicina.   **2.** Yo recommendaría la ingeniería.   **3.** Es necesario hacer la solicitud.   **4.** Es difícil encontrar trabajo hoy día.   **5.** Si yo necesito un puesto, le pediré a mi profesor de español que me recomiende.

B, page 114:   *(Answers will vary.)*

Para comprender y escribir

A, page 115:   **1.** (b) un ascenso.   **2.** (a) una beca.   **3.** (c) se pone nervioso.   **4.** (b) un ingeniero.

B, page 115:   **1.** Es difícil que Uds. vean al señor Ruiz.   **2.** Es importante que nosotros nos graduemos de la universidad.   **3.** Es más fácil que yo aprenda el español en Puerto Rico.   **4.** Es mejor que Uds. hagan la solicitud ya.   **5.** Es imposible que la señorita White traduzca esos versos.   **6.** Es necesario que el candidato sea bilingüe.   **7.** Es preciso que tú escribas la carta ya.   **8.** Es posible que yo consiga un buen trabajo.

C, page 115:   **1.** Aquella chica a quien él conoce es una estudiante de esta universidad.   **2.** El señor a quien llamé es el gerente de la empresa.   **3.** Aquellas jóvenes a quienes saludamos son secretarias de esta compañía.   **4.** Aquel señor a quien conocí es un ingeniero que trabaja en Puerto Rico.

D, page 115:   El director de la Escuela de Ingeniería Agrícola acaba de recibir una carta del señor Ruiz, gerente de una compañía que tiene una sucursal en Puerto Rico. El señor Ruiz le pregunta si el director conoce a alguien que pueda trabajar como agente en la isla. Cuando su secretaria, la señorita White, ve pasar a Miguel Ramos, lo llama y comienza a hablarle sobre la carta. El director cree que es posible que le interese el puesto. Miguel, que se graduará de ingeniero en junio, le contesta que será necesario que él encuentre trabajo pronto.

Lección 20

Preguntas sobre los diálogos, page 119:   **1.** (Alberto y Silvia) Decidieron pasar su luna de miel en Suramérica.   **2.** (Ellos) Siempre habían deseado conocer Machu Picchu (la gran ciudad de piedra cerca de Cuzco).   **3.** (Ellos) Escogieron la agencia de viajes del padre de un amigo (la que está cerca del parque).   **4.** No, no hay vuelos directos a Cuzco. Se llega a Lima y desde allí se continúa el viaje (en una línea interna) hasta Cuzco.   **5.** (A ellos) Les gustaría salir el quince de agosto.   **6.** (Ellos) No pueden salir en el vuelo de la mañana porque no quedan asientos (a menos que alguien cancele).   **7.** (Ellos) Tienen que regresar el día treinta. (Tienen que regresar antes de que comiencen las clases en la universidad. *or* Tienen que regresar para esa fecha porque comienzan…)   **8.** (Ellos) Podrán pagar con tarjeta de crédito o cheque personal.

Práctica 1, page 121:   **1.** envío   **2.** continúen   **3.** me dirijo   **4.** escojan   **5.** continúas   **6.** envían   **7.** escogen   **8.** continúan   **9.** se dirijan   **10.** continuemos   **11.** envíe   **12.** escogemos

Práctica 2, page 123:   **1.** Entraremos en la sala cuando empiece la conferencia.   **2.** Cerraremos los libros en cuanto el profesor llegue.   **3.** Haremos la excursión aunque continúe lloviendo.   **4.** Iremos a la boda a menos que Ana se enferme.   **5.** Lo visitaré después de que él vuelva de clase.   **6.** Veremos a Laura antes de que se gradúe en junio.   **7.** Dígaselo para que ella no escoja otra universidad.   **8.** Le mandaré flores antes de que ella regrese del hospital.

Práctica 3, page 124:   **1.** se acerque   **2.** asisto   **3.** facture   **4.** oigamos   **5.** dice   **6.** cancele   **7.** traiga   **8.** podamos   **9.** ve   **10.** maneja

Práctica 4, page 125:   **1.** Sí, compré el suyo.   **2.** Sí, vengo al suyo.   **3.** Sí, traemos los nuestros.   **4.** Sí, hallamos las suyas (tuyas).   **5.** Sí, facturé la suya (tuya).   **6.** Sí, envolví los suyos (tuyos).   **7.** Sí, vimos la suya (tuya).   **8.** Sí, el suyo es de oro (es de oro el suyo).

Práctica 5, page 125:   **1.** Este carro y el del profesor no son caros.   **2.** Me llevo este anillo y el que Isabel escogió.   **3.** Vamos a enviarle este mapa y el de Inés.   **4.** Me gustan esta clase y la de francés.   **5.** Estas maletas y las de Carolina son muy caras.   **6.** Me interesan esas comedias y las que recomendó Ud.

Práctica 6, page 126:   **1.** sino   **2.** pero   **3.** pero   **4.** sino   **5.** pero   **6.** sino

Repaso

A, page 127:   **1.** de viajes   **2.** la luna de miel   **3.** la computadora   **4.** personal   **5.** el boleto   **6.** la maleta   **7.** de la salida   **8.** el pasaporte   **9.** interna   **10.** directo

B, page 127:   **1.** Alberto y Silvia han decidido pasar su luna de miel en el Perú.   **2.** Aprenden que hay varios vuelos diarios; pero no son directos a Cuzco, sino a Lima.   **3.** (Ellos) Esperan partir (*or* salir) el quince de agosto, con tal (de) que haya un vuelo de la mañana (*or* de día).   **4.** El agente de viajes consulta la computadora y encuentra que no quedan asientos en ese vuelo; Silvia le pide (*or* ruega) que los ponga en la lista de espera.   **5.** (Ellos) Compraron boletos de ida y vuelta, porque tienen que regresar (*or* volver) el treinta de agosto.

Expansión

A, page 127:   (*Answers will vary.*)   **1.** Puedo comprarlos en una agencia de viajes.   **2.** Las pago con tarjeta de crédito.   **3.** Prefiero facturar mis maletas.   **4.** Pienso ir

a… porque mi familia vive allí.   **5.** Para poder entrar en muchos países, uno necesita llevar el pasaporte.   **6.** Sí, me gustaría poder estudiar en…, porque es un país muy interesante.

B, page 128:   (*Answers will vary.*)

Para comprender y escribir

A, page 128:   **1.** (b) azafata.   **2.** (c) el pasaporte.   **3.** (a) un boleto de ida y vuelta.   **4.** (a) despedirse.   **5.** (c) no quedan asientos.

B, page 128:   **1.** Yo te digo las fechas para que tú hagas las reservas.   **2.** Queremos regresar en agosto antes de que comiencen las clases.   **3.** Luis comprará los boletos cuando nosotros le demos el dinero.   **4.** Pasaremos una semana en Cuzco con tal de que tengamos suficiente tiempo.   **5.** Haremos el viaje en julio aunque haga bastante frío.   **6.** Visitaremos otras ciudades en Suramérica a menos que el boleto de avión cueste mucho.

C, page 129:   **1.** Silvia tiene los suyos.   **2.** Juan lleva la suya.   **3.** Dame el tuyo, por favor.   **4.** El suyo es de oro.   **5.** El mío no es pequeño.   **6.** Ponte la suya.   **7.** La nuestra es argentina.   **8.** Los nuestros llegan mañana.

D, page 129:   Alberto y Silvia han decidido pasar su luna de miel en el Perú. Lo que quieren ver es Machu Picchu, la gran ciudad de piedra cerca de Cuzco. Buscan una agencia de viajes y escogen la del señor Ponce, el padre de un amigo suyo. Hay varios vuelos diarios, pero no van directos a Cuzco, sino a Lima. Les gustaría salir el quince de agosto, con tal de que haya un vuelo de la mañana. Tienen que regresar el treinta de agosto, antes de que comiencen las clases.

Lección 21

Preguntas sobre el diálogo, page 132:   **1.** (Alberto y Silvia *or* Ellos) Se encuentran con José Soto (un ingeniero cubano muy simpático).   **2.** (Silvia y Alberto *or* Ellos) Pensaban llamarlo (*or* llamar a José) porque querían pedirle algunos consejos.   **3.** (Si volviera por Chile durante el invierno, José [*or* él]) Llevaría ropa de lana, un abrigo ligero y unos guantes.   **4.** (Silvia *or* Ella) Piensa llevar un suéter. Necesitarán impermeables y un paraguas.   **5.** (El padre de Silvia *or* Él) Les aconsejó que compraran una (cámara) vídeo porque (a él) le gustaría que tomaran algunas películas de los Andes.   **6.** Es lástima (que no hubieran llamado a José antes) porque (él) los habría ayudado a escoger la (cámara) vídeo.   **7.** (Los tres *or* Ellos) Van a encontrarse enfrente de la casa de correos (mañana por la mañana). (Ellos) Piensan ir a varias tiendas para comparar las diferentes marcas y precios de las cámaras vídeo.

Práctica 1, page 134:   **1.** escribiera   **2.** compraran   **3.** llevaran   **4.** compraran   **5.** recibieran   **6.** llamaran   **7.** prometiera   **8.** llamáramos/llamásemos   **9.** viviéramos   **10.** comprendieran/comprendiesen

Práctica 2, page 135:   **1.** Ella no creía que estos boletos costaran más que aquéllos.   **2.** Yo temía que la policía me pidiera el carnet.   **3.** Yo le dije que devolviera la cámara cinematográfica. **4.** Nos alegramos de que Uds. se divirtieran en la fiesta. **5.** Querían que nos encontráramos enfrente de la casa de correos. **6.** Alberto me pidió que le recomendara un buen hotel. **7.** Fue mejor que ellos durmieran anoche en la residencia. **8.** Fue lástima que lloviera anoche durante la fiesta.

Práctica 3, page 135: **1.** trajéramos **2.** leyera **3.** pusiéramos **4.** fuera **5.** fuera **6.** supiese **7.** quisiese **8.** creyesen **9.** estuviesen **9.** oyésemos

Práctica 4, page 136: **1.** Yo no creía que Alberto hubiera comprado la cámara. **2.** Es extraño que ellas no hubieran visto esa película. **3.** No parecía posible que Ana se lo hubiera dicho al profesor. **4.** Me molestó que él todavía no lo hubiera traducido. **5.** Todos dudaban que nosotros le hubiéramos dado el dinero. **6.** Sentíamos que Uds. no nos hubieran escrito algunas líneas.

Práctica 5, page 138: **1.** No había nadie que comprendiera eso. **2.** Alberto buscaba una cámara que le gustara. **3.** No fue cierto que Jaime conociera la ciudad. **4.** Querían que nos encontráramos enfrente de la casa de correos. **5.** Sería posible que ella escogiera otra marca. **6.** Les traje las fotos para que Uds. las vieran. **7.** Yo le aconsejé a Luis que les mostrara la carta. **8.** José recomendó que nosotros fuéramos a otra tienda.

Práctica 6, page 139: **1.** tuviera **2.** hagamos **3.** estuviera **4.** partiera **5.** quisiera **6.** busque **7.** escogieran **8.** volvieran

Práctica 7, page 140: **1.** pudiera **2.** hubiera **3.** hacen **4.** hubieras **5.** llevas **6.** permitieran **7.** me encuentro **8.** fuera

Práctica 8, page 140: **1.** Si el profesor lo recomendara, yo compraría el libro. **2.** Si tuviéramos estampillas, le enviaríamos una tarjeta. **3.** Si quedaran asientos en ese vuelo, te acompañaríamos. **4.** Si estuviera amueblado, ellos alquilarían el apartamento. **5.** Si estuviera lloviendo, Luis llevaría un paraguas. **6.** Si él me consultara, yo le daría algunos consejos.

Práctica 9, page 141: **1.** vale/valdrá/valdría/valga **2.** vale/valdrá/valdría **3.** valen/valdrán/valdrían **4.** valgan **5.** Valdría **6.** valga

Repaso

A, page 142: **1.** la pena **2.** la lana **3.** de película **4.** mañana **5.** el impermeable **6.** fotográfica **7.** áerea **8.** falta

B, page 142: **1.** Al salir de la casa de correos, Alberto y Silvia se encuentran con José Soto. **2.** Éste es un ingeniero cubano muy simpático que ha viajado por Suramérica tres o cuatro veces. **3.** Quieren pedirle algunos consejos porque parten (*or* salen) para Chile la semana que viene. **4.** Si José lo hubiera sabido antes, los habría invitado a su casa para ver las transparencias de su último viaje. **5.** El padre de Silvia les aconsejó que, además de la cámara fotográfica, (ellos) deberían llevar una cámara vídeo. **6.** Si ellos tuvieran una cámara vídeo, traerían recuerdos inolvidables.

Expansión

A, page 142: (*Answers will vary.*) **1.** Yo visitaría los estados de California y Colorado porque nunca los he visitado. **2.** Yo tendría que comprar unos pantalones y varias camisas. **3.** Si yo necesitara dinero durante mi viaje, se lo pediría a mis padres. **4.** Les escribiría a mi novio(-a) y a mis mejores amigos durante el viaje. **5.** Sí, (yo) saco muchas fotografías cuando viajo. **6.** Sí, habría tenido problemas con la lengua.

B, page 143: (*Answers will vary.*)

Para comprender y escribir

A, page 143: **1.** (a) unos guantes. **2.** (b) Todavía no. **3.** (c) el equipaje? **4.** (b) una línea aérea. **5.** (b) vale la pena.

B, page 144: **1.** Yo buscaba una cámara que me gustara. **2.** Mi hermano sentía mucho que no tuviera nada que hacer. **3.** No había nadie que pudiera ir a la estación conmigo. **4.** Era mejor que Uds. me llamaran a menudo. **5.** Nos alegrábamos de que ellos hicieran un viaje por el Perú. **6.** Yo no conocía a ningún estudiante que viviera en Quito. **7.** Lo llamé por teléfono para que viniera temprano. **8.** Tuvieron que bajar el precio antes de que yo lo comprara.

C, page 144: **1.** Sí, si me pagaran bien, yo viviría en Puerto Rico. **2.** Sí, si yo pudiera hacer un viaje, me gustaría ir a Lima. **3.** Sí, si yo estuviera en Cozumel ahora, miraría el paisaje. **4.** Sí, si fuera verano ahora, yo practicaría el tenis y la natación. **5.** Sí, si yo no tuviera que estudiar esta noche, iría al teatro. **6.** Sí, si yo tuviera libre el próximo fin de semana, iría de compras.

D, page 144: Al salir de la casa de correos, Alberto y Silvia se encuentran con José Soto. José es un ingeniero cubano muy simpático que ha viajado mucho por Suramérica. Quieren pedirle algunos consejos porque salen para Chile la próxima semana. Si José lo hubiera sabido antes, los habría invitado a su casa para ver las transparencias de su último viaje. José sabe que si tuvieran una cámara, sacarían muchas fotos muy bonitas.

Lección 22

Preguntas sobre los diálogos, page 148: **1.** (Antes de marcharse de la universidad, Jorge y sus compañeros) Se reúnen para almorzar. **2.** (El restaurante) Les ha sido recomendado por Miguel Ramos. **3.** (Miguel) No pudo asistir a la reunión porque estaba muy ocupado preparando su partida a Puerto Rico. **4.** (Isabel) Piensa pasar el verano en la costa. **5.** (La casa) Fue construida por sus abuelos (hace casi cien años). **6.** (El padre de Jorge) Le sugirió que volviera a Madrid. **7.** Él quisiera que Jorge llegara a ser el gerente de su compañía. **8.** La frase «No digamos adiós, sino hasta luego» está escrita en el pastel (que Miguel ha enviado).

Práctica 1, page 149: **1.** No, no volváis ahora. Volved más tarde. **2.** No, no salgáis ahora. Salid más tarde. **3.** No, no almorcéis ahora. Almorzad más tarde. **4.** No, no os levantéis ahora. Levantaos más tarde. **5.** No, no os lavéis ahora. Lavaos más tarde. **6.** No, no se lo déis ahora. Dádselo más tarde.

Práctica 2, page 150: **1.** Sí, el pasaporte fue recibido por Alberto. **2.** Sí, las becas fueron solicitadas por muchos estudiantes. **3.** Sí, esas fotos fueron sacadas por los estudiantes. **4.** Sí, las maletas serán facturadas por José mañana. **5.** Sí, la fecha del examen será anunciada por el profesor.

Práctica 3, page 150: **1.** fue; está **2.** está; fue **3.** están (*or* fueron) **4.** está; fue **5.** fueron; están

Práctica 4, page 151: **1.** nos vemos **2.** se entienden **3.** nos escribimos **4.** nos conocemos **5.** se visitan **6.** se quieran

Práctica 5, page 152: **1.** quisiera **2.** quisiéramos **3.** Debiera **4.** debieran **5.** pudieras **6.** Pudiera

Práctica 6, page 152: **1.** ¡Ojalá (que) Beatriz estudie arte en España! **2.** ¡Ojalá (que) los estudiantes lleguen a tiempo al concierto! **3.** ¡Ojalá (que) pasáramos el verano en la costa! **4.** ¡Ojalá (que) se graduaran Uds. en junio! **5.** ¡Ojalá (que) yo hubiera podido visitar la fábrica con Uds.! **6.** ¡Ojalá (que) el profesor hubiera podido darle una buena recomendación!

Práctica 7, page 153: **1.** Se reúnen **2.** nos reunimos **3.** te reúnas **4.** se reúna **5.** me reúno **6.** Reúnete

Práctica 8, page 154: **1.** construyeron **2.** construyan **3.** construí **4.** construida **5.** Construye **6.** construyera

Práctica 9, page 155: **1.** para **2.** por **3.** Por **4.** para **5.** para **6.** por **7.** por **8.** para **9.** para **10.** por **11.** para **12.** por **13.** para **14.** por **15.** Por **16.** por **17.** por **18.** por **19.** por **20.** por

Repaso

A, page 155: **1.** podamos/antes de **2.** pasado/de menos **3.** se alegrarán/sepan **4.** se haría/consiguiera **5.** por casualidad/despedirnos **6.** para

B, page 156: **1.** Al terminar sus exámenes y antes de marcharse (*or* irse) de la universidad, varios compañeros se reúnen para almorzar (*or* tomar el almuerzo). **2.** El restaurante les fue recomendado por Miguel Ramos, que (*or* quien) no pudo asistir a la reunión. **3.** Jorge, que (*or* quien) es español, dice que si Miguel no hubiera estado tan ocupado preparando su partida a Puerto Rico, habría almorzado (*or* habría tomado el almuerzo) con ellos. **4.** Isabel va a pasar dos meses en la costa en la casa que fue construida por su abuelo hace casi cien años. **5.** Jorge va a recibir la maestría en administración de negocios, y a su padre le gustaría (*or* y su padre quisiera) que él llegara a ser el gerente de su compañía. **6.** Por fin Jorge anuncia: —Amigos, ya es tarde. Levantaos y despidámonos. ¡Ojalá (*or* Espero) que nos veamos otra vez (*or* volvamos a vernos) pronto!

Expansión

A, page 156: (*Answers will vary.*) **1.** Sí, me reúno de vez en cuando con algunos compañeros para cenar. Vamos a un restaurante. **2.** Me gusta ir de vacaciones con amigos porque nos divertimos mucho. **3.** Sí, pienso continuar mis estudios de español. **4.** Espero conseguir un puesto... **5.** Sí, pienso que saber hablar español me podría ayudar en el trabajo porque...

B, page 157: (*Answers will vary.*)

Para comprender y escribir

A, page 157: **1.** (a) ¡Cuánto me alegro! **2.** (c) No digamos adiós, sino hasta luego. **3.** (c) ¡No dejes de escribirnos! **4.** (a) Un pastel. **5.** (b) Por la noche.

B, page 157: **1.** No lo hagáis esta tarde. **2.** No enviéis por el equipaje. **3.** No os sentéis en el comedor. **4.** No os pongáis esas gafas. **5.** No os acerquéis a la esquina. **6.** No os vayáis con ellos.

C, page 158: **1.** Yo quisiera llegar a ser gerente de una compañía. **2.** A Ana le gustaría almorzar en el centro hoy. **3.** Debiéramos esperar enfrente de la casa de correos. **4.** Él quisiera estudiar arquitectura. **5.** ¡Ojalá que Uds. tengan mucho éxito! **6.** Ellos debieran reunirse mañana. **7.** Yo quisiera que nos viéramos otra vez. **8.** ¿Pudiera yo conseguir un puesto en su compañía?

D, page 158: Al terminar sus exámenes y antes de salir de la universidad, varios compañeros se reúnen para almorzar. El restaurante les fue recomendado por Miguel Ramos, quien no pudo asistir a la reunión. Jorge, que es español, dice que si Miguel no estuviera tan ocupado preparándose para ir a Puerto Rico, habría almorzado con ellos. Beatriz dice que es hora de hablar sobre sus planes para el verano. Después de una conversación muy animada, Jorge anuncia que es hora de despedirse.

Repaso 3: Lecciones 12–15 (Appendix C)

A, page 181: **1.** (No,) Nosotros no volvemos **2.** (No,) Nosotros no jugamos **3.** (No,) Yo no les devolví **4.** (No,) Yo no oigo **5.** (No,) Yo no pagué **6.** (No,) Yo no comencé **7.** (No,) Nosotros no pudimos **8.** (No,) Nosotros no vinimos **9.** (No,) Yo no les traje **10.** (No,) Yo no estuve **11.** (No,) Ellos no han visto **12.** (No,) Yo no he hecho **13.** (No,) Yo no les he escrito **14.** (No,) Nosotros no nos habíamos puesto **15.** (No,) Yo no había abierto **16.** (No,) Nosotros no habíamos hecho **17.** (No,) Tú no tendrás (*or* Ud. no tendrá) **18.** (No,) Yo no me pondré **19.** (No,) Tú no podrías (*or* Ud. no podría) **20.** (No,) Ellos no harían

B, page 181: **1.** Sí, se la di (a ella). **2.** Sí, se lo traje (a Luis). **3.** Sí, se los devolví (a ellos). **4.** Sí, me los puse. **5.** Sí, ella estaba arreglándoselo (*or* se lo estaba arreglando).   **6.** Sí, se las pude entregar (*or* pude entregárselas) (a él).

C, page 181:   **1.** ya habremos regresado   **2.** ya habré vuelto   **3.** ya (la) habrán recibido   **4.** ya habrá llamado   **5.** ya (la) habrá tenido   **6.** la habríamos escuchado   **7.** las habría visto   **8.** lo habríamos leído   **9.** lo habría hecho   **10.** las habríamos traído

D, page 182:   **1.** Me gustan estos bailes.   **2.** A ella le encanta esta música.   **3.** ¿Qué te parece esta blusa?   **4.** Nos gusta esa cartera (blanca).   **5.** Se ven (muchos) artículos finos en las vitrinas.   **6.** Se abre la peluquería a las nueve.

E, page 182:   **1.** a   **2.** por   **3.** por; a   **4.** con   **5.** de   **6.** de; en   **7.** a; en   **8.** a; en   **9.** de   **10.** entre (*or* de)   **11.** por   **12.** a   **13.** en; a   **14.** de; del (*or* para el)   **15.** de   **16.** para (*or* de)

F, page 182:   (*Answers will vary.*)

G, page 183:   **1.** (Probablemente) Las chicas (*or* muchachas) irán (*or* van a ir) al cine.   **2.** Las vimos hace una hora (*or* Hace una hora que las vimos).   **3.** Ellas fueron a España en el verano de mil novecientos noventa y seis y compraron muchos regalos.   **4.** Mis amigos (*or* amigos y amigas) me dieron un regalo.   **5.** ¡Claro! (¡Cómo no!)   **6.** Hacía mucho frío y las ventanas estaban abiertas.   **7.** ¿Qué hora será?   **8.** Volveré (*or* Voy a volver, Vuelvo, [Regresaré, *or* voy a regresar]) el domingo por la noche.   **9.** Estamos muy contentos (*or* contentas) de verte.   **10.** ¿Nos quedamos adentro?   **11.** Se come (*or* Uno come) muy bien aquí.   **12.** ¿Hizo Tomás una excursión con Uds.?   **13.** Yendo en avión se llega (*or* uno llega) rápido; para las cinco de la tarde él habrá llegado.   **14.** —¿En qué puedo servirle? —Nada, gracias.   **15.** Hay que (*or* Es necesario) decidir eso hoy.   **16.** El señor y la señora (*or* Los señores) Sierra acaban de entrar en la joyería.   **17.** Aquella (*or* Esa) pulsera y ésta son preciosas.   **18.** A los muchachos (*or* chicos) les habría gustado asistir a la Copa Mundial.   **19.** Me gustaría visitar muchos (*or* varios) lugares interesantes (*or* de interés).   **20.** (Él) No se ha puesto su traje de baño todavía.   **21.** Miguel se cansó mucho. (Él) Está cansado de bucear.   **22.** Nos levantamos poco después.

Para comprender y escribir

A.   **1.** la pesca, la bicicleta, el equipo, la raqueta   **2.** abierta, los aretes, el oro, la vitrina   **3.** el cinturón, el traje de baño, pagar, el regalo   **4.** amables, el esposo, la recepcionista   **5.** la cocina, el hielo, el palto, el hambre   **6.** el tocadiscos para compactos, el cumpleaños, las bebidas, puntual, la fecha

B.   **1.** el corredor   **2.** el traje   **3.** el cinturón   **4.** envolver   **5.** la hamaca   **6.** el llavero   **7.** registrarse   **8.** la toalla   **9.** la vista   **10.** la plaza   **11.** el corredor   **12.** la empanada   **13.** el hielo   **14.** el postre   **15.** la paella

C.   **1.** tarde   **2.** nunca   **3.** la última vez   **4.** la esposa   **5.** pequeño   **6.** subir   **7.** rápido   **8.** viejo   **9.** primero   **10.** negro   **11.** tampoco   **12.** nadie

Repaso 4: Lecciones 16–19 (Appendix C)

A, page 183:   **1.** Sí, es más nuevo que aquél. Es el más nuevo de todos.   **2.** Sí, son más hermosas que aquéllas. Son las más hermosas de todas.   **3.** Sí, es mejor que aquél. Es el mejor de todos.   **4.** Sí, son más altos que aquéllos. Son los más altos de todos.   **5.** Sí, es más importante que aquélla. Es la más importante de todas.   **6.** Sí, son más trabajadores que aquéllos. Son los más trabajadores de todos.   **7.** Sí, es más competente que aquélla. Es la más competente de todas.   **8.** Sí, es más amable que aquél. Es el más amable de todos.

B, page 183:   **1.** Mis sobrinos son altísimos.   **2.** Sus padres son felicísimos.   **3.** Sus hijas son inteligentísimas.   **4.** Su novio es buenísimo.   **5.** Mi esposa es guapísima.

C, page 184:   **1.** Sugiero que Ud. alquile un apartamento; no compre una casa.   **2.** Recomiendo que Ud. hable con el gerente; no llame a la dueña.   **3.** Deseo que Ud. sirva las bebidas ahora; no comience a cocinar.   **4.** Recomiendo que Ud. vaya a la conferencia; no se quede en la biblioteca.   **5.** Le digo a Ud. que escriba el resumen ahora; no pague las cuentas.   **6.** Prefiero que Ud. ponga este disco; no busque otro.

D, page 184:   **1.** Me alegro de que Alberto y Silvia quieran casarse.   **2.** Yo sé que ellos son muy felices.   **3.** Me extraña que ellos no hayan dicho nada todavía.   **4.** Es posible que Silvia ya haya vuelto de la Argentina.   **5.** Temo que sus amigas no lo hayan visto todavía.   **6.** Estoy seguro de que Alberto se ha puesto muy contento.   **7.** No dudo que nosotros les daremos una gran fiesta.   **8.** Espero que ellos reciban muchos regalos.

E, page 184:   **1.** que no hayas vuelto   **2.** que no hayas visto   **3.** que no le hayas escrito   **4.** que no le hayas dicho   **5.** que no hayas ido   **6.** que no hayas venido   **7.** que no te hayas enfermado   **8.** que no hayas hecho

F, page 184:   **1.** escribe   **2.** sepa   **3.** es   **4.** pueda   **5.** tenga   **6.** esté

G, page 185:   **1.** desde hace   **2.** ocupadísimo   **3.** graduarme de   **4.** case   **5.** un tiempo   **6.** quien   **7.** volvamos   **8.** decir   **9.** difícil   **10.** puesto   **11.** no creo   **12.** amueblar   **13.** nuevo   **14.** Quizás   **15.** traduciendo   **16.** irnos   **17.** nuestra boda   **18.** guapísima   **19.** Escríbeme   **20.** Tu

H, page 185:   **1.** Lavémonos las manos.   **2.** Vámonos ahora.   **3.** No nos sentemos todavía.   **4.** Que lo haga Jorge.   **5.** Que sigan adelante.   **6.** Hace una semana que Juan está aquí *or* Juan está aquí desde hace una semana.   **7.** ¿Cuánto tiempo hace que ellos trabajan aquí?   **8.** (Ellos) Se hicieron muy ricos hace unos años *or* Hace unos años que (ellos) se hicieron muy ricos.   **9.** Quizás (*or* Tal vez) no venga Roberto. Lo dudo.   **10.** ¿Cómo te sientes hoy? **11.** La mayor parte de los estudiantes fué a la conferencia. **12.** Juan tiene dolor de cabeza *or* A Juan le duele la cabeza. **13.** A Ricardo le duele el brazo. **14.** A propósito, ¿qué le pasa a (*or* ¿qué tiene) Tomás? **15.** ¿Por qué no dan Uds. un paseo conmigo? **16.** Antonio llegó a ser un buen médico. **17.** ¿Hay alguien aquí que la conozca? **18.** Oímos decir (*or* Hemos oído decir) que él consiguió (*or* obtuvo) el puesto. **19.** Sentimos que la hermana de Juan haya estado enferma. **20.** Déjenme (a mí) manejar esta tarde.

Para comprender y escribir

A. **1.** el brazo, enfermarse, la rodilla, el cuello **2.** la ambulancia, la enfermera, los antibióticos, la fiebre **3.** amueblada, alquilar, el barrio, la cocina **4.** el anillo, la lista de regalos, casarse, la luna de miel, feliz **5.** la aspiradora, eléctricos, la cafetera, la batidora, la plancha **6.** la avería, la licencia de conducir, manejar, chocar, el tráfico **7.** la empleada, el ascenso, el sueldo, el gerente

B. **1.** la solicitud **2.** obtener **3.** la maquinaria **4.** la ambulancia **5.** la policía **6.** calmarse **7.** el ordenador **8.** la sartén **9.** el regalo **10.** la lista **11.** cercano **12.** la pierna **13.** la mesa **14.** al menos **15.** ir a pescar

C. **1.** dormirse **2.** poquísimo **3.** rico **4.** mejorarse **5.** por la derecha **6.** terminar

Repaso 5: Lecciones 20–22 (Appendix C)

A, page 186: **1.** No, nosotros no los escogemos. Sí, Ud. los escoge. **2.** No, nosotros no la dirigimos. Sí, Ud. la dirige. **3.** No, yo no la continúo. Sí, Ud. la continúa. **4.** No, yo no se los envío. Sí, se los envía la oficina del departamento de español. **5.** No, los estudiantes de francés no se reúnen aquí. Sí, nosotros nos reunimos aquí. **6.** No, yo no los construyo. Sí, un grupo de ingenieros los construye.

B, page 186: **1.** …que José consiga… **2.** …que Beatriz escoja… **3.** …que Lupe envíe… **4.** …que ese carro no continúe… **5.** …que ese carro se detenga… **6.** …que el policía dirija… **7.** …que el policía le pida… **8.** …que la gente se vaya… **9.** …que la ciudad construya… **10.** …que eso valga…

C, page 186: **1.** No, no traigo las suyas. **2.** No, no llevo el suyo. **3.** No, no necesito los suyos (*or* tuyos). **4.** No, no quiero el suyo (*or* tuyo). **5.** No, no hago las suyas (*or* las de Uds. *or* las nuestras). **6.** No, no conduzco el suyo (*or* el de Uds. *or* el nuestro).

D, page 186: **1.** Sí, él quería que yo escuchara la conferencia. **2.** Sí, él prefería que yo tradujera los versos. **3.** Sí, ella prefería que nosotros hiciéramos la solicitud.

4. Sí, ellos esperaban que nosotros fuéramos buenos amigos. **5.** Sí, ellos no creían que yo pudiera ser mal empleado. **6.** Sí, ellos esperaban que Ud. construyera (*or* tú construyeras) un futuro mejor para nosotros. **7.** Sí, él esperaba que su secretaria escribiera mejores resúmenes. **8.** Sí, ella esperaba que nosotros leyéramos más artículos.

E, page 187: **1.** …para que tú escogieras… **2.** …que durmieran… **3.** …que nos hiciera… **4.** …que Lola consiguiera… **5.** …de que Ana saliera… **6.** …que ellos llevaran…

F, page 187: **1.** hubiera asientos libres en ese vuelo, partiríamos el sábado. **2.** te hubiera visto antes, te habría avisado de la reunión. **3.** supiera traducir, podría conseguir un buen puesto en Suramérica. **4.** me hubieran invitado, habría ido. **5.** hubieran tenido paciencia, habrían sacado mejores fotos. **6.** tuviera suficiente para mí, te daría más dinero.

G, page 187: **1.** volví **2.** tuvieran **3.** buscaran **4.** sirvieran (*or* hayan servido) **5.** llovió **6.** tuviéramos **7.** gustara **8.** llegue (*or* llegara *or* haya llegado) **9.** construyera **10.** hubieran **11.** fuera **12.** estamos

H, page 188: **1.** No pensábamos ir a una película, sino a un concierto. **2.** De nada (*or* No hay de qué). **3.** Nos veíamos a menudo, pero nunca nos conocimos. **4.** Vale la pena pasar algún tiempo en un país extranjero. **5.** Me encontré con Jorge hace una hora. **6.** Los regalos son para Isabel. **7.** Jaime salió (*or* partió) para España anoche. **8.** Mandad (*or* Enviad) por Rita mañana por la mañana. **9.** Tienen mucho éxito. **10.** ¿Compró él un boleto de ida y vuelta? **11.** Éste es para Ud. **12.** Los versos fueron traducidos por Miguel. **13.** Las tarjetas fueron escritas por mi hermana. **14.** Si yo hubiera visto a Juan, le habría dado las fotos. **15.** Si yo tuviera el dinero, compraría una cámara vídeo. **16.** Yo quisiera (*or* Me gustaría) viajar por este país. **17.** ¡Ojalá que los muchachos (*or* chicos) estuvieran aquí ahora! **18.** Roberto ha solicitado una beca para estudiar ingeniería. **19.** Pagué veinte dólares por los guantes. **20.** (Ellos) Debieran (*or* Deben) estar enfrente del restaurante para las seis.

Para comprender y escribir

A. **1.** el equipaje, la maleta, el pasajero, la agencia, despedirse **2.** la computadora, el ascenso, informar, la reunión, emplear **3.** aéreo, el aeromozo, la ida, una línea interna **4.** el abrigo, el guante, la marca, el impermeable, el suéter **5.** felicitar, reunirse, el pastel, animada

B. **1.** el asiento **2.** la falta **3.** el camarero **4.** detener **5.** el piropo **6.** la duda **7.** la azafata **8.** el consejo **9.** la cámara **10.** sin embargo

C. **1.** recibir **2.** olvidar **3.** despedirse **4.** la vuelta **5.** el pasado **6.** último

TAPESCRIPTS: ACTIVIDADES Y PRÁCTICA, PARA COMPRENDER Y ESCRIBIR, REPASO SELF-TESTS

Lección 12

Actividades y práctica

A. Repeat the model sentence and then substitute each new subject. You will hear a confirmation of your response.

1. Los señores Ramos hicieron un viaje a Córdoba. //
   Los señores Ramos hicieron un viaje a Córdoba.
   Las muchachas //
   Las muchachas hicieron un viaje a Córdoba.
   Yo //
   Yo hice un viaje a Córdoba.
   Diana //
   Diana hizo un viaje a Córdoba.
   Ustedes //
   Ustedes hicieron un viaje a Córdoba.
   Nosotros //
   Nosotros hicimos un viaje a Córdoba.
2. Ellos vinieron sin hacer reservas. //
   Ellos vinieron sin hacer reservas.
   Miguel //
   Miguel vino sin hacer reservas.
   Ustedes //
   Ustedes vinieron sin hacer reservas.
   Jaime y yo //
   Jaime y yo vinimos sin hacer reservas.
   Tú //
   Tú viniste sin hacer reservas.
   Yo //
   Yo vine sin hacer reservas.
3. La recepcionista les dijo el precio. //
   La recepcionista les dijo el precio.
   Yo //
   Yo les dije el precio.
   Los señores //
   Los señores les dijeron el precio.
   Él //
   Él les dijo el precio.
   Nosotros //
   Nosotros les dijimos el precio.
   Tú //
   Tú les dijiste el precio.
4. Ellos quisieron ver la habitación. //
   Ellos quisieron ver la habitación.
   Nosotros //
   Nosotros quisimos ver la habitación.
   Rita //
   Rita quiso ver la habitación.
   Yo //
   Yo quise ver la habitación.
   Ustedes //

Ustedes quisieron ver la habitación.
Tú //
Tú quisiste ver la habitación. //

B. Listen to the questions and confirm the information you hear. Use the present progressive tense in your responses and pay close attention to the position of the pronouns. Listen to the correct answer.

> MODEL: Y los periódicos, ¿quién los compra? ¿Lupe?
> **Sí, Lupe está comprándolos.**

1. Y las reservas, ¿quién las hace? ¿Roberto? //
   Sí, Roberto está haciéndolas.
2. Y, ¿quiénes se desayunan ahora? ¿Ustedes? //
   Sí, nosotros estamos desayunándonos ahora.
3. Y las cartas, ¿quién las escribe? ¿Tú? //
   Sí, yo estoy escribiéndolas.
4. Y las toallas, ¿quién las trae? ¿La criada? //
   Sí, la criada está trayéndolas.
5. Y, ¿quiénes se registran? ¿Los señores? //
   Sí, los señores están registrándose.
6. Y la ropa, ¿quién la lava? ¿Elena? //
   Sí, Elena está lavándola. //

C. Answer each question, following the model. You will hear a confirmation of your response.

> MODEL: ¿Está haciendo Ana las reservas?
> **No, no está haciéndolas todavía, pero va a hacerlas en seguida.**

1. ¿Están ustedes registrándose? //
   No, no estamos registrándonos todavía, pero vamos a registrarnos en seguida.
2. ¿Está la criada buscando las llaves? //
   No, no está buscándolas todavía, pero va a buscarlas en seguida.
3. ¿Estás tú arreglándote? //
   No, no estoy arreglándome todavía, pero voy a arreglarme en seguida.
4. ¿Están ustedes preparándose para salir? //
   No, no estamos preparándonos para salir todavía, pero vamos a prepararnos para salir en seguida.
5. ¿Está la recepcionista preparando la cuenta? //
   No, no está preparándola todavía, pero va a prepararla en seguida. //

D. Answer each question affirmatively, using a construction with **se.** Follow the model and then listen to the correct response.

> MODEL: ¿Hablan español aquí?
> **Sí, señor, se habla español aquí.**

203

1. ¿Podemos llamar a México? //
   Sí, señor, se puede llamar a México.
2. ¿Aceptan ustedes tarjetas de crédito? //
   Sí, señor, se aceptan tarjetas de crédito.
3. ¿Abren los bancos temprano? //
   Sí, señor, se abren los bancos temprano.
4. ¿Venden ustedes periódicos extranjeros. //
   Sí, señor, se venden periódicos extranjeros.
5. ¿Cobran ustedes por el estacionamiento? //
   Sí, señor, se cobra por el estacionamiento.
6. ¿Podemos comer algo ahora? //
   Sí, señor, se puede comer algo ahora. //

Now answer each question using a construction with **se**.
Follow the model and then listen to the correct response.

> MODEL: ¿Podemos comprar las entradas aquí?
> **Perdone, pero las entradas se compran
> allá.**

7. ¿Podemos hacer las reservas aquí? //
   Perdone, pero se hacen las reservas allá.
8. ¿Podemos pagar las cuentas aquí? //
   Perdone, pero se pagan las cuentas allá.
9. ¿Puedo comprar el *ABC* aquí? //
   Perdone, pero se compra el *ABC* allá.
10. ¿Puedo cambiar el cheque aquí? //
    Perdone, pero se cambia el cheque allá.
11. ¿Pueden entregarnos los boletos aquí? //
    Perdone, pero se entregan los boletos allá.
12. ¿Pueden ustedes poner este anuncio aquí? //
    Perdone, pero se pone el anuncio allá. //

E. Answer each question affirmatively, using a prepositional
pronoun, as in the model. Then listen for confirmation of
your response.

> MODEL: ¿Para quién son las llaves? ¿Para mí?
> **Sí, las llaves son para ti. (Sí, las llaves son
> para usted.)**

1. ¿Para quién son las mantas? ¿Para mí? //
   **Sí, las mantas son para ti. (Sí, las mantas son para
   usted.)**
2. ¿Para quién son las toallas? ¿Para usted? //
   Sí, las toallas son para mí.
3. ¿Para quién es el jabón? ¿Para él? //
   Sí, el jabón es para él.
4. ¿Para quién es la ropa de cama? ¿Para ella? //
   Sí, la ropa de cama es para ella.
5. ¿Para quiénes son las bebidas? ¿Para ustedes? //
   **Sí, las bebidas son para nosotros. (Sí, las bebidas son
   para nosotras.)**
6. ¿Para quiénes son los periódicos? ¿Para nosotros? //
   **Sí, los periódicos son para ustedes. (Sí, los periódicos
   son para nosotros.) //**

F. Answer each question negatively, using the next lower
ordinal number, as in the model. You will hear a
confirmation of your response.

> MODEL: ¿Le dieron a usted la segunda reserva?
> **No, me dieron la primera.**

1. ¿Es su tercer viaje a España? //
   **No, es mi segundo. (No, es su segundo. No, es nuestro
   segundo.)**
2. ¿Tomó usted la quinta habitación? //
   No, tomé la cuarta.
3. ¿Subió usted al octavo piso? //
   No, subí al séptimo.
4. ¿Estudiaron ustedes sobre Carlos Segundo? //
   No, estudiamos sobre Carlos Primero.
5. ¿Vieron ustedes el sexto programa? //
   No, vimos el quinto.
6. ¿Escucharon ustedes la décima canción? //
   No, escuchamos la novena. //

Para comprender y escribir

A. From the three choices offered, select the one that best
completes the statement or answers the question you
hear and circle it.

1. Para bajar al primer piso se puede usar...
   (a) la vista.
   (b) el ascensor.
   (c) el siglo. //
2. Como no queremos dejar el coche en la calle,
   necesitamos encontrar...
   (a) una cama.
   (b) una criada.
   (c) un garaje. //
3. Mi hermano me dio cuatrocientas pesetas y mi mamá me
   dio quinientas pesetas. Ahora tengo...
   (a) setecientas pesetas.
   (b) novecientas pesetas.
   (c) mil pesetas. //
4. ¿Cuál es la fecha de la independencia de los Estados
   Unidos?
   (a) El cuatro de junio de mil novecientos setenta y seis.
   (b) El cuatro de julio de mil setecientos setenta y seis.
   (c) El cuatro de julio de mil seiscientos sesenta y
   seis. //

B. Listen to the statement and the question that follows it.
Write the response, according to the model.

> MODEL: Ellos fueron a Granada en coche. ¿Cómo
> fueron ustedes?
> **Nosotros también fuimos en coche.**

1. Ellos quisieron descansar. ¿Qué quisieron ustedes? //
2. Ellos vinieron en una excursión. ¿Cómo vinieron
   ustedes? //
3. Ellos hicieron las reservas. ¿Qué hiciste tú? //
4. Ellos decidieron tomar la habitación. ¿Qué decidiste
   tú? //
5. Ellos dijeron que era cómoda. ¿Qué dijiste tú? //

C. Dictado

You will hear a short paragraph about travel. You will hear the narrative three times. Listen the first time. Write what you hear on the lines provided the second time. Make any necessary corrections the third time.

La hermana de Alicia Martí // hizo un viaje a Granada el año pasado. // Fue con dos amigas de la universidad. // Una de las muchachas, // Isabel, // tenía familia en España. // El avión las llevó a Madrid // y entonces decidieron ir hasta Granada en tren. // Fueron a un hotel muy agradable // cerca de una plaza. // Allí conocieron a muchas personas // de todo el mundo // que también estaban de viaje por el país. //

End of **Lección doce.**

Lección 13

Actividades y práctica

A. Repeat the model sentence and then substitute each new subject. You will hear a confirmation of your response.

1. Nosotros estuvimos en Yucatán. //
   Nosotros estuvimos en Yucatán.
   Yo //
   Yo estuve en Yucatán.
   Ella //
   Ella estuvo en Yucatán.
   Ustedes //
   Ustedes estuvieron en Yucatán.
   Antonio y Carlos //
   Antonio y Carlos estuvieron en Yucatán.
2. Nosotros pudimos visitar las ruinas. //
   Nosotros pudimos visitar las ruinas.
   Miguel //
   Miguel pudo visitar las ruinas.
   Tú //
   Tú pudiste visitar las ruinas.
   Yo //
   Yo pude visitar las ruinas.
   Ustedes //
   Ustedes pudieron visitar las ruinas.
3. Durante el viaje nosotros tuvimos mucha suerte. //
   Durante el viaje nosotros tuvimos mucha suerte.
   tú //
   Durante el viaje tú tuviste mucha suerte.
   mis amigos //
   Durante el viaje mis amigos tuvieron mucha suerte.
   ustedes //
   Durante el viaje ustedes tuvieron mucha suerte.
   yo //
   Durante el viaje yo tuve mucha suerte.
4. ¿Dónde pusiste tú los boletos? //
   ¿Dónde pusiste tú los boletos?
   ustedes //
   ¿Dónde pusieron ustedes los boletos?

Diana //
¿Dónde puso Diana los boletos?
ellos //
¿Dónde pusieron ellos los boletos?
usted //
¿Dónde puso usted los boletos?
5. ¿Cuándo supieron ustedes la hora de llegada? //
   ¿Cuándo supieron ustedes la hora de llegada?
   tú //
   ¿Cuándo supiste tú la hora de llegada?
   tus padres //
   ¿Cuándo supieron tus padres la hora de llegada?
   él //
   ¿Cuándo supo él la hora de llegada?
   yo //
   ¿Cuándo supe yo la hora de llegada? //

B. Listen to each question and the cue. Respond affirmatively with the appropriate object pronoun. You will hear a confirmation of your answer.

> MODEL: ¿Quién te dio el collar? ¿Él?
> **Sí, él me lo dio.**

1. ¿Quién te dio la pulsera? ¿Él? //
   Sí, él me la dio.
2. ¿Quién te puso los aretes? ¿Ella? //
   Sí, ella me los puso.
3. ¿Quién les enseñó los anillos a ustedes? ¿Yo? //
   Sí, usted nos los enseñó. (Sí, tú nos los enseñaste.)
4. ¿Quién les compró el prendedor a ustedes? ¿Yo? //
   Sí, usted nos lo compró. (Sí, tú nos lo compraste.)
5. ¿Quién me buscó la mercancía? ¿Usted? //
   Sí, yo se la busqué.
6. ¿Quién me mandó el regalo? ¿Ustedes? //
   Sí, nosotros se lo mandamos. (Sí, nosotros te lo mandamos.)
7. ¿Quién nos sacó las fotos? ¿Usted? //
   Sí, yo se las saqué.
8. ¿Quién nos pagó la cuenta? ¿Usted? //
   Sí, yo se la pagué.
9. ¿Quién se llevó los paquetes? ¿Ella? //
   Sí, ella se los llevó.
10. ¿Quién se compró la camisas típicas? ¿Tú? //
    Sí, yo me las compré. //

C. Listen to each question. Respond negatively to the first question and affirmatively to the second one, using formal commands. Follow the models and listen for confirmation of your answer.

> MODELS: ¿Le devuelvo la pulsera a ella?
> **No, no se la devuelva usted a ella.**
> ¿Se la devuelvo a usted?
> **Sí, devuélvamela usted a mí.**

1. ¿Le devuelvo las llaves a él? //
   No, no se las devuelva usted a él.
   ¿Se las devuelvo a usted? //
   Sí, devuélvamelas usted a mí.

2. ¿Le traigo los paquetes a ella? //
   No, no se los traiga usted a ella.
   ¿Se los traigo a usted? //
   Sí, tráigamelos usted a mí.
3. ¿Les vendo el coche a ellos? //
   No, no se lo venda usted a ellos.
   ¿Se lo vendo a ustedes? //
   Sí, véndanoslo usted a nosotros.
4. ¿Les doy los relojes a ella? //
   No, no se los dé usted a ella.
   ¿Se los doy a ustedes? //
   Sí, dénoslos usted a nosotros.
5. ¿Les saco la foto a ustedes? //
   No, no nos la saque usted a nosotros.
   ¿Se la saco a ellas? //
   Sí, sáquesela usted a ellas.
6. ¿Les entrego los recibos a ustedes? //
   No, no nos los entregue usted a nosotros.
   ¿Se los entrego a ellos? //
   Sí, entrégueselos usted a ellos.
7. ¿Te hago las reservas? //
   No, no me las haga usted a mí.
   ¿Se las hago a ellas? //
   Sí, hágaselas usted a ellas.
8. ¿Me compro yo el sombrero? //
   No, no se lo compre usted.
   ¿Te lo compro a ti? //
   Sí, cómpremelo usted a mí. //

D. Answer the first question affirmatively and the second question negatively, using demonstrative pronouns, as in the model. Then listen for confirmation of your response.

> MODELS: ¿Te gustan esos llaveros?
> **Sí, ésos me gustan mucho.**
> ¿Y estos aretes?
> **No, éstos no me gustan.**

1. ¿Te gusta este prendedor? //
   Sí, éste me gusta.
   ¿Y aquel cinturón? //
   No, aquél no me gusta.
2. ¿Te gustan estos anillos? //
   Sí, éstos me gustan.
   ¿Y esa hamaca? //
   No, ésa no me gusta.
3. ¿Te gusta aquella joyería? //
   Sí, aquélla me gusta.
   ¿Y esa cerámica? //
   No, ésa no me gusta.
4. ¿Te gusta ese collar? //
   Sí, ése me gusta.
   ¿Y estos regalos? //
   No, éstos no me gustan.
5. ¿Te gusta esta camisa? //
   Sí, ésta me gusta.
   ¿Y aquellas camisas? //
   No, aquéllas no me gustan. //

E. Answer each question negatively, giving an explanation. Follow the model. You will hear a response, but yours may vary slightly as to the reasons.

> MODEL: ¿Tienes sueño?
> **No, no tengo sueño porque acabo de despertarme.**

1. ¿Tienes hambre? //
   No, no tengo hambre porque acabo de comer.
2. ¿Quieres salir? //
   No, yo no quiero salir porque acabo de entrar.
3. ¿Vas a lavar la ropa? //
   No, no voy a lavar la ropa porque acabo de lavarla.
4. ¿Piensas ir a la biblioteca? //
   No, no pienso ir a la biblioteca porque acabo de volver de la biblioteca.
5. ¿Quieres leer el libro? //
   No, yo no quiero leer el libro porque acabo de leerlo. //

Para comprender y escribir

A. From the three choices offered, select the one that best completes the statement or answers the question you hear and circle it.

1. Clara y Marta tienen ganas de comprarse unos aretes. ¿Adónde van a ir?
   (a) A una joyería.
   (b) A una vitrina.
   (c) A una joya. //
2. Después de darle el llavero que compró, el dependiente le da a Alberto...
   (a) el recibo.
   (b) la paja.
   (c) el par. //
3. No me gusta este collar. Creo que voy a...
   (a) volverlo.
   (b) envolverlo.
   (c) devolverlo. //
4. Quiero llevarles regalos de plata a mis amigas. Pienso comprar unos aretes, una pulsera y...
   (a) una hamaca.
   (b) un prendedor.
   (c) un paquete. //
5. ¿Dónde está el mercado?
   (a) En un par de semanas.
   (b) En el cinturón.
   (c) En el centro. //

B. Listen to the question and write a response, following the model.

> MODEL: ¿Vas a estar en la universidad hoy?
> **No, estuve en la universidad ayer.**

1. ¿Vas a hacerlo hoy? //
2. ¿Vas a tener tiempo hoy? //
3. ¿Vas a buscar a Diana hoy? //
4. ¿Quieres almorzar con ella hoy? //

5. ¿Vas a comenzar a trabajar hoy? //
6. ¿Van ustedes a llevarse los paquetes hoy? //

C. Answer the questions affirmatively, using an object pronoun, as in the model.

> MODEL: ¿Quién buscó las llaves ayer?
> **Yo las busqué ayer.**

1. ¿Quién sacó las fotos ayer? //
2. ¿Quién practicó el baile ayer? //
3. ¿Quién tocó ese disco ayer? //
4. ¿Quién entregó las joyas ayer? //
5. ¿Quién pagó la cuenta ayer? //
6. ¿Quién cruzó el río ayer? //

D. Dictado

You will hear a short paragraph about the trip señor and señora Ramos took to Mexico. You will hear the paragraph three times. Listen the first time. Write what you hear on the lines provided the second time. Make any necessary corrections the third time.

El año pasado // los señores Ramos estuvieron en México // un par de semanas. // Durante ese viaje // pudieron visitar las ruinas de Yucatán // y otros lugares interesantes. // Un día encontraron una joyería típica. // El dependiente les mostró muchos artículos // de oro y de plata. // La señora Ramos quería comprar algo especial // para sus dos hijas. // El señor Ramos vio unas pulseras de plata // que le gustaron mucho. // Cuando regresaron a los Estados Unidos, // les encantaron los regalos a sus hijas. //

End of **Lección trece.**

Lección 14

Actividades y práctica

A. Answer as in the models, saying that you have already done what is being suggested. You will hear a confirmation of your response.

> MODELS: Oye, ¿quieres cenar?
> **Gracias, pero ya he cenado.**
> Oye, quieren ustedes cenar?
> **Gracias, pero ya hemos cenado.**

1. Oye, ¿quieres desayunarte? //
   Gracias, pero ya me he desayunado.
2. Oye, ¿quieres bañarte en el mar? //
   Gracias, pero ya me he bañado en el mar.
3. Oye ¿quieres tomar el sol? //
   Gracias, pero ya he tomado el sol.
4. Oye, ¿quieres nadar? //
   Gracias, pero ya he nadado.
5. Oye, ¿quieren ustedes ir a bucear? //
   Gracias, pero ya hemos ido a bucear.

6. Oye, ¿quieren ustedes salir a almorzar? //
   Gracias, pero ya hemos salido a almorzar.
7. Oye, ¿quieren ustedes ir a pescar? //
   Gracias pero ya hemos ido a pescar.
8. Oye, ¿quieren ustedes hacer una excursión? //
   Gracias, pero ya hemos hecho una excursión. //

B. Answer each question negatively, as in the model, and then listen for confirmation of your response.

> MODEL: ¿Ya visitaron ustedes México?
> **No, ya habíamos visitado México antes.**

1. ¿Estuvieron ustedes en Yucatán? //
   No, ya habíamos estado en Yucatán antes.
2. ¿Vieron ustedes las ruinas mayas? //
   No, ya habíamos visto las ruinas mayas antes.
3. ¿Fueron ustedes a Cozumel? //
   No, ya habíamos ido a Cozumel antes.
4. ¿Conociste Cancún también? //
   No, yo ya había conocido Cancún antes.
5. ¿Hiciste el viaje en coche? //
   No, yo ya había hecho el viaje en coche antes.
6. ¿Visitaste la ciudad de México? //
   No, yo ya había visitado la ciudad de México antes. //

C. Respond to each question, saying the action was already done, as in the model. You will hear a confirmation of your response.

> MODEL: ¿Prepararon ustedes la cena?
> **No, ya estaba preparada.**

1. ¿Hicieron ustedes el almuerzo? //
   No, ya estaba hecho.
2. ¿Cocinaron ustedes la paella? //
   No, ya estaba cocinada.
3. ¿Cubrieron ustedes la comida? //
   No, ya estaba cubierta.
4. ¿Cerraste las ventanas? //
   No, ya estaban cerradas.
5. ¿Arreglaste el tocadiscos para compactos? //
   No, ya estaba arreglado.
6. ¿Lavaste las coches? //
   No, ya estaban lavados. //

D. Answer each question affirmatively, using the information given. Then listen for confirmation of your response.

> MODEL: ¿Dónde has estado hoy? ¿En el centro?
> **Sí, hoy he estado en el centro.**

1. ¿A quiénes has visto esta semana? ¿A Ana y a Ramón? //
   Sí, esta semana he visto a Ana y a Ramón.
2. ¿Qué hay que hacer este fin de semana? ¿Estudiar? //
   Sí, este fin de semana hay que estudiar.
3. ¿Dónde habían vivido ustedes antes? ¿En Colombia? //
   Sí, antes habíamos vivido en Colombia.
4. ¿Qué hay que hacer para mañana? ¿Leer este artículo? //
   Sí, para mañana hay que leer este artículo. //

E. Answer each question affirmatively, following the model. Then listen for confirmation of your response.

> MODEL: Miguel llegó hace un mes, ¿verdad?
> **Sí, hace un mes que Miguel llegó.**

1. Ellos volvieron hace una semana, ¿verdad? //
   Sí, hace una semana que volvieron.
2. Marta nos visitó hace dos días, ¿verdad? //
   Sí, hace dos días que Marta nos visitó.
3. Tu hermana salió hace un par de horas, ¿verdad? //
   Sí, hace un par de horas que mi hermana salió.
4. Ellos hicieron el viaje hace un año, ¿verdad? //
   Sí, hace un año que hicieron el viaje.
5. Nosotros regresamos al hotel hace media hora, ¿verdad? //
   Sí, hace media hora que regresamos al hotel.
6. Silvia llamó por teléfono hace un rato, ¿verdad? //
   Sí, hace un rato que Silvia llamó por teléfono. //

F. Repeat the model sentence and then substitute each new subject. You will hear a confirmation of your response.

1. El señor Ramos no oye muy bien. //
   El señor Ramos no oye muy bien.
   Yo //
   Yo no oigo muy bien.
   Ana y yo //
   Ana y yo no oímos muy bien.
   Tú //
   Tú no oyes muy bien.
   Rita y Laura //
   Rita y Laura no oyen muy bien.
2. Jaime no lo creyó. //
   Jaime no lo creyó.
   Ellos //
   Ellos no lo creyeron.
   Yo //
   Yo no lo creí.
   Luis y yo //
   Luis y yo no lo creímos.
   Tú //
   Tú no lo creíste.
3. Yo tampoco leí su carta. //
   Yo tampoco leí su carta.
   Sus padres //
   Sus padres tampoco leyeron su carta.
   Mario y yo //
   Mario y yo tampoco leímos su carta.
   Ella //
   Ella tampoco leyó su carta.
   Ustedes //
   Ustedes tampoco leyeron su carta. //

Para comprender y escribir

A. From the three choices offered, select the one that best completes the statement or answers the question you hear and circle it.

1. En Cozumel se puede disfrutar de muchos deportes acuáticos como bucear, nadar y...
   (a) preocuparse.
   (b) pescar.
   (c) oír. //
2. Chichén Itzá fue muy importante durante la época de los mayas. Es una ciudad muy...
   (a) abierta.
   (b) cubierta.
   (c) antigua. //
3. Yo no quiero conformarme con eso. ¿Y tú?
   (a) Yo tampoco.
   (b) Yo es fin.
   (c) Yo también. //
4. Mis vacaciones en Cancún no fueron muy agradables porque dejé en casa mi...
   (a) peluquería.
   (b) traje de baño.
   (c) piscina. //
5. ¿Has visitado las ruinas de Tikal...
   (a) alguna vez?
   (b) hace media hora?
   (c) poco después? //

B. Write negative answers to the questions, as in the model. Be sure to use object pronouns where possible.

> MODEL: ¿Ya les compraste los regalos?
> **No, todavía no se los he comprado.**

1. ¿Ya les hiciste las reservas? //
2. ¿Ya les entregaste los boletos de avión? //
3. ¿Ya le enseñaste las fotos del hotel? //
4. ¿Ya le dijiste el horario de comidas? //
5. ¿Ya le devolviste su tarjeta de crédito? //

C. Answer the questions affirmatively, following the model.

> MODEL: ¿Has escrito la carta?
> **Sí, está escrita.**

1. ¿Has cobrado los cheques? //
2. ¿Has pagado la cuenta? //
3. ¿Has abierto el regalo? //
4. ¿Han envuelto ustedes el paquete? //
5. ¿Han escrito ustedes las tarjetas? //
6. ¿Han puesto ustedes las estampillas? //

D. Dictado

You will hear a short narrative about how the Ramoses spent their vacation in Cozumel. You will hear the narrative three times. Listen the first time. Write what you hear the second time. Make any necessary corrections the third time.

El año pasado los señores Ramos // hicieron un viaje a México. // Ellos fueron a Yucatán // y pasaron una semana en la isla de Cozumel. // Todas las mañanas // ellos se levantaban temprano // y bajaban a la playa; //

nadaban un rato, // y luego se desayunaban. // Después del desayuno, // les gustaba sentarse en la arena // y tomar el sol. // Como se encontraban muy cansados, // pasaban muchas horas en la playa, // leyendo y descansando. //

End of **Lección catorce.**

Lección 15

Actividades y práctica

A. Repeat the model sentence and then substitute the new subject you hear. Listen for confirmation of your response.

1. Luis irá al apartamento de Jorge. //
   Luis irá al apartamento de Jorge.
   Yo //
   Yo iré al apartamento de Jorge.
   Nosotros //
   Nosotros iremos al apartamento de Jorge.
   Ustedes //
   Ustedes irán al apartamento de Jorge.
   Ellos //
   Ellos irán al apartamento de Jorge.
2. Ellos mirarán un partido de la Copa Mundial. //
   Ellos mirarán un partido de la Copa Mundial.
   Nosotros //
   Nosotros miraremos un partido de la Copa Mundial.
   Mis amigos //
   Mis amigos mirarán un partido de la Copa Mundial.
   Yo //
   Yo miraré un partido de la Copa Mundial.
   Tú //
   Tú mirarás un partido de la Copa Mundial.
3. El equipo colombiano jugará muy bien. //
   El equipo colombiano jugará muy bien.
   Ustedes //
   Ustedes jugarán muy bien.
   Usted //
   Usted jugará muy bien.
   Ellos //
   Ellos jugarán muy bien.
   Tú //
   Tú jugarás muy bien.
4. Alberto te escribirá después del juego. //
   Alberto te escribirá después del juego.
   Yo //
   Yo te escribiré después del juego.
   Nosotros //
   Nosotros te escribiremos después del juego.
   Ellos //
   Ellos te escribirán después del juego.
   Ella //
   Ella te escribirá después del juego.
5. Mañana leeremos las noticias en el periódico. //
   Mañana leeremos las noticias en el periódico.

yo //
Mañana yo leeré las noticias en el periódico.
tú //
Mañana tú leerás las noticias en el periódico.
ustedes //
Mañana ustedes leerán las noticias en el periódico.
usted //
Mañana usted leerá las noticias en el periódico. //

B. Repeat the model sentence and then substitute the new subject you hear. Listen for confirmation of your response.

1. Yo necesitaría mirar la guía. //
   Yo necesitaría mirar la guía.
   Nosotros //
   Nosotros necesitaríamos mirar la guía.
   Jorge //
   Jorge necesitaría mirar la guía.
   Tú //
   Tú necesitarías mirar la guía.
   Ustedes //
   Ustedes necesitarían mirar la guía.
2. Ellos estarían en el estadio de México ayer. //
   Ellos estarían en el estadio de México ayer.
   Yo //
   Yo estaría en el estadio de México ayer.
   Nosotros //
   Nosotros estaríamos en el estadio de México ayer.
   Alberto //
   Alberto estaría en el estadio de México ayer.
   Tú //
   Tú estarías en el estadio de México ayer.
3. Usted gozaría más del partido. //
   Usted gozaría más del partido.
   Los muchachos //
   Los muchachos gozarían más del partido.
   Yo //
   Yo gozaría más del partido.
   Tú //
   Tú gozarías más del partido.
   Mario //
   Mario gozaría más del partido.
4. Nosotros participaríamos de la emoción. //
   Nosotros participaríamos de la emoción.
   Yo //
   Yo participaría de la emoción.
   Usted //
   Usted participaría de la emoción.
   Tú //
   Tú participarías de la emoción.
   Alberto y Luis //
   Alberto y Luis participarían de la emoción. //

C. Repeat the model sentence and then substitute the new subject you hear. Listen for confirmation of your response.

1. Mis amigos vendrán esta tarde. //
   Mis amigos vendrán esta tarde.

Luis //
Luis vendrá esta tarde.
Yo //
Yo vendré esta tarde.
Alberto y yo //
Alberto y yo vendremos esta tarde.
Las chicas //
Las chicas vendrán esta tarde.

2. Nosotros podremos mirar el partido de fútbol. //
Nosotros podremos mirar el partido de fútbol.
Tú //
Tú podrás mirar el partido de fútbol.
Los muchachos //
Los muchachos podrán mirar el partido de fútbol.
Él //
Él podrá mirar el partido de fútbol.
Usted //
Usted podrá mirar el partido de fútbol.

3. ¿Dirías tú que los Estados Unidos pueden ganar? //
¿Dirías tú que los Estados Unidos pueden ganar?
usted //
¿Diría usted que los Estados Unidos pueden ganar?
ustedes //
¿Dirían ustedes que los Estados Unidos pueden ganar?
él //
¿Diría él que los Estados Unidos pueden ganar?
ellos //
¿Dirían ellos que los Estados Unidos pueden ganar?

4. Nosotros tendríamos una fiesta. //
Nosotros tendríamos una fiesta.
Yo //
Yo tendría una fiesta.
Ellos //
Ellos tendrían una fiesta.
Tú //
Tú tendrías una fiesta.
Ustedes //
Ustedes tendrían una fiesta. //

D. Listen to each statement and confirm the information, using the future tense. Follow the model and listen for confirmation of your response.

MODEL: Llámame para jugar al tenis.
Te llamaré mañana y jugaremos al tenis.

1. Llámame para practicar algún deporte. //
Te llamaré mañana y practicaremos algún deporte.
2. Llámame para hacer el aeróbic en el gimnasio. //
Te llamaré mañana y haremos el aeróbic en el gimnasio.
3. Búscame para correr en el estadio. //
Te buscaré mañana y correremos en el estadio.
4. Búscame para nadar en la piscina de la universidad. //
Te buscaré mañana y nadaremos en la piscina de la universidad.
5. Avísame para buscar una cancha de tenis. //
Te avisaré mañana y buscaremos una cancha de tenis.
6. Avísame para traer las raquetas de tenis. //
Te avisaré mañana y traeremos las raquetas de tenis. //

E. Listen to the question and confirm what is being asked, following the model. Then listen for confirmation of your response.

MODEL: ¿Te dijo Luis si él vendría a ver el partido?
Sí, Luis me dijo que él vendría a ver el partido.

1. ¿Te dijo Luis si su hermana podría venir? //
Sí, Luis me dijo que su hermana podría venir.
2. ¿Te dijo Alberto si él buscaría a las chicas? //
Sí, Alberto me dijo que él buscaría a las chicas.
3. ¿Te avisaron ellos si saldrían a tiempo? //
Sí, ellos me avisaron que saldrían a tiempo.
4. ¿Te dijo Alberto si sus amigos sabrían la dirección? //
Sí, Alberto me dijo que sus amigos sabrían la dirección.
5. ¿Te avisaron ellos si Luis traería las bebidas? //
Sí, ellos me avisaron que Luis traería las bebidas.
6. ¿Te dijeron ellos si él tendría suficiente dinero? //
Sí, ellos me dijeron que él tendría suficiente dinero.
7. ¿Te avisaron las chicas si ellas prepararían unos bocaditos? //
Sí, las chicas me avisaron que ellas prepararían unos bocaditos.
8. ¿Te dijo Alberto si ellos llegarían antes de las dos? //
Sí, Alberto me dijo que ellos llegarían antes de las dos. //

F. Respond to each question, as in the model, implying conjecture. You will hear a confirmation of your response.

MODEL: ¿Sabes si ya son las ocho?
Posiblemente ya serán las ocho.

1. ¿Sabes si Marta ya está en su apartamento? //
Posiblemente ya estará en su apartamento.
2. ¿Sabes si ella estudia ahora? //
Posiblemente estudiará ahora.
3. ¿Sabes si ella tiene exámenes finales? //
Posiblemente tendrá exámenes finales.
4. ¿Sabes si tus amigos salen de excursión mañana? //
Posiblemente saldrán de excursión mañana.
5. ¿Sabes si ellos van a las montañas? //
Posiblemente irán a las montañas.
6. ¿Sabes si ellos se quedan unos días allí? //
Posiblemente se quedarán unos días allí.

MODEL: ¿Salió Alberto con Luis?
Sí, probablemente saldría con Luis.

7. ¿Fue Alberto a ver el juego? //
Sí, probablemente iría a ver el juego.
8. ¿Jugaba el equipo de Luis? //
Sí, probablemente jugaría el equipo de Luis.
9. ¿Llamó Alberto a Jorge? //
Sí, probablemente llamaría a Jorge.
10. ¿Invitaron ellos a las chicas también? //
Sí, probablemente invitarían a las chicas también.
11. ¿Tenían ellos boletos? //
Sí, probablemente tendrían boletos.

12. ¿Salieron ellos a comer después del partido? // //
Sí, probablemente saldrían a comer después del partido. //

Para comprender y escribir

A. From the three choices offered, select the one that best completes the statement or answers the question you hear and circle it.

1. A Luis le encanta el tenis. De verdad es un...
   (a) maní.
   (b) aficionado.
   (c) guía. //
2. Vamos a jugar al fútbol el domingo, pero nos falta un jugador. ¿Quieres estar en...
   (a) la pelota?
   (b) el gimnasio?
   (c) el equipo? //
3. No me gusta hacer el aeróbic. Para ejercicio, prefiero alzar...
   (a) los deportes.
   (b) la natación.
   (c) las pesas. //
4. Soy muy aficionado a los deportes. Me gustaría jugar más al...
   (a) basquetbol.
   (b) estadio.
   (c) timbre. //
5. Ayer el equipo de los Estados Unidos ganó la Copa Mundial.
   (a) ¡Cuánto me alegro!
   (b) ¡No lo sé!
   (c) ¡Me acerco mucho! //

B. Answer the questions affirmatively. Then give an alternate negative response, as in the model.

> MODEL: ¿Van a ir ustedes al juego esta noche o van a regresar a la biblioteca?
> **Nosotros iremos al juego; no regresaremos a la biblioteca.**

1. ¿Van a ir ustedes al cine o van a mirar la televisión? //
2. ¿Van a cenar ustedes en un restaurante o van a comer aquí? //
3. ¿Vas a ir a la fiesta o vas a estudiar? //
4. ¿Vas a salir temprano o vas a llegar tarde? //
5. ¿Van a hacer ellos ejercicio o van a alzar las pesas? //

C. Write contradictions to the statements made, using the conditional, as in the model.

> MODEL: Voy a comprar una casa en México.
> **¡Yo no compraría una casa en México!**

1. Voy a ingresar en la escuela de verano. //
2. Vamos a poner la televisión antes de comenzar el partido. //
3. Van a decir los nombres de los jugadores. //
4. Voy a ir al estadio en bicicleta. //
5. Van a mostrarle las canchas de tenis. //

D. Dictado

You will hear a short narrative about plans Jorge and Alberto have for going to a basketball game. You will hear the narrative three times. Listen the first time. Write what you hear on the lines provided the second time. Make any necessary corrections the third time.

Es sábado que viene, // Jorge y yo iremos al partido de basquetbol. // Yo compraré los boletos // mañana por la mañana. // Jorge y yo saldremos de casa // a las doce menos cuarto. // Tomaremos el almuerzo en la cafetería. // Creo que varios amigos estarán allí también. // Será necesario llegar al estadio // antes de la una y media // porque habrá mucha gente allí para el juego. // Luis dijo que él vendría // a nuestro apartamento a las once. // Yo sabía que él haría eso. // Algunos de los jugadores me dijeron anoche // que sería un partido muy emocionante. // Yo diría eso también. //

End of Lección quince.

Lección 16

Actividades y práctica

A. Repeat the model sentence and then substitute the new subject you hear. Listen for confirmation of your response.

1. Ana se sintió mal anoche. //
   Ana se sintió mal anoche.
   Yo //
   Yo me sentí mal anoche.
   Las chicas //
   Las chicas se sintieron mal anoche.
   Nosotros //
   Nosotros nos sentimos mal anoche.
   Tú //
   Tú te sentiste mal anoche.
2. Ella durmió muy poco. //
   Ella durmió muy poco.
   Nosotras //
   Nosotras dormimos muy poco.
   Yo //
   Yo dormí muy poco.
   Ustedes //
   Ustedes durmieron muy poco.
   Usted //
   Usted durmió muy poco.
3. Ella le pidió algo a la enfermera. //
   Ella le pidió algo a la enfermera.
   Tú //
   Tú le pediste algo a la enfermera.
   Yo //
   Yo le pedí algo a la enfermera.
   Nosotras //
   Nosotras le pedimos algo a la enfermera.
4. Ana se divirtió con la visita de Rita. //
   Ana se divirtió con la visita de Rita.

Nosotros / /
Nosotros nos divertimos con la visita de Rita.
Tú / /
Tú te divertiste con la visita de Rita.
Ustedes / /
Ustedes se divirtieron con la visita de Rita.
Yo / /
Yo me divertí con la visita de Rita.
5. Ellos se rieron mucho. / /
Ellos se rieron mucho.
Ana / /
Ana se rió mucho.
Yo / /
Yo me reí mucho.
Nosotros / /
Nosotros nos reímos mucho.
Tú / /
Tú te reíste mucho. / /

B. Answer each question affirmatively, using a familiar singular command, as in the model. Then listen for confirmation of your response.

MODEL: ¿Compro yo las entradas?
Sí, por favor, compra tú las entradas.

1. ¿Hago yo las reservas? / /
Sí, por favor, haz tú las reservas.
2. ¿Voy yo al estadio? / /
Sí, por favor, ve tú al estadio.
3. ¿Salgo yo ahora? / /
Sí, por favor, sal tú ahora.
4. ¿Devuelvo yo las entradas? / /
Sí, por favor, devuelve tú las entradas.
5. ¿Se lo digo yo a Mario? / /
Sí, por favor, díselo tú a Mario.
6. ¿Le recuerdo yo la fecha? / /
Sí, por favor, recuérdale tú la fecha.
7. ¿Le pido yo el dinero? / /
Sí, por favor, pídele tú el dinero. / /

MODEL: ¿Busco a Carolina ahora o la busco más tarde?
Búscala más tarde; no la busques ahora.

Answer each question affirmatively and then negatively, using familiar commands, as in the model. Then listen for confirmation of your response.

8. ¿Saco las fotos ahora o las saco más tarde? / /
Sácalas más tarde; no las saques ahora.
9. ¿Pago la cuenta ahora o la pago después? / /
Págala después; no la pagues ahora.
10. ¿Toco este disco compacto ahora o lo toco después? / /
Tócalo después; no lo toques ahora.
11. ¿Cruzo la calle ahora o la cruzo después de ese coche? / /
Crúzala después de ese coche; no las cruces ahora.
12. ¿Juego al tenis ahora o juego esta noche? / /
Juega al tenis esta noche; no juegues ahora.
13. ¿Almuerzo ahora o almuerzo con los invitados? / /
Almuerza con los invitados; no almuerces ahora. / /

C. Listen to each infinitive phrase and respond with a familiar command, following the model. Then listen to the correct answer.

MODEL: despertarse ya
Oye, Rita, es muy tarde, ¡despiértate ya!

1. levantarse en seguida / /
Oye, Rita, es muy tarde, ¡levántate en seguida!
2. lavarse la cara rápido / /
Oye, Rita, es muy tarde, ¡lávate la cara rápido!
3. no bañarse ahora / /
Oye, Rita, es muy tarde, ¡no te bañes ahora!
4. no peinarse tanto / /
Oye, Rita, es muy tarde, ¡no te peines tanto!
5. no desayunarse hoy / /
Oye, Rita, es muy tarde, ¡no te desayunes hoy!
6. ponerse la ropa rápido / /
Oye, Rita, es muy tarde, ¡ponte la ropa rápido!
7. no arreglarse mucho / /
Oye, Rita, es muy tarde, ¡no te arregles mucho!
8. no afeitarse las piernas hoy / /
Oye, Rita, es muy tarde, ¡no te afeites las piernas hoy! / /

D. Compare life in your hometown or city to life in the place where you are now living. Answer each question following the model. You will hear a confirmation of your response.

MODEL: ¿Es agradable la vida en tu ciudad?
Sí, la vida en mi ciudad es más agradable que la vida aquí.

1. ¿Es interesante la vida en tu ciudad? / /
Sí, la vida en mi ciudad es más interesante que la vida aquí.
2. ¿Son caros los restaurantes allí? / /
Sí, los restaurantes allí son más caros que los restaurantes aquí.
3. ¿Es buena la comida allí? / /
Sí, la comida allí es mejor que la comida aquí.
4. ¿Son baratas las tiendas en tu ciudad? / /
Sí, las tiendas en mi ciudad son más baratas que las tiendas aquí.
5. ¿Es fina la ropa allí? / /
Sí, la ropa allí es más fina que la ropa aquí.
6. ¿Son buenos los conciertos en tu ciudad? / /
Sí, los conciertos en mi ciudad son mejores que los conciertos aquí. / /

E. Repeat the model sentence and then substitute each new element you hear. You will hear a confirmation of your response.

1. Este apartamento no es tan grande como aquél. / /
Este apartamento no es tan grande como aquél.
Estas casas / /
Estas casas no son tan grandes como aquéllas.
Estos cuartos / /
Estos cuartos no son tan grandes como aquéllos.

Esta universidad / /
Esta universidad no es tan grande como aquélla.
Este hospital / /
Este hospital no es tan grande como aquél.
2. Yo no tengo tanto tiempo como tú. / /
Yo no tengo tanto tiempo como tú.
calor / /
Yo no tengo tanto calor como tú.
hambre / /
Yo no tengo tanta hambre como tú.
clases / /
Yo no tengo tantas clases como tú.
amigas / /
Yo no tengo tantas amigas como tú.
3. Hay tantos estudiantes como profesores. / /
Hay tantos estudiantes como profesores.
enfermeras/médicos / /
Hay tantas enfermeras como médicos.
chicos/chicas / /
Hay tantos chicos como chicas.
comida/bebidas / /
Hay tanta comida como bebidas.
vino/cerveza / /
Hay tanto vino como cerveza.
4. Lola habla el inglés tan bien como tú. / /
Lola habla el inglés tan bien como tú.
mal / /
Lola habla el inglés tan mal como tú.
claro / /
Lola habla el inglés tan claro como tú.
rápido / /
Lola habla el inglés tan rápido como tú.
despacio / /
Lola habla el inglés tan despacio como tú.
5. Yo me divierto tanto como ustedes. / /
Yo me divierto tanto como ustedes.
trabajo / /
Yo trabajo tanto como ustedes.
estudio / /
Yo estudio tanto como ustedes.
juego / /
Yo juego tanto como ustedes.
viajo / /
Yo viajo tanto como ustedes. / /

F. Answer each question affirmatively, using the absolute superlative. Follow the model and then listen for confirmation of your answer.

MODEL: ¿Era grande el teatro?
Sí, el teatro era grandísimo.

1. ¿Fue bueno el concierto? / /
Sí, el concierto fue buenísimo.
2. ¿Era famoso el cantante? / /
Sí, el cantante era famosísimo.
3. ¿Eran populares las canciones? / /
Sí, las canciones eran popularísimas.
4. ¿Eran divertidos tus amigos? / /
Sí, mis amigos eran divertidísimos. / /

Para comprender y escribir

A. From the three choices offered, select the one that best completes the statement or answers the question you hear and circle it.

1. Oye, parece que no puedes andar muy bien. ¿Te pasa algo en...
(a) el tobillo?
(b) el cuello?
(c) la nariz? / /
2. Esta noche voy a comer muy poco. Me duele mucho...
(a) la rodilla.
(b) la garganta.
(c) la oreja. / /
3. No puedo escribir bien porque ayer me lastimé...
(a) los pulmones.
(b) las piernas.
(c) los dedos. / /
4. Mi mamá no puede tomar penicilina porque es...
(a) enfermera.
(b) alérgica.
(c) divertida. / /
5. Creo que tengo todos los síntomas de un resfriado:
(a) tos, fiebre y dolor de cabeza.
(b) píldoras, paciencia y congestión.
(c) jarabe, penicilina y sueño. / /

B. Answer the first question you hear negatively and the second question affirmatively, as in the model.

MODEL: ¿Dormiste bien anoche?
No, no dormí bien.
¿Y tu compañero de cuarto?
Él sí durmió bien.

1. ¿Sentiste frío anoche? / /
¿Y tu compañera de cuarto? / /
2. ¿Pediste otra manta? / /
¿Y tu compañero de cuarto? / /
3. ¿Sintieron calor ustedes? / /
¿Y tus amigos? / /
4. ¿Pidieron ustedes una habitación con aire acondicionado? / /
¿Y Jaime? / /
5. ¿Se divirtieron ustedes en el cine? / /
¿Y Laura? / /
6. ¿Se rieron ustedes mucho con la película? / /
¿Y Luis? / /

C. Answer each question first with an affirmative command and then with a negative command, as in the model.

MODEL: ¿Busco a Carolina más tarde o la busco ahora?
Búscala más tarde; no la busques ahora.

1. ¿Saco las fotos más tarde o las saco ahora? / /
2. ¿Pago la cuenta después o la pago ahora? / /
3. ¿Toco este disco compacto más tarde o lo toco ahora? / /
4. ¿Cruzo la calle después de ese coche o la cruzo ahora? / /
5. ¿Juego al tenis más tarde o juego ahora? / /

6. ¿Almuerzo en un restaurante o almuerzo en la cafetería? / /

D. Dictado

You will hear a short narrative about a visit Rita and Jaime made to a friend in the hospital. You will hear the narrative three times. Listen the first time. Write what you hear the second time. Make any necessary corrections the third time.

Un domingo, después de asistir a misa, / / Rita y Jaime fueron al hospital / / a visitar a una amiga suya. / / Ana se puso muy contenta / / cuando vio a sus amigos. / / Rita le dio a Ana unas flores / / que le habían traído. / / Ana les dijo a Rita y a Jaime / / que le dolía todo el cuerpo: / / la espalda, la garganta y el pecho. / / También tenía mucha fiebre y mucha tos. / / El médico le había recetado un jarabe / / y unas gotas para la nariz. / / A Ana no le divierte estar en el hospital / / y espera mejorarse pronto. / /

End of **Lección dieciséis.**

Lección 17
Actividades y práctica

A. Repeat the model sentence and then substitute each new subject in the dependent clause. You will hear a confirmation of your response.

1. Quiero que tú hables conmigo sobre la lista de regalos. / /
   Quiero que tú hables conmigo sobre la lista de regalos.
   Jaime / /
   Quiero que Jaime hable conmigo sobre la lista de regalos.
   ellas / /
   Quiero que ellas hablen conmigo sobre la lista de regalos.
   usted / /
   Quiero que usted hable conmigo sobre la lista de regalos.
2. Preferimos que ustedes dedican la fecha de la boda. / /
   Preferimos que ustedes decidan la fecha de la boda.
   tú / /
   Preferimos que tú decidas la fecha de la boda.
   Silvia / /
   Preferimos que Silvia decida la fecha de la boda.
   sus hermanas / /
   Preferimos que sus hermanas decidan la fecha de la boda.
3. Insisten en que yo escriba las invitaciones. / /
   Insisten en que yo escriba las invitaciones.
   ellos / /
   Insisten en que ellos escriban las invitaciones.
   nosotros / /
   Insisten en que nosotros escribamos las invitaciones.
   tú / /
   Insisten en que tú escribas las invitaciones.

4. Sugieren que Silvia vaya a la iglesia hoy. / /
   Sugieren que Silvia vaya a la iglesia hoy.
   yo / /
   Sugieren que yo vaya a la iglesia hoy.
   nosotros / /
   Sugieren que nosotros vayamos a la iglesia hoy.
   ustedes / /
   Sugieren que ustedes vayan a la iglesia hoy. / /

B. Repeat the model sentence and then substitute each new verb phrase you hear. Don't forget to conjugate the verb! You will hear a confirmation of your response.

1. Quiero que Silvia esté contenta. / /
   Quiero que Silvia esté contenta.
   ser feliz / /
   Quiero que Silvia sea feliz.
   volver pronto / /
   Quiero que Silvia vuelva pronto.
   conocer a mis padres / /
   Quiero que Silvia conozca a mis padres.
2. Prefiero que ustedes nos den otra cosa. / /
   Prefiero que ustedes nos den otra cosa.
   traer flores / /
   Prefiero que ustedes nos traigan flores.
   hacer una lista de regalos / /
   Prefiero que ustedes nos hagan una lista de regalos.
   buscar un apartamento / /
   Prefiero que ustedes nos busquen un apartamento.
3. Nos recomiendan que vayamos hoy. / /
   Nos recomiendan que vayamos hoy.
   estar allí temprano / /
   Nos recomiendan que estemos allí temprano.
   salir ahora / /
   Nos recomiendan que salgamos ahora.
   ver otro apartamento / /
   Nos recomiendan que veamos otro apartamento. / /

C. Respond negatively to each statement you hear, recommending that the person not do the action. Follow the model and then listen for confirmation of your answer.

> MODEL: Sabes, nosotros queremos tener una casa grande.
> **Mira, les recomiendo que no tengan una casa grande.**

1. Sabes, nosotros queremos alquilar un apartamento pequeño. / /
   Mira, les recomiendo que no alquilen un apartamento pequeño.
2. Sabes, nosotros vamos a hacer una cita con el dueño. / /
   Mira, les recomiendo que no hagan una cita con el dueño.
3. Sabes, nosotros necesitamos comprar unos muebles baratos. / /
   Mira, les recomiendo que no compren unos muebles baratos.

4. Sabes, voy a llevar el estéreo a la fiesta. //
   Mira, te recomiendo que no lleves el estéreo a la fiesta.
5. Sabes, voy a traer la videograbadora a clase. //
   Mira, te recomiendo que no traigas la videograbadora a clase.
6. Sabes, voy a vender el ordenador. //
   Mira, te recomiendo que no vendas el ordenador. //

D. Answer the first question you hear negatively and the second one affirmatively. Follow the model and listen for confirmation of your response.

> MODEL: ¿Le escribo la carta a su madre?
> **No, le ruego a usted que no le escriba la carta a ella.**
> ¿Y a su padre?
> **Sí, prefiero que usted le escriba a él.**

1. ¿Le aviso la fecha a su hermano? //
   No, le ruego a usted que no le avise la fecha a él.
   ¿Y a su hermana? //
   Sí, prefiero que usted le avise la fecha a ella.
2. ¿Le pido el dinero a Rita? //
   No, le ruego a usted que no le pida el dinero a ella.
   ¿Y a Jaime? //
   Sí, prefiero que usted le pida el dinero a él.
3. ¿Le digo la verdad a él? //
   No, le ruego a usted que no le diga la verdad a él.
   ¿Y a ella? //
   Sí, prefiero que usted le diga la verdad a ella.
4. ¿Le entrego el cheque a la dueña? //
   No, le ruego a usted que no le entregue el cheque a ella.
   ¿Y al gerente? //
   Sí, prefiero que usted le entregue el cheque a él.
5. ¿Le doy los regalos a Alberto? //
   No, le ruego a usted que no le dé los regalos a él.
   ¿Y a Silvia? //
   Sí, prefiero que usted le dé los regalos a ella.
6. ¿Le muestro la casa a Jorge? //
   No, le ruego a usted que no le muestre la casa a él.
   ¿Y a Mario? //
   Sí, prefiero que usted le muestre la casa a él. //

E. Respond affirmatively to each statement you hear, following the model. Then listen for confirmation of your response.

> MODEL: Oye, Alberto insiste en que conoce el barrio.
> **Sí, y él insiste en que yo conozca el barrio también.**

1. Oye, Jaime me dice que va a ver el apartamento. //
   Sí, y él me dice que yo vaya a ver el apartamento también.
2. Oye, Juan me escribe que asiste al concierto. //
   Sí, y él me escribe que yo asista al concierto también.
3. Oye, Elena me avisa que ella traerá unas bebidas. //
   Sí, y ella me avisa que yo traiga unas bebidas también.
4. Oye, Juan me dice que va a alquilar unos muebles. //
   Sí, y él me dice que yo alquile unos muebles también.
5. Oye, Luisa insiste en que va a almorzar temprano. //
   Sí, y ella insiste en que yo almuerce temprano también. //

Para comprender y escribir

A. From the three choices offered, select the one that best completes the statement or answers the question you hear and circle it.

1. Mañana vamos a ir al almacén para comprar...
   (a) un gerente.
   (b) un apartamento.
   (c) una batidora. //
2. ¡Este apartamento me encanta! ¿Sabes cuánto es...
   (a) la ganga?
   (b) el alquiler?
   (c) la almohada? //
3. Tengo ganas de conocer mejor el barrio. ¿Quieres dar...
   (a) un paseo?
   (b) un mantel?
   (c) una plancha? //
4. ¡Qué regalo tan bonito nos trajiste!
   (a) ¡Cuántas cosas quieres...!
   (b) ¡Eres un encanto!
   (c) ¡Qué barbaridad! //
5. La sala ya está casi completamente amueblada, pero nos hace falta todavía...
   (a) un dueño.
   (b) una tostadora.
   (c) un sillón. //

B. Write an answer to the question, saying you don't want it to happen yet, as in the model.

> MODEL: ¿Puedo regresar ahora?
> **No, no quiero que regreses todavía.**

1. ¿Puedo salir ahora? //
2. ¿Puedo ir ahora? //
3. ¿Puedo llamar ahora? //
4. ¿Podemos entrar ahora? //
5. ¿Podemos jugar al tenis ahora? //
6. ¿Podemos venir ahora? //

C. Answer each question negatively and then affirmatively, following the models.

> MODELS: ¿Quieres verlo tú?
> **No, no quiero verlo; quiero que tú lo veas.**
> ¿Quieren verlo ustedes?
> **No, no queremos verlo; queremos que ustedes lo vean.**

1. ¿Quieres conocerlo tú? //
2. ¿Quieren saberlo ustedes? //
3. ¿Deseas invitarlas tú? //
4. ¿Desean traerlos ustedes? //
5. ¿Prefieres hacerlo tú? //
6. ¿Prefieren tenerla ustedes? //

D. Dictado

You will hear a short narrative about Silvia and Alberto's marriage plans. You will hear the narrative three times. Listen the first time. Write what you hear on the lines provided the second time. Make any necessary corrections the third time.

Silvia y Alberto han decidido casarse // este verano. // Están buscando un apartamento; // quieren que esté amueblado // y que sea pequeño y barato. // Silvia le muestra a su novio // la lista de aparatos que necesitan // para su casa. // Algunos de los artículos son // una batidora, una cafetera y una tostadora. // También necesitan sábanas y mantas // para la cama. // Alberto le sugiere a Silvia // que ponga los artículos // en la lista de regalos // que tienen en los almacenes. //

End of **Lección diecisiete**.

Lección 18

Actividades y práctica

A. Repeat the model sentence and then substitute the cue you hear. You will hear a confirmation of your response.

1. Yo no creo que tú y yo lleguemos a tiempo. //
   Yo no creo que tú y yo lleguemos a tiempo.
   que ustedes //
   Yo no creo que ustedes lleguen a tiempo.
   que tú //
   Yo no creo que tú llegues a tiempo.
   que ella //
   Yo no creo que ella llegue a tiempo.
   que ellos //
   Yo no creo que ellos lleguen a tiempo.
2. Ellos esperan que tú busques a la policía. //
   Ellos esperan que tú busques a la policía.
   que nosotros //
   Ellos esperan que nosotros busquemos a la policía.
   que usted //
   Ellos esperan que usted busque a la policía.
   que yo //
   Ellos esperan que yo busque a la policía.
   que Roberto //
   Ellos esperan que Roberto busque a la policía.
3. Roberto duda que la conferencia empiece a tiempo. //
   Roberto duda que la conferencia empiece a tiempo.
   que las clases //
   Roberto duda que las clases empiecen a tiempo.
   que ustedes //
   Roberto duda que ustedes empiecen a tiempo.
   que tú //
   Roberto duda que tú empieces a tiempo.
   que nosotros //
   Roberto duda que nosotros empecemos a tiempo.
4. Yo me alegro de que ese taxista no siga adelante. //
   Yo me alegro de que ese taxista no siga adelante.
   que ustedes //
   Yo me alegro de que ustedes no sigan adelante.

que nosotros //
Yo me alegro de que nosotros no sigamos adelante.
que usted //
Yo me alegro de que usted no siga adelante.
que ellos //
Yo me alegro de que ellos no sigan adelante. //

B. Contradict each statement you hear, using **dudo que** or **no estoy seguro de que**. Follow the models and listen for confirmation of your response.

MODELS: Yo creo que la conferencia empezará a las cuatro.
Yo dudo que la conferencia empiece a las cuatro.
Yo estoy seguro de que la conferencia empezará a las cuatro.
Yo no estoy seguro de que la conferencia empiece a las cuatro.

1. Yo creo que el economista hablará en español. //
   Yo dudo que el economista hable en español.
2. Yo estoy seguro de que será una buena conferencia. //
   Yo no estoy seguro de que sea una buena conferencia.
3. Yo creo que tenemos que asistir. //
   Yo dudo que tengamos que asistir.
4. Yo estoy seguro de que habrá mucha gente. //
   Yo no estoy seguro de que haya mucha gente.
5. Yo creo que debemos hacer un resumen. //
   Yo dudo que debamos hacer un resumen.
6. Yo estoy seguro de que podré comprender todo. //
   Yo no estoy seguro de que pueda comprender todo. //

C. Listen to each sentence and then form a new one, using a subjunctive construction. Follow the model and listen for confirmation of your response.

MODEL: No le permitas a Isabel salir sólo con norteamericanos.
No le permitas a Isabel que salga sólo con norteamericanos.

1. No le permitas a Isabel hablar en inglés. //
   No le permitas a Isabel que hable en inglés.
2. Yo te aconsejo practicar más con ella. //
   Yo te aconsejo que practiques más con ella.
3. Yo les recomiendo a ustedes asistir a conferencias. //
   Yo les recomiendo a ustedes que asistan a conferencias.
4. Yo les sugiero a ellos leer más en español. //
   Yo les sugiero a ellos que lean más en español.
5. Déjalas a ellas escribir el resumen. //
   Déjalas a ellas que escriban el resumen.
6. Permítanme ustedes sugerirles algunas ideas. //
   Permítanme ustedes que les sugiera algunas ideas. //

D. Respond negatively to each command you hear and say that José should do the action. Follow the model and listen for the correct answer.

MODEL: Empiécelo usted.
Yo no puedo; que lo empiece José.

1. Tráigalo usted. //
   Yo no puedo; que lo traiga José.
2. Búsquelos usted. //
   Yo no puedo; que los busque José.
3. Organícela usted. //
   Yo no puedo; que la organice José.
4. Sírvalas usted. //
   Yo no puedo; que las sirva José.
5. Páguelas usted. //
   Yo no puedo; que las pague José.
6. Alquílelo usted. //
   Yo no puedo; que lo alquile José. //

E. Listen to the questions. Respond affirmatively to the first question and negatively to the second group. Use **nosotros** commands and follow the models. Then listen for confirmation of your response.

> MODELS: ¿Pagamos la cuenta?
> **Sí, paguémosla.**
> ¿Que le parece a usted? ¿La pagamos?
> **No, no la paguemos.**

1. ¿Tomamos el autobús? //
   Sí, tomémoslo.
   ¿Qué le parece a usted? ¿Lo tomamos? //
   No, no lo tomemos.
2. ¿Visitamos el barrio? //
   Sí, visitémoslo.
   ¿Qué le parece a usted? ¿Lo visitamos? //
   No, no lo visitemos.
3. ¿Buscamos al gerente? //
   Sí, busquémoslo.
   ¿Qué le parece a usted? ¿Lo buscamos? //
   No, no lo busquemos.
4. ¿Alquilamos el apartamento? //
   Sí, alquilémoslo.
   ¿Qué le parece a usted? ¿Lo alquilamos? //
   No, no lo alquilemos.
5. ¿Le entregamos un cheque? //
   Sí, entreguémoselo.
   ¿Qué le parece a usted? ¿Se lo entregamos? //
   No, no se lo entreguemos.
6. ¿Compramos los muebles? //
   Sí, comprémoslos.
   ¿Qué le parece a usted? ¿Los compramos? //
   No, no los compremos. //

F. Listen to the question and respond with an expression of hope, following the model. You will hear a confirmation of your response.

> MODEL: ¿Sabes si los chicos llegaron ya?
> **Espero que hayan llegado.**

1. ¿Sabes si tus amigos salieron ya? //
   Espero que hayan salido.
2. ¿Sabes si sus padres volvieron ya? //
   Espero que hayan vuelto.
3. ¿Sabes si su prima vino ya? //
   Espero que haya venido.

4. ¿Sabes si tu compañero se despertó ya? //
   Espero que se haya despertado.
5. ¿Sabes si Ana se arregló ya? //
   Espero que se haya arreglado.
6. ¿Sabes si Mario se afeitó ya? //
   Espero que se haya afeitado. //

Para comprender y escribir

A. From the three choices offered, select the one that best completes the statement or answers the question you hear and circle it.

1. Cuando hay un accidente grave, ¿qué debemos hacer?
   (a) Buscar un taxista.
   (b) Seguir adelante.
   (c) Avisar a la policía. //
2. Este autobús no va a salir a tiempo porque no hay...
   (a) un herido.
   (b) un conductor.
   (c) un carro. //
3. Los comentarios sobre la conferencia han sido muy buenos.
   (a) ¡Cuánto me alegro!
   (b) ¡Cuánto me canso!
   (c) ¡Cuánto me preocupa! //
4. Parece que la persona que manejaba no pudo parar.
   (a) Le fallarían los frenos.
   (b) Seguramente moderó la marcha.
   (c) Tendría que esperar mucho. //
5. —Por favor, necesito tu ayuda. El carro no funciona.
   — Sí, parece que ha tenido...
   (a) un volante.
   (b) un apuro.
   (c) una avería. //

B. Write a new sentence using the subjunctive in the dependent clause, as in the model.

> MODEL: Juan va a la conferencia. (Me alegro de que)
> **Me alegro de que Juan vaya a la conferencia.**

1. El profesor Ramos va a darnos una conferencia. (Nos alegramos de que) //
2. Inés viene a la conferencia con nosotros. (Me gusta que) //
3. Juan llegará temprano. (Estamos contentos de que) //
4. Roberto almuerza en la cafetería. (No me extraña que) //
5. Ellos no hablarán en español. (Sentimos que) //
6. Los señores Soto no se divierten. (Temo que) //
7. Alberto nunca dice la verdad. (Nos molesta que) //
8. Tú tendrás unas vacaciones magníficas. (Espero que) //

C. Respond in writing to the question you hear, using a logical statement such as **¡Cuánto me alegro de que...!**, **Me extraña que...**, **Siento mucho que...**, or **Me molesta que...**

1. ¡Sabes que Silvia se casa con Alberto! //
2. ¡Sabes ustedes que Ana está en el hospital! //

3. ¡Sabes que mi novia llega mañana! //
4. ¡Saben ustedes que Juan ya no me escribe! //
5. ¡Sabes tú que Marta no me ha llamado! //
6. ¡Saben ustedes que nosotros hemos conseguido el apartamento! //
7. ¡Sabes tú que mis amigos han tenido un choque! //
8. ¡Saben ustedes que mi familia no me ha dicho nada! //

D. Dictado

You will hear a short description of Silvia and Alberto's problems. You will hear the passage three times. Listen the first time. Write what you hear the second time. Make any necessary corrections the third time.

Silvia y Alberto quizás se casen // el verano próximo, // pero yo lo dudo. // Ella necesita volver a su país // y los padres de Alberto // esperan que él siga sus estudios de medicina. // Me extraña mucho // que ellos tengan tantos problemas, // porque creo que ellos son muy felices. // A Alberto no le gusta que Silvia vuelva a su país. // También le molesta que sus padres no lo comprendan. // Yo espero ver a Silvia mañana // y le diré que se quede. // No creo que ella me haga mucho caso, // pero dudo que Alberto la deje ir. // ¡Yo creo que sólo ellos deben decidir sus vidas! //

End of Lección dieciocho.

Lección 19

Actividades y práctica

A. Repeat the model sentence and then substitute each cue you hear. You will hear a confirmation of your response.

1. Juan conduce muy bien. //
   Juan conduce muy bien.
   Yo //
   Yo conduzco muy bien.
   Tú //
   Tú conduces muy bien.
   Mis hermanos //
   Mis hermanos conducen muy bien.
   Ustedes //
   Ustedes conducen muy bien.
2. Miguel tradujo la carta. //
   Miguel tradujo la carta.
   Las secretarias //
   Las secretarias tradujeron la carta.
   Nosotros //
   Nosotros tradujimos la carta.
   Yo //
   Yo traduje la carta.
   Tú //
   Tú tradujiste la carta.
3. Es necesario que ustedes produzcan más. //
   Es necesario que ustedes produzcan más.
   que tú //
   Es necesario que tú produzcas más.

que nosotros //
Es necesario que nosotros produzcamos más.
que la compañía //
Es necesario que la compañía produzca más.
que usted //
Es necesario que usted produzca más. //

B. You will hear a statement followed by a question. Listen carefully and then respond with the appropriate impersonal expression and a verb in the indicative or the subjunctive, as in the model. You will hear a confirmation of your response.

> MODEL: Oigo decir que Carmen vuelve mañana. ¿Es verdad?
> **Sí, es verdad que Carmen vuelve mañana.**

1. Oigo decir que Miguel se gradúa. ¿Es posible? //
   Sí, es posible que Miguel se gradúe.
2. Oigo decir que él no recibirá la beca. ¿Es cierto? //
   Sí, es cierto que él no recibirá la beca.
3. Oigo decir que ustedes lo ayudarán. ¿Es urgente? //
   Sí, es urgente que nosotros lo ayudemos.
4. Oigo decir que a ellos les interesa el puesto. ¿Es probable? //
   Sí, es probable que a ellos les interese el puesto.
5. Oigo decir que los candidatos son bilingües. ¿Es importante? //
   Sí, es importante que los candidatos sean bilingües.
6. Oigo decir que hay muchos puestos vacantes. Eso es dudoso, ¿verdad? //
   Sí, es dudoso que haya muchos puestos vacantes.
7. Oigo decir que Miguel no tiene una entrevista allí. Es una lástima, ¿verdad? //
   Sí, es una lástima que Miguel no tenga una entrevista allí.
8. Oigo decir que sus profesores lo recomendarán. ¿Es necesario? //
   Sí, es necesario que sus profesores lo recomienden. //

C. You will hear two separate sentences. Combine them into one sentence, using the relative pronoun **que**. Follow the model and listen for confirmation of your response.

> MODEL: Juan tiene trabajo. Es estupendo.
> **El trabajo que Juan tiene es estupendo.**

1. El nuevo jefe comienza mañana. Es amigo suyo. //
   El nuevo jefe que comienza mañana es amigo suyo.
2. Las solicitudes llegaron ayer. Son excelentes. //
   Las solicitudes que llegaron ayer son excelentes.
3. La candidata está de visita. Es muy competente. //
   La candidata que está de visita es muy competente.
4. Los empleados son de Puerto Rico. Son muy trabajadores. //
   Los empleados que son de Puerto Rico son muy trabajadores. //

Now combine the two sentences, using **quien** or **quienes**, following the model.

MODEL: Conocimos a la ingeniera. Es muy
inteligente.
**Conocimos a la ingeniera, quien es muy
inteligente.**

5. Conocí al dueño de la fábrica. Es una persona muy
rica. //
**Conocí al dueño de la fábrica, quien es una persona
muy rica.**
6. Llamé al señor Ruiz. Es un importante hombre de
negocios. //
**Llamé al señor Ruiz, quien es un importante hombre
de negocios.**
7. Saludamos al gerente. Es un ingeniero agrícola. //
Saludamos al gerente, quien es un ingeniero agrícola.
8. Conocimos a los empleados. Son muy competentes. //
**Conocimos a los empleados, quienes son muy
competentes. //**

Now combine the two sentences, using **el cual, la cual,
los cuales,** or **las cuales,** following the model.

MODEL: El padre de Ana es médico. Estudió en esta
universidad.
**El padre de Ana, el cual es médico,
estudió en esta universidad.**

9. Mi hermano es estudiante de ingeniería. Se gradúa
pronto. //
**Mi hermano, el cual es estudiante de ingeniería, se
gradúa pronto.**
10. Mis compañeras de trabajo son bilingües. Ellas han
abierto una agencia de empleo. //
**Mis compañeras de trabajo, las cuales son bilingües,
han abierto una agencia de empleo.**
11. Sus tíos son abogados. Tienen su oficina en San Juan. //
**Sus tíos, los cuales son abogados, tienen su oficina en
San Juan.**
12. La secretaria de mi novio busca trabajo. Ha tenido varias
entrevistas. //
**La secretaria de mi novio, la cual busca trabajo, ha
tenido varias entrevistas. //**

D. Confirm each of the statements you hear, as in the
model. Then listen for the correct answer.

MODEL: Ellos buscan una casa, pero debe ser grande.
Es cierto; buscan una casa que sea grande.

1. Silvia y Alberto buscan un apartamento, pero debe estar
en un buen barrio. //
**Es cierto; buscan un apartamento que esté en un buen
barrio.**
2. Mis amigos necesitan una habitación, pero debe tener
aire acondicionado. //
**Es cierto; tus amigos necesitan una habitación que
tenga aire acondicionado.**
3. Mi familia quiere comprar un carro nuevo, pero no debe
ser caro. //
**Es cierto; tu familia quiere comprar un carro que no
sea caro.**

4. El señor Ruiz busca un ingeniero agrícola, pero debe
hablar español. //
**Es cierto; el señor Ruiz busca un ingeniero agrícola
que hable español.**
5. Su compañía necesita una secretaria, pero debe saber
traducir bien el español. //
**Es cierto; su compañía necesita una secretaria que
sepa traducir bien el español.**
6. Nosotros buscamos a alguien, pero debe entender de
ordenadores. //
**Es cierto; ustedes buscan a alguien que entienda de
ordenadores.**
7. La sucursal de San Juan busca a alguien, pero debe
conocer la isla. //
**Es cierto; la sucursal de San Juan busca a alguien que
conozca la isla.**
8. Nosotros necesitamos a alguien, pero debe entender de
negocios. //
**Es cierto; ustedes necesitan a alguien que entienda de
negocios. //**

E. Listen to the question and the cue. Respond according to
the model, then listen for the correct answer.

MODEL: ¿Cuánto tiempo hace que ustedes esperan
aquí? ¿Una hora?
Sí, esperamos aquí desde hace una hora.

1. ¿Cuánto tiempo hace que ustedes están en los Estados
Unidos? ¿Mucho tiempo? //
**Sí, estamos en los Estados Unidos desde hace mucho
tiempo.**
2. ¿Cuánto tiempo hace que usted la conoce? ¿Poco
tiempo? //
Sí, la conozco desde hace poco tiempo.
3. ¿Cuánto tiempo hace que ustedes son amigos? ¿Varias
semanas? //
Sí, somos amigos desde hace varias semanas.
4. ¿Cuánto tiempo hace que ella no regresa a su país? ¿Un
año? //
Sí, ella no regresa a su país desde hace un año. //

Now respond to these questions and cues, following the
model. Listen for the correct answer.

MODEL: ¿Cuánto tiempo hace que estudias español?
¿Unos meses?
Sí, hace unos meses que estudio español.

5. ¿Cuánto tiempo hace que vives en esta ciudad? ¿Poco
tiempo? //
Sí, hace poco tiempo que vivo en esta ciudad.
6. ¿Cuánto tiempo hace que no vas a tu casa? ¿Unas
semanas? //
Sí, hace unas semanas que no voy a mi casa.
7. ¿Cuánto tiempo hace que no llamas a tu familia? ¿Unos
días? //
Sí, hace unos días que no llamo a mi familia.

8. ¿Cuánto tiempo hace que no recibes noticias de tu mejor amigo? ¿Mucho tiempo? //
   Sí, hace mucho tiempo que no recibo noticias de mi mejor amigo. //

F. Answer each question affirmatively, as in the model. Then listen for confirmation of your response.

> MODEL: Yo vi a Miguel pasar por el corredor. ¿Y tú?
> **Yo también vi a Miguel cuando él pasaba por el corredor.**

1. Yo vi a Marta bailar el merengue. ¿Y tú? //
   Yo también vi a Marta cuando ella bailaba el merengue.
2. Nosotros vimos a Silvia y Alberto bailar salsa. ¿Y ustedes? //
   Nosotros también vimos a Silvia y Alberto cuando ellos bailaban salsa.
3. Yo oí a Ana cantar en la fiesta. ¿Y tú? //
   Yo también oí a Ana cuando ella cantaba en la fiesta.
4. Nosotros oímos a Miguel Bosé cantar esa canción. ¿Y ustedes? //
   Nosotros también oímos a Miguel Bosé cuando él cantaba esa canción.
5. Yo escuché al profesor dar la conferencia. ¿Y tú? //
   Yo también escuché al profesor cuando él daba la conferencia.
6. Ellos vieron a los heridos llegar al hospital. ¿Y ustedes? //
   Nosotros también vimos a los heridos cuando ellos llegaban al hospital.
7. La familia oyó a los policías hablar del accidente. ¿Y ustedes? //
   Nosotros también oímos a los policías cuando ellos hablaban del accidente.
8. Nosotros escuchamos a la gente contar lo que pasó. ¿Y tú? //
   Yo también escuché a la gente cuando contaba lo que pasó. //

Para comprender y escribir

A. From the three choices offered, select the one that best completes the statement or answers the question you hear.

1. Hace cinco años que trabajo con esta compañía. Es hora que me den...
   (a) un asunto.
   (b) un ascenso.
   (c) un agente. //
2. Para que puedas terminar tus estudios, quizás la universidad pueda ofrecerte...
   (a) una beca.
   (b) un empleado.
   (c) una sucursal. //
3. No le gustan las entrevistas. Cada vez que tiene una entrevista,...
   (a) hace una recomendación.
   (b) se gradúa de ingeniero.
   (c) se pone nervioso. //

4. Una persona que trabaja con maquinaria agrícola es...
   (a) una empresa.
   (b) un ingeniero.
   (c) un negocio. //

B. Write a new sentence using the cues you hear, as in the model.

> MODEL: Es bueno trabajar. (que ustedes)
> **Es bueno que ustedes trabajen.**

1. Es difícil ver al señor Ruiz. (que ustedes) //
2. Es importante graduarse de la universidad. (que nosotros) //
3. Es más fácil aprender el español en Puerto Rico. (que yo) //
4. Es mejor hacer la solicitud ya. (que ustedes) //
5. Es imposible traducir estos versos. (que la señorita White) //
6. Es necesario ser bilingüe. (que el candidato) //
7. Es preciso escribir la carta ya. (que tú) //
8. Es posible conseguir un buen trabajo. (que yo) //

C. Combine the two sentences you hear, using **a quien** or **a quienes**, as in the model.

> MODEL: Vimos a la joven. Es española.
> **La joven a quien vimos es española.**

1. Él conoce a aquella chica. Es una estudiante de esta universidad. //
2. Llamé al señor. Es el gerente de la empresa. //
3. Saludamos a aquellas jóvenes. Son secretarias de esta compañía. //
4. Conocí a aquel señor. Es un ingeniero que trabaja en Puerto Rico. //

D. Dictado

You will hear a short narrative about a letter the director of the School of Agricultural Engineering received and what he plans on doing with it. You will hear the passage three times. Listen the first time. Write what you hear the second time. Make any necessary corrections the third time.

El director de la Escuela de Ingeniería Agrícola // acaba de recibir una carta // del señor Ruiz, // gerente de una compañía // que tiene una sucursal en Puerto Rico. // El señor Ruiz // le pregunta si el director conoce a alguien // que pueda trabajar como agente en la isla. // Cuando su secretaria, la señorita White, // ve pasar a Miguel Ramos, // lo llama y comienza a hablarle // sobre la carta. // El director cree que es posible // que le interese el puesto. // Miguel, // que se graduará de ingeniero en junio, // le contesta que será necesario // que él encuentre trabajo pronto. //

End of **Lección diecinueve.**

Lección 20

Actividades y práctica

A. Repeat the model sentence and then substitute each new subject. You will hear a confirmation of your response.

1. Alberto escoge un vuelo directo. //
   Alberto escoge un vuelo directo.
   Yo //
   Yo escojo un vuelo directo.
   Carlos y yo //
   Carlos y yo escogemos un vuelo directo.
   Usted //
   Usted escoge un vuelo directo.
   Ellos //
   Ellos escogen un vuelo directo.
2. La agencia de viajes les envía los boletos. //
   La agencia de viajes les envía los boletos.
   Nosotros //
   Nosotros les enviamos los boletos.
   Tú //
   Tú les envías los boletos.
   Yo //
   Yo les envío los boletos.
   Ustedes //
   Ustedes les envían los boletos.
3. Ellos continúan el viaje hasta Cuzco. //
   Ellos continúan el viaje hasta Cuzco.
   Ramón //
   Ramón continúa el viaje hasta Cuzco.
   Alberto y Silvia //
   Alberto y Silvia continúan el viaje hasta Cuzco.
   Yo //
   Yo continúo el viaje hasta Cuzco.
   Nosotros //
   Nosotros continuamos el viaje hasta Cuzco.
4. Recomiendan que nosotros escojamos clase turista. //
   Recomiendan que nosotros escojamos clase turista.
   que ustedes //
   Recomiendan que ustedes escojan clase turista.
   que tú //
   Recomiendan que tú escojas clase turista.
   que yo //
   Recomiendan que yo escoja clase turista.
   que usted //
   Recomiendan que usted escoja clase turista.
5. Sugiero que tú envíes las maletas y continúes el viaje. //
   Sugiero que tú envíes las maletas y continúes el viaje.
   que nosotros //
   Sugiero que nosotros enviemos las maletas y continuemos el viaje.
   que usted //
   Sugiero que usted envíe las maletas y continúe el viaje.
   que ustedes //
   Sugiero que ustedes envíen las maletas y continúen el viaje.
   que ella //
   Sugiero que ella envíe las maletas y continúe el viaje. //

B. Respond to each question in the negative; then listen for confirmation of your response.

1. ¿Estabas en casa cuando ellos llegaron? //
   No, yo no estaba en casa cuando ellos llegaron.
2. ¿Estarás aquí cuando lleguen mis amigos? //
   No, no estaré aquí cuando lleguen tus amigos.
3. ¿Compraste los boletos después de que Carlos te dio el dinero? //
   No, no compré los boletos después de que Carlos me dio el dinero.
4. ¿Comprarás las maletas después de que te paguen? //
   No, no las compraré después de que me paguen.
5. ¿No saliste hasta que te llamamos por teléfono? //
   No, no salí hasta que ustedes me llamaron por teléfono.
6. ¿No saldrás de tu cuarto hasta que te llamemos? //
   No, no saldré de mi cuarto hasta que ustedes me llamen.
7. ¿Fuiste a escoger un asiento en cuanto fue posible? //
   No, no fui a escoger un asiento en cuanto fue posible.
8. ¿Irás a escogerlo en cuanto tengas tiempo? //
   No, no iré a escogerlo en cuanto tenga tiempo. //

C. Answer the first question affirmatively and the second question negatively, as in the model. You will hear a confirmation of your response.

> MODEL: ¿Te gusta la blusa que tiene Ana?
> **Sí, me gusta mucho la que ella tiene.**
> ¿Te gusta la mía?
> **No, no me gusta la tuya.**

1. ¿Te gusta la pulsera que tiene Lupe? //
   Sí, me gusta mucho la que ella tiene.
   ¿Te gusta la mía? //
   No, no me gusta la tuya.
2. ¿Te gusta el reloj que lleva Miguel? //
   Sí, me gusta mucho el que él lleva.
   ¿Te gusta el mío? //
   No, no me gusta el tuyo.
3. ¿Te gustan las gafas que compró Mario? //
   Sí, me gustan mucho las que él compró.
   ¿Te gustan las mías? //
   No, no me gustan las tuyas.
4. ¿Te gustan los aretes que trajo Marta? //
   Sí, me gustan mucho los que ella trajo.
   ¿Te gustan los míos? //
   No, no me gustan los tuyos.
5. ¿Te gusta el carro que tienen ellos? //
   Sí, me gusta mucho el que ellos tienen.
   ¿Te gusta el nuestro? //
   No, no me gusta el suyo.
6. ¿Te gusta la casa que alquilaron ellas? //
   Sí, me gusta mucho la que ellas alquilaron.
   ¿Te gusta la nuestra? //
   No, no me gusta la suya.
7. ¿Te gustan los muebles que compraron ellos? //
   Sí, me gustan mucho los que ellos compraron.

¿Te gustan los nuestros? //
No, no me gustan los suyos.
8. ¿Te gustan las artesanías que trajeron ellas? //
Sí, me gustan mucho las que ellas trajeron.
¿Te gustan las nuestras? //
No, no me gustan las suyas. //

D. Listen to the two sentences; then combine them by using **pero** or **sino**, as appropriate. Follow the model; then listen for confirmation of your response.

> MODEL: Este verano no vamos a México. Vamos al Perú.
> **Este verano no vamos a México sino al Perú.**

1. Queremos salir la semana que viene. No quedan asientos. //
Queremos salir la semana que viene, pero no quedan asientos.
2. No hay vuelos diarios. Hay vuelos sólo los martes y los viernes. //
No hay vuelos diarios sino vuelos sólo los martes y los viernes.
3. No puedo comprar los boletos hoy. Sólo puedo hacer las reservas. //
No puedo comprar los boletos hoy, pero puedo hacer las reservas.
4. No tengo suficiente dinero. Puedo pagar con tarjeta de crédito. //
No tengo suficiente dinero, pero puedo pagar con tarjeta de crédito.
5. Nos gustaría visitar otros lugares. No tendremos mucho tiempo. //
Nos gustaría visitar otros lugares, pero no tendremos mucho tiempo.
6. Ahora no es verano en Suramérica. Ahora es invierno. //
Ahora no es verano en Suramérica sino invierno. //

Para comprender y escribir

A. From the three choices offered, select the one that best completes the statement or answers the question you hear and circle it.

1. Como a Carmen le gusta tanto viajar, está buscando un trabajo como...
   (a) parada.
   (b) azafata.
   (c) vuelo. //
2. Cuando uno llega a un país extranjero, al pasar por la aduana, hay que presentar...
   (a) el asiento.
   (b) el pasajero.
   (c) el pasaporte. //
3. Quiero salir el día quince y regresar el día treinta. Me hace falta...
   (a) un boleto de ida y vuelta.
   (b) una lista de espera.
   (c) una línea interna. //

4. No sé cómo se fueron tan rápido sin...
   (a) despedirse.
   (b) partir.
   (c) salir. //
5. No pueden tomar ese vuelo a Cuzco porque...
   (a) no salen de viaje.
   (b) no hacen la maleta.
   (c) no quedan asientos. //

B. Combine the two sentences you hear, using the conjunction suggested. Follow the model.

> MODEL: Ana no partirá. Su familia le envía el dinero. (hasta que)
> **Ana no partirá hasta que su familia le envíe el dinero.**

1. Yo te digo las fechas. Tú haces las reservas. (para que) //
2. Queremos regresar en agosto. Comienzan las clases. (antes de que) //
3. Luis comprará los boletos. Nosotros le daremos el dinero. (cuando) //
4. Pasaremos una semana en Cuzco. Tendremos suficiente tiempo. (con tal de que) //
5. Haremos el viaje en julio. Hace bastante frío. (aunque) //
6. Visitaremos otras ciudades en Suramérica. El boleto de avión costará mucho. (a menos que) //

C. Write an alternative form for the sentence you hear, using a possessive pronoun. Follow the model.

> MODEL: Tengo el libro de Ana.
> **Tengo el suyo.**

1. Silvia tiene sus boletos. //
2. Juan lleva su maleta. //
3. Dame tu paquete, por favor. //
4. El reloj de Marta es de oro. //
5. Mi apartamento no es pequeño. //
6. Ponte la camisa de Luis. //
7. Nuestra profesora es argentina. //
8. Nuestros hijos llegan mañana. //

D. Dictado

You will hear a short passage about Silvia and Alberto's honeymoon plans. You will hear the passage three times. Listen the first time. Write what you hear the second time. Make any necessary corrections the third time.

Alberto y Silvia han decidido pasar // su luna de miel en el Perú. // Lo que quieren ver es Machu Picchu, // la gran ciudad de piedra cerca de Cuzco. // Buscan una agencia de viajes // y escogen la del señor Ponce, // el padre de un amigo suyo. // Hay varios vuelos diarios, // pero no van directos a Cuzco, sino a Lima. // Les gustaría salir el quince de agosto, // con tal de que haya un vuelo de la mañana. // Tienen que regresar el treinta de agosto, // antes de que comiencen las clases. //

End of **Lección veinte.**

Lección 21

Actividades y práctica

A. Repeat the model sentence and then substitute each new subject. You will hear a confirmation of your response.

1. Esperaban que José comprara una cámara. //
   Esperaban que José comprara una cámara.
   que ustedes //
   Esperaban que ustedes compraran una cámara.
   que nosotros //
   Esperaban que nosotros compráramos una cámara.
   que yo //
   Esperaban que yo comprara una cámara.
   que tú //
   Esperaban que tú compraras una cámara.
2. Trajeron las transparencias para que Ana las viera. //
   Trajeron las transparencias para que Ana las viera.
   para que yo //
   Trajeron las transparencias para que yo las viera.
   para que ustedes //
   Trajeron las transparencias para que ustedes las vieran.
   para que nosotros //
   Trajeron las transparencias para que nosotros las viéramos.
   para que tú //
   Trajeron las transparencias para que tú las vieras.
3. Sería mejor que ellos no se durmieran durante el viaje. //
   Sería mejor que ellos no se durmieran durante el viaje.
   que Sara //
   Sería mejor que Sara no se durmiera durante el viaje.
   que tú //
   Sería mejor que tú no te durmieras durante el viaje.
   que tus amigos //
   Sería mejor que tus amigos no se durmieran durante el viaje.
   que nosotros //
   Sería mejor que nosotros no nos durmiéramos durante el viaje.
4. Yo quería que ellos pudieran ver los Andes. //
   Yo quería que ellos pudieran ver los Andes.
   que tú //
   Yo quería que tú pudieras ver los Andes.
   que ustedes //
   Yo quería que ustedes pudieran ver los Andes.
   que nosotros //
   Yo quería que nosotros pudiéramos ver los Andes.
   que usted //
   Yo quería que usted pudiera ver los Andes. //

B. Repeat the model sentence and then substitute each new subject. You will hear a confirmation of your response.

1. Sentían que Elena no hubiera vuelto. //
   Sentían que Elena no hubiera vuelto.
   que yo //
   Sentían que yo no hubiera vuelto.
   que nosotros //
   Sentían que nosotros no hubiéramos vuelto.
   que tú //
   Sentían que tú no hubieras vuelto.
   que ustedes //
   Sentían que ustedes no hubieran vuelto.
2. Yo no creía que José no hubiera llevado una vídeo. //
   Yo no creía que José no hubiera llevado una vídeo.
   que ustedes //
   Yo no creía que ustedes no hubieran llevado una vídeo.
   que tú //
   Yo no creía que tú no hubieras llevado una vídeo.
   que los chicos //
   Yo no creía que los chicos no hubieran llevado una vídeo.
   que usted //
   Yo no creía que usted no hubiera llevado una vídeo.
3. Todos dudaban que tú hubieras escrito el artículo. //
   Todos dudaban que tú hubieras escrito el artículo.
   que Jaime //
   Todos dudaban que Jaime hubiera escrito el artículo.
   que ellos //
   Todos dudaban que ellos hubieran escrito el artículo.
   que ustedes //
   Todos dudaban que ustedes hubieran escrito el artículo.
4. Yo esperaba que tú me hubieras aconsejado mejor. //
   Yo esperaba que tú me hubieras aconsejado mejor.
   que ustedes //
   Yo esperaba que ustedes me hubieran aconsejado mejor.
   que ellos //
   Yo esperaba que ellos me hubieran aconsejado mejor.
   que mis amigos //
   Yo esperaba que mis amigos me hubieran aconsejado mejor.
   que Lupe //
   Yo esperaba que Lupe me hubiera aconsejado mejor. //

C. Listen to the statements; then confirm each one using ¡Claro!, as in the model. You will hear a confirmation of your response.

> MODEL: Si llevo una cámara fotográfica, podré sacar fotos.
> **¡Claro! Si llevaras una cámara fotográfica, podrías sacar fotos.**

1. Si voy al Perú, me encontraré con muchos amigos. //
   ¡Claro! Si fueras al Perú, te encontrarías con muchos amigos.
2. Si José viaja conmigo, se divertirá. //
   ¡Claro! Si viajara contigo, se divertiría.
3. Si ellos sacan buenas fotos, tendrán recuerdos inolvidables. //
   ¡Claro! Si sacaran buenas fotos, tendrían recuerdos inolvidables.
4. Si visitamos Cuzco ahora, necesitaremos llevar suéteres. //
   ¡Claro! Si visitaran Cuzco ahora, necesitarían llevar suéteres.

5. Si Ana recibe el dinero, ella traerá alguna artesanía
antigua. //
¡**Claro! Si recibiera el dinero, traería alguna artesanía
antigua.**
6. Si ellos tienen tiempo, irán a otras ciudades. //
¡**Claro! Si tuvieran tiempo, irían a otras ciudades. //**

D. Listen to each statement and respond with a contrary-to-
fact condition. Follow the model and listen for
confirmation of your response.

> MODEL: Yo no visité el Perú; por eso no fui a Cuzco.
> **Pero si hubieras visitado el Perú, habrías
> ido a Cuzco.**

1. Yo no hice las reservas a tiempo; por eso no salí hoy. //
**Pero si hubieras hecho las reservas a tiempo, habrías
salido hoy.**
2. Yo no llevé un abrigo pesado; por eso pesqué un
resfriado. //
**Pero si hubieras llevado un abrigo pesado, no habrías
pescado un resfriado.**
3. Yo no entregué la solicitud; por eso no recibí la beca. //
**Pero si hubieras entregado la solicitud, habrías
recibido la beca.**
4. Yo no llamé a tiempo; por eso no conseguí ese puesto. //
**Pero si hubieras llamado a tiempo, habrías conseguido
ese puesto.**
5. Ellos no me pidieron consejos; por eso no les envíe los
papeles. //
**Pero si ellos te hubieran pedido consejos, les habrías
enviado los papeles.**
6. Ellos no me invitaron; por eso no valía la pena llevarles
un regalo. //
**Pero si te hubieran invitado, habría valido la pena
llevarles un regalo.**
7. Nosotros no asistimos a la conferencia; por eso no
conocimos al economista. //
**Pero si hubieran asistido a la conferencia, habrían
conocido al economista.**
8. Nosotros no revelamos el rollo de película; por eso no
tenemos fotos. //
**Pero si hubieran revelado el rollo de película, habrían
tenido fotos. //**

Para comprender y escribir

A. From the three choices offered, select the one that best
completes the statement or answers the question you
hear and circle it.

1. Porque es posible que haga frío en los Andes, es preciso
que llevemos un abrigo y...
(a) unos guantes.
(b) unas marcas.
(c) una transparencia. //
2. Sé que te encanta esta película sobre Suramérica, pero
ya es tarde. ¿No quieres que regresemos a casa, querida?
(a) Hasta mañana.
(b) Todavía no.
(c) Pasado mañana. //

3. Es la primera vez que estoy en este aeropuerto. ¿Dónde
se puede buscar...
(a) la cámara?
(b) el paraguas?
(c) el equipaje? //
4. La mejor manera para ir de aquí hasta Lima es por...
(a) la casa de correos.
(b) una línea aérea.
(c) un impermeable bueno. //
5. Espero que ustedes puedan visitar las ruinas de Machu
Picchu. La verdad es que...
(a) viajan por carro.
(b) vale la pena.
(c) se preocupan mucho. //

B. Change the sentences from the present to the past, as in
the model.

> MODEL: Quieren que yo lleve un abrigo ligero.
> **Querían que yo llevara un abrigo ligero.**

1. Yo busco una cámara que me guste. //
2. Mi hermano siente mucho que no tenga nada que
hacer. //
3. No hay nadie que pueda ir a la estación conmigo. //
4. Es mejor que ustedes me llamen a menudo. //
5. Nos alegramos de que ellos hagan un viaje por el
Perú. //
6. Yo no conozco a ningún estudiante que viva en Quito. //
7. Lo llamo por teléfono para que venga temprano. //
8. Tienen que bajar el precio antes de que yo le compre. //

C. Respond affirmatively to the questions you are asked, as
in the model.

> MODEL: ¿Qué harías si consiguieras trabajo en
> España? ¿Vivir allí?
> **Sí, si yo consiguiera trabajo en España,
> viviría allí.**

1. ¿Dónde vivirías si te pagaran bien? ¿En Puerto Rico? //
2. ¿Adónde te gustaría ir si pudieras hacer un viaje? ¿A
Lima? //
3. ¿Qué harías si estuvieras en Cozumel ahora? ¿Mirar el
paisaje? //
4. ¿Qué deportes practicarías si fuera verano ahora? ¿El
tenis y la natación? //
5. ¿Adónde irías si no tuvieras que estudiar esta noche? ¿Al
teatro? //
6. ¿Qué te gustaría hacer si tuvieras libre el próximo fin de
semana? ¿Ir de compras? //

D. Dictado

You will hear a short narrative about Silvia and Alberto's
encounter with José Soto. You will hear the narrative
three times. Listen the first time. Write what you hear
the second time. Make any necessary corrections the
third time.

Al salir de la casa de correos, // Alberto y Silvia se
encuentran con José Soto. // José es un ingeniero cubano

muy simpático // que ha viajado mucho por Suramérica. // Quieren pedirle algunos consejos // porque salen para Chile la próxima semana. // Si José lo hubiera sabido antes, // los habría invitado a su casa // para ver las transparencias de su último viaje. // José sabe que si tuvieran una cámara, // sacarían muchas fotos muy bonitas. //

End of **Lección veintiuno**.

Lección 22

Actividades y práctica

A. Listen to each statement and respond with an affirmative **vosotros** command. You will hear a confirmation of your response.

> MODEL: Los estudiantes no quieren leer este artículo.
> **Estudiantes, leed este artículo.**

1. Los estudiantes no quieren hablar en español. //
Estudiantes, hablad en español.
2. Los muchachos no tienen ganas de venir a clase. //
Muchachos, venid a clase.
3. Las chicas no tienen ganas de escuchar la conferencia. //
Chicas, escuchad la conferencia.
4. Miguel y José no desean escribir el resumen. //
Miguel y José, escribid el resumen.
5. Las muchachas no quieren tener la fiesta. //
Muchachas, tened la fiesta.
6. Marta y Luis no quieren bailar el merengue. //
Marta y Luis, bailad el merengue.
7. Ana y Mario no desean cantar otra canción. //
Ana y Mario, cantad otra canción.
8. Los chicos no tienen ganas de regresar a casa. //
Chicos, regresad a casa. //

B. Listen to the question and the cue. Respond, using the passive voice, as in the model. Then listen for confirmation of your response.

> MODEL: ¿Quién tomó la película? ¿Ana?
> **Sí, la película fue tomada por Ana.**

1. ¿Quién hizo las reservas? ¿El agente de viajes? //
Sí, las reservas fueron hechas por el agente de viajes.
2. ¿Quién escribió la carta de recomendación? ¿La profesora? //
Sí, la carta de recomendación fue escrita por la profesora.
3. ¿Quién preparó el examen de español? ¿Un grupo de profesores? //
Sí, el examen de español fue preparado por un grupo de profesores.
4. ¿Quién hizo los planes para la reunión? ¿El gerente? //
Sí, los planes para la reunión fueron hechos por el gerente.

5. ¿Quiénes enviaron las invitaciones? ¿Los padres de la novia? //
Sí, las invitaciones fueron enviadas por los padres de la novia.
6. ¿Quién construyó este edificio? ¿Una compañía extranjera? //
Sí, el edificio fue construido por una compañía extranjera.
7. ¿Quién escogió a los secretarios? ¿El nuevo jefe? //
Sí, los secretarios fueron escogidos por el nuevo jefe.
8. ¿Quiénes alquilaron el apartamento? ¿Unos estudiantes extranjeros? //
Sí, el apartamento fue alquilado por unos estudiantes extranjeros. //

C. Listen to the question and confirm the information, using a se construction. Follow the model and then listen for confirmation of your response.

> MODEL: Cierran los bancos a las dos, ¿verdad?
> **Es cierto, se cierran los bancos a las dos.**

1. Abren las tiendas los domingos, ¿verdad? //
Es cierto, se abren las tiendas los domingos.
2. Hablan español en los almacenes, ¿verdad? //
Es cierto, se habla español en los almacenes.
3. Sólo venden mercancía muy fina, ¿verdad? //
Es cierto, sólo se vende mercancía muy fina.
4. Aceptan tarjetas de crédito aquí, ¿verdad? //
Es cierto, se aceptan tarjetas de crédito aquí.
5. Venden periódicos extranjeros en la librería, ¿verdad? //
Es cierto, se venden periódicos extranjeros en la librería.
6. Toman vino en España, ¿verdad? //
Es cierto, se toma vino en España.
7. Encontramos mucha artesanía bonita en México, ¿verdad? //
Es cierto, se encuentra mucha artesanía bonita en México.
8. Vemos estilos muy diferentes allí, ¿verdad? //
Es cierto, se ven estilos muy diferentes allí. //

D. Answer each question with a softened statement, as in the model. You will hear a confirmation of your response.

> MODEL: ¿Quieres hablar conmigo?
> **Sí, yo quisiera hablar contigo.**

1. ¿Quieres invitarme a salir? //
Sí, yo quisiera invitarte a salir.
2. ¿Puedes llevarme a cenar? //
Sí, yo podría llevarte a cenar.
3. ¿Debo arreglarme ya? //
Sí, debieras arreglarte ya.
4. ¿Quieren ustedes ir conmigo? //
Sí, quisiéramos ir contigo.
5. ¿Pueden ustedes pasar por mí? //
Sí, podríamos pasar por ti.
6. ¿Deben ellos llegar a eso de las seis? //
Sí, debieran llegar a eso de las seis. //

Para comprender y escribir

A. From the three choices offered, select the one that best completes the statement or answers the question you hear and circle it.

1. Oí decir que vas a trabajar con tu padre.
   (a) ¡Cuánto me alegro!
   (b) ¡Espero que no tengas éxito!
   (c) ¡Ojalá que consigas empleo! //

2. Parece que no vamos a vernos hasta septiembre y voy a echarlos de menos.
   (a) Firmen aquí, por favor.
   (b) Ojalá que soliciten el puesto.
   (c) No digamos adiós, sino hasta luego. //

3. Y a Jorge, que regresa a España en unos días, sólo podemos decirle...
   (a) ¡Échenos piropos!
   (b) ¡Es hora de hacerse rico!
   (c) ¡No dejes de escribirnos! //

4. ¿Qué te gustaría comer en la fiesta en mi casa?
   (a) Un pastel.
   (b) Una costa.
   (c) Unas formas. //

5. ¿Cuándo estudias generalmente?
   (a) En la reunión.
   (b) Por la noche.
   (c) Es hora de estudiar. //

B. Make each of the commands you hear negative, as in the model.

> MODEL: Solicitad las becas.
> **No solicitéis las becas.**

1. Hacedlo esta tarde. //
2. Enviad por el equipaje. //
3. Sentaos en el comedor. //
4. Poneos esas gafas. //
5. Acercaos a la esquina. //
6. Idos con ellos. //

C. Write a new sentence with the cue you hear.

1. Yo quiero llegar a ser gerente de una compañía. (Yo quisiera) //
2. Ana quisiera almorzar en el centro hoy. (A Ana le gustaría) //
3. Debemos esperar enfrente de la casa de correos. (Debiéramos) //
4. A él gustaría estudiar arquitectura. (Él quisiera) //
5. ¡Cuánto me alegro de que ustedes tengan mucho éxito! (¡Ojalá que...!) //
6. Ellos deben reunirse mañana. (Ellos debieran) //
7. ¡Ojalá que nos viéramos otra vez! (Yo quisiera) //
8. ¿Puedo yo conseguir un puesto en su compañía? (Pudiera yo) //

D. Dictado

You will hear a short narrative about a group of students gathering for lunch before leaving the university for the summer. You will hear the narrative three times. Listen the first time. Write what you hear the second time. Make any corrections the third time.

Al terminar sus exámenes // y antes de salir de la universidad, // varios compañeros se reúnen para almorzar. // El restaurante les fue recomendado por Miguel Ramos, // quien no pudo asistir a la reunión. // Jorge, // que es español, // dice que si Miguel no estuviera tan ocupado // preparándose para ir a Puerto Rico, // habría almorzado con ellos. // Beatriz dice que es hora de hablar // sobre sus planes para el verano. // Después de una conversación muy animada, // Jorge anuncia que es hora de despedirse. //

End of **Lección veintidós**.

Repaso 3: Lecciones 12–15

I. Verbs

A. Listen to the statement and the question that follows. Answer negatively, using the same tense and the subject pronoun for emphasis.

1. Ellos vuelven al centro hoy. ¿Y ustedes? //
   No, nosotros no volvemos al centro hoy.
2. Pablo y Lupe juegan al tenis los sábados. ¿Y ustedes? //
   No, nosotros no jugamos al tenis los sábados.
3. Nosotras les devolvimos la sección de deportes. ¿Y tú? //
   No, yo no les devolví la sección de deportes.
4. Ellos oyen my bien. ¿Y tú? //
   No, yo no oigo muy bien.
5. Mis amigos pagaron la cuenta. ¿Y usted? //
   No, yo no pagué la cuenta.
6. Marta comenzó a trabajar ayer. ¿Y usted? //
   No, yo no comencé a trabajar ayer.
7. Ellos pudieron esperar hasta las seis. ¿Y ustedes? //
   No, nosotros no pudimos esperar hasta las seis.
8. Ellos vinieron sin dinero. ¿Y ustedes? //
   No, nosotros no vinimos sin dinero.
9. Miguel y yo les trajimos regalos. ¿Y tú? //
   No, yo no les traje regalos.
10. Yo estuve el año pasado en Cozumel. ¿Y usted? //
    No, yo no estuve el año pasado en Cozumel.
11. Yo he visto esas playas. ¿Y tus amigos? //
    No, ellos no han visto esas playas.
12. Nosotros hemos hecho esa excursión. ¿Y usted? //
    No, yo no he hecho esa excursión.
13. Lola les ha escrito a menudo. ¿Y tú? //
    No, yo no les he escrito a menudo.
14. Ella se había puesto muy bronceada. ¿Y ustedes? //
    No, nosotros no nos habíamos puesto muy bronceados.
15. Luis había abierto las ventanas. ¿Y usted? //
    No, yo no había abierto las ventanas.
16. Nosotros habíamos hecho los reservas. ¿Y ustedes? //
    No, nosotros no habíamos hecho las reservas.
17. Ustedes tendrán que cambiarlas. ¿Y yo? //
    No, tú no tendrás que cambiarlas. (No, usted no tendrá que cambiarlas.)

18. Ella se pondrá el vestido nuevo. ¿Y tú? / /
No, yo no me pondré el vestido nuevo.
19. Ustedes podrían sacar las fotos ahora. ¿Y yo? / /
No, tú no podrías sacar las fotos ahora. (No, usted no podría sacar las fotos ahora.)
20. Luisa haría el viaje en coche. ¿Y sus amigos? / /
No, ellos no harían el viaje en coche. / /

B. You will hear a statement followed by a question. Answer affirmatively, using the present perfect tense. Follow the model.

MODEL: Yo he visto esas playas. ¿Y tus amigos?
Sí, ellos han visto esas playas también.

1. Yo he hecho esa excursión. ¿Y ustedes? / /
Sí, nosotros hemos hecho esa excursión también.
2. Lola ha escrito a su familia. ¿Y ellos? / /
Sí, ellos han escrito a su familia también.
3. Ella se había puesto las gafas. ¿Y usted? / /
Sí, yo me había puesto las gafas también.
4. Luis había abierto las cartas. ¿Y ustedes? / /
Sí, nosotros habíamos abierto las cartas también.
5. Nosotros habíamos hecho la comida. ¿Y tu compañera? / /
Sí, mi compañera había hecho la comida también. / /

C. Listen to each statement and question. Answer negatively, using the future or conditional tenses. Follow the model.

MODEL: Yo le diré la verdad. ¿Y ustedes?
No, nosotros no le diremos la verdad.

1. Ustedes tendrán que pagarlo. ¿Y yo? / /
No, tú no tendrás que pagarlo.
2. Ella se pondrá el vestido nuevo. ¿Y tú? / /
No, yo no me pondré el vestido nuevo.
3. Yo sabré la dirección. ¿Y ustedes? / /
No, nosotros no sabremos la dirección.
4. Ustedes podrían sacar las fotos. ¿Y yo? / /
No, tú no podrías sacar las fotos. (No, usted no podría sacar las fotos.)
5. Luisa haría el viaje. ¿Y ellos? / /
No, ellos no harían el viaje.
6. Yo vendría temprano. ¿Y ustedes? / /
No, nosotros no vendríamos temprano. / /

II. Pronouns

D. Answer each question affirmatively, substituting the appropriate direct object pronoun for the noun.

1. ¿Le diste tú a ella la pulsera? / /
Sí, se la di.
2. ¿Le trajiste a Luis el reloj? / /
Sí, se lo traje.
3. ¿Les devolviste a ellos los anillos? / /
Sí, se los devolví.
4. ¿Se puso usted los aretes de oro? / /
Sí, me los puse.

5. ¿Estaba ella arreglándose el pelo? / /
Sí, ella estaba arreglándoselo. (Sí, ella se lo estaba arreglando.)
6. ¿Pudiste entregarle a él las gafas? / /
Sí, se las pude entregar. (Sí, pude entregárselas.) / /

E. Listen to each sentence and the cue. Repeat the sentence, substituting the new subject and making any other changes necessary.

1. Se usan mucho estos vestidos. (esta blusa) / /
Se usa mucho esta blusa.
2. Se vende este coche a precio especial. (estos zapatos) / /
Se venden estos zapatos a precios especiales.
3. Se ve mucha mercancía en las vitrinas. (artículos finos) / /
Se ven muchos artículos finos en las vitrinas.
4. Se abren las tiendas a las nueve. (la peluquería) / /
Se abre la peluquería a las nueve. / /

III. Demonstrative pronouns

F. Listen to each statement and agree with what is said, substituting a demonstrative pronoun where appropriate. Follow the model.

MODEL: Me gusta este disco.
A mí me gusta éste también.

1. Ese muchacho va a clase conmigo. / /
Ése va a clase conmigo también.
2. Siempre voy a aquel hotel. / /
Yo siempre voy a aquél también.
3. Esos libros tienen mil páginas. / /
Ésos tienen mil páginas también.
4. Esa persona vive cerca de mi casa. / /
Ésa vive cerca de mi casa también.
5. Me encantan esas pulseras. / /
Me encantan ésas también. / /

IV. Vocabulario—Para comprender y escribir

A. Write the words that belong to each category listed. You will hear the words only once. Not all the words or expressions you hear will belong to the category mentioned, so listen carefully.

1. Los deportes /
la pesca / / las ruinas / / la llave / / la bicicleta / / el equipo / / la cocina / / la cita / / la raqueta / /
2. La joyería /
la arena / / abierta / / los aretes / / la hamaca / / el oro / / la razón / / la vitrina / / el patio / /
3. La ropa /
el cinturón / / el jabón / / el traje de baño / / despacio / / pagar / / el regalo / / el partido / / la pelota / /
4. Las personas /
amables / / el fondo / / la estampilla / / la cartera / / el esposo / / la recepcionista / / la manta / / el timbre / /
5. El restaurante /
la cocina / / traer / / el hielo / / el disco compacto / / el plato / / tocar / / el hambre / / la chimenea / /

6. La fiesta /
el tocadiscos para compactos // dejar // el cumpleaños // el recado // el sueño // las bebidas // puntual // la fecha //

B. You will hear three words or phrases spoken once. Write the one word or phrase that does NOT belong with the other two.

1. la arena / la playa / el corredor //
2. la estampilla / el traje / la tarjeta postal //
3. el collar / el cinturón / los aretes //
4. pagar / envolver / la cuenta //
5. la hamaca / la vitrina / la tienda //
6. la guayabera / la camisa / el llavero //
7. el ascensor / registrarse / subir //
8. la toalla / la manta / la cama //
9. los cheques de viajero / el dinero / la vista //
10. las reservas / la plaza / el hotel //
11. el corredor / la plata / el oro //
12. la empanada / el fondo / los corales //
13. el recado / el hielo / el teléfono //
14. las servilletas / las copas / el postre //
15. el vino / la cerveza / la paella //

C. Write the opposite for the words you hear.

1. temprano //
2. siempre //
3. la primera vez //
4. el esposo //
5. grande //
6. bajar //
7. despacio //
8. nuevo //
9. último //
10. blanco //
11. también //
12. alguien //

End of **Repaso tres.**

Repaso 4: Lecciones 16–19

I. Verbs

A. In Lessons 16 through 19 you learned about the subjunctive mood, which expresses an attitude about a fact rather than simply indicating the fact itself (which the indicative does). The subjunctive is usually used in a dependent clause. In this exercise, you are asked to use the subjunctive in noun clauses. Listen to the question and answer in the affirmative with an alternate negative response, as in the model.

> MODEL: ¿Envuelvo el regalo o busco otra cosa? ¿Qué prefiere usted?
> **Prefiero que usted envuelva el regalo; no busque otra cosa.**

1. ¿Alquilo un apartamento o compro una casa? ¿Qué sugiere usted? //
   Sugiero que usted alquile un apartamento; no compre una casa.
2. ¿Hablo con el gerente o llamo a la dueña? ¿Qué recomienda usted? //
   Recomiendo que usted hable con el gerente; no llame a la dueña.
3. ¿Sirvo las bebidas ahora o comienzo a cocinar? ¿Qué desea usted? //
   Deseo que usted sirva las bebidas ahora; no comience a cocinar.
4. ¿Voy a la conferencia o me quedo en la biblioteca? ¿Qué recomienda usted? //
   Recomiendo que usted vaya a la conferencia; no se quede en la biblioteca.
5. ¿Escribo el resumen ahora o pago las cuentas? ¿Qué me dice usted? //
   Le digo que usted escriba el resumen ahora; no pague las cuentas.
6. ¿Pongo este disco o busco otro? ¿Qué prefiere usted? //
   Prefiero que usted ponga ese disco; no busque otro. //

B. Listen to the sentence and the question that follows it. Answer affirmatively, using the present perfect subjunctive. Follow the model.

> MODEL: Hace tiempo que no llamo a Lupe. Te extraña, ¿verdad?
> **Sí, me extraña que no la hayas llamado.**

1. Hace tiempo que no vuelvo a casa. Te extraña, ¿verdad? //
   Sí, me extraño que no hayas vuelto a casa.
2. Hace tiempo que no veo a Miguel. Lo sientes, ¿verdad? //
   Sí, siento que no hayas visto a Miguel.
3. Hace un año que no le escribo. Lo dudas, ¿verdad? //
   Sí, dudo que no le hayas escrito.
4. Hace meses que no le digo nada. Es importante, ¿verdad? //
   Sí, es importante que no le hayas dicho nada.
5. Hace semanas que no voy al cine. Es posible, ¿verdad? //
   Sí, es posible que no hayas ido al cine.
6. Hace días que no vengo a clases. Te preocupa, ¿verdad? //
   Sí, me preocupa que no hayas venido a clases.
7. Hace tiempo que no me enfermo. Es extraño, ¿verdad? //
   Sí, es extraño que no te hayas enfermado.
8. Hace meses que no hago nada interesante. Es lástima, ¿verdad? //
   Sí, es lástima que no hayas hecho nada interesante. //

C. Listen to each sentence and the cue that follows. Form a new sentence, using the subjunctive or indicative in the noun clause as needed. Follow the model.

> MODEL: Alberto los ha invitado a su boda. (Dudo mucho que)

Dudo mucho que Alberto los haya invitado a su boda.

1. Alberto y Silvia quieren casarse. (Me alegro de que) //
   Me alegro de que Alberto y Silvia quieran casarse.
2. Ellos son muy felices. (Yo sé que) //
   Yo sé que ellos son muy felices.
3. Ellos no han dicho nada todavía. (Me extraña que) //
   Me extraña que ellos no hayan dicho nada todavía.
4. Silvia ya ha vuelto de la Argentina. (Es posible que) //
   Es posible que Silvia ya haya vuelto de la Argentina.
5. Sus amigas no lo han visto todavía. (Temo que) //
   Temo que sus amigas no lo hayan visto todavía.
6. Alberto se ha puesto muy contento. (Estoy seguro de que) //
   Estoy seguro de que Alberto se ha puesto muy contento.
7. Nosotros les daremos una gran fiesta. (No dudo que) //
   No dudo que nosotros les daremos una gran fiesta.
8. Ellos recibirán muchos regalos. (Espero que) //
   Espero que ellos reciban muchos regalos. //

D. Listen to the two sentences; then combine them using **que** and a verb in the indicative or the subjunctive, as appropriate.

1. Tengo una secretaria. Escribe bien en español. //
   Tengo una secretaria que escribe bien en español.
2. Necesitamos a alguien. Sabe traducir del inglés. //
   Necesitamos a alguien que sepa traducir del inglés.
3. Conozco a una persona. Es bilingüe. //
   Conozco a una persona que es bilingüe.
4. ¿Hay alguien aquí? ¿Puede recomendar bien a Miguel? //
   ¿Hay alguien aquí que pueda recomendar bien a Miguel?
5. Buscan un joven. Debe tener dos años de experiencia. //
   Buscan un joven que tenga dos años de experiencia.
6. No conozco a nadie. Nadie está sin trabajo ahora. //
   No conozco a nadie que esté sin trabajo ahora. //

II. Adjectives

E. Confirm the statement you hear, using a comparison and then a superlative. Follow the model.

> MODEL: Este apartamento es cómodo.
> **Sí, es más cómodo que aquél. Es el más cómodo de todos.**

1. Este edificio es nuevo. //
   Sí, es más nuevo que aquél. Es el más nuevo de todos.
2. Estas calles son hermosas. //
   Sí, son más hermosas que aquéllas. Son las más hermosas de todas.
3. Ese equipo es bueno. //
   Sí, es mejor que aquél. Es el mejor de todos.
4. Esos jugadores son altos. //
   Sí, son más altos que aquéllos. Son los más altos de todos.

5. Esta empresa es importante. //
   Sí, es más importante que aquélla. Es la más importante de todas.
6. Estos empleados son trabajadores. //
   Sí, son más trabajadores que aquéllos. Son los más trabajadores de todos.
7. Esa secretaria es competente. //
   Sí, es más competente que aquélla. Es la más competente de todas.
8. Este jefe es amable. //
   Sí, es más amable que aquél. Es el más amable de todos. //

F. Listen to the statement and the question that follows. Respond according to the model.

> MODEL: La hija de él es muy bonita. ¿Y las hijas de usted?
> **Mis hijas son bonitísimas.**

1. El sobrino de Miguel es muy alto. ¿Y los sobrinos de usted? //
   Mis sobrinos son altísimos.
2. Los padres de él son muy felices. ¿Y los padres de ella? //
   Sus padres son felicísimos.
3. El hijo de los señores Ruiz es muy inteligente. ¿Y las hijas de ellos? //
   Sus hijas son inteligentísimas.
4. El novio de Marta es muy bueno. ¿Y el novio de Silvia? //
   Su novio es buenísimo.
5. La esposa del señor Ramos es muy guapa. ¿Y la esposa de usted? //
   Mi esposa es guapísima. //

III. Time expressions

G. Answer each question using **hacer**, and the cue given, as in the model.

> MODEL: ¿Cuánto tiempo has estudiado aquí? ¿Dos años?
> **Sí, hace dos años que estudio aquí.**

1. ¿Cuánto tiempo han vivido ellos en ese apartamento? ¿Seis meses? //
   Sí, hace seis meses que viven en ese apartamento.
2. ¿Cuánto tiempo has hablado por teléfono? ¿Veinte minutos? //
   Sí, hace veinte minutos que hablo por teléfono.
3. ¿Cuánto tiempo han jugado ese partido? ¿Media hora? //
   Sí, hace media hora que juegan ese partido.
4. ¿Cuánto tiempo han dormido los chicos? ¿Siete horas? //
   Sí, hace siete horas que duermen los chicos.
5. ¿Cuánto tiempo hemos asistido a esta clase? ¿Un semestre? //
   Sí, hace un semestre que asistimos a esta clase. //

IV. Vocabulario—Para comprender y escribir

A. Write the words that belong to each category listed. You will hear the words once. Not all the words or expressions you hear will belong to the category mentioned, so listen carefully.

1. El cuerpo /
   el almacén / el brazo / enfermarse / el comentario / la rodilla / el cuello / la sorpresa / el jugo //
2. El hospital /
   la ambulancia / el resumen / la fábrica / la enfermera / los antibióticos / traducir / la fiebre / la funda //
3. La casa /
   la beca / la empresa / amueblada / alquilar / el barrio / la entrevista / la cocina / la pulmonía //
4. La boda /
   el anillo / la conferencia / la lista de regalos / la ganga / casarse / el cubierto / la luna de miel / feliz //
5. Los aparatos /
   la sirena / el lugar / la aspiradora / eléctricos / la almohada / la cafetera / la batidora / la plancha //
6. El automóvil /
   la avería / la vacante / la licencia de conducir / la sucursal / manejar / chocar / el tráfico //
7. El trabajo /
   el freno / el herido / la empleada / el ascenso / dudar / adelante / el sueldo / el gerente //

B. You will hear three words or phrases spoken once. Write the one word or phrase that does NOT belong with the other two.

1. la sábana / la solicitud / la funda //
2. conducir / manejar / obtener //
3. el candidato / la maquinaria / las referencias //
4. la ambulancia / el carro / el coche //
5. la economía / los negocios / la policía //
6. calmarse / lastimarse / doler //
7. el sillón / el ordenador / el sofá //
8. el estéreo / la grabadora / la sartén //
9. el regalo / el refrigerador / el hielo //
10. el almacén / la lista / la tienda //
11. la ganga / barato / cercano //
12. la pierna / la congestión / la pulmonía //
13. la iglesia / la misa / la mesa //
14. al menos / a cada rato / de vez en cuando //
15. pescar un resfriado / ir a pescar / enfermarse //

C. Write the opposite for the words you hear.

1. despertarse //
2. muchísimo //
3. pobre //
4. enfermarse //
5. por la izquierda //
6. empezar //

End of **Repaso cuatro.**

Repaso 5: Lecciones 20–22

I. Verbs

A. Listen to each statement and then confirm it, using the introductory phrase suggested. Follow the model.

> MODEL: Ana pedirá permiso para salir temprano.
> (Quiero que)
> **Quiero que Ana pida permiso para salir temprano.**

1. José conseguirá un puesto de ingeniero. (Espero que) //
   Espero que José consiga un puesto de ingeniero.
2. Beatriz escogerá la carrera de medicina. (Es posible que) //
   Es posible que Beatriz escoja la carrera de medicina.
3. Lupe enviará una solicitud a la Escuela de Arquitectura. (Quiero que) //
   Quiero que Lupe envíe una solicitud a la Escuela de Arquitectura.
4. Ese carro no continuará por esa calle. (Espero que) //
   Espero que ese carro no continúe por esa calle.
5. Ese carro se detendrá a tiempo. (Dudo que) //
   Dudo que ese carro se detenga a tiempo.
6. El Policía dirigirá el tráfico mejor. (Espero que) //
   Espero que el policía dirija el tráfico mejor.
7. El policía le pedirá el carnet a ese conductor. (Es posible que) //
   Es posible que el policía le pida el carnet a ese conductor.
8. La gente se irá pronto. (Es probable que) //
   Es probable que la gente se vaya pronto.
9. La ciudad construirá mejores avenidas. (Insisten en que) //
   Insisten en que la ciudad construya mejores avenidas.
10. Eso valdrá la pena. (No creo que) //
    No creo que eso valga la pena. //

B. Rephrase the sentence you hear, using the suggested conjunction. Some sentences will take an indicative and some will take a subjunctive in the adverbial clause. Listen to the models.

> MODELS: Voy a visitar a Ana al salir de clase.
> (cuando)
> **Voy a visitar a Ana cuando yo salga de clase.**
> Fui a visitar a Ana al salir de clase.
> (cuando)
> **Fui a visitar a Ana cuando salí de clase.**

1. Debes evitar el tráfico y llegaremos a tiempo. (para que) //
   Debes evitar el tráfico para que lleguemos a tiempo.
2. Van a despedirse porque ya sale el vuelo. (antes de que) //
   Van a despedirse antes de que salga el vuelo.

3. Los novios entraron pero antes se sentaron los invitados. (después que) //
Los novios entraron después que se sentaron los invitados.
4. ¿Quieres acompañarme hasta irme? (hasta que) //
¿Quieres acompañarme hasta que me vaya?
5. Nos vamos pero no hemos comido postre. (aunque) //
Nos vamos aunque no hemos comido postre.
6. Preferimos seguir sus consejos si no tienes otra idea. (a menos que) //
Preferimos seguir sus consejos a menos que tengas otra idea.
7. Visité a mis primos al viajar por España. (cuando) //
Visité a mis primos cuando viajé por España.

C. Listen to each statement and then confirm it, following the model.

MODEL: Miguel quiere que tú vayas al concierto.
Sí, él quería que yo fuera al concierto.

1. El profesor quiere que tú escuches la conferencia. //
Sí, él quería que yo escuchara la conferencia.
2. Antonio prefiere que tú traduzcas los versos. //
Sí, él prefería que yo tradujera los versos.
3. Carmen prefiere que ustedes hagan la solicitud. //
Sí, ella prefería que nosotros hiciéramos la solicitud.
4. Sus padres esperan que ustedes sean buenos amigos. //
Sí, ellos esperaban que nosotros fuéramos buenos amigos.
5. Ellos no creen que usted pueda ser mal empleado. //
Sí, ellos no creían que yo pudiera ser mal empleado.
6. Ellos esperan que yo construya un futuro mejor para ustedes. //
Sí, ellos esperaban que usted construyera un futuro mejor para nosotros.
(Sí, ellos esperaban que tú construyeras un futuro mejor para nosotros.)
7. El jefe espera que su secretaria escriba mejores resúmenes. //
Sí, él esperaba que su secretaria escribiera mejores resúmenes.
8. La profesora espera que ustedes lean más artículos. //
Sí, ella esperaba que nosotros leyéramos más artículos. //

D. Rephrase each sentence you hear, using a **si**-clause, as in the models. Observe the appropriate tense agreement.

MODELS: No solicito el puesto porque no quiero mudarme.
Si quisiera mudarme, solicitaría el puesto.
No solicité el puesto porque no quería mudarme.
Si hubiera querido mudarme, habría solicitado el puesto.

1. No partimos el sábado porque no hay asientos libres en ese vuelo. //
Si hubiera asientos libres en ese vuelo, partiríamos el sábado.

2. No te avisé de la reunión porque no te había visto antes. //
Si te hubiera visto antes, te habría avisado de la reunión.
3. Carolina no sabe traducir; por eso no puede conseguir un buen puesto en Suramérica. //
Si Carolina supiera traducir, podría conseguir un buen puesto en Suramérica.
4. Como ellos no me invitaron a su fiesta de bodas, no fui. //
Si ellos me hubieran invitado a su fiesta de bodas, habría ido.
5. Ustedes no tuvieron paciencia; por eso no sacaron mejores fotos. //
Si ustedes hubieran tenido paciencia, habrían sacado mejores fotos.
6. No te doy más dinero porque no tengo suficiente para mí. //
Si yo tuviera suficiente para mí, te daría más dinero. //

II. Pronouns

E. Listen to the question and respond negatively, using the appropriate possessive pronoun. Follow the model.

MODEL: ¿Tienes mi pasaporte?
No, no tengo el tuyo.

1. ¿Traes las maletas de Rita? //
No, no traigo las suyas.
2. ¿Llevas el equipaje de Miguel? //
No, no llevo el suyo.
3. ¿Necesita usted los boletos míos? //
No, no necesito los suyos.
No, no necesito los tuyos.
4. ¿Quiere usted el asiento mío? //
No, no quiero el suyo.
No, no quiero el tuyo.
5. ¿Hace usted las reservas nuestras? //
No, no hago las suyas.
No, no hago las nuestras.
6. ¿Conduces el carro nuestro? //
No, no conduzco el suyo.
No, no conduzco el nuestro. //

III. Passive voice

F. Answer the questions affirmatively, using a passive construction. Follow the model.

MODEL: ¿Quién construyo la casa? ¿José?
Sí, la casa fue construida por José.

1. ¿Quién confirmó las reservas? ¿La recepcionista? //
Sí, las reservas fueron confirmadas por la recepcionista.
2. ¿Quién escogió la pulsera? ¿Inés? //
Sí, la pulsera fue escogida por Inés.
3. ¿Quién solicitó el puesto? ¿Miguel? //
Sí, el puesto fue solicitado por Miguel.

4. ¿Quiénes anunciaron los resultados? ¿Los profesores? / /
Sí, los resultados fueron anunciados por los profesores. / /

IV. Vocabulario—Para comprender y escribir

A. Write the words that belong to each category listed. You will hear the words only once. Not all the words or expressions you hear will belong to the category mentioned, so listen carefully.

1. El viaje /
   el equipaje / el compromiso / guapo / la maleta / delicioso / el pasajero / la agencia / despedirse / /
2. La oficina /
   la computadora / el ascenso / informar / la reunión / el ecuador / la piedra / el pasaporte / emplear / /
3. El vuelo /
   firmar / la maestría / aéreo / el aeromozo / el paraguas / la ida / la casa de correos / una línea interna / /
4. La ropa /
   el abrigo / encontrarse / el guante / la marca / sencillo / el impermeable / la parada / el suéter / /
5. La fiesta de despedida /
   el boleto / felicitar / preocuparse / el ingeniero / enviar / reunirse / el pastel / animada / /

B. You will hear three words or phrases spoken once. Write the one word or phrase that does NOT belong with the other two.

1. el equipaje / la maleta / el asiento / /
2. la costa / la falta / el mar / /
3. el camarero / el arte / el museo / /
4. solicitar / detener / el puesto / /
5. el pastel / delicioso / el piropo / /
6. la boda / la duda / la luna de miel / /
7. el paraguas / la lluvia / la azafata / /
8. el consejo / el boleto / la entrada / /
9. el collar / el anillo / la cámara / /
10. sin duda / sin falta / sin embargo / /

C. Write the opposite for the words you hear.

1. enviar / /
2. recordar / /
3. saludar / /
4. la ida / /
5. el futuro / /
6. primero / /

End of **Repaso cinco.**

✠✠✠ *Vocabulario*

The Spanish-English Vocabulary lists in alphabetical order the words, expressions, and phrases that appear in Volumes I and II of **Spanish on Your Own**. Phrases are also listed under the entries for the most important words in each phrase. Active vocabulary items (the words and expressions that you are expected to know) are followed by a number in parentheses indicating the lesson in which each word is introduced. The reference (1), for example, indicates that the item was introduced in **Lección 1**.

The English-Spanish Vocabulary lists the words and expressions that are needed to complete the translations in the **Repaso** section of each lesson, as well as the **Repaso** self-tests in Appendix C.

The following abbreviations are used in the vocabulary lists.

adj.	adjective	*Mex.*	Mexican
adv.	adverb	*n.*	noun
Am.	Latin American	*obj.*	object
conj.	conjunction	*p.p.*	past participle
dir.	direct	*part.*	participle
etc.	and so forth	*pl.*	plural
f.	feminine	*prep.*	preposition
fam.	familiar	*pres.*	present
i.e.	that is	*pron.*	pronoun
indef.	indefinite	*reflex.*	reflexive
indir.	indirect	*s./sing.*	singular
inf.	infinitive	*subj.*	subjunctive
lit.	literally	*U.S.*	United States
m.	masculine	+	followed by

Spanish-English

A

a *prep.*   to, at, in (3)

   a cada rato   every short while (moment) (16)

   a casa de su amigo (**Ramón**)   to his friend (Raymond)'s house (6)

   a cualquier hora   at any time (hour) (21)

   a eso de   at about (*time*) (3)

   a (**la**) **medianoche**   at midnight (3)

   a la una   at one o'clock (12)

   a menos que *conj.*   unless (20)

   a menudo   often, frequently (6)

   a orillas de   on the banks of

   a partir de   beginning with (19)

   a precio especial   on sale, at a special price, at special prices (7)

   a propósito   by the way (9)

   ¿a qué hora… ?   (at) what time . . . ? (3)

   a tiempo   on time (11)

   a veces   at times (11); sometimes

   a ver   let's (let me) see (13)

abandonar   to abandon

abarcar   to include

abierto, -a *p.p. of* **abrir** *and adj.*   open, opened (14)

la **abogada**   lawyer (*f.*) (6)

el **abogado**   lawyer (*m.*) (6)

el **abono**   fertilizer

el **abrigo**   topcoat, overcoat, coat (21)

   abril   April (5)

   abrir   to open (6)

la **abuela**   grandmother

el **abuelo**   grandfather; *pl.* grandparents (*m. and f.*) (10)

aburrido, -a   boring (4)

acabar   to end, finish (13)

   acabar de + *inf.*   to have just + *p.p.* (13)

la **academia**   academy

el **accidente**   accident (18)

   el **accidente de tráfico**   traffic accident (18)

la **acción** (*pl.* **acciones**)   action (7)

   el **Día de Acción de Gracias**   Thanksgiving Day (7)

aceptar   to accept (12)

acercarse (**a** + *obj.*)   to approach (15)

acompañar   to accompany, go with (21)

acondicionado: el aire ___   air conditioning (12)

aconsejar   to advise (17)

acostarse (**ue**)   to go to bed, lie down (8)

la **actividad**   activity

el **actor**   actor

la **actriz** (*pl.* **actrices**)   actress

la **actualidad**   present time (4)

   de actualidad   contemporary, of the present time (4)

acuerdo: de ___   agreed, I agree, O.K. (4)

adelante *adv.*   ahead, forward (18)

   seguir (**i, i**) **adelante**   to continue (go on) ahead (18)

además *adv.*   besides (7)

adentro *adv.*   inside, within (14)

¡adiós!   good-bye! (9)

el **adjetivo**   adjective

la **administración** (*pl.* **administraciones**)   administration (6)

   la **administración de negocios**   business administration (6)

   la **Facultad de Administración de Negocios**   Business School, School of Business Administration (6)

¿adónde?   where? (*with verbs of motion*) (3)

adquirir (**ie**)   to acquire

la **aduana**   customs

aéreo, -a *adj.*   air (21)

   la **línea aérea**   airline (21)

el **aeróbic**   aerobics (15)

   hacer el aeróbic   to do aerobics (15)

el **aeromozo**   flight attendant (*m.*) (20)

el **aeropuerto**   airport (20)

afeitarse   to shave (8)

afuera *adv.*   outside (14)

la **agencia**   agency (20)

   la **agencia de empleo**   employment agency (19)

   la **agencia de viajes**   travel agency (20)

el (la) **agente**   agent (19)

   el (la) **agente de viajes**   travel agent (20)

   como agente   as an agent (19)

agosto   August (5)

agradable   pleasant, nice (2)

   ¡qué encuentro más agradable!   what a pleasant encounter (meeting)!

agradecer   to be grateful (thankful) for (19)

   ¡cuánto se lo agradezco!   how grateful I am to you for it (that)! (19)

agrícola (*m. and f.*) *adj.*   agricultural, farm (19)

   la **Ingeniería Agrícola**   Agricultural Engineering (19)

el **agua** (*f. pl.* las **aguas**)   water (10)

   esquiar en el agua   to water-ski (10)

¡ah!   ah! oh! (1)

ahí *adv.*   there (*near or related to person addressed*) (7)

los **ahijados**   godson and goddaughter

ahora *adv.*   now (1)

   por ahora   for the present, for now

el **aire**   air

   el **aire acondicionado**   air conditioning (12)

   al aire libre   outdoor, open-air

al = **a** + **el**   to the (3)

   al + *inf.*   on, upon + *pres. part.* (6)

   al día   per day (12)

   al día siguiente   (on) the following or next day (8)

   al lado de *prep.*   beside, next to, at the side of (8)

   al mediodía   at noon (3)

   al menos   at least (16)

   al mes   a (per) month, monthly (17)

   al poco rato   after a short while (13)

   al sur de(l)   south of (21)

   al suroeste   southwest

Alberto   Albert

alegrarse (**mucho**) **de** (+ *inf.*)   to be (very) glad to (+ *verb*) (15)

   alegrarse de que   to be glad that (18)

   ¡cuánto me alegro!   how glad I am! (22)

alegre (*m. or f.*)   cheerful, joyful, happy (5)

la **alegría**   joy (5)

   ¡qué alegría!   what joy! (5)

el **alemán**   German (*the language*) (1)

   la **lección de alemán**   German lesson (1)

   el **profesor** (la **profesora**) **de alemán**   the German teacher (professor) (1)

Alemania   Germany (15)

alérgico, -a allergic (16)

   ser alérgico(-a) a to be allergic to (16)

algo *pron.* anything, something (6)

   algo más something more, anything else (13)

   tomar algo to have *or* take something to eat *or* drink (6)

algo *adv.* somewhat (16)

el **algodón** cotton (7)

alguien *pron.* someone, somebody, anyone, anybody (9)

algún (*used for* **alguno** *before m. sing. nouns*) some, any (11)

alguno, -a (-os, -as) *adj. and pron.* some, any, someone; *pl.* some, a few, several, any (9)

   alguna vez sometime; ever (14)

allá there (*often used after verbs of motion*) (3)

   ¡vamos allá! let's go there!

allí there (*distant*) (2)

   allí llega there comes (arrives) (2)

el **almacén** (*pl.* **almacenes**) department store (17)

la **almohada** pillow (17)

almorzar (ue) to have (eat) lunch (8)

el **almuerzo** lunch (3)

   tomar el almuerzo to eat *or* have lunch (3)

¡aló! hello! (*telephone*)

alquilar to rent (17)

el **alquiler** rent, rental (*property*) (17)

alrededor de around

el **altar** altar

la **altiplanicie** highland plain

alto *adv.* loudly (14)

   hablar más alto to talk louder (14)

alto, -a high; tall (16)

la **alumna** pupil, student (*f.*) (1)

el **alumno** pupil, student (*m.*) (1)

   los **alumnos de la profesora** students of (the) professor (*f.*) (2)

alzar to lift (15)

   alzar (las) pesas to lift weights (15)

amable (*m. or f.*) friendly, kind (12)

amarillo, -a yellow (2)

ambiente: el medio _____ environment

la **ambulancia** ambulance (18)

   no hay heridos ni ambulancias there aren't any injured persons or ambulances (there are no . . . nor . . .) (18)

América America

   la **América Latina** Latin America

   la **América del Sur** South America

americano, -a American

   el **fútbol americano** football (15)

la **amiga** friend (*f.*) (4)

el **amigo** friend (*m.*) (4)

ampliar to broaden

amueblar to furnish (17)

   sin amueblar unfurnished (17)

Ana Ann, Anne, Anna

andar to go, walk

   anda (*fam. sing. command*) go, come on (now); *often used in an exclamation* (5)

el **ángel** (*pl.* **ángeles**) angel

el **anillo** ring (13)

   (el **anillo**) **de plata** silver (ring) 13

animadamente *adv.* animatedly (22)

animado, -a animated, lively (12)

anoche *adv.* last night (9)

antes *adv.* before (*time*), first (5)

   antes de *prep.* before (*time*) (9)

   antes de (entrar) before (entering) (9)

   antes (de que) *conj.* before (20)

el **antibiótico** antibiotic (16)

antiguo, -a ancient, old; former (*before a noun*) (14)

Antonio Anthony, Tony

anunciar to announce (22)

el **anuncio** ad(vertisement) (8)

el **año** year (5)

   Año Nuevo New Year (11)

   el **año (mes) pasado** last year (month) (9)

   ¿cuántos años tienes (tiene Ud.)? how old are you? (11)

   ¿cuántos años vas a cumplir (tú)? how old are you going to be? (11)

   cumplir… años to be . . . years old (i.e., reach the age of . . . years) (11)

   en este tiempo del año in (at) this time of (the) year (12)

   las **estaciones del año** the seasons of the year (5)

   tener… años to be . . . years old (11)

el **aparador** buffet (17)

el **aparato (eléctrico)** (electrical) appliance (17)

el **apartamento** apartment (3)

   la **compañera de apartamento** apartment mate, roommate (*f.*) (4)

   el **compañero de apartamento** apartment mate, roommate (*m.*) (4)

   el **edificio de apartamentos** apartment building (6)

apenas *adv.* scarcely, hardly (14)

   hace apenas (unos minutos) que it has been scarcely (a few minutes) since (14)

el **apogeo** apogee, highest point

apreciar to appreciate

aprender to learn (2)

apurado, -a in a hurry (*Am.*) (9)

   estar apurado, -a to be in a hurry (*Am.*) (9)

el **apuro** hurry, rush (18)

   ¿cuál es el apuro? what's the hurry (rush)? (18)

aquel, aquella (-os, -as) *adj.* that, those (*distant*) (6)

aquél, aquélla (-os, -as) *pron.* that, that one (those) (13)

aquello *neuter pron.* that (13)

aquí *adv.* here (2)

   aquí tiene(n) Ud(s). (la llave) here is (the key) (*lit.*, here you have . . .) (12)

   por aquí by (around) here, this way (5)

árabe (*m. and f.*) *also noun* Arab, Arabic

la **arena** sand (14)

el **arete** earring (13)

   (el **arete**) **de oro** gold earring (13)

la **Argentina** Argentina (5)

argentino, -a *also noun* Argentine (2)

el **arpa** (*f.*) harp

arqueológico, -a archeological

la **arquitecta** architect (*f.*) (6)

el **arquitecto** architect (*m.*) (6)

la **arquitectura** architecture (6)

   la **Facultad de Arquitectura** School of Architecture

arreglar to arrange, fix (14); *reflex.* to get ready (fixed up) (8)

   arreglarse el pelo to have one's hair done (14)

el **arte** (*f. pl.* las **artes**) art (6)

   las **artes liberales** liberal arts (6)

   la **clase de historia del arte** art history class

la **artesanía** handicraft (13)

   los **artículos de artesanía** handiwork, work of craftspeople (13)

el **artículo** article (4)

   los **artículos de artesanía** handiwork, work of craftspeople (13)

el **ascenso** promotion (19)

el **ascensor** elevator (12)

   tomar el ascensor to take the elevator (12)

así *adv.* so, thus, that way (8)

   así como as well as

   así es so it is (8)

   así que *conj.* so, so that (15); as soon as (20)

el **asiento** seat (20)

no quedan asientos   no seats are left (remain), there aren't any seats left
asistir (a)   to attend (16)
asomado, -a a   looking out from
asomarse a   to look out, lean out
asombrarse   to be amazed, be surprised (22)
la **aspiradora**   vacuum cleaner (17)
la **aspirina**   aspirin (16)
el **asunto**   matter, affair (19)
aún *adv.*   even; still, yet (15)
aunque *conj.*   although, even though (4)
el **autobús** (*pl.* **autobuses**)   bus (8)
   en autobús   by (in a) bus (8)
avanzar   to advance (15)
la **aventura**   adventure (10)
la **avería**   breakdown, failure (*of motor vehicle*) (18)
   tener una avería   to have a breakdown, failure (*in the car*) (18)
el **avión** (*pl.* **aviones**)   (air)plane (4)
   el boleto de avión   (air)plane ticket (8)
   en avión   by (in a) plane (5)
   por avión   by airmail, by plane (4)
avisar   to inform, notify (11)
¡ay!   ah! oh! (5)
ayer *adv.*   yesterday (9)
   ayer por la mañana (tarde)   yesterday morning (afternoon) (14)
la **ayuda**   aid
ayudar (a + *inf.*)   to help or to aid (19)
la **azafata**   flight attendant (*f.*) (20)
azul (*m. or f.*)   blue (2)

B

bailar   to dance (9)
el **bailarín** (*pl.* **bailarines**)   dancer (*m.*) (9)
la **bailarina**   dancer (*f.*)
el **baile**   dance (9)
   el número de baile   dance number (9)
bajar   to go down, descend (12)
el **baluarte**   bulwark
el **banco**   bank (7)
bañarse   to bathe (8)
el **baño**   bath, bathroom (12)
   el traje de baño   bathing suit (14)
barato, -a   inexpensive, cheap (7)
la **barba**   beard (8)
barbaridad: ¡qué ____!   how awful! (16)

el **barco**   ship, boat (8)
   el equipo de barcos de vela   sailing team
   en barco   by (in a) boat (8)
el **barrio**   quarter, district, neighborhood (17)
el **basquetbol**   basketball (15)
bastante *adv.*   quite, quite a bit; rather; *adj.* enough, sufficient (1)
   venir bastante cansado, -a   to be quite tired (5)
la **batidora**   mixer, beater, blender (17)
Beatriz   Beatrice
beber   to drink (3)
la **bebida**   drink (11)
la **beca**   scholarship (19)
el **béisbol**   baseball (15)
la **belleza**   beauty
bello, -a   beautiful, pretty
benéfico, -a   beneficent, good
la **biblioteca**   library (3)
   en la biblioteca   at (in) the library (3)
la **bicicleta**   bicycle (15)
   en bicicleta   by (on a) bicycle (15)
bien *adv.*   well (1)
   estar (muy) bien   to be (very) well (5)
   ¡muy bien!   very well! (that's) fine! (1)
   ¡qué bien!   good! great! (6)
   (ella) se ve muy bien   (she) looks very well (14)
   ¿(te, le, les) parece bien?   is it all right with (you)? does it seem O.K. to (you)? (7)
bilingüe (*m. and f.*)   bilingual (4)
la **billetera**   wallet (*Am.*) (7)
blanco, -a   white (2)
la **blusa**   blouse (7)
los **bocaditos**   appetizers (11)
la **boda**   wedding (17)
   el regalo de boda   wedding gift (17)
el **boleto**   ticket (*transportation*) (5)
   el boleto de avión   (air)plane ticket (8)
   el boleto sencillo (de ida y vuela)   one-way (round-trip) ticket (20)
la **bolsa**   purse, pocketbook, bag (7)
   la bolsa de cuero   leather purse (bag) (7)
bonito, -a   beautiful, pretty (2)
el **borde**   edge
el **brazo**   arm (16)
brillante (*m. or f.*)   brilliant (12)
bronceado, -a   tanned (14)
bucear   to (skin *or* scuba) dive (10)
buen   *used for* **bueno** *before m. sing. nouns* (9)

¡buen viaje!   (have) a good *or* fine trip! (9)
   hace buen tiempo   the weather is fine (nice) (10)
   pasar un buen rato   to have a good time (11)
   ¡qué buen rato!   what a good time! what fun! (11)
bueno *adv.*   well, well now (then), all right, O.K. (2)
bueno, -a   good (1)
   buenas noches   good evening, good night (1)
   buenas tardes   good afternoon (1)
   ¡bueno!   hello! (*telephone*) (*Mex.*) (7)
   buenos días   good morning, good day (1)
   es bueno   it's good (19)
buscar   to look for, seek, get (5)
   en busca de   in search of (8)

C

la **cabeza**   head (16)
   tener dolor de cabeza   to have a headache (16)
la **cablevisión**   cable TV
cada (*m. and f.*)   each, every
   a cada rato   every short while (moment) (16)
el **café**   coffee (3); café
   el café solo   black coffee
   tomar una taza de café   to have or drink a cup of coffee (3)
la **cafetera**   coffee pot, percolator (17)
la **cafetería**   cafeteria (2)
el **calcetín** (*pl.* **calcetines**)   sock (7)
el **Califato**   caliphate (*dominion of a caliph*) (12)
la **calle**   street (6)
   la calle (Constitución)   (Constitution) Street (7)
calmar   to calm; *reflex.* to calm oneself, become calm, calm down (16)
el **calor**   heat, warmth (10)
   hacer (mucho) calor   to be (very) hot (*weather*) (10)
   tener calor   to be hot (*living beings*) (11)
caluroso, -a   warm, hot (10)
la **cama**   bed (12)
   la cama doble   double bed (12)
   las camas sencillas   single beds (12)
   la ropa de cama   bed linens (sheets, pillowcases, etc.), bedclothes (blankets, sheets, etc.) (12)

el **sofá-cama** sofa bed (17)
la **cámara** camera (21)
la **cámara vídeo** video camera (21)
el **camarero** waiter (22)
cambiar to change (12)
el **cambio** change, exchange (4)
el **camino** road, way (10)
(**ir**) **camino de** (to be or go) on the (one's) way to (10)
la **camisa** shirt (7)
la **camiseta** T-shirt, sportshirt (7); undershirt
el **campeón** (pl. **campeones**) champion
el **campo** country, field (10)
el **campo de juego** court (ball)
la **cana** gray hair
el **canal** channel (15); canal
cancelar to cancel (20)
la **cancha** (tennis) court (15)
la **canción** (pl. **canciones**) song (9)
la **candidata** candidate (applicant for a job, position) (f.) (19)
el **candidato** candidate (applicant for a job, position) (m.) (19)
cansado, -a tired (5)
venir bastante cansado, -a to be quite tired (5)
cansarse to get tired (14)
el (la) **cantante** singer (9)
cantar to sing (9)
cántaros: llover (**ue**) **a** _____ to rain cats and dogs (10)
la **capital** capital (city) (5)
la **cara** face (8)
lavarse la cara to wash one's face (8)
pintarse la cara to put on make-up (8)
¡caramba! goodness! gosh! gee! good gracious! (6)
el **Caribe** Caribbean Sea (area) (10)
Carlos Charles
Carmen Carmen
el **carnet** license
el **carnet** (la **licencia**) **de manejar** driver's license (18)
caro, -a expensive, dear (7)
Carolina Caroline
la **carrera** career; field, course of study (6)
el **carro** car (Am.) (18)
el **carro patrulla** patrol (police) car (18)
la **carta** letter (3)
la **carta de recomendación** letter of recommendation (19)
el **papel de cartas** (**de escribir**) writing paper
el **cartel** poster (2)

la **casa** house, home (1)
a casa de su amigo (**Ramón**) to his friend (Raymond)'s (house) (6)
la **casa de correos** post office (21)
de casa de (**Diana**) from (Diane)'s house (6)
en casa at home (1)
la **especialidad de la casa** the specialty of the house
estar en casa to be at home (8)
invitar a casa to invite to one's house (21)
(**llegar**) **a casa** (to arrive) home (3)
volver (**ue**) **a casa** to return or go back home; to come back home (8)
casado, -a married (5)
estar casado, -a to be married (5)
casarse to get married (17)
casi almost, nearly (3)
casi no se oye one can hardly (scarcely) hear (14)
casi que really, truly (15)
el **caso** case
hacer caso a to notice, listen to, pay attention to (16)
en caso de que conj. in case (the event) that (20)
la **casualidad** chance, accident (9)
por casualidad by chance (11)
¡qué casualidad! what a coincidence! (9)
la **catarata** cataract, waterfall
catorce fourteen (3)
la **celebración** (pl. **celebraciones**) celebration
celebrar to celebrate (11)
celebramos los veintiún años de (**...**) we celebrate (are celebrating) (...)'s twenty-first birthday (11)
celeste (m. or f.) light blue (7)
el **cementerio** cemetery
cenar to eat (have) supper (3)
el **cenicero** ashtray (13)
el **centavo** cent (U.S.) (7)
central (m. or f.) central
el **centro** downtown, center (4)
(**estar**) **en el centro** (to be) downtown (13)
ir al centro to go downtown (4)
(**llegar**) **al centro** (to arrive) downtown (7)
Centroamérica Central America
centroamericano, -a also noun Central American
la **cerámica** ceramics, pottery (13)
los **objetos de cerámica** ceramics, pottery objects, pieces of pottery (13)

cerca adv. near (10)
cerca de prep. near, close to (3)
cercano, -a nearby, neighboring (18)
la **ceremonia** ceremony
cero zero
cerrar (**ie**) to close (8)
la **cerveza** beer (11)
la **chaqueta** jacket (7)
charlar to chat (6)
el **cheque** check (7)
los **cheques de viajero** traveler's checks (12)
la **chica** girl (6)
el **chico** boy; pl. boys and girls, young people (6)
chileno, -a also noun Chilean (2)
la **chimenea** chimney, fireplace (11)
chocar (**con**) to hit, collide (with) (18)
el **choque** collision (18)
la **ciencia** science (6)
la **ciencia-ficción** science fiction (9)
las **ciencias naturales** (**sociales**) natural (social) sciences (6)
la **película de ciencia-ficción** science-fiction movie or film (9)
ciento (**cien**) one (a) hundred (12)
cien mil one hundred thousand (12)
ciento (**dos**) one hundred (two) (12)
cierto, -a (a) certain, sure (5)
por cierto certainly, surely, for certain (sure), by the way (10)
cinco five (2)
cincuenta fifty (6)
el **cine** movie(s) (9)
el **cinturón** (pl. **cinturones**) belt (13)
la **cita** date, appointment (15)
la **ciudad** city (4)
la **ciudad de México** Mexico City (13)
la (**ciudad**) **de piedra** stone (city) (20)
la **civilización** (pl. **civilizaciones**) civilization (12)
Clara Clara, Clare, Claire
claro adv. clearly, of course (2)
¡claro! I see! sure! of course! certainly! (6)
claro, -a adj. clear (14)
la **clase** class, classroom (1)
la **clase de español** (**francés, inglés**) Spanish (French, English) class (1)
la **clase turista** tourist (economy) class (20)
la **compañera de clase** classmate (f.) (3)
el **compañero de clase** classmate (m.) (3)

en clase   in class (1)
la **primera clase**   first class (20)
la **sala de clase**   classroom (2)
el **clima**   climate
cobrar   to cash (*a check*) (7); to charge, collect (12)
el **cobre**   copper
la **cocina**   kitchen (15); kitchen stove (17)
cocinar   to cook (11)
el **coche**   car (*Spain*) (8)
en coche   by (in a) car (8)
el **colegio**   school; college
el **collar**   necklace (13)
colombiano, -a *also noun*   Colombian (2)
el **color**   color (2)
¿de qué color... ?   what color . . . ? (2)
las **fotografías a colores**   color photographs (2)
la **comedia**   comedy (9)
la **comedia musical**   musical comedy or play (9)
el **comedor**   dining room (hall) (3)
el **comentario**   commentary, comment (18)
comenzar (**ie**) (**a** + *inf.*)   to begin or commence (to) (9)
comer   to eat, dine, eat dinner (2)
comercial (*m. or f.*)   commercial, business
la **comida**   food, meal, dinner (3)
el **horario de las comidas**   meal hours, time (schedule) of meals (3)
el **Comisionado Residente**   Resident Commissioner
como *adv.*   as, like (5); since (10)
como agente   as an agent (19)
como en España, ¿no?   like (as) in Spain, right? (3)
como si   as if (21)
¡cómo!   how!
¡cómo no!   of course! certainly! (4)
¡cómo se ve que... !   one can tell that . . . ! (16)
¿cómo?   how? (1)
¿cómo se dice... ?   how do you say . . . ?
¿cómo es (son)... ?   what is (are) . . . like? (2)
¿cómo lo han pasado?   how have things gone? (14)
¿cómo se llama Ud. (te llamas)?   what's your name?, how/what do you call yourself?
¿cómo te sientes?   how do you (*fam. sing.*) feel? (16)
cómodo, -a   comfortable (7)

el **compacto**   compact disk (11)
el **disco compacto**   compact disk, CD (11)
el **tocadiscos** (**para compactos**)   record (compact disk) player (11)
los **compadres**   parents and godparents of a child
la **compañera**   companion (*f.*) (3)
la **compañera de apartamento**   apartment mate; roommate (*f.*) (4)
la **compañera de clase**   classmate (*f.*) (3)
la **compañera de cuarto**   roommate (*f.*) (3)
la **compañera de viaje**   traveling companion (*f.*) (8)
el **compañero**   companion (*m.*) (3)
el **compañero de apartamento**   apartment mate, roommate (*m.*) (4)
el **compañero de clase**   classmate (*m.*) (3)
el **compañero de cuarto**   roommate (*m.*) (3)
el **compañero de viaje**   traveling companion (*m.*) (8)
la **compañía**   company (19)
comparar   to compare (21)
competente (*m. or f.*)   competent, qualified (19)
completamente *adv.*   completely (15)
completo, -a   complete, full (12)
el **desayuno completo**   full breakfast (12)
la **compra**   purchase (7)
(**ir**) **de compras**   (to go) shopping (7)
comprar   to buy, purchase (4)
comprender   to understand, comprehend (4)
el **compromiso**   engagement, commitment (22)
la **computadora**   computer (20)
común (*m. or f., pl.* **comunes**)   common
por lo común   usually, commonly, generally (10)
la **comunidad**   community
con   with (1)
con (sin) el desayuno completo   with (without) a full breakfast (12)
con mucho gusto   gladly, with great pleasure (5)
con nosotros   with us (5)
con tal (de) que *conj.*   provided (that) (20)
el **concierto**   concert (9)

conducir   to drive (*Spain*) (18)
el **conductor**   driver (*m.*) (18)
la **conductora**   driver (*f.*) (18)
la **conferencia**   lecture (18)
confirmar   to confirm (20)
conformar   to adapt, adjust (14)
conformarse con   to resign oneself to (14)
la **congestión**   congestion (16)
conmigo   with me (12)
conocer   to know, be acquainted with, meet (5)
encantado, -a de conocerte   delighted to meet you (*fam. sing.*)
mucho gusto en conocerla   (I am) pleased (glad) to know you *or* nice meeting (to meet) you (*formal f. sing.*) (20)
la **conquista**   conquest
conseguir (**i, i**) (*like* **seguir**)   to get, obtain (18)
el **consejero**   adviser
el **consejo**   piece of advice (16)
dar un consejo   to give (a piece of, some) advice (16)
conservar   to preserve; to conserve
el **conservatorio**   conservatory
la **constitución** (*pl.* **constituciones**)   constitution (7)
la **calle** (**Constitución**)   (Constitution) Street (7)
la **construcción** (*pl.* **construcciones**)   construction
construir   to construct, build (22)
los **consuegros**   fathers and mothers whose children are married to each other; in-laws
consultar   to consult (20)
el **consultorio médico**   medical clinic
contar (**ue**)   to tell, relate; to count (9)
contento, -a   happy, pleased, glad (5)
estar contento, -a   to be happy (5)
contestar   to answer (1)
conteste (**Ud.**) (*pl.* **contesten** [**Uds.**])   answer (1)
contigo   with you (*fam. sing.*) (12)
continuar   to continue, go on (20)
contra *prep.*   against (15)
convenir (*like* **venir**)   to be advisable (12)
la **conversación** (*pl.* **conversaciones**)   conversation (1)
la **copa**   glass (*for wine*), goblet (11); cup (15)
la **Copa Mundial**   World Cup (15)
los **corales**   coral (14)
Córdoba   Cordova (*city in southern Spain*) (12)
el **corredor**   corridor, hall (14)

el **correo** mail, postal service

correos: la **casa de** _____ post office (21)

correr to run (10)

correr las olas to surf (10)

corrientemente currently

corto, -a short (4)

los **pantalones cortos** shorts (7)

la **cosa** thing (7)

¡**cuántas cosas quieres… !** how many things you want . . . ! (17)

la **costa** coast (22)

costar (**ue**) to cost (8)

crear to create

crecer to grow

el **crédito** credit (12)

la **tarjeta de crédito** credit card (12)

creer to believe, think (2)

¡**ya lo creo!** of course! certainly! (21)

la **criada** maid (12)

cruzar to cross (10)

el **cuaderno** notebook (2)

el **cuaderno de ejercicios** workbook (2)

¿**cuál?** (_pl._ ¿**cuáles?**) what?, which one(s)? (7)

¿**cuál es el apuro?** what's the hurry (rush)? (18)

¿**cuál es la fecha?** what's the date? (12)

cualquier, -a (_pl._ **cualesquier, -a**) any (one at all); just any (one at all) (21)

a cualquier hora at any time (hour) (21)

en cualquier momento (at) any moment (17)

cuando when (6)

de vez en cuando from time to time, once in a while, occasionally (6)

¿**cuándo?** when? (3)

¡**cuánto** + _verb_! how . . . ! (18)

¡**cuánto me alegro!** how glad I am! (22)

¡**cuánto me alegro de que… !** how glad I am that . . . ! (18)

¡**cuánto me gustaría viajar… !** how I should (would) like to travel . . . ! (22)

¡**cuánto se lo agradezco!** how grateful I am to you for it (that)! (19)

¿**cuánto -a (-os, -as)?** how much? (5)

¡**cuántas cosas quieres… !** how many things you want! (17)

¿**cuánto tiempo hace que Uds. volvieron?** how long has it been since you (_pl._) returned? (14)

¿**cuánto tiempo hace?** how long is it (has it been)? (19)

¿**cuánto tiempo?** how much time? how long? (5)

¿**cuántos años tienes** (**tiene Ud.**)? how old are you? (11)

¿**cuántos años vas a cumplir** (**tú**)? how old are you going to be? (11)

cuarenta forty (6)

cuarenta minutos forty minutes (3)

cuarto, -a fourth (12)

el **cuarto** room; quarter (_of an hour_) (3)

la **compañera de cuarto** roommate (_f._) (3)

el **compañero de cuarto** roommate (_m._) (3)

cuatro four (3)

cuatrocientos, -as four hundred (12)

cubano, -a _also noun_ Cuban (4)

los **cubiertos** place setting (knife, fork, and spoon) (17)

cubierto, -a (**de**) _p.p. of_ **cubrir** _and adj._ covered (with) (14)

cubrir to cover (14)

el **cuello** neck (16)

la **cuenta** bill, account (12)

el **cuero** leather (7)

la **bolsa de cuero** leather purse (bag) (7)

el **cuerpo** body (16)

todo el cuerpo (the) whole or entire body

el **cuidado** care (11)

tener (**mucho**) **cuidado** to be (very) careful (11)

cultivable (_m. or f._) cultivable, arable

cultural (_m. or f._) cultural

las **funciones culturales** cultural events

la **cumbia** _a Colombian dance_ (11)

el **cumpleaños** (_pl._ los **cumpleaños**) birthday (11)

la **fiesta de cumpleaños** birthday party (11)

cumplir to reach one's birthday, be (_years old_) (11)

¿**cuántos años vas a cumplir** (**tú**)? how old are you going to be? (11)

cumplir… años to be . . . years old (i.e., reach the age of . . . years) (11)

los **cuñados** brothers _or_ sisters-in-law

Cuzco _Cuzco, ancient capital of the Incan empire_

D

daño: hacerse _____ to hurt oneself, get hurt (18)

dar to give (7)

dar a to face, open onto (12)

dar calabazas to reject (_lit._ to give pumpkins)

dar un consejo to give (a piece of, some) advice (16)

dar un paseo to take a walk (ride) (17)

lo (**la**) **damos por** we are offering (selling) it (_m. or f._) for (7)

de of, from, about (1); to with, as; in (_with time_) (3); than (_before numerals_)

de actualidad contemporary, of the present time (4)

de acuerdo agreed, I agree, O.K. (4)

de casa de (**Diana**) from (Diane's house (6)

¿**de dónde?** (from) where? (2)

de ninguna manera (in) no way (16)

de noche at (by) night (8)

de la mañana (**tarde, noche**) in the morning (afternoon, evening) (_when a specific hour is given_) (3)

de postre for dessert (11)

¿**de qué color… ?** what color . . . ? (2)

¿**de quién** (_pl._ ¿**de quiénes?**) **es** (**son**)? whose is it (are they)? (3)

de todos modos in any case (20)

de veras really, truly (15)

de vez en cuando from time to time, once in a while, occasionally (6)

de visita on (for) a visit (5)

estar de visita to visit, be visiting, be on a visit (5)

debajo de below

deber to owe; must, should, ought to (15)

la **decadencia** decadence

decidir to decide (10)

décimo, -a tenth (12)

decir to say, tell (7)

¿**cómo se dice… ?** how do you say . . . ?

diga, dígame hello (_telephone_) (11)

dinos = **di** (_fam. sing. command of_ **decir**) + **nos** tell us (16)

oír decir que to hear (it said) that (19)

querer (**ie**) **decir** to mean (20)

el **dedo**   finger (16)

dejar   to leave (behind) (11); to let, allow, permit (18)

  no dejar de + *inf.*   not to fail to + *verb* (22)

del = **de** + **el**   of (from) the (3)

delante de   in front of

deleitar   to delight

delicioso, -a   delicious (22)

la **dependienta**   clerk (*f.*) (4)

el **dependiente**   clerk (*m.*) (4)

el **deporte**   sport (15)

  practicar un deporte   to play a sport (15)

  la **sección de deportes**   sports section (15)

derecho, -a *adj.*   right

  a la derecha   to (on, at) the right

  por la derecha   on (to) the right (18)

el **derecho**   law (6)

desarrollar   to develop; *reflex.* to be developed

desayunar(se)   to have (eat) breakfast (8)

el **desayuno**   breakfast (3)

  con (**sin**) **el desayuno completo**   with (without) a full breakfast (12)

  desayuno completo   full breakfast (12)

  tomar el desayuno   to eat *or* have breakfast (3)

descansar   to rest (5)

  descansar un rato   to rest for a while (5)

desconocido, -a   unknown

describir   to describe

desde *prep.*   since, from (12); for (*time*)

desear   to desire, wish, want (8)

  no deseamos nada más   we don't want anything else

desgraciadamente   unfortunately (8)

el **desierto**   desert

desocupado, -a   unoccupied, vacant (12)

despacio   slowly (14)

la **despedida**   farewell (11)

  la **fiesta de despedida**   farewell party (11)

despedirse (**i, i**) (**de** + *obj.*)   to say good-bye (to), take leave (of) (20)

despejado, -a   clear (*weather*) (10)

despertar (**ie**)   to arouse, awake; *reflex.* to wake up (8)

despierto, -a   awake (16)

después *adv.*   afterwards, later (5)

  después de *prep.*   after (2)

  después (**de**) **que** *conj.*   after (20)

poco después   shortly afterward (14)

detener (*like* **tener**)   to detain, stop; *reflex.* to stop (oneself) (12)

devolver (**ue**)   to return, give *or* take back (13)

el **día** (*note gender*)   day (1)

  al día   per day (12)

  al día siguiente   (on) the following *or* next day (8)

  buenos días   good morning, good day (1)

  el **Día de Acción de Gracias**   Thanksgiving Day (7)

  hoy día   nowadays (6)

  todos los días   every day (*lit.*, all the days) (1)

  el **vuelo de día**   daytime flight, flight by day (20)

Diana   Diane, Diana

diario, -a   daily (20)

el **diccionario**   dictionary (4)

diciembre   December (5)

diecinueve   nineteen (3)

dieciocho   eighteen (3)

dieciséis   sixteen (3)

diecisiete   seventeen (3)

el **diente**   tooth (8)

diez   ten (3)

diferente (*m. or f.*)   different (21)

difícil (*m. or f.*)   difficult, hard (4)

  no son difíciles de comprender   (they) are not difficult to understand (4)

dígame   hello (*telephone*) (11)

el **dinero**   money (6)

  el **dinero en efectivo**   cash (12)

Dios   God (11)

  ¡Dios mío!   heavens! (my God!) (11)

la **dirección** (*pl.* **direcciones**)   direction, address (4)

directo, -a   direct (20)

  el **vuelo directo**   non-stop (direct) flight (20)

el **director**   director (*m.*) (19)

la **directora**   director (*f.*) (19)

dirigir   to direct (13); **dirigirse a** *reflex.* to turn to, direct oneself to, address (*a person*) (13)

el **disco**   record (*phonograph*); disk (11)

  el **disco compacto**   compact disk (11)

disfrutar (**de** + *obj.*)   to enjoy (14)

divertido, -a   amused, amusing (9)

divertir (**ie, i**)   to divert, amuse; *reflex.* to amuse oneself or enjoy oneself, have a good time (16)

doble (*m. or f.*)   double

  la **cama doble**   double bed (12)

doce   twelve (3)

el **dólar**   dollar (*U.S.*) (7)

doler (**ue**)   to ache, pain, hurt (16)

el **dolor**   ache, pain (16); sorrow

  tener dolor de cabeza   to have a headache (16)

doméstico, -a   domestic

dominar   to dominate

el **domingo**   (on) Sunday (3)

  el **domingo por la mañana**   (on) Sunday morning (8)

donde   where, in which (3)

¿dónde?   where? (2)

  ¿de dónde?   (from) where? (2)

dormir (**ue, u**)   to sleep; *reflex.* to fall asleep, go to sleep (16)

el **dormitorio**   bedroom, dormitory (17)

dos   two (2)

  dos mil   two thousand (12)

  los (las) **dos**   both, the two (6)

doscientos, -as   two hundred (12)

el **drama** (*note gender*)   drama (9)

la **duda**   doubt (21)

  sin duda   doubtless, no doubt (21)

dudar   to doubt (18)

dudoso, -a   doubtful (19)

la **dueña**   owner (*f.*) (17)

el **dueño**   owner (*m.*) (17)

durante *prep.*   during, for (8)

E

e   and (*used for* **y** *before* **i-**, **hi-** *but not* **hie-**)

echar   to throw, cast (22); put (in)

  echar de menos   to miss (someone or something) (22)

  echar piropos   to pay compliments (22)

la **ecología**   ecology

la **economía** (*sing.*)   economics (6)

el (la) **economista**   economist (6)

el **ecuador**   equator (21)

el **edificio**   building, edifice (2)

  el **edificio de apartamentos**   apartment building (6)

  el **edificio principal**   main building (2)

Eduardo   Edward

efectivo: el **dinero en** _____   cash (12)

¿eh?   eh? right? (8)

el **ejemplo**   example (4)

  por ejemplo   for example (4)

el **ejercicio**   exercise (1)

  el **cuaderno de ejercicios**   workbook (2)

el **ejercicio de pronunciación** pronunciation exercise (1)

hacer ejercicio to exercise (15)

el (*pl.* **los**) the (*m.*)

el de that of; the one of (with, in)

el que that; who; which, he (who, whom) that (which)

él he; him, it (*m.*) (*after prep.*) (12)

la **elección** (*pl.* **elecciones**) election (4)

eléctrico, -a electric (17)

la **sartén eléctrica** electric skillet (17)

Elena Helen, Ellen

ella she; her, it (*f.*) (*after prep.*) (12)

ello *neuter pron.* it

ellos, -as they; them (*after prep.*)

embargo: sin _____ however

eminente (*m. or f.*) eminent

la **emoción** (*pl.* **emociones**) excitement; emotion (15)

emocionante (*m. or f.*) exciting, thrilling (15)

la **empanada** turnover, small meat pie (11)

empezar (**ie**) (**a** + *inf.*) to begin to (18)

la **empleada** employee (*f.*) (19)

el **empleado** employee (*m.*) (19)

emplear to employ, use (22)

el **empleo** employment, job

la **agencia de empleo** employment agency (19)

la **empresa** company, firm, house (*business*) (19); industrial enterprise

en in, on, at (1)

en autobús by (in a) bus (8)

en avión by (in a) plane (5)

en barco by (in a) boat (8)

en bicicleta by (on a) bicycle (15)

en busca de in search of (8)

en casa at home (1)

en caso de que *conj.* in case (the event) that (20)

en clase in class (1)

en coche by (in a) car (8)

en cualquier momento (at) any moment (17)

en cuanto *conj.* as soon as (20)

en efectivo cash, in cash (12)

en el mes de (**agosto**) during the month of (August) (5)

en el número (**cincuenta**) at number (fifty) (6)

en este tiempo del año in (at) this time of (the) year (12)

en fin in short (14)

en la biblioteca at (in) the library (3)

en la universidad at the university (1)

en la vida never in my life (16)

en punto on the dot, sharp (*time*) (3)

¿en qué puedo servirle(s)? what can I do for you? how can I help you? (13)

en seguida at once, immediately (12)

en serio seriously (9)

en todas partes everywhere

en tren by (in a) train (8)

estar en casa to be at home (8)

encantador, -ora enchanting, charming (14)

encantar to charm, delight (7)

me encanta el estilo I love (am delighted with, charmed by) the style (7)

encanto: ¡eres un _____! you're a dear! (17)

encontrar (**ue**) to meet, encounter, find (8); *reflex.* to find oneself, be found, be (14)

encontrarse (**ue**) (**con**) to meet, run across, run into someone (21)

enero January (5)

enfermarse to get sick (ill) (16)

la **enfermera** nurse (*f.*) (16)

el **enfermero** nurse (*m.*) (16)

enfermo, -a ill, sick (5)

estar enfermo, -a to be ill, sick (5)

enfrente de *prep.* across from, in front of (6)

estar enfrente de to be across from (6)

Enriqueta Henrietta

enseñar to teach (1)

enseñar a + *inf.* to show, teach (how to) (7)

entender (**ie**) to understand (19)

entender de (**asuntos de maquinaria agrícola**) to understand *or* have experience in (matters of agricultural machinery) (19)

la **entonación** intonation

entonces *adv.* then, well then, at that time (3)

la **entrada** ticket (*for admission*) (9)

entrar (**en** + *obj.*) to enter, go *or* come in (into) (6)

entre *prep.* between, among (3)

entregar to hand (over) (13); to turn in

entremetido, -a meddlesome (18)

la **entrevista** interview (19)

enviar to send (20)

envolver (**ue**) to wrap (up) (13); to involve

la **época** epoch, period

el **equipaje** baggage, luggage (21)

el **equipo** team (15)

la **era** era

de la era cristiana Christian era

el **escaparate** shop window (7)

la **escena** scene (15)

el **esclavo** slave

escoger to choose, select (20)

escribir to write (3)

el **papel de cartas** (**de escribir**) writing paper (4)

el **escritor** writer

escuchar to listen (to) (1)

escuchar la radio (**las noticas**) listen to the radio (news) (4)

escuche (**Ud.**) (*pl.* **escuchen** [**Uds.**]) listen

la **escuela** school (10)

la **escuela secundaria** secondary school, high school (15)

la **escuela de verano** summer school (15)

la **Escuela Técnica** (Superior/Advanced) Technological School

la **escultura** sculpture

ese, esa (**-os, -as**) *adj.* that (those) (*nearby*) (6)

ése, ésa (**-os, -as**) *pron.* that, that one (those) (*nearby*) (13)

eso *neuter pron.* that (13)

a eso de at about (*time*) (3)

por eso because of that, for that reason, that's why (16)

la **espalda** back (10)

España Spain (2)

como en España, ¿no? like (as) in Spain, right? (3)

español, -ola Spanish: *noun* Spaniard; *pl.* Spanish (*persons*) (2)

la **tortilla española** potato omelet (*Spain*)

el **español** Spanish (*the language*) (1)

la **clase de español** Spanish class (1)

los **estudiantes de español** students of Spanish (2)

la **lección de español** Spanish lesson (1)

el **profesor** (**la profesora**) **de español** Spanish teacher (1)

especial (*m. or f.*) special (7)

a precio especial on sale, at a special price, at special prices (7)

la **especie** species

el **espectáculo** show (9), public function, performance; spectacle la **espera**   wait

la **lista de espera**   waiting list (20)

esperar   to wait, wait for; to expect, hope (6)

esperar mucho   to wait long (*a long time*) (18)

la **esposa**   wife (12)

el **esposo**   husband (12)

esquiar   to ski (10)

esquiar en el agua   to water-ski (10)

establecer   to establish; *reflex.* to settle, establish oneself

el **establecimiento**   establishment, settlement

la **estación** (*pl.* **estaciones**)   season; station (5)

las **estaciones del año**   the seasons of the year (5)

el **estacionamiento**   parking (12)

el **estadio**   stadium (15)

el **estado**   state

el **Estado Libre Asociado**   Associated Free State (Commonwealth)

los **Estados Unidos**   the United States (1)

estadounidense (*m. or f.*)   US, American

el **torneo estadounidense**   US Open

la **estampilla**   stamp (14)

estar   to be (5)

estar apurado, -a   to be in a hurry (*Am.*) (9)

estar casado, -a   to be married (5)

estar contento, -a   to be happy (5)

estar de vacaciones   to be on vacation (5)

estar de visita   to visit, be visiting, be on a visit (5)

estar en casa   to be at home (8)

(**estar**) **en el centro**   (to be) downtown (13)

estar enfermo, -a   to be ill, sick (5)

estar enfrente de   to be across from (6)

estar (**muy**) **bien**   to be (very) well (5)

está (**muy**) **de moda**   it's (very) much in fashion (7)

estar nublado   to be cloudy (*sky*) (10)

estar regular   to be so-so (5)

estar seguro, -a de que   to be sure that (6)

este, esta (**-os, -as**) *adj.*   this (these) (6)

esta misma tarde   this very afternoon (17)

esta vez   this time (11)

éste, ésta (**-os, -as**) *pron.*   this, this one (these); the latter (13)

el **este**   east

el **estéreo**   stereo (17)

el **estilo**   style (7)

me encanta el estilo   I love (am delighted with, charmed by) the style (7)

esto *neuter pron.*   this (13)

el **estómago**   stomach (16)

el (la) **estudiante**   student (1)

los **estudiantes de español**   students of Spanish (2)

la **residencia** (**de estudiantes**)   (student) dormitory, residence hall (3)

estudiar   to study (1)

tener mucho que estudiar   to have a great deal to study (6)

el **estudio**   study (6)

estupendo, -a   stupendous, great, wonderful (8)

(**ella**) **se ve estupenda**   (she) looks great (14)

evidente (*m. or f.*)   evident

el **examen** (*pl.* **exámenes**)   exam (11)

los **exámenes finales**   final exams, finals (11)

excelente (*m. or f.*)   excellent (4)

la **excursión** (*pl.* **excursiones**)   excursion, trip (10)

hacer una excursión   to take (make) an excursion (a trip) (15)

salir de excursión   to go (set out) on an excursion (10)

excusar   to excuse; *reflex.* to excuse oneself (20)

el **éxito**   success, "hit" (9)

tener (**mucho**) **éxito**   to be (very) successful (22)

la **expresión** (*pl.* **expresiones**)   expression(s) (1)

extenso, -a   extensive

extranjero, -a   foreign (4)

la **librería de libros extranjeros**   foreign bookstore (4)

extrañar   to surprise (18)

me extraña   I am surprised, it surprises me (18)

extraño, -a   strange (19)

F

la **fábrica**   factory (19); fabric

fácil (*m. or f.*)   easy (4)

facturar   to check (*baggage*) (20)

la **Facultad**   School (*in a university*) (6)

la **Facultad de Administración de Negocios**   Business School, School of Business Administration (6)

la **Facultad de Arquitectura**   School of Architecture

la **Facultad de Ingeniería**   School of Engineering

la **Facultad de Medicina**   Medical School, School of Medicine (6)

la **falda**   skirt (7)

fallar   to fail (18)

la **falta**   lack, want (21)

sin falta   without fail (21)

la **familia**   family (1)

familiar (*m. or f.*)   familiar

famoso, -a   famous (9)

fantasía: las joyas de _____   costume jewelry (13)

fantástico, -a   fantastic, "great" (9)

farmacéutico, -a   pharmaceutical

la **farmacia**   drugstore, pharmacy (6)

el **favor**   favor (11)

hága(n)me *or* **haga(n) el favor de** + *inf.*   please + *verb*

¿**nos hace Ud. el favor de decirnos... ?**   will you please tell us . . . ?

por favor   please (1)

febrero   February (5)

la **fecha**   date (12)

¿**cuál es la fecha?**   what's the date? (12)

¿**para qué fecha(s)?**   for (by) what date(s)? (12)

felicitar   to congratulate (22)

Felipe   Philip

feliz (*m. or f.*; *pl.* **felices**)   happy (17)

feo, -a   ugly (4)

Fernando   Ferdinand

festejar   to honor, entertain

el **festival**   festival

la **fiebre**   fever (16)

tener (**muchísima**) **fiebre**   to have a (very high) fever (16)

la **fiesta**   party, festival, holiday (11)

la **fiesta de cumpleaños** (**despedida, Año Nuevo**)   birthday (farewell, New Year's) party (11)

figurar   to figure

fijo, -a   fixed (7)

tener precio fijo   to have fixed prices (7)

el **fin**   end

en fin   in short (14); in sum

el **fin de semana**   the weekend (8)

por fin   finally (6)

final (*m. or f.*)   final (11)

los **exámenes finales**   final exams, finals (11)

la **final**   final match (*game*), finals (*sports*) (15)

la **semifinal**   semifinal match (15)

fino, -a   fine, nice (7)

firmar   to sign (22)

firme (*m. or f.*)   firm, solid

fiscal (*m. or f.*)   fiscal

el **flan**   flan (*a custard*) (11)

la **flor**   flower (16)

el **fondo**   bottom, depth (14)

la **forma**   form (22)

la **foto**   photo (12)

  sacar fotografías (**fotos** [*f.*])   to take photographs (photos) (12)

la **fotografía**   photograph, picture (2)

  las **fotografías a colores**   color photographs (2)

  sacar fotografías (**fotos** [*f.*])   to take photographs (photos) (12)

el **francés**   French (*the language*) (1)

  la **clase de francés**   French class (1)

  la **lección de francés**   French lesson (1)

  el **profesor** (la **profesora**) **de francés**   French teacher

  el **torneo francés**   French Open

francés, -esa   French; *noun* Frenchman, Frenchwoman; *pl.* French (*persons*) (2)

la **frase**   sentence, expression (4)

el **freno**   brake (*of a car*) (18)

fresco, -a   cool (10)

el **fresco**   coolness (10)

  hacer (**mucho**) **fresco**   to be (very) cool (*weather*) (10)

el **frío**   cold (10)

  hacer (**mucho**) **frío**   to be (very) cold (*weather*) (10)

  tener (**mucho**) **frío**   to be (very) cold (*living beings*) (11)

frío, -a   cold (10)

la **frontera**   frontier, border (10)

la **función** (*pl.* **funciones**)   function, event

  las **funciones culturales**   cultural events

la **funda**   pillowcase (17)

el **fútbol**   soccer, football (15)

  el **fútbol americano**   football (15)

  el **jugador de fútbol**   soccer player

el **futuro**   future (22)

G

el **gabinete**   cabinet, display case; office (*of a doctor or lawyer*); advisory council (*government*)

las **gafas**   (eye)glasses, spectacles (8)

el **ganado**   cattle, livestock (10)

ganar   to gain, earn, win (6)

ganas: tener _____ de   to feel like

la **ganga**   bargain (17)

el **garaje**   garage (12)

la **garganta**   throat (16)

la **gasolina**   gasoline (8)

la **generación** (*pl.* **generaciones**)   generation

generalmente   generally (3)

el **genio**   genius (18)

  (**tú**) **eres un genio en el volante**   you are a genius at the wheel (18)

la **gente**   people (*requires sing. verb*) (10)

el (la) **gerente**   manager (17)

el **gimnasio**   gym (15)

gitano, -a *also noun*   gypsy

el **gobierno**   government (6)

el **golf**   golf (15)

la **gota**   drop (16)

gozar (**de** + *obj.*)   to enjoy (10)

la **grabadora**   (tape)recorder (17)

  la **videograbadora**   video recorder (VCR) (17)

gracias   thank you, thanks (5)

  el **Día de Acción de Gracias**   Thanksgiving Day (7)

el **grado**   degree (*weather*) (10)

  hacer… grados   to be … degrees (*temperature*) (10)

graduarse (**de**)   to graduate (as *or* from) (19)

gran *adj.*   large, great (*used before sing. noun*) (16)

grande   large, big (2)

  las **grandes ligas**   big leagues (16)

  más grande   (the) larger, largest (16)

grave (*m. or f.*)   grave, serious (18)

el **grupo**   group (2)

el **guacamole**   guacamole salad; avocado salad (11)

el **guante**   glove (21)

guapo, -a   handsome, good-looking (2)

la **guayabera**   *shirt with fancy work, worn outside trousers* (13)

la **guerra**   war

  la **película de guerra**   war movie *or* film (9)

la **guía**   guidebook; guide (*f.*) (15)

gustar   to like, be pleasing to (someone) (7)

  ¡cuánto me gustaría viajar… !   how I should (would) like to travel … ! (22)

me gusta que…   I like it that . . . (18)

el **gusto**   pleasure, delight (5)

  con mucho gusto   gladly, with great pleasure (5)

  el **gusto es mío**   the pleasure is mine (20)

  mucho gusto en conocerla   (I am) pleased (glad) to know you *or* nice meeting (to meet) you (*formal f. sing.*) (20)

H

haber   to have (*auxiliary*); to be (*impersonal*) (14)

había   there was, there were (10)

hay   there is, there are (2); *See separate entry under* **hay** *for the list of expressions with* **hay**

la **habitación** (*pl.* **habitaciones**)   room (12)

  la **habitación para dos**   double room (a room for two) (12)

hablar   to speak, talk (1)

  hablar más alto   to talk louder, more loudly (14)

  háblele (**Ud.**) **de cómo…**   speak to him (her) about how . . . (9)

  (**te**) **habla Silvia**   Sylvia is speaking (to you); this is Sylvia speaking *or* talking (to you) (7)

hacer   to do, make (8); to be (*weather*) (10); *reflex.* (19)

  ¿cuánto tiempo hace?   how long is it (has it been)? (19)

  ¿cuánto tiempo hace que Uds. volvieron?   how long has it been since you returned? (14)

  hace apenas (**unos minutos**) **que**   it has been scarcely (a few minutes) since (14)

  hace buen tiempo   the weather is fine (nice) (10)

  hace poco   a short while ago, not long ago (10)

  hacer aeróbic   to do aerobics (15)

  hacer (**mucho**) **calor/fresco/frío/ sol/viento**   to be (very) hot/cool/cold/sunny/windy (*weather*) (10)

  hacer caso a   to notice, listen to, pay attention to (16)

  hacer ejercicio   to exercise (15)

  hacer el viaje   to make (take) the trip (8)

  hacer… grados   to be … degrees (*temperature*) (10)

hacer juego con   to match, go (or make a set) with (13)

hacer la maleta   to pack one's bag (20)

hacer la solicitud   to apply, submit the application (19)

hacer reservas   to make reservations (a reservation) (12)

hacer una excursión   to take (make) an excursion (a trip) (15)

hacer una pregunta (a)   to ask a question (of) (21)

hacer una recomendación   to give a recommendation (19)

hacerse daño   to hurt oneself, get hurt (18)

hága(n)me or haga(n) Ud(s). el favor de + *inf.*   please + *verb* (11)

hazle = haz (*fam. sing. command of* **hacer**) + **le**   do (something) for him or her (16)

no tener nada que hacer   not to have anything (to have nothing) to do (21)

¿qué tiempo hace/hacía?   how is/was the weather? (10)

hallar   to find; *reflex.* to find oneself, be found, be (14)

la **hamaca**   hammock (13)

el **hambre** (*f., pl.* las **hambres**) hunger (11)

tener hambre   to be hungry (11)

hasta *prep.*   until, to, up to (3)

hasta el viernes   until (see you) Friday (11)

hasta la vista   until (see you) later (20)

hasta luego   so long, until later, see you later (3)

hasta mañana   until (see you) tomorrow (21)

hasta pronto   until (see you) soon (5)

hasta que *conj.*   until (20)

hay   there is, there are (2)

hay que + *inf.*   one (you, we, people, etc.) must *or* it is necessary to + *verb* (14)

no hay de qué   you're welcome, don't mention it (20)

no hay heridos ni ambulancias   there aren't any injured persons or ambulances (there are no . . . nor . . .) (18)

no hay problema   there is no (isn't any) problem (8)

¿qué distancia hay?   how far is it?

¿qué hay de nuevo?   what's new? what do you know? (5)

el **hemisferio**   hemisphere

el **herido**   wounded (injured) person (*m.*) (18)

la **hermana**   sister (5)

el **hermano**   brother; *pl.* brothers, brother(s) and sister(s) (5)

hermoso, -a   beautiful, handsome (14)

el **hielo**   ice (11)

el **hierro**   iron

la **hija**   daughter; dear (*f.*) (*in direct address*) (5)

el **hijo**   son; *pl.* children (*m. and f.*) (5)

el **hilo**   linen (7)

hispánico, -a   Hispanic (4)

hispano, -a   Spanish, Hispanic (15)

Hispanoamérica   Spanish America (2)

hispanoamericano, -a *also noun*   Spanish American (2)

la **historia**   history (6)

la **clase de historia del arte**   art history class

hojear   to turn the pages of (15)

¡hola!   hello! hi! (1)

el **hombre**   man (10)

el **hombre de negocios**   businessman (19)

el **honor**   honor

la **hora**   hour, time (*of day*) (3)

a cualquier hora   at any time (*hour*) (21)

¿a qué hora... ?   (at) what time . . . ? (3)

¿qué hora es?   what time is it? (3)

¿qué hora será?   I wonder what time it is? (15)

ser hora de   to be time to (22)

el **horario**   timetable (3)

el **horario de las comidas**   meal hours, time (schedule) of meals (3)

el **horno**   oven (17)

el **horno microondas**   microwave oven (17)

horrible (*m. or f.*)   horrible (10)

el **hospital**   hospital (16)

el **hotel**   hotel (12)

hoy *adv.*   today (3)

hoy día   nowadays (6)

la **humedad**   humidity (10)

I

la **ida**   departure (20)

el **boleto de ida y vuelta**   round-trip ticket (20)

la **idea**   idea (8)

ideal (*m. or f.*)   ideal (17)

el **idioma** (*note gender*)   language

la **iglesia**   church (16)

imaginarse   to imagine (19)

impenetrable (*m. or f.*)   impenetrable

el **impermeable**   raincoat (21)

importante (*m. or f.*)   important (6)

imposible (*m. or f.*)   impossible (7)

la **industria**   industry

industrial (*m. or f.*)   industrial

Inés   Inez, Agnes

la **inestabilidad**   instability

inferior (*m. or f.*)   inferior

la **influencia**   influence

influir   to influence

la **información**   information (20)

informar   to inform (20)

la **informática**   computer science (6)

la **ingeniera**   engineer (*f.*) (6)

la **ingeniería**   engineering (6)

la **Facultad de Ingeniería**   School of Engineering

la **Ingeniería Agrícola**   Agricultural Engineering (19)

el **ingeniero**   engineer (*m.*) (6)

el **inglés**   English (*the language*) (1)

la **clase de inglés**   English class (1)

la **lección de inglés**   English lesson (1)

el **profesor** (la **profesora**) **de inglés**   English teacher (1)

ingresar (**en** + *obj.*)   to enter, enroll (in) (15)

innumerable (*m. or f.*)   innumerable

inolvidable (*m. or f.*)   unforgettable (21)

insistir en   to insist upon (17)

inspirar   to inspire

el **instituto**   institute

intelectual (*m. or f.*)   intellectual

inteligente (*m. or f.*)   intelligent

interesante (*m. or f.*)   interesting (2)

interesar   to interest (12)

el **interior**   interior; *also adj.*

internacional (*m. or f.*)   international

interno, -a   internal, domestic (20)

la **línea interna**   domestic airline (20)

la **interpretación** (*pl.* las **interpretaciones**)   interpretation

el **invierno**   winter (5)

la **invitación** (*pl.* **invitaciones**)   invitation (11)

el **invitado**   guest (*m.*) (11)

invitar (**a** + *inf.*)   to invite (to) (6)

invitar a casa   to invite to one's house (21)

ir (**a** + *inf.*)   to go (to + *verb*) (3); *reflex.* to go (away), leave (18)

ir al centro to go downtown (4)

(**ir**) **camino de** (to be *or* go) on the (one's) way to (10)

(**ir**) **de compras** (to go) shopping (7)

ir de pesca to go fishing (14)

ir de vacaciones to go on a vacation (5)

¡que les vaya bien! good luck! (*lit.*, may it go well with you! [*pl.*])

vamos (**a otra tienda**) let's go *or* we are going (to another store) (7)

Isabel Isabel, Elizabeth, Betty

la isla island (19)

Italia Italy (15)

el italiano Italian (*the language*) (1); *also adj.*

izquierdo, -a left

por la izquierda on (to) the left (18)

J

el jabón (*pl.* **jabones**) soap (12)

Jaime James, Jim

el japonés Japanese (*the language*) (1); *also adj.*

el jarabe syrup (16)

el jarabe para la tos cough syrup (16)

el jardín (*pl.* **jardines**) garden

el (la) jefe boss (19)

Jesucristo: antes de ____ B.C.

Jorge George

José Joseph

joven (*pl.* **jóvenes**) young (6)

el joven young man; *pl.* young men, young people (6)

la joven young woman, girl (6)

la joya jewel; *pl.* jewels, jewelry (13)

las joyas de fantasía costume jewelry (13)

la joyería jewelry shop (store) (13)

Juan John

el juego game (15)

hacer juego con to match, go (or make a set) with (13)

el jueves (on) Thursday (3)

el jueves por la noche (on) Thursday evening (7)

el jugador player (*m.*) (15)

la jugadora player (*f.*) (15)

jugar (**ue**) (**a** + *obj.*) to play (a game) (15)

el jugo juice (16)

julio July (4)

junio June (5)

junto a *prep.* near (to), close to (11)

juvenil (*m. or f.*) youthful, young-looking (7)

K

el kilómetro kilometer (5/8 mile)

L

la (*pl.* **las**) the (*f.*)

la(**s**) **de** that (those) of; the one(s) of (with, in)

la(**s**) **que** who; that; which; she (those) who (whom, which); the one(s) who (that, whom, which)

la *dir. obj. pron.* her, it (*f.*), you (*formal f. sing.*) (6)

el labio lip (8)

pintarse los labios to put on lipstick (8)

el laboratorio laboratory (1)

el lado side (8)

al lado de *prep.* beside, next to, at the side of (8)

el lago lake (10)

la lana wool (21)

la ropa de lana wool clothes, woolen clothing (21)

el lápiz (*pl.* **lápices**) pencil(s) (2)

largo, -a long (4)

a lo largo de throughout

las *dir. obj. pron.* them (*f.*), you (*f. pl.*) (6)

la lástima pity, shame (5)

es una lástima it's a pity (too bad) (19)

¡qué lástima! too bad! what a pity (shame)! (5)

lastimarse to get hurt, to hurt oneself (16)

me lastimé el (*or* **la**)**...** I hurt (injured) my . . . (16)

latino, -a Latin

América Latina Latin America

Laura Laura

la lavadora de platos dishwasher (17)

lavar to wash (something); *reflex.* to wash (oneself) (8)

lavarse la cara (**las manos, el pelo**) to wash one's face (hands, hair) (8)

le *dir. obj. pron.* him, you (*formal m. sing.*); *indir. obj. pron.* (to, for) him, her, it, you (*formal sing.*) (7)

la lección (*pl.* **lecciones**) lesson(s) (1)

la lección de español (**alemán, francés, inglés**) The Spanish (German, French, English) lesson (1)

la lectura reading (selection)

leer to read (1)

lea (**Ud.**) (*pl.* **lean** [**Uds.**]) read

lejos de *prep.* far from (3)

la lengua language, tongue (1)

el lenguaje language

les *indir. obj. pron.* (to, for) them, you (*pl.*) (7)

les indica... que sigan adelante he or she indicates to them . . . to continue ahead

levantar to raise; *reflex.* to get up, rise

la ley law

liberal: las artes ____ es liberal arts (6)

libre (*m. or f.*) free, available (15)

al aire libre outdoor, open-air

el Estado Libre Asociado Associated Free State (Commonwealth)

el tiempo libre free time (15)

la librería bookstore (4)

la librería de libros extranjeros foreign bookstore (4)

el libro book (2)

el libro (**de español**) (Spanish) book (2)

la licencia de manejar (**conducir**) driver's license (18)

la liga league

las grandes ligas big leagues

ligero, -a light (*weight*) (21)

el limón (*pl.* **limones**) lemon

la línea line (*telephone*) (5)

la línea aérea airline (21)

la línea interna domestic airline (20)

la lista list (13)

la lista de espera waiting list (20)

la lista de regalos gift registry; gift list (17)

listo, -a ready (21)

llamar to call; to knock (at the door) (5); *reflex.* to be called, be named (8)

llamar a la puerta to knock, knock at (on) the door (5)

llamar por teléfono to telephone (call), talk by (on the) telephone (5)

la llanura plain

la llave key (12)

el llavero key chain, key ring (13)

la llegada arrival (5)

llegar to arrive (2)

ahí llega there comes (arrives) (2)

(**llegar**) **a casa** (to arrive) home (3)

(**llegar**) **al centro**   (to arrive) downtown (7)

lleno, -a   full (7)

llevar   to take, carry (8); to wear, take (21); to bear; *reflex.* to take (away with oneself) (13)

llover (**ue**)   to rain (10)

llover a cántaros   to rain cats and dogs (10)

lo *dir. obj. pron.*   him, you (*formal m. sing.*), it (*m. and neuter*) (6)

lo *neuter article*   the

loco, -a   crazy, wild, mad (19)

volverse (**ue**) **loco, -a**   to become *or* go crazy (wild, mad) (19)

el **lodo**   mud (10)

Lola   Lola

los *dir. obj. pron.*   them, you (*m. pl.*) (6)

los   the (*m. pl.*)

los de   those of; the ones of (with, in)

los (**las**) **dos**   both, the two (6)

los que   who; that; which; the ones *or* those who (that, which, whom)

Los Ángeles   Los Angeles (8)

luego *adv.*   then, next, later (6)

desde luego   of course

hasta luego   so long, until later, see you later (3)

luego que *conj.*   as soon as (20)

el **lugar**   place (13)

en lugar de   instead of, in place of

Luis   Louis

Luisa   Louise

la **luna**   moon (10)

la **luna de miel**   honeymoon (20)

el **lunes**   (on) Monday (3)

M

la **madre**   mother (5)

la **maestría**   master's degree (M.A., M.B.A., M.S., etc.) (22)

magnífico, -a   magnificent, fine (21)

mal *adv.*   badly (1); *adj. used for* **malo** *before m. sing. nouns* (9)

(**ella**) **se ve** (**muy**) **mal**   (she) looks (very) bad/ill (14)

la **maleta**   suitcase, bag (20)

hacer la maleta   to pack one's bag (20)

malo, -a   bad (2)

¡qué mala suerte!   what bad luck! (18)

la **mamá**   mama, mom, mother (5)

mandar   to send, order (4)

manejar   to drive (*Am.*) (18)

la **licencia de manejar** (**conducir**)   driver's license (18)

la **manera**   manner, way

de ninguna manera   (in) no way (16)

la **mano** (*note gender*)   hand (8)

lavarse las manos   to wash one's hands (8)

la **manta**   blanket (12)

el **mantel**   tablecloth (17)

la **mañana**   morning (3)

ayer por la mañana   yesterday morning (14)

de la mañana   in the morning (*when a specific hour is given*) (3)

el **domingo por la mañana**   (on) Sunday morning (8)

hasta mañana   until (see you) tomorrow (21)

mañana por la mañana (**tarde, noche**)   tomorrow morning (afternoon, night *or* evening) (14)

por la mañana   in the morning (*no specific hour given*) (3)

el **vuelo de la mañana**   morning flight (20)

mañana *adv.*   tomorrow (7)

pasado mañana   the day after tomorrow (21)

el **mapa** (*note gender*)   map (2)

la **maquinaria**   machinery (19)

el **mar**   sea, ocean

el **mar Caribe**   Caribbean Sea

la **maravilla**   marvel, wonder

la **marca**   brand, kind, make (21)

marcha: moderar la ____   to slow down (18)

marcharse (**de** + *obj.*)   to leave (from) (22)

Margarita   Margaret, Marguerite

María   Mary

marrón (*m. or f.*)   brown (7)

Marta   Martha

el **martes**   (on) Tuesday (3)

marzo   March (5)

más *adv.*   more, most (1)

algo más   something more, anything else (13)

lo más pronto posible   as soon as possible (17)

más + *adj.* + (**que**)   more + *adj.* or *adj.* + -er + (than) (7)

más + *adv.* + **que**   -er + than *or* more + -ly + than

más de   more than

más o menos   more or less, approximately (3)

más que nunca   more than ever (9)

más tarde   later (11)

valer más   to be better (21)

la **máscara**   mask

maya (*m. or f.*) *also noun*   Maya, Mayan (14)

mayo   May (5)

(el, la) **mayor**   (the) older, greater, oldest, greatest (16)

la **mayor parte de**   most (of), the greater part of (16)

la **Plaza Mayor**   Main Square (*in center of Old Madrid*)

me *obj. pron.*   me (6); to (for) me (7); (to, for) myself

la **medianoche**   midnight (3)

a (**la**) **medianoche**   at midnight (3)

la **medicina**   medicine (6)

la **Facultad de Medicina**   Medical School, School of Medicine (6)

medicinal (*m. or f.*)   medicinal

médico, -a   medical

el **consultorio médico**   medical clinic

el **médico**   doctor, physican (*m.*) (16)

medio, -a   half, a half (3)

el **mediodía**   noon (3)

al mediodía   at noon (3)

mejor *adj. and adv.*   better, best (12); el, la **mejor**   the better, best (16)

mejorar   to improve; *reflex.* to get better (16)

(el, la) **menor**   (the) smaller, younger, smallest, youngest (16)

menos   less (3); least; fewer; except

a menos que *conj.*   unless (20)

al menos   at least (16)

echar de menos   to miss (someone or something) (22)

más o menos   more or less, approximately (3)

menos + *adj.* + (**que**)   *adj.* + -er + (than) *or* less + *adj.* + (than) (7)

menos + *adv.* + **que**   -er + than *or* less + -ly + than

menudo: a ____   often, frequently (6)

el **mercado**   market (13)

la **mercancía**   merchandise

merecer   to deserve

el **merengue**   *a Caribbean dance* (11)

el **mes**   month (5)

al mes   a (per) month, monthly (17)

en el mes de (**agosto**)   during the month of (August) (5)

el **mes pasado**   last month (9)

la **mesa**   table, desk (2)

mexicano, -a *also noun*   Mexican (2)

México   Mexico (2)

el **golfo de México**   Gulf of Mexico

la **mezcladora**   mixer (17)

mi(s) *adj.*   my (4)

mí *pron.* me, myself (*after prep.*) (12)

miel: la luna de ___ honeymoon (20)

mientras (que) *conj.* while, as long as (3)

el **miércoles** (on) Wednesday (3)

el (**miércoles**) **que viene** next (Wednesday) (9)

Miguel Michael, Mike

mil one thousand, a thousand (12); *pl.* thousands

cien mil one hundred thousand (12)

dos mil two thousand (12)

militar (*m. or f.*) military

el **millón** (*pl.* **millones**) (**de**) million (12)

el **minuto** minute (*time*) (3)

mío, -a *adj.* my, (of) mine (11)

¡Dios mío! heavens! (my God!)

(**el**) **mío,** (**la**) **mía,** (**los**) **míos,** (**las**) **mías** *pron.* mine (20)

el gusto es mío the pleasure is mine (20)

mirar to look at, watch (3)

(**él**) **mira el reloj** (he) looks at the (his) watch (clock) (3)

mirar la televisión (**las noticias**) to look at (watch) television (the news) (4)

mirar por televisión to watch on TV (15)

la **misa** mass (16)

la **misión** (*pl.* **misiones**) mission (8)

mismo, -a same (7)

esta misma tarde this very afternoon (17)

por sí mismo, -a by itself, himself, herself

el **misterio** mystery (9)

la **película de misterio** mystery movie *or* film (9)

misterioso, -a mysterious

el **mocasín** (*pl.* **mocasines**) moccasin (7)

la **moda** style, fashion, fad (7)

está (**muy**) **de moda** it's (very) much in fashion (7)

moderar la marcha to slow down (18)

moderno, -a modern (17)

el **modo** manner, means, ways (7)

de todos modos in any case (20)

¡ni modo! no way! certainly not! (7)

molestar to bother, disturb, molest (11)

la **molestia** bother, annoyance (16)

el **momento** moment (6)

en cualquier momento (at) any moment (17)

la **monarquía** monarchy

la **moneda** money

la **montaña** mountain (10)

mostrar (**ue**) to show (15)

la **muchacha** girl (2)

el **muchacho** boy (2)

muchísimo *adv.* very much (16)

muchísimo, -a (**-os, -as**) very much (many) (16)

mucho *adv.* much, a lot, a great deal (1)

esperar mucho to wait long (a long time) (18)

mucho, -a (**-os, -as**) much, a lot of; (*pl.*) many (2)

con mucho gusto gladly, with great pleasure (5)

mucho gusto (I am) pleased *or* glad to know *or* meet you

mucho gusto en conocerla (I am) pleased (glad) to know you *or* nice meeting (to meet) you (*formal f. sing.*) (20)

los **muebles** furniture (17)

la **fábrica de muebles** furniture factory

la **mujer** woman (10)

la **mujer de negocios** businesswoman (19)

la **mujer policía** police officer (*f.*) (18)

mundial *adj.* world (15)

la **Copa Mundial** World Cup (15)

el **mundo** world (4)

todo el mundo everybody (9)

mural *adj. m. or f., also m. noun* mural

la **música** music (9)

musical (*m. or f.*) musical (9)

la **comedia musical** musical comedy *or* play (9)

la **película musical** musical movie *or* film (9)

musulmán, -ana *also noun* Mussulman, Moslem (12)

muy *adv.* very (1)

¡muy bien! very well! (that's) fine! (1)

N

nada *pron.* nothing, (not) … anything (9)

de nada you're welcome, don't mention it

no deseamos nada más we don't want anything else

no tener nada que hacer not to have anything (to have nothing) to do (21)

nadar to swim (10)

nadie *pron.* no one, nobody, (not) … anybody (anyone) (9)

la **nariz** (*pl.* **narices**) nose (16)

la **natación** swimming (15)

natal (*m. or f.*) natal

natural (*m. or f.*) natural; *noun* native

las **ciencias naturales** natural sciences (6)

naval (*m. or f.*) naval

la **Navidad** Christmas (8)

las **vacaciones de Navidad** Christmas vacation (8)

la **neblina** fog (10)

necesario, -a necessary (4)

necesitar to need (1)

el **negocio** business (company); *pl.* business

la **administración de negocios** business administration (6)

la **Facultad de Administración de Negocios** Business School, School of Business Administration (6)

el **hombre de negocios** businessman (19)

la **mujer de negocios** businesswoman (19)

el **viaje de negocios** business trip (19)

negro, -a black (2)

nervioso, -a nervous

ponerse nervioso, -a to get (become) nervous (19)

nevar (**ie**) to snow (10)

ni neither, nor, (not) … or (7)

¡ni modo! no way! certainly not! (7)

ni… ni neither … nor, no (not) … any … or

la **niebla** fog (10)

los **nietos** grandchildren

la **nieve** snow (10)

ningún (*used for* **ninguno** *before m. sing. nouns*) no, none, (not) … any

ninguno, -a *adj. and pron.* no one, none, (not) … any (anybody, anyone); nobody (9)

de ninguna manera (in) no way (16)

la **niñez** childhood (10)

no no, not (1)

¡cómo no! of course!, certainly! (4)

hoy no not today

¿no? aren't you?, isn't it?, do you?, etc. (3)

no dejar de + *inf.* not to fail to + *verb* (22)

¿(no es) verdad? aren't you?, isn't it?, do you?, etc. (3)

no hay de qué you're welcome, don't mention it (20)

no hay heridos ni ambulancia there aren't any injured persons or ambulance (there are no . . . nor . . .) (18)

no hay problema there is no (isn't any) problem (8)

no lo sé I don't know (15)

no quedan asientos no seats are left (remain), there aren't any seats left (20)

no tener nada que hacer not to have anything (to have nothing) to do (21)

todavía no not yet (21)

noble (*m. or f.*) noble

la **noche** night, evening (1)

buenas noches good evening, good night (1)

de la noche in the evening (*when a specific hour is given*) (3)

de noche at (by) night (8)

esta noche tonight

el jueves por la noche (on) Thursday evening (7)

mañana por la noche tomorrow night *or* evening (14)

por la noche in the evening (*no specific hour given*) (3)

los sábados por la noche (on) (Saturday) evenings/nights (9)

todas las noches every night (3)

el **nordeste** northeast

Norteamérica North America (9)

norteamericano, -a *also noun* North American (2)

nos *obj. pron.* us (6); to (for) us (7); (to, for) ourselves

nosotros, -as we (1); us; ourselves (*after prep.*) (12)

la **nota** note, grade

notable (*m. or f.*) notable, noteworthy

la **noticia** notice, news item, piece of news; *pl.* news (4)

escuchar las noticias listen to the news (4)

mirar las noticias to watch the news (4)

novecientos, -as nine hundred (12)

noveno, -a ninth (12)

noventa ninety (6)

la **novia** girlfriend (steady); fiancée, bride (17)

el **noviazgo** courtship

noviembre November (5)

el **novio** boyfriend (steady); fiancé, groom (17)

la **nube** cloud (10)

nublado, -a cloudy (10)

estar nublado to be cloudy (sky) (10)

la **nuera** daughter-in-law

nuestro, -a *adj.* our (4); of ours (11) (**el**) **nuestro**, (**la**) **nuestra**, (**los**) **nuestros**, (**las**) **nuestras** *pron.* ours (20)

nueve nine (3)

nuevo, -a new (4)

el **Año Nuevo** New Year (11)

¿qué hay de nuevo? what's new? what do you know? (5)

el **número** number (6)

en el número (**cincuenta**) at number (fifty) (6)

el **número de baile** dance number (9)

nunca *adv.* never, (not) . . . ever (9)

más que nunca more than ever (9)

O

o or (2)

el **objeto** object (13)

los **objetos de cerámica** ceramics, pottery objects, pieces of pottery (13)

obstante: no _____ nevertheless

obtener (*like* **tener**) to obtain, get (19)

occidental (*m. or f.*) western

ochenta eighty (6)

ocho eight (3)

ochocientos, -as eight hundred (12)

octavo, -a eighth (12)

octubre October (5)

ocupado, -a occupied, busy (5)

el **oeste** west (9)

la **película del oeste** western movie *or* film (9)

oficial (*m. or f.*) official

la **oficina** office (5)

la **oficina del periódico** newspaper office (8)

ofrecer to offer (11)

oír to hear, listen (14)

casi no se oye one can hardly (scarcely) hear (14)

oír decir que to hear (it said) that (19)

¡ojalá (**que**)**!** would that! I wish that! (22)

el **ojo** eye (8)

pintarse los ojos to put on eye makeup (8)

la **ola** wave

correr las olas to surf (10)

olvidar to forget (4)

once eleven (3)

la **opinión** (*pl.* **opiniones**) opinion (17)

la **oportunidad** opportunity, chance (21)

tener la oportunidad de + *inf.* to have the opportunity of (to) + *verb* (21)

la **oposición** (*pl.* **oposiciones**) competitive examination

optativo, -a optional

el **orden** (*pl.* **órdenes**) order (arrangement)

de primer orden of high rank, first-class

la **orden** (*pl.* **órdenes**) order, command; religious order

el **ordenador** word processor, computer (17)

la **oreja** (outer) ear (16)

organizar to organize (18)

oriental (*m. or f.*) oriental, eastern

el **origen** (*pl.* **orígenes**) origin

originar(se) to originate

la **orilla** bank, shore

a orillas de on the banks of

el **oro** gold (13)

(**el arete**) **de oro** gold (earring) (13)

os *obj. pron.* you (*fam. pl.*) (6); to (for) you (7); (to, for) yourselves

el **otoño** fall, autumn (5)

otro, -a another, other; *pl.* other(s) (1)

otra vez again (9)

¡oye! (*fam. sing. command of* **oír**, to hear) listen! say! hey! (3)

P

Pablo Paul

la **paciencia** patience (16)

tener paciencia to be patient (18)

el **padre** father; *pl.* parents (5)

los **padrinos** godfather and godmother of a child

la **paella** paella (*a rice dish containing chicken, meat, shellfish, and vegetables cooked with saffron*) (11)

pagar to pay, pay for (12)

pagar con tarjeta de crédito to pay with a credit card (12)

pagar en efectivo to pay cash (12)

la **página** page

el **país** (*pl.* **países**) country (4)

la **paja** straw (13)

la **palabra** word (1)

Panamá Panama (2)

panameño, -a *also noun* Panamanian (2)

los **pantalones**   trousers, pants, slacks (7)

los **pantalones cortos**   shorts (7)

el **papá**   papa, dad, father (5)

el **papel**   paper (2)

el **papel de cartas (de escribir)** writing paper (4)

la **servilleta de papel**   paper napkin (11)

el **paquete**   package (13)

el **par**   pair, couple (13)

un **par de (semanas)**   a couple of (weeks) (13)

para *prep.*   for + *inf.* to, in order to (3)

para que *conj.*   in order (so) that (20)

¿para qué fecha(s)?   for (by) what date(s)? (12)

¿para quién (es)?   for whom (is it)? (4)

partir para   to depart (leave) for (20)

la **parada**   stop (20)

el (los) **paraguas**   umbrella(s) (21)

parar   to stop (18)

parecer   to seem, appear, appear to be (7)

me parece raro…   it seems strange to me . . . (18)

¿qué te parece si… ?   what do you think if . . . ? how does it seem to you if . . . ? (8)

¿(te, le, les) parece bien?   is it all right with (you)? does it seem O.K. to (you)? (7)

la **pared**   wall (2)

el (la) **pariente**   relative

el **parque**   park (20)

la **parte**   part (10)

en todas partes   everywhere

la mayor parte de   most (of), the greater part of (16)

por otra parte   on the other hand

por todas partes   everywhere (10)

participar   to participate (15)

particular (*m. or f.*)   particular; private

la **partida**   departure (20)

el **partido**   game, match (15)

partir (de)   to depart, leave (from) (20)

a partir de   beginning with (19)

partir (para)   to depart, leave (for) (20)

pasado, -a   past, last (9)

el año pasado   last year (9)

el mes pasado   last month (9)

pasado mañana   day after tomorrow (21)

la semana pasada   last week (9)

la **pasajera**   passenger (*f.*) (20)

el **pasajero**   passenger (*m.*) (20)

el **pasaporte**   passport (20)

pasar   to pass or come (by), spend (*time*) (5)

¡pasa (tú)!   come in! (15)

pasar las vacaciones (de verano) to spend the (summer) vacation (5)

pasar un buen rato   to have a good time (11)

¿qué te pasa?   what's the matter with you? what's wrong with you? (16)

pasear   to walk, stroll (12)

el **paseo**   walk, stroll, ride (17)

dar un paseo   to take a walk (ride) (17)

la **pasión** (*pl.* **pasiones**)   passions

el **pastel**   cake (22)

el **patio**   patio, courtyard (13)

partrulla: el carro ____   patrol (police) car (18)

el **pecho**   chest (16)

pedir (i, i)   to ask, ask for, request (16)

peinar   to comb; *reflex.* to comb oneself (8)

pelar la pava   to converse (in courtship) (*lit.*, to pluck the hen turkey)

la **película**   movie, film (9)

la **película de ciencia-ficción** science-fiction movie *or* film (9)

la **película de guerra**   war movie *or* film (9)

la **película de misterio**   mystery movie *or* film (9)

la **película de terror**   horror movie *or* film (9)

la **película del oeste**   western movie *or* film (9)

la **película musical**   musical movie *or* film (9)

el **rollo de película**   roll of film (21)

tomar una película   to film (a movie) (21)

peligroso, -a   dangerous (10)

el **pelo**   hair (8)

arreglarse el pelo   to have one's hair done (14)

lavarse el pelo   to wash one's hair (8)

la **pelota**   ball (*game*) (15)

la **peluquería**   beauty parlor (shop), barber shop (14)

pena: valer la ____   to be worthwhile (21)

la **penicilina**   penicillin (16)

peninsular (*m. or f.*)   peninsular (*of Spain*) (22)

pensar (ie)   to think, think over, consider, + *inf.* to intend, plan (8)

pensar en + *obj.*   to think of (about) (11)

piénsalo   think about it (*fam.*) (8)

peor *adv.*   worse, **el**, **la peor**   the worst (16)

pequeño, -a   small, little (*size*) (4)

más pequeño   (the) smaller, smallest (16)

perdonar   to pardon, excuse (9)

perdóname   pardon me, excuse me (*fam.*) (9)

perdone(n) Ud(s).   excuse (pardon) me (us) (11)

perfecto *adv.*   perfectly (15)

el **periódico**   newspaper (4)

la **oficina del periódico** newspaper office (8)

permanente (*m. or f.*)   permanent

permitir   to permit, allow, let (12)

¿nos permite Ud. ver?   may we see? (*lit.* do you permit *or* allow us to see?) (12)

pero *conj.*   but (1)

la **persona**   person (12)

personal (*m. or f.*)   personal (20)

el **Perú**   Peru (20)

peruano, -a *also noun*   Peruvian (4)

la **pesa**   weight (15)

alzar (las) pesas   to lift weights (15)

la **pesca**   fishing (14)

ir de pesca   to go fishing (14)

pescar   to fish (14)

pescar una pulmonía (un virus, un resfriado)   to catch (or come down with) pneumonia (a virus, a cold) (16)

la **peseta**   peseta (*Spanish monetary unit*) (12)

el **petróleo**   petroleum, oil

el **pie**   foot (16)

la **piedra**   stone (20)

la **(ciudad) de piedra**   stone (city) (20)

la **pierna**   leg (16)

la **píldora**   pill (16)

pintar   to paint; *reflex.* to put makeup on (8)

pintarse la cara   to put on makeup (8)

pintarse los labios   to put on lipstick (8)

pintarse los ojos   to put on eye makeup (8)

el **piropo**   compliment (22)

echar piropos   to pay compliments (22)

la **piscina**   swimming pool (14)

el **piso** floor, story (12)

  el **piso principal** first (main) floor (12)

la **pizarra** (chalk) board (2)

el **plan** plan (20)

la **plancha (eléctrica)** (electric) iron (17)

la **plata** silver (13)

  (el **anillo**) **de plata** silver (ring) (13)

la **plática** conversation

el **plato** plate, dish; course (*at meals*) (11)

  la **lavadora de platos** dishwasher (17)

la **playa** beach (10)

la **plaza** plaza, square (12)

la **pluma** pen (2)

pluvial: el bosque ___ rain forest

pobre (*m. or f.*) poor

poco, -a *adj.* little (*quantity*) (16); *also pron. and adv.* (1); *pl.* a few (1)

  al poco rato after a short while (13)

  hace poco a short while ago, not long ago (10)

  poco después shortly afterward (14)

  un poco (de + *noun*) a little *or* some (+ *noun*)

poder (ue) to be able, can (6)

  ¿en qué puedo servirle(s)? what can I do for you? how can I help you? (13)

la **policía** police (*force*) (18)

el **policía** police officer (*m.*) (18)

  la **mujer policía** police officer (*f.*) (18)

poner to put, place; to turn on (15); *reflex.* to put on (oneself) (8)

  ponerse + *adj.* to become, get (14)

  ponerse nervioso, -a to get (become) nervous (19)

  ponerse rojo, -a to blush, become (get) red (19)

  se ha puesto (muy) popular it has become (very) popular (15)

popular (*m. or f.*) popular (9)

por *prep.* for, in, by, along, during, through (3); with, because of, around, for the sake of, on account of, about, per, in exchange of

  por aquí by (around) here, this way (5)

  por avión by airmail, by plane (4)

  por casualidad by chance (11)

  por cierto certainly, surely, for certain (sure), by the way (10)

  por ejemplo for example (4)

por eso because of that, for that reason, that's why (16)

por favor please (1)

por fin finally (6)

por la derecha on (to) the right (18)

por la izquierda on (to) the left (18)

por la mañana (tarde, noche) in the morning (afternoon, evening) (*no specific hour given*) (3)

por lo común commonly, generally (10)

por otra parte on the other hand

por primera vez for the first time (12)

¿por qué? why? for what reason? (5)

por sí mismo, -a by himself, herself, itself

por suerte luckily (10)

¡por supuesto! of course! (5)

por todas partes everywhere (10)

porque *conj.* because, for (5)

el **portugués** Portuguese (*the language*) (1)

posible (*m. or f.*) possible (19)

  lo más pronto posible as soon as possible (17)

posiblemente *adv.* possibly (15)

el **postre** dessert (11)

  de postre for dessert (11)

practicar to practice (1)

  practicar un deporte to play a sport (15)

el **precio** price (7)

  a precio especial on sale, at a special price, at special prices (7)

  ¿qué precio tiene(n)… ? what is the price (cost) of … ? (7)

  tener precio fijo to have fixed prices (7)

precioso, -a precious, beautiful (9)

  (te) quedan preciosos they look great on (you) (13)

precisamente *adv.* precisely (19)

preciso, -a necessary (19)

precolombino, -a pre-Columbian (*before the arrival of Columbus*)

el **precursor** precursor

predominantemente predominantly

preferir (ie, i) to prefer (17)

la **pregunta** question

  hacer una pregunta (a) to ask (*a question*) (of) (21)

preguntar to ask (*a question*) (1)

  preguntar por to ask (inquire) about (13)

el **prendedor** pin, brooch (13)

preocupado, -a worried, preoccupied (8)

preocuparse (por) to worry, to be *or* get worried (about) (14)

  me preocupo tanto I get so worried (19)

preparar to prepare (1)

  prepararse para to prepare (oneself) for *or* to get ready for (8)

presentar to present, introduce (20); *reflex.* to present oneself, appear

preguntar por to ask (inquire) about (13)

la **presión** (blood) pressure (16)

  tomarle la presión (a uno) to take (one's) blood pressure (16)

el **préstamo** loan

el **pretendiente** suitor

la **prima** cousin (*f.*)

la **primavera** spring (5)

primer *used for* **primero** *before m. sing. nouns* first (10)

primero, -a, first (1); *also adv.* first (22)

  la **primera clase** first class (20)

  por primera vez for the first time (12)

el **primo** cousin (*m.*) (9)

principal (*m. or f.*) principal, main (2)

  el **edificio principal** main building (2)

  el **piso principal** first (main) floor (12)

principalmente principally, mainly

privado, -a private (12)

probable (*m. or f.*) probable (19)

probablemente *adv.* probably (15)

el **problema** (*note gender*) problem (8)

  no hay problema there is no (isn't any) problem (8)

proclamar to proclaim

producir to produce (19)

la **profesión** profession (15)

profesional (*m. or f.*) professional (15)

el **profesor** teacher, professor (*m.*) (1)

  el **profesor de español (alemán, italiano, inglés)** Spanish (German, Italian, English) teacher (*m.*) (1)

la **profesora** teacher, professor (*f.*) (1)

  la **profesora de español (alemán, italiano, inglés)** the Spanish (German, Italian, English) teacher (*f.*) (1)

el **programa** (*note gender*) program (4)

  el **programa de televisión** television program (4)

prohibir   to prohibit
prometer   to promise (11)
pronto   soon, quickly (5)
  hasta pronto   until (see you) soon (5)
  lo más pronto posible   as soon as possible (17)
la **pronunciación**   pronunciation (1)
  el **ejercicio de pronunciación**   pronunciation exercise (1)
pronunciar   to pronounce (1)
propósito: a ____   by the way (9)
la **propuesta**   proposal
la **provisión**   provision
próximo, -a   next (9)
  la **próxima vez**   next time (11)
el **público**   audience, public (15)
el **pueblo**   town, village (10)
el **puente**   bridge
la **puerta**   door (5)
  llamar a la puerta   to knock, knock at (on) the door (5)
  el **timbre de la puerta**   doorbell (15)
  tocar a la puerta   to knock on the door (15)
el **puerto**   port (shipping) (19)
pues *adv.*   well, well then, then (4)
el **puesto**   position, place, job (19)
  el **puesto vacante**   available position (job), job opening (19)
el **pulmón** (*pl.* **pulmones**)   lung (16)
la **pulmonía**   pneumonia (16)
  pescar una pulmonía   to catch (*or* come down with) pneumonia (16)
  tener una pulmonía viral   to have viral pneumonia (16)
la **pulsera**   bracelet (13)
punto: en ____   on the dot, sharp (*time*) (3)
puntual (*m. or f.*)   punctual, on time (11)
puro, -a   pure (7)

Q

que *relative pron.*   that, which, who, whom; *conj.* that (2); than, (7) since; *indir. command,* have, let, may, I wish (hope)
  el (**la, los, las**) **que**   that, which, who, whom; he (she, those) who (etc.); the one(s) who, (etc.)
  es que   the fact is (that) (14)
  la hora en que   the time (hour) when
  lo que   what, that which, which

¡que les vaya bien!   good luck (*lit.,* may it go well with you [*pl.*])!
¿qué?   what? which? (1)
  ¿a qué hora... ?   (at) what time . . . ? (3)
  ¿qué hay de nuevo?   what's new? what do you know? (5)
  ¿qué hora es?   what time is it? (3)
  ¿qué hora será?   I wonder what time it is? (15)
  ¿qué precio tiene(n)... ?   what is the price (cost) of . . . ? (7)
  ¿qué tal?   how goes it? how are you? (5)
  ¿qué tal (**el viaje**)**?**   how about (the trip)? how is *or* was (the trip)? (5)
  ¿qué te parece si... ?   what do you think if . . . ? how does it seem to you if . . . ? (8)
  ¿qué te pasa?   what's the matter with you? what's wrong with you? (16)
  ¿qué tiempo hace/hacía?   how is/was the weather?
¡qué + *noun*!   what (a *or* an) . . . ! (5)
  ¡qué alegría!   what joy! (5)
  ¡qué barbaridad!   how awful! (16)
  ¡qué bien!   good! great! (6)
  ¡qué buen rato!   what a good time!, what fun! (11)
  ¡qué casualidad!   what a coincidence! (9)
  ¡qué lástima!   too bad! what a pity (shame)! (5)
  ¡qué mala suerte!   what bad luck! (18)
  ¡qué sorpresa tan agradable!   what a pleasant surprise (16)
  ¡qué va!   of course not! (16)
¡qué + *adj. or adv.*!   how . . . ! (7)
quedar(se)   to stay, remain; to be (9); to be left (20)
  no quedan asientos   no seats are left (remain), there aren't any seats left (20)
  (**te**) **quedan preciosos**   they look great on(you) (13)
querer (**ie**)   to wish, want (4)
  ¡cuántas cosas quieres... !   how many things you want . . . ! (17)
  querer decir   to mean (20)
querido, -a   dear (5)
quien (*pl.* **quienes**)   who, whom (*after prep.*); he (those) who, the one(s) (19)
¿quién? (*pl.* **¿quiénes?**)   who? (1)
  ¿de quién (*pl.* **de quiénes**) **es** (**son**)?   whose is it (are they)? (3)

¿para quién (**es**)**?**   for whom (is it)? (4)
químico, -a   chemical
quince   fifteen (3)
quinientos, -as   five hundred (12)
quinto, -a   fifth (12)
el **quiosco de periódicos**   newsstand
quizás   perhaps (13)

R

la **radio**   radio (*means of communication*) (4)
  escuchar la radio   listen to the radio (4)
Ramón   Raymond
rancheros: los huevos ____   ranch-style eggs
rápidamente *adv.*   fast, rapidly (16)
rápido *adv.*   fast (14)
rápido, -a   fast, quick
la **raqueta**   racket (15)
raro, -a   strange (18)
  me parece raro   it seems strange to me (18)
el **rato**   short time, a while (5)
  a cada rato   every short while (moment) (16)
  al poco rato   after a short while (13)
  descansar un rato   to rest for a while (5)
  pasar un buen rato   to have a good time (11)
  ¡qué buen rato!   what a good time!, what fun! (11)
  un rato   a short time, a while (5)
la **razón** (*pl.* **razones**)   reason (11)
  tener razón   to be right (11)
el **recado**   message (11)
el (la) **recepcionista**   receptionist (12)
recetar   to prescribe (16)
rechazar   to reject
el **recibidor**   reception area (room) (11)
recibir   to receive (3)
el **recibo**   receipt (invoice) (13)
la **recomendación** (*pl.* **recomendaciones**)   recommendation (19)
  la **carta de recomendación**   letter of recommendation (19)
  hacer una recomendación   to give a recommendation
recomendar (**ie**)   to recommend (17)
reconquistar   to reconquer
recordar (**ue**)   to recall, remember (9); to remind (someone) (10)
el **recuerdo**   memory, remembrance; *pl.* regards, best wishes (9)
los **recursos**   means
la **red**   network

la **referencia**   reference (19)

el **refresco**   cold (soft) drink, soda (11)

el **refrigerador**   refrigerator (17)

el **regalo**   gift (13)

   el **regalo de boda**   wedding gift (17)

regatear   to haggle, bargain (7)

registrarse   to register (12)

regresar (a)   to return (to) (3)

   regresar (de)   to return (from) (3); to go (come) back home (5)

   tenemos que regresar el día (treinta)   we have to return on the (thirtieth) (20)

el **regreso**   return (10)

regular *adv.*   fair, not bad, so-so (5)

   estar regular   to be so-so (5)

reír (i, i) (*also reflex.*)   to laugh (16)

la **reja**   grille, grating (*of a window*)

religioso, -a   religious

el **reloj**   watch, clock (3)

repetir (i, i)   to repeat (1)

   repita (Ud.) (*pl.* **repitan [Uds.]**)   repeat (1)

representar   to represent

la **república**   republic

la **República Dominicana**   Dominican Republic (11)

res: la carne de _____   beef

las **reservas**   reservation(s) (12)

   hacer reservas   to make reservations (a reservation) (12)

el **resfriado**   cold (illness) (16)

   pescar un resfriado   to catch (*or* come down with) a cold (16)

   tener un resfriado   to have a cold (16)

la **residencia**   residence hall, dormitory (3)

   la **residencia (de estudiantes)**   (student) dormitory, residence hall (3)

Residente: el Comisionado _____   Resident Commissioner

residir   to reside (19)

el **restaurante**   restaurant (3)

el **resumen** (*pl.* **resúmenes**)   summary (18)

la **reunión** (*pl.* **reuniones**)   meeting, gathering (22)

reunirse   to gather, get together, meet (22)

revelar   to develop (*film*) (21)

la **revista**   magazine, journal (4)

la **revolución** (*pl.* **revoluciones**)   revolution

rico, -a   rich (19)

el **riego**   irrigation

la **riqueza**   wealth

Rita   Rita

el **rito**   rite

Roberto   Robert, Bob

la **rodilla**   knee (16)

rogar (ue)   to ask, beg (17)

rojo, -a   red (2)

   ponerse rojo, -a   to blush, become (get) red (19)

el **rollo**   roll

   el **rollo de película**   roll of film (21)

romántico, -a   romantic (19)

la **ropa**   clothes, clothing (7)

   la **ropa de cama**   bed linens (sheets, pillowcases, etc.), bedclothes (blankets, sheets, etc.) (12)

   la **ropa de lana**   wool clothes, woolen clothing (21)

rosado, -a   pink (7)

la **rueda**   wheel

la **ruina**   ruin (13)

rural (*m. or f.*)   rural

S

el **sábado**   (on) Saturday (3)

   los (**sábados**) **por la noche**   (on) (Saturday) evenings/nights (9)

la **sábana**   sheet (17)

saber   to know (*a fact*), know how (to) (4)

   no lo sé   I don't know (15)

sacar   to obtain (*a grade or degree*); to take (out) (12)

   sacar (de)   to take out of (13)

   sacar fotografías (fotos [*f.*])   to take photographs (photos) (12)

la **sala**   room (2); living room, lounge (6)

   la **sala de clase**   classroom (2)

salir (de + *obj.*)   to leave, go *or* come out (of) (6)

   salir de excursión   to go (set out) on an excursion (10)

   salir de viaje   to leave on the (one's) trip (20)

   salir para   to leave for (9)

la **salsa**   Latin rhythm; sauce (11)

saludar   to greet, speak to, say hello to (6)

san   saint, *used for santo before m. name of saints not beginning with* **Do-, To-** (16)

la **sandalia**   sandal (7)

el **San(to)**   Saint (St.) (16)

Sara   Sara, Sarah

la **sartén** (*pl.* **sartenes**)   skillet (17)

   la **sartén eléctrica**   electric skillet (17)

se   *pron. used for* **le, les** to (for) him, her, it, them, you (*formal*); *reflex.* (to, for) himself, herself, etc.; *indef. subject* one, people, you, etc.; *used with verbs as substitute for the passive voice*

la **sección** (*pl.* **secciones**)   section (15)

   la **sección de deportes**   sports section (15)

la **secretaria**   secretary (*f.*) (19)

el **secretario**   secretary (*m.*) (19)

secundario, -a   secondary (15)

   la **escuela secundaria**   secondary school, high school (15)

la **sed**   thirst (11)

   tener sed   to be thirsty (11)

seguida: en _____   at once, immediately (12)

   volver (ue) en seguida   to be right back, to return at once

seguir (i, i)   to follow, continue, go on (18)

   seguir adelante   to continue (go on) ahead (18)

segundo, -a   second (12)

seguramente *adv.*   surely, certainly (10)

seguro, -a   sure, certain (6)

   estar seguro, -a de que   to be sure that (6)

seis   six (3)

seiscientos, -as   six hundred (12)

la **semana**   week (4)

   el **fin de semana**   the weekend (8)

   la **semana pasada**   last week (9)

   todas las semanas   every week (*lit.*, all the weeks) (4)

   un par de (semanas)   a couple of (weeks) (13)

el **semestre**   semester (10)

la **semifinal**   semifinal match (15)

sencillo, -a   simple, single (12)

   el **boleto sencillo**   one-way ticket (20)

   las **camas sencillas**   single beds (12)

sentado, -a   seated (8)

sentarse (ie)   to sit down (9)

sentir (ie, i)   to feel; to regret, be sorry; *reflex.* to feel (well, ill, happy, etc.)

   ¿cómo te sientes?   how do you (*fam. sing.*) feel? (16)

   lo siento mucho   I am very sorry (7)

señalar   to point at (to, out), indicate (12)

el **señor**   gentleman; (*pl. and in direct address*) gentlemen, madam and sir, ladies and gentlemen (12)

la **señora**   woman, lady (12); (*in direct address*) madam, ma'am (12) los **señores** (**Ramos**) Mr. and Mrs. (Ramos) (12)

la **señorita** Miss, young lady (woman) (1); (*in direct address*) miss, ma'am (1)

septiembre September (5)

séptimo, -a seventh (12)

ser to be (2)

  conseguir (**i, i**) **ser** to succeed in being

  ¡eres un encanto! you're a dear! (17)

  es (**una**) **lástima** it's a pity (too bad) (19)

  es decir that is

  es que the fact is (that) (14)

  es verdad it is true (3)

  fue confiada was entrusted

  llegar a ser to become

  no son difíciles de comprender (they) are not difficult to understand

  ¿qué hora será? I wonder what time it is? (15)

  ser aficionado, -a (**a**) to be fond (of) (15)

  ser alérgico(-a) a to be allergic to (16)

  ser fuente to be a source

  ser hora de to be time to (22)

  ser premiado, -a to be awarded

  soy yo it is I (8)

  tú eres un genio en el volante you are a genius at the wheel (18)

la **serie** series

serio, -a serious (8)

  en serio seriously (9)

el **servicio** service

la **servilleta** napkin (11)

  la **servilleta de papel** paper napkin (11)

servir (**i, i**) to serve

sesenta sixty (6)

setecientos, -as seven hundred (12)

setenta seventy (6)

sexto, -a sixth (12)

si *conj.* if, whether (1)

  como si as if (21)

sí yes (1)

la **sicología** psychology (6)

el **sicólogo** psychologist (*m.*)

siempre *adv.* always (1)

siete seven (3)

el **siglo** century (12)

siguiente following, next (8)

  al día siguiente (on) the following *or* next day (8)

la **silla** chair (2)

el **sillón** (*pl.* **sillones**) armchair (17)

simpático, -a charming, likeable, nice (21)

simple: el juego ____ singles (*tennis*)

sin *prep.* without

  sin amueblar unfurnished (17)

  sin duda doubtless, no doubt (12)

  sin embargo however

  sin falta without fail (21)

  sin que *conj.* without (20)

sino *conj.* but, but rather (20)

el **síntoma** (*note gender*) symptom (16)

la **sirena** siren (18)

sobre *prep.* on, upon, about, concerning (4)

social (*m. or f.*) social

  las **ciencias sociales** social sciences (6)

el **sofá** (*note gender*) sofa (17)

  el **sofá-cama** sofa bed (17)

el **sol** sun (10)

  hacer (**mucho**) **sol** to be (very) sunny (*weather*) (10)

  tomar el sol to sunbathe (10)

solamente *adv.* only (20)

solicitar to apply for, ask for (22)

la **solicitud** application (19)

  hacer la solicitud to apply, submit the application (19)

sólo *adv.* only (1)

  no sólo… sino (**también**) not only . . . but (also)

  no sólo es… sino que es not only is . . . but is

  sólo quería avisarles que I just (only) wanted to inform you (*pl.*) (let you know) that (11)

el **sombrero** hat (13)

sonar (**ue**) to sound; ring (8)

la **sorpresa** surprise (16)

  ¡qué sorpresa tan agradable! what a pleasant surprise! (16)

Sr. = **señor**

Sra. = **señora**

Srta. = **señorita**

su (**s**) *adj.* his, her, its, your (*formal sing.*); their, your (*formal pl.*) (4)

subir (**a**) to go up (to), climb up (into) (12)

la **sucursal** branch (*of a company*) (19)

los **suegros** mother- and father-in-law

el **sueldo** salary (19)

el **sueño** sleepiness; sleep (11)

  tener sueño to be sleepy (11)

la **suerte** luck (10)

  por suerte luckily (10)

  ¡qué mala suerte! what bad luck! (18)

  tener (**mucha**) **suerte** to be (very) lucky (11)

el **suéter** sweater (21)

suficiente (*m. or f.*) enough (8)

sugerir (**ie, i**) to suggest (17)

la **superficie** surface

los **Supertazones** Superbowls

supuesto: ¡por ____! of course! (5)

el **sur** south (21)

  al sur de(**l**) south of (21)

Suramérica South America (2)

suramericano, -a *also noun* South American (5)

suyo, -a *adj.* his, her, your (*formal sing. pl.*), its, their; of his, of hers, of yours (*formal sing. pl.*), of theirs (11)

  (**el**) **suyo**, (**la**) **suya**, (**los**) **suyos**, (**las**) **suyas** *pron.* his, hers, theirs, yours (*formal sing. pl.*) (20)

T

tal such, such a

  con tal (**de**) **que** *conj.* provided that (20)

  ¿qué tal? how goes it? how are you? (5)

  ¿qué tal (**el viaje**)? how about (the trip)? how is *or* was (the trip)? (5)

  tal vez perhaps (18)

la **talla** size (*of a garment*) (7)

el **tamaño** size (of) (7)

también *adv.* also, too (1)

tampoco *adv.* neither, (not) . . . either (9)

  (**yo**) **tampoco** neither can (I), (I) cannot either (14)

tan *adv.* so, as (3)

  tan + *adj. or adv.* as (so) . . . as (16)

tanto, -a (**-os, -as**) *adj. and pron.* as (so) much; *pl.* as (so) many; *adv.* as (so) much, so many (11)

  me preocupo tanto I get so worried (19)

  tanto como as (so) much (16)

  tanto, -a (**-os, -as**)**… como** as (so) much (many, well) . . . as (16)

la **tarde** afternoon (1)

  ayer por la tarde yesterday afternoon (14)

  buenas tardes good afternoon (1)

  de la tarde in the afternoon (*when a specific hour is given*) (3)

  esta misma tarde this very afternoon (17)

  mañana por la tarde tomorrow afternoon (14)

  por la tarde in the afternoon (*no specific hour given*) (3)

todas las tardes every afternoon (3)

tarde *adv.* late (3)

más tarde later (11)

la **tarjeta** card (12)

la **tarjeta de crédito** credit card (12)

la **tarjeta postal** postcard (14)

el (la) **taxista** taxi driver (18)

la **taza** cup (3)

tomar una taza de café to have *or* drink a cup of coffee (3)

te *obj. pron.* you (*fam. sing.*) (6); to (for) you (*fam. sing.*) (7); (to, for) yourself

el **teatro** theater (9)

el **teléfono** telephone (5)

llamar por teléfono to telephone (call), talk by (on the) telephone (5)

la **televisión** television, TV (4)

mirar la televisión to watch television (4)

mirar por televisión to watch on TV (15)

el **programa de televisión** television program (4)

el **tema** (*note gender*) theme, topic, subject (4)

temer to fear, suspect (18)

el **temor** fear

la **temperatura** temperature (10)

tomarle la temperatura (a uno) to take (one's) temperature (16)

temprano *adv.* early (3)

tener to have (*possess*) (2); *in pret.* to get, receive

¿cuántos años tienes (tiene Ud.)? how old are you? (11)

no tener nada que hacer not to have anything (to have nothing) to do (21)

¿qué precio tiene(n)… ? what is the price (cost) of . . . ? (7)

tenemos que regresar el día (treinta) we have to return on the (thirtieth) (20)

tener calor to be hot (11)

tener cuidado to be careful (11)

tener dolor de cabeza to have a headache (16)

tener frío to be cold (11)

tener ganas de… to feel like (having), to be in the mood for . . . (11)

tener hambre to be hungry (11)

tener la oportunidad de + *inf.* to have the opportunity of (to) + *verb* (21)

tener (muchísima) fiebre to have a (very high) fever (16)

tener (mucho) cuidado to be (very) careful (11)

tener (mucho) éxito to be (very) successful (22)

tener mucho que estudiar to have a great deal to study (6)

tener paciencia to be patient (18)

tener precio fijo to have fixed prices (7)

tener que + *inf.* to have to, must + *verb* (2)

tener razón to be right (11)

tener (mucha) sed to be (very) thirsty (11)

tener sueño to be sleepy (11)

tener suerte to be lucky (11)

tener tiempo para to have time to (for) (11)

tener un resfriado (una pulmonía viral) to have a cold (viral pneumonia) (16)

tener una avería to have a breakdown, failure (*in the car*) (18)

tener… años to be . . . years old (11)

el **tenis** tennis (15)

tercer *used for* **tercero** *before m. sing. nouns* third (12)

tercero, -a third (12)

terminar to end, finish (6)

terrible (*m. or f.*) terrible (16)

territorial (*m. or f.*) territorial

el **terror** horror, terror (9)

la **película de terror** horror movie *or* film (9)

textil (*m. or f.*) textile

ti *pron.* you (*fam. sing.*), yourself (*after prep.*) (12)

la **tía** aunt (9)

el **tiempo** time (*in general sense*) (5); weather (10)

a tiempo on time (11)

¿cuánto tiempo hace? how long is it (has it been)? (19)

¿cuánto tiempo hace que Uds. volvieron? how long has it been since you (*pl.*) returned? (14)

en este tiempo del año in (at) this time of (the) year (12)

faltar mucho tiempo para (las siete) to be a long time before (seven)

hace buen tiempo the weather is fine (nice) (10)

¿qué tiempo hace/hacía? how is/was the weather? (10)

tener tiempo para to have time to (for) (11)

tiempo libre free time (15)

la **tienda** store, shop (7)

la **tienda de ropa** clothing store

vamos a (otra tienda) let's go *or* we are going (to another store) (7)

el **timbre** (door)bell (15)

el **timbre de la puerta** doorbell (15)

tocar el timbre to ring the doorbell (15)

el **tío** uncle; *pl.* uncles, uncle(s) and aunt(s) (9)

típico, -a typical (11)

el **tipo** type (9)

el **título** degree (*university*); title (6)

la **toalla** towel (12)

el **tobillo** ankle (16)

el **tocadiscos (para compactos)** (*pl.* los **tocadiscos**) record (compact disk) player (11)

tocar to play (*music*) (11)

tocar a la puerta to knock on the door (15)

tocar el timbre to ring the doorbell (15)

todavía *adv.* still, yet (5)

todavía no not yet (21)

todo, -a all, every (1); (*pl.* **todos, -as**) all, everybody (9)

de todos modos in any case (20)

en todas partes everywhere

por todas partes everywhere (10)

todas las noches (tardes) every night (afternoon) (3)

todas las semanas every week (4)

todo el mundo everybody (9)

todos los días every day (*lit.* all the days) (1)

tomar to take, eat, drink (3)

tomar algo to have *or* take something to eat *or* drink (6)

tomar el almuerzo (desayuno) to eat *or* have lunch (breakfast) (3)

tomar el ascensor to take the elevator (12)

tomar el desayuno to eat *or* have breakfast (3)

tomar el sol to sunbathe (10)

tomarle la temperatura (presión) (a uno) to take (one's) temperature (blood pressure) (16)

tomar una película to film (a movie) (21)

tomar una taza de café to have *or* drink a cup of coffee (3)

Tomás   Thomas, Tom
la **tormenta**   storm (10)
la **tos**   cough (16)
   el **jarabe para la tos**   cough syrup (16)
toser   to cough (16)
la **tostadora**   toaster (17)
trabajador, -ora   industrious, hard-working (19)
trabajar   to work (5)
el **trabajo**   work, employment, position, job (19)
la **tradición** (*pl.* **tradiciones**)   tradition
traducir   to translate (19)
traer   to bring (6)
el **tráfico**   traffic (18)
   el **accidente de tráfico**   traffic accident (18)
el **traje**   suit (14)
   el **traje de baño**   bathing suit (14)
tranquilo, -a   quiet (17)
la **transparencia**   transparency, slide (21)
tratar   to treat
   tratar de + *inf.*   to try to + *verb* (9)
   tratar de + *obj.*   to treat, deal (with) (9)
   tratarse de   to be a question of
trece   thirteen (3)
treinta   thirty (3)
   treinta y dos   thirty-two (3)
   treinta y un(o), -a   thirty-one (3)
el **tren**   train (8)
   en tren   by (in a) train (8)
tres   three (3)
trescientos, -as   three hundred (12)
el **tribunal examinador**   examining board (committee)
tridimensional (*m. or f.*)   three-dimensional
el **trimestre**   trimester, quarter (19)
tropical (*m. or f.*)   tropical (10)
   la **selva tropical**   rainforest
tu(s) *adj.*   your (*fam. sing.*) (4)
tú   you (*fam. sing. subject pron.*) (1)
el **turismo**   tourism
   el **campo de turismo**   tourist camp, campground
el (la) **turista**   tourist
   la **clase turista**   tourist (economy) class (20)
turístico, -a   tourist
tuyo, -a *adj.*   your (*fam.*), of yours (*fam.*) (11)
el **tuyo**, (**la**) **tuya**, (**los**) **tuyos**, (**las**) **tuyas** *pron.*   yours (*fam.*) (20)

U

último, -a   last (*in a series*) (14)
   la **última vez**   the last time (11)
últimamente   lately
un, **uno, una**   a, an, one
   a la una   at one o'clock (2)
Unidos: los Estados ____   United States (1)
la **universidad**   university (1)
   en la universidad   at the university (1)
uno (*n.*)   one (3)
unos, -as   some, a few, several; about (*quantity*) (19)
urgente (*m. or f.*)   urgent (19)
el **Uruguay**   Uruguay (5)
uruguayo, -a *also noun*   Uruguayan (5)
usar   to use (2)
usted (**Ud.**)   you (*formal sing.*) (1); *pl.* you (*fam. and formal*) (1)
útil (*m. or f.*)   useful

V

las **vacaciones**   vacation (5)
   estar de vacaciones   to be on vacation (5)
   ir de vacaciones   to go on a vacation (5)
   pasar las vacaciones (**de verano**)   to spend the (summer) vacation (5)
   las **vacaciones de Navidad**   Christmas vacation (8)
la **vacante**   job opening (19); *also adj.* (*m. or f.*) unfilled, unoccupied (19)
   el **puesto vacante**   available position (job), job opening
vale   O.K., all right (9)
   valenciano, -a   Valencian, from *or* of Valencia (*Spain*) (11)
valer   to be worth (21)
   valer la pena   to be worthwhile (21)
   valer más   to be better (21)
la **variedad**   variety
varios, -as   various, several (4)
vecino, -a   neighboring
veinte   twenty (3)
veinticinco   twenty-five (3)
veinticuatro   twenty-four (3)
veintidós   twenty-two (3)
veintinueve   twenty-nine (3)
veintiocho   twenty-eight (3)
veintiséis   twenty-six (3)
veintisiete   twenty-seven (3)
veintitrés   twenty-three (3)

ventiuno (**veintiún, veintiuna**)   twenty-one (3)
vencer   to conquer
el **vendedor**   salesman, clerk (*m.*) (7)
la **vendedora**   saleslady, clerk (*f.*) (7)
vender   to sell (4)
venir   to come (4)
   el (**viernes**) **que viene**   next (Friday) (11)
   venir (**bastante**) **cansado, -a**   to be (quite) tired (5)
la **ventana**   window (2)
ver   to see (6); to look
   a ver   let's (let me) see (13)
   (**ella**) **se ve estupenda** (**muy bien/mal**)   she looks great (very good/well, bad/ill) (14)
el **verano**   summer (5)
   la **escuela de verano**   summer school (15)
   las **vacaciones de verano**   summer vacation (5)
veras: de ____   really, truly (15)
la **verdad**   truth (3)
   es verdad   it is true (3)
   ¿(no) es verdad?   aren't you?, isn't it?, do you?, etc. (3)
   ¿verdad?   do you?, is it true?, really? (3)
verde (*m. or f.*)   green (2)
   verde-azul (*m. or f.*)   greenish blue (14)
el **verso**   verse (19)
el **vestido**   dress (7)
el **vestigio**   vestige
la **vez** (*pl.* **veces**)   time (*in a series*) (6)
   a veces   at times (11); sometimes
   alguna vez   sometime, ever (14)
   de vez en cuando   from time to time, once in a while, occasionally (6)
   esta vez   this time (11)
   otra vez   again (9)
   la próxima vez   next time (11)
   tal vez   perhaps (18)
   la última vez   the last time (11)
viajar   to travel
   ¡cuánto me gustaría viajar!   how I should (would) like to travel! (22)
   viajar por   to travel in (through) (21)
el **viaje**   trip, journey (5)
   la **agencia de viajes**   travel agency (20)
   el (la) **agente de viajes**   travel agent (20)
   ¡buen viaje!   (have) a good *or* fine trip! (9)

la **compañera de viaje**   traveling companion (*f.*) (8)

el **compañero de viaje**   traveling companion (*m.*) (8)

hacer el viaje   to make (take) the trip (8)

salir de viaje   to leave on the (one's) trip (20)

su viaje por España   their (his, her, your [*formal*]) trip around Spain (13)

el **viaje de negocios**   business trip (19)

el **viajero**   traveler (*m.*) (12)

los **cheques de viajero**   traveler's checks (12)

la **vida**   life (10)

en la vida   never in my life (16)

el **vídeo**   video (20)

la **videograbadora**   video recorder (VCR) (17)

viejo, -a   old (4)

el **viento**   wind (10)

hacer (mucho) viento   to be (very) windy (10)

el **viernes**   (on) Friday (3)

hasta el viernes   until (see you) Friday (11)

el **(viernes) que viene**   next (Friday) (11)

el **vino**   wine (11)

el **vino tinto**   red wine

viral (*m. or f.*)   viral (16)

el **virus**   virus (16)

pescar un virus   to catch (come down with) a virus (16)

la **visita**   visit, call (5)

de visita   on (for) a visit (5)

estar de visita   to visit, be visiting, be on a visit (5)

visitar   to visit, call on (8)

la **vista**   view (12)

hasta la vista   until (see you) later (20)

la **vitrina**   showcase (13)

la **vivienda**   housing

vivir   to live (3)

el **volante**   steering wheel (18)

tú eres un genio en el volante   you are a genius at the wheel (18)

el **voleibol**   volleyball (15)

volver (ue)   to return *or* go back; to come back (8)

volver a casa   to return *or* go back home; to come back home (8)

volver a (llamar)   (to call) again (11)

volverse loco, -a   to become *or* go crazy (mad, wild) (19)

vosotros, -as   you (*fam. pl. subject pron.*) (1); you, yourselves (*fam. pl.*) (*after prep.*) (12)

el **vuelo**   flight (20)

el **vuelo de día**   daytime flight, flight by day (*in the daytime*) (20)

el **vuelo de la mañana**   morning flight (20)

el **vuelo directo**   non-stop (direct) flight (20)

la **vuelta**   return; turn (20)

el **boleto de ida y vuelta**   round-trip ticket (20)

dar vuelta (a)   to turn (to)

vuestro, -a *adj.*   your (*fam. pl.*) (4); of yours (*fam. pl.*) (11)

(el) vuestro, (la) vuestra, (los) vuestros, (las) vuestras *pron.*   yours (*fam. pl.*) (20)

Y

y   and (1)

ya *adv.*   already, now (1); *sometimes used only for emphasis*

¡ya lo creo!   of course! certainly! (21)

el **yerno**   son-in-law

yo   I (*subject pron.*) (1)

soy yo   it is I (8)

yucateco, -a   of (pertaining to) Yucatan (13)

Z

el **zapato**   shoe (7)

English-Spanish

A

a, **an**   un, una; *often untranslated*
  a bit   un poco
  a few   unos, -as, algunos, -as
  a little   un poco
  a lot *adv.*   mucho
  a lot of *adj.*   mucho, -a (-os, -as)
A.M.   de la mañana
able: be ____   poder
about   de, sobre, acerca de (*for probability, use future or conditional tenses*)
  at about (*time*)   a eso de
accompany (**to**)   acompañar
ache (**to**)   doler (ue)
  does his stomach ache?   ¿le duele (a él) el estómago?
  her entire body ached   (a ella) le dolía todo el cuerpo
  my head doesn't ache   no me duele la cabeza
acquainted: is ____ **with**   conoce a
  get acquainted   conocer
across: run ____   encontrarse (ue) con
ad   el anuncio
address   la dirección (*pl.* direcciones)
administration   la administración
  business administration   la administración de negocios
advice   los consejos
  to ask for some advice   pedir (i, i) consejos
  to give (**some**) **advice**   dar un / algún consejo
advise (**to**)   aconsejar
afraid: be ____ (**that**)   tener miedo (de que)
  be afraid to   tener miedo de
after *conj.*   después que
after *prep.*   después de
afternoon   la tarde
  good afternoon   buenas tardes
  in the afternoon   por la tarde
  one Sunday afternoon   un domingo por la tarde
  that afternoon   esa tarde
  tomorrow afternoon   mañana por la tarde
afterward *adv.*   después
  shortly afterward   poco después
again   volver (ue) a (+ *inf.*); otra vez
agency   la agencia
  travel agency   la agencia de viajes
agent   el agente, la agente
Agnes   Inés

ago: a couple of hours ____   hace un par de horas
  a few months ago   hace unos meses
  a hundred years ago   hace cien años
  an hour ago   hace una hora
agricultural   agrícola (*m. or f.*)
  agricultural machinery   la maquinaria agrícola
  School of Agricultural Engineering   la Escuela de Ingeniería Agrícola (*or de* Agronomía)
ahead *adv.*   adelante
  go on (**continue**) **ahead**   seguir (i, i) *or* continuar adelante
  may they continue ahead   que sigan (continúen) adelante
air conditioning   el aire acondicionado
airmail   el correo aéreo
Albert   Alberto
all   todo, -a; *pl.* todos, -as
almost   casi
already   ya
also   también
although   aunque
always   siempre
America: South ____   Suramérica
American: North ____   norteamericano, -a
  South American: suramericano, -a
  Spanish American   hispanoamericano, -a
among   entre
ancient   antiguo, -a
and   y
Ann   Ana
announce (**to**)   anunciar
another   otro, -a
  (in order) to take leave of one another   para despedirse (i, i)
  one another (*m.*)   uno al otro
answer (**to**)   contestar
Anthony   Antonio
any *adj. and pron.*   alguno, -a; (*before m. sing. nouns*) algún; *often not translated*
  at any hour   a cualquier hora
anymore (*after negative*)   más
anyone   alguien; (*after negative*) nadie
anything   algo; (*after negative*) nada
  not to have anything to do   no tener nada que hacer
apartment   el apartamento

apartment building   el edificio (la casa) de apartamentos
appliance   el aparato
apply (**to**)   solicitar
appointment   la cita
approach (**to**)   acercarse (a + *obj.*)
April   abril
architecture   la arquitectura
Argentine   argentino, -a
arm   el brazo
arrive (**to**)   llegar (a + *obj.*)
  arrive downtown   llegar al centro
  arrive home   llegar a casa
  arrive on time   llegar a tiempo
arriving: on ____   al llegar
article   el artículo
as *conj.*   como
  as + *adj. or adv.* + **as**   tan… como
  as an agent   como agente
  as if   como si
  so much as   tanto como
ask (**to**) (*question*)   preguntar; (*request*) pedir (i, i)
ask for   preguntar por; (*request*) pedir (i, i)
at   a, en, de
  at (**a movie**)   en (un cine)
  at about (*time*)   a eso de
  at home   en casa
  at nine o'clock   a las nueve
  at once   en seguida
  at this time of the year   en este tiempo del año
  at what time?   ¿a qué hora?
attend (**to**)   asistir a
attention   la atención
  pay attention to   hacer (+ *ind. obj. pron.*) caso a
  (that John) not pay attention to   (que Juan) no le haga caso a
attractive   atractivo, -a
audience   el público
August   agosto
aunt   la tía
away: right ____   en seguida

B

back (*body*)   la espalda
bad   malo, -a
badly   mal
bank   el banco
bargain   la ganga
  it's a bargain   es una ganga
basketball   el basquetbol

bath   el baño
bathing suit   el traje de baño
bathroom   el cuarto de baño
be (to)   estar, ser; encontrarse (ue),
  hallarse, verse
  be able   poder
  be afraid (that)   tener miedo (de
    que)
  be afraid to   tener miedo de
  be a (great) hit   ser un (gran) éxito
  be (a little) hungry   tener (un poco
    de) hambre
  be a success   tener éxito
  be cloudy   estar nublado
  be cold (*weather*)   hacer frío
  be cold (*living beings*)   tener frío
  be fantastic   ser fantástico, -a
  be fond of   ser aficionado, -a a
  be fortunate   tener suerte
  be glad that   alegrarse de que
  be in a hurry   estar apurado, -a
  be ill   estar enfermo, -a
  be lucky   tener suerte
  be (nineteen)   cumplir (diecinueve)
    años
  be on a visit   estar de visita
  be on one's (the) way to   ir camino
    de
  be patient   tener paciencia
  be pleasant   ser agradable
  be possible   ser posible
  be (quite) tired   estar (bastante)
    cansado, -a
  be right   tener razón
  be sure that   estar seguro, -a de
    que
  be time to   ser hora de
  be tired of + *ing*   estar cansado, -a
    de + *inf.*
  be unable to   no poder
  be urgent   ser urgente
  be (very) glad to   alegrarse
    (mucho) de + *inf.*
  be (very much) in fashion   estar
    (muy) de moda
  be (very) sleepy   tener (mucho)
    sueño
  be (very) successful   tener
    (mucho) éxito
  be (very) windy   hacer (mucho)
    viento
  be worthwhile   valer la pena
  be . . . years old   tener (cumplir)…
    años
  how glad I am that . . . !   ¡cuánto
    me alegro de que… !
  how glad I would be to (travel)!
    ¡cuánto me alegraría de (viajar)!
  I'll be there at 11:00 A.M.   estoy
    allí a las once de la mañana

it is (a week) since (they came)
  hace (una semana) que
  (vinieron) *or* (vinieron) hace
  (una semana)
(it) is being played   se juega
it is I   soy yo
it is sunny   hace (hay) sol
it must be half past ten   serán las
  diez y media
there are probably many people
  habrá mucha gente
there has been   ha habido
there is (are)   hay
there was (were)   había
there were people   había gente
there will be   habrá
they have been lucky   han tenido
  suerte
they would be happy   estarían
  contentos (felices)
what time can it be?   ¿qué hora
  será?
you're welcome   de nada, no hay
  de qué
beach   la playa
Beatrice   Beatriz
beautiful   bonito, -a; hermoso, -a;
  precioso, -a
beauty parlor   la peluquería
because   porque
become   ponerse + *adj.*; hacerse,
  llegar a ser + *noun*
  become calm   ponerse calmado, -a;
    calmarse
  become rich   hacerse rico, -a
  become (very) tired   ponerse
    (muy) cansado, -a; cansarse
    mucho
bed   la cama
  go to bed   acostarse (ue)
  single bed   la cama sencilla
before *adv.* antes; *prep.* antes de;
  conj. antes (de) que
begin (to)   comenzar (ie) (a + *inf.*),
  empezar (ie) (a + *inf.*)
besides   además (de)
best, better   mejor
Betty   Isabel
bicycle   la bicicleta
  take bicycle tours   hacer
    excursiones en bicicleta
bilingual   bilingüe (*m. or f.*)
bill   la cuenta
birthday   el cumpleaños
  a birthday party   una fiesta de
    cumpleaños
blanket   la manta
blender   la batidora
blouse   la blusa
blue: light ____   celeste (*m. or f.*)

blush (to)   ponerse rojo, -a
book   el libro
bookstore   la librería
border   la frontera
boring   aburrido, -a
bother (to)   molestar
  it bothers him   le molesta
bottom   el fondo
boy   el chico, el muchacho
boyfriend   el novio
bracelet   la pulsera
brakes   los frenos
branch (*business*)   la sucursal
breakfast   el desayuno
  full breakfast   el desayuno
    completo
  take (eat) breakfast   desayunarse,
    tomar el desayuno
bring (to)   traer
build (to)   construir
building   el edificio
  apartment building   el edificio de
    apartamentos
  main building   el edificio principal
business   el negocio
  business trips   los viajes de
    negocios
  business administration   la
    administración de negocios
busy   ocupado, -a
  be busy   estar ocupado, -a
but   pero; (*after negative*) sino
buy (to)   comprar
  buy (for) oneself   comprarse
  I'll buy them (*m.*) **for you** (*fam.
    sing.*)   te los compro
  that he would buy it (*f.*) **for them**
    que él se la compraría
by   por, de, en; *not translated when
    used with Spanish gerund*
  by bus   en autobús
  by car   en coche *or* carro
  by plane   en avión
  by seeing it   viéndolo
  by the way   a propósito

C

cafeteria   la cafetería
cake   la torta
call (to)   llamar, llamar por teléfono
calm down (to)   calmarse
camera   la cámara
  video camera   la (cámara) vídeo
can   poder; (*know how*) saber; *for
    conjecture use future tense*
  what time can it be?   ¿qué hora
    será?
candidate   el candidato, la candidata

car el carro (*Am.*); el coche (*Spain*)
  (**go**) **by car** (ir) en carro (coche)
  going by car yendo en coche
    (carro)
  in John's car en el coche (carro) de
    Juan
  (**leave**) **by car** (salir) en carro
    (coche)
  patrol car el carro patrulla
card la tarjeta
  credit card la tarjeta de crédito
career la carrera
Caroline Carolina
carry (**to**) llevar
cash (**to**) cambiar
  cash a check cobrar un cheque
cattle el ganado
celebrate (**to**) celebrar
cent el centavo
chair la silla
channel (*television*) el canal
charge (**to**) cobrar
Charles Carlos
charming encantador, encantadora
  (-es, -as)
chat (**to**) charlar, hablar
cheap barato, -a
cheaper más barato, -a
check el cheque
  cash a check cambiar un cheque
chest el pecho
childhood la niñez
  childhood memory el recuerdo de
    niñez
children (*family*) los hijos (*m. and f.*);
  niños, -as
Chilean chileno, -a
chili chile
choose (**to**) escoger
Christmas la Navidad
  Christmas vacation las vacaciones
    de Navidad
city la ciudad
class la clase
  go to class ir a clase
  have a class tener clase
  in class en (la) clase
classmate el compañero (la
  compañera) de clase
classroom la sala de clase (*pl.* las salas
  de clase)
cleaner: vacuum ___ la aspiradora
clear claro, -a
clerk el dependiente, el vendedor
  (*m.*); la dependienta, la vendedora
  (*f.*)
close (**to**) cerrar (ie)
closed cerrado, -a
cloud la nube
cloudy nublado

it was cloudy estaba nublado
coast la costa
coffee el café
  cup of coffee la taza de café
  have coffee tomar café
cold (*weather*) el frío; (*illness*) el
  resfriado
  be cold (*weather*) hacer frío;
    (*living beings*) tener frío
  catch a cold pescar un resfriado
  I caught a (**terrible**) **cold** pesqué
    un resfriado (terrible)
  cold drink el refresco
cold, *adj.* frío, -a
collision el choque
Colombian colombiano, -a
color el color
  photographs in color las
    fotografías a colores
come (**to**) venir
  come back volver (ue), regresar
  come by pasar por
  come in entrar; (*fam. sing.*
    command) pasa (tú)
comfortable cómodo, -a
comment el comentario
compact disk player el tocadiscos
  para compactos
companion el compañero (*m.*), la
  compañera (*f.*)
  travelling companion (*m.*) el
    compañero (la compañera) de
    viaje
companions los compañeros (*m. and
  f.*)
company la compañía
compare (**to**) comparar
competent competente (*m. or f.*)
completely completamente
computer la computadora, el
  ordenador (*Spain*)
concert el concierto
confirm (**to**) confirmar
congratulate (**to**) felicitar
constitution la constitución
  Constitution Street la calle
    Constitución
consult (**to**) consultar
continue (**to**) continuar
cook (**to**) cocinar
cool el fresco
  be cool (*weather*) hacer fresco
coral el coral (*pl.* corales)
Cordova Córdoba
cost (**to**) costar (ue)
cotton el algodón
cough la tos
  a cough syrup un jarabe para la
    tos
cough (**to**) toser

could *imp., pret., cond., or imp. subj. of*
  poder
country el campo; (*nation*) el país (*pl.*
  países)
couple el par
  a couple of hours (**weeks**) **ago**
    hace un par de horas (semanas)
course: of ___! ¡cómo no! ¡claro! ¡ya
  lo creo! ¡por supuesto!
court (*sports*) la cancha
  tennis court la cancha de tenis
cousin el primo (*m.*), la prima (*f.*), los
  primos (*m. and f.*)
covered cubierto, -a
crazy loco, -a
  go crazy volverse (ue) loco, -a
credit el crédito
  credit card la tarjeta de crédito
Cuban cubano, -a
cumbia la cumbia
cup la taza
  cup of coffee la taza de café

D

daily diario, -a
dance el baile
  at the dance en el baile
  dance number el número de baile
dance (**to**) bailar
date (*appointment*) la cita; (*calendar*)
  la fecha
  make a date hacer una cita
daughter la hija
day (*m.*) el día
  a day al día
  on the following day al día
    siguiente
daytime de día
  daytime flight el vuelo de día
deal: a great ___ mucho, -a
dear querido, -a
decide (**to**) decidir
degree (*university*) el título
  master's degree el título de
    maestría, la maestría
departure la partida
dessert el postre
  for dessert de postre
Diane Diana
dictionary el diccionario
difficult difícil (*m. or f.*)
dining room el comedor (*pl.*
  comedores)
direct directo, -a
director el director (*m.*), la directora
  (*f.*)
discotheque la discoteca
dish el plato

dishwasher la lavadora de platos

district el barrio

dive (to) bucear

do (to) hacer; *not expressed as an auxiliary*

  do that gladly hacer eso con (mucho) gusto

  doesn't he? doesn't she? don't they? ¿(no es) verdad?

  not to have anything to do no tener nada que hacer

  what can I do for you (*pl.*)? ¿en qué puedo servirles?

doctor el médico

dollar el dólar (U.S.); (*pl.* dólares)

door la puerta

doorbell el timbre (de la puerta)

dormitory la residencia, el dormitorio

  university dormitories las residencias (los dormitorios) de la universidad

doubt (to) dudar

down: calm ___ calmarse

  go down bajar

  lie down acostarse (ue)

  sit down sentarse (ie)

  slow down moderar la marcha

downtown (*city*) el centro

  go downtown ir al centro

dress el vestido

drink la bebida

  cold (soft) drink el refresco

  take something (to drink) tomar algo

drive (to) manejar (*Am.*), conducir (*Spain*)

  they don't let him drive no le permiten manejar (conducir)

driver el conductor (*pl.* conductores)

  taxi driver el (la) taxista

drop la gota

  nose drops las gotas para la nariz

during durante

E

each: we used to see ___ other nos veíamos

early temprano

earn (to) ganar

earrings los aretes

  gold earrings los aretes de oro

easier más fácil

easy fácil (*m. or f.*)

  be easy ser fácil

  it is easy es fácil

eat (to) comer

  eat breakfast desayunarse, tomar el desayuno

eat lunch almorzar (ue), tomar el almuerzo

eat supper cenar

economics la economía

  economics professor (teacher) el profesor (la profesora) de economía

economist el (la) economista

eight ocho

eighteen dieciocho

either (*after negative*) tampoco

elections las elecciones

elevator el ascensor

eleven once

  at eleven A.M. a las once de la mañana

encounter (to) encontrar (ue)

engineer el ingeniero, la ingeniera

engineering la ingeniería

  Engineering School la Facultad de Ingeniería

  engineering student el (la) estudiante de ingeniería

  School of Agricultural Engineering la Escuela de Ingeniería Agrícola (*or de* Agronomía)

English (*the language*) el inglés

enjoy (to) gozar (de + *obj.*), disfrutar (de + *obj.*)

  enjoy (oneself) divertirse (ie, i) *reflex.*

  may you (*pl.*) **enjoy yourselves** que se diviertan Uds.

enough bastante, suficiente (*m. or f.*)

enter (to) entrar (en *or* a + *obj.*); ingresar (en + *obj.*)

  enter the university ingresar en la universidad

entering: on ___ al entrar

entire: her ___ body todo el cuerpo

equator el ecuador

evening la noche

  Friday evening el viernes por la noche

  in the evening por la noche

  on Thursday evening el jueves por la noche

ever (*after negative*) nunca

  more than ever más que nunca

every todo, -a

  every day todos los días

  every night (week) todas las noches (semanas)

everybody todo el mundo

exam el examen (*pl.* exámenes)

excitement la emoción

exclaim (to) exclamar

excursion la excursión (*pl.* excursiones)

go on an excursion salir de excursión

take an excursion hacer una excursión

exercise el ejercicio

  do exercise hacer ejercicio

expensive caro, -a

  the most expensive one (*f.*) la más cara

F

face (to) dar a

  that face the (square) que dan a la (plaza)

fail (to) dejar de; fallar (*brakes*)

  don't fail to no dejéis de (*fam.* vosotros *form*)

  not to fail to no dejar de + *inf.*

  without fail sin falta

fall el otoño

family la familia

fantastic fantástico, -a

far *adv.* lejos

  far from lejos de

fashion la moda

  be (very much) in fashion estar (muy) de moda

  is very much in fashion está muy de moda

fast *adv.* rápido

father el padre, el papá

fear (to) temer

feel (to) sentir(se) (ie, i)

  feel somewhat better sentirse (ie, i) algo mejor

  feel (well) sentirse (ie, i) (bien)

  how do you feel? ¿cómo te sientes (se siente Ud.)?

feel like (to) + *ing* tener ganas de + *inf.*

  they feel like dancing ellos tienen ganas de bailar

fever la fiebre

few: a ___ unos, -as; algunos, -as

fifteenth: the ___ of el quince de

film la película

final match la final

finally al (por) fin

finals los exámenes finales

find (to) encontrar (ue), hallar

find oneself (to) encontrarse (ue)

fine (quality) fino, -a

finish (to) terminar

fireplace la chimenea

firm la empresa, la compañía

first primero, -a; (*before m. sing. nouns*) primer

fishing la pesca

go fishing ir de pesca
five cinco
fixed: ___ **price** el precio fijo
flan el flan
flight el vuelo
  a daytime flight un vuelo de día
  direct flights los vuelos directos
floor el piso
  on the third floor en el tercer piso
  main (**first**) **floor** el piso principal
  third floor (*Spain*) el piso segundo (el segundo piso)
flower la flor
following siguiente (*m. or f.*)
  on the following day al día siguiente
fond (**of**) aficionado, -a a
  be fond of ser aficionado, -a a
football el fútbol
  football match el partido de fútbol
for para, por
  ask for (**to**) pedir (i, i)
  for a long time hace mucho tiempo *or* desde hace mucho tiempo
foreign extranjero, -a
forget (**to**) olvidar
fortunately afortunadamente
forty-nine cuarenta y nueve
four cuatro
free libre (*m. or f.*)
French (*the language*) el francés
French *adj.* francés, francesa (*pl.* franceses, francesas)
Friday el viernes
  Friday evening el viernes por la noche
  on Friday morning el viernes por la mañana
  next Friday el viernes que viene
friend el amigo (*m.*), la amiga (*f.*)
from de
  from Diane's house de casa de Diana
  from the university de la universidad
front: in ___ **of** *prep.* enfrente de
full lleno, -a
  full breakfast el desayuno completo
furnished amueblado, -a

G

game (*match*) el partido
gasoline la gasolina
gather (**to**) reunirse
gathering la reunión

generally generalmente, por lo común
George Jorge
get (**to**) obtener, conseguir (i, i)
  get *or* **become acquainted** conocer(se)
  get *or* **become** (**well**) ponerse (bien), mejorarse
  get dressed, fixed up arreglarse
  get hurt hacerse daño
  get married casarse
  get ready (*for something*) prepararse
  get tanned ponerse bronceado, -a
  get together reunirse
  get up levantarse
  let's get going, then! ¡vámonos, pues!
  let's get together vamos a reunirnos, reunámonos
  let's not get up no nos levantemos
  we have gotten quite tanned nos hemos puesto bastante bronceados
gift el regalo
  gift list la lista de regalos
girl la muchacha, la chica
give (**to**) dar
  give (**some**) **advice** dar un (algún) consejo
glad: be ___ **that** alegrarse de que
  be (**very**) **glad to** alegrarse (mucho) de (+ *inf.*)
  how glad I am that . . . ! ¡cuánto me alegro de que… !
  how glad I would be to (**travel**)! ¡cuánto me alegraría de (viajar)!
gladly! ¡con mucho gusto!
glasses (*spectacles*) las gafas; (*water*) los vasos
  puts on his glasses se pone las gafas
gloves los guantes
go (**to**) ir (a + *inf.* or *obj.*)
  go ahead pasar, seguir (i, i) adelante
  go back regresar, volver (ue)
  go crazy volverse (ue) loco, -a
  go down bajar
  go fishing ir de pesca
  go into entrar en (+ *obj.*)
  go on ahead seguir (i, i) *or* continuar adelante
  go on an excursion salir de excursión
  go out salir
  go shopping ir de compras
  go to bed acostarse (ue)
  go to sleep dormirse (ue, u)
  go up (**to**) subir (a)

going by car yendo en coche
how have things gone? ¿cómo lo han pasado?
  let's go (**to**) vamos (a + *obj.*)
  let's not go to class no vayamos a clase
gold el oro
  gold (**earrings**) (los aretes) de oro
good bueno, -a; (*before m. sing. nouns*) buen
  good afternoon buenas tardes
  good morning buenos días
  have a good time divertirse (ie, i)
  have a good trip! ¡buen viaje!
good-looking guapo, -a
good-bye adiós
  let's not say good-bye no digamos adiós
graduate (**to**) graduarse
grandfather el abuelo
great (*before sing. nouns*) gran
  they look great on you (*fam. sing.*) (**her, him**) te (le) quedan preciosos
  great! ¡estupendo!
  she looked great se veía estupenda
greet (**to**) saludar
group el grupo
  a group of un grupo de
guacamole: a ___ (**salad**) un guacamole
guide (*person*) el (la) guía
guidebook la guía

H

haggle (**to**) regatear
hair el pelo
  have one's hair done arreglarse el pelo
half medio, -a
  it's half past seven (**nine**) son las siete (nueve) y media
hall el corredor
  residence hall la residencia
  student residence hall la residencia de estudiantes
  university residence hall la residencia de la universidad
hammock la hamaca
hand la mano
hand (**over**) (**to**) entregar
handsome guapo, -a
happy contento, -a; feliz (*pl.* felices)
hard: study ___ (estudiar) mucho
have (**to**) tener; (*auxiliary*) haber
  have *indir. command* que + *pres. subj. tense*

have a class   tener clase
have a cup of coffee   tomar una taza de café
have a good time   divertirse (ie, i)
have a good trip!   ¡buen viaje!
have (a great deal) to do   tener (mucho) que hacer
have a party   tener una fiesta
have bad luck   tener mala suerte
have (George) do it   que lo haga (Jorge)
have just + *p.p.*   acabar de + *inf.*
have lunch   tomar el almuerzo, almorzar (ue)
have news   recibir (tener) noticias
have one's hair done   arreglarse el pelo
have supper   cenar
have the opportunity to   tener la oportunidad de
have time to   tener tiempo para
have to   tener que + *inf.*
not to have anything to do   no tener nada que hacer
he   él
headache   el dolor de cabeza
to have a headache   tener dolor de cabeza
hear (to)   oír, escuchar
heavens!   ¡Dios mío!
Helen   Elena
hello (*telephone*)   diga, dígame, hola, bueno
help (to)   ayudar
Henrietta   Enriqueta
her *adj.*   su(s)
her   *dir. obj.* la; *indir. obj.* le, se; *after prep.* ella
here   aquí
hers   *pron.*(el) suyo, (la) suya, etc.; (el, la, los, las) de ella
of hers *adj.*   suyo(s), -a(s); de ella
high school   la escuela secundaria
him   *dir. obj.* lo, le; *indir. obj.* le, se; *after prep.* él
his   *adj.* su(s); *pron.*(el) suyo, (la) suya, etc.; (el, la, los, las) de él
of his *adj.*   suyo(s), -a(s); de él
Hispanic   hispánico, -a
hit (*success*)   el éxito
be a great hit   ser un gran éxito
home   la casa, el hogar
(arrive) home   (llegar) a casa
at home   en casa
honeymoon   la luna de miel
hope (to)   esperar
horrible   horrible (*m. or f.*)
hospital   el hospital
hot   caliente (*m. or f.*)

be (very) hot (*weather*)   hacer (mucho) calor
hotel   el hotel
hour   la hora
meal hours (*schedule*)   el horario de las comidas
how + *adj. or adv.!*   ¡qué… !
how pretty it is!   ¡qué bonito es!
how + *verb!*   ¡cuánto… !
how glad I am that . . . !   ¡cuánto me alegro de que… !
how: know ___ to   saber + *inf.*
how?   ¿cómo?
how long (*time*)**?**   ¿cuánto tiempo?
how much (many)?   ¿cuánto, -a (-os, -as)?
how old is (Charles)?   ¿cuántos años tiene (Carlos)?
how have things gone?   ¿cómo lo han pasado?
how was the trip?   ¿qué tal el viaje?
hungry: be (a little) ___   tener (un poco de) hambre
hurry: be in a ___   estar apurado, -a
hurt (to)   doler (ue)
get hurt   hacerse daño
her chest hurts   la duele (a ella) el pecho
my leg and arm hurt   me duelen la pierna y el brazo
husband   el marido, el esposo

I

I   yo
idea   la idea
if   si
ill   enfermo, -a
be ill   estar enfermo, -a
important   importante (*m. or f.*)
in   en, por, de; (*after a superlative*) de
in order to *prep.*   para
in the afternoon (morning, evening)   por la tarde (mañana, noche)
travel in   viajar por
industrious   trabajador, -ora
inexpensive   barato, -a
inform (to)   informar, avisar
injured person (*m.*)   el herido
intend (to)   pensar (ie) + *inf.*
interest (to)   interesar
interesting   interesante (*m. or f.*)
into: go ___   entrar en + *obj.*
run into   encontrarse (ue) con
introduce (to) (*a person*)   presentar
invite (to)   invitar
island   la isla

it   *dir. obj.* lo (*m. and neuter*), la (*f.*); *indir. obj.* le; (*usually omitted as subject*) él (*m.*), ella (*f.*); *after prep.* él (*m.*), ella (*f.*)
it has   tiene
Italian (*the language*)   el italiano
item: news ___   la noticia
its *adj.*   su(s)

J

jacket   la chaqueta
James   Jaime
jewel   la joya
jewelry store   la joyería
job   el trabajo
job opening   el puesto vacante, la vacante
John   Juan
Joseph   José
just: have ___   acabar de + *inf.*

K

keep on + *ing*   seguir (*or* continuar) + *-ndo*
tells him to keep on driving   le dice que siga (continúe) manejando (conduciendo)
key   la llave
kitchen   la cocina
knock (to)   llamar
knock at the door   llamar a la puerta
know (to)   (*a fact*) saber; (*be acquainted with*) conocer

L

laboratory   el laboratorio
language   la lengua
large   grande, gran (*before m. or f. nouns*)
very large   muy grande; grandísimo, -a
last   pasado, -a; (*in a series*) último, -a
last night   anoche
last week   la semana pasada
last year   el año pasado
the last day   el último día
late   tarde
later   después, más tarde, luego
see you later   hasta luego
until later   hasta luego
latter: the ___   éste, ésta
learn (to)   aprender (a + *inf.*)

leave (**to**)   salir, partir, irse, *or* marcharse (de + *obj.*); *trans.* dejar
 leave for   salir (partir, irse, marcharse) para
 leave her (**his**) **house**   salir de su casa
 leave home   salir de casa
 let's take leave of each other (**one another**)   despidámonos
 take leave of   despedirse (i, i) de
 upon leaving   al salir
lecture   la conferencia
left: be ___   quedar
 haven't left him   no le han dejado
 no seats are (**there are no seats**) **left**   no quedan asientos
 on the left   por la izquierda
less   menos
 more or less   más o menos
lesson   la lección (*pl.* lecciones)
 (**Spanish**) **lesson**   la lección (de español)
let (**to**)   dejar, permitir
 let (*pl.*) **me** (**drive**)   déjenme *or* permítanme (Uds.) (manejar *or* conducir)
   let's (**let us**) + *verb*   vamos a + *inf. or first-person pl. pres. subj. tense*
 let's get going, then!   ¡vámonos, pues!
 let's go (**to the lecture**)   vamos (a la conferencia)
 let's see   a ver
letter   la carta
library   la biblioteca
lie down (**to**)   acostarse (ue)
life   la vida
light (*weight*)   ligero, -a
like (**to**)   gustar
 I (**he, we, they**) **should** *or* **would like**   me (le, nos, les) gustaría; yo (él) quisiera (quisiéramos, quisieran)
 would you (*fam. sing.*) **like to stay here?**   ¿te gustaría quedarte aquí?
likeable   simpático, -a
list   la lista
 gift list   la lista de regalos
 waiting list   la lista de espera
listen (**to**)   escuchar
little: a ___   un poco (de)
live (**to**)   vivir
living room   la sala
long   largo, -a
 for a long time   hace mucho tiempo *or* desde hace mucho tiempo
 how long? (*time*)   ¿cuánto tiempo?

too long   demasiado tiempo
wait long   esperar mucho
look (**at**) (**to**)   mirar
 they (*m.*) **look great on you** (*fam. sing.*)   te quedan preciosos
look for (**to**)   buscar
look great (**to**)   verse estupendo, -a
looking: good- ___   guapo, -a
 young-looking   juvenil (*m. or f.*)
looking: while ___ **at**   mirando
lot: a ___ *adv.*   mucho
 a lot of *adj.*   mucho, -a (-os, -as)
lots (*adv.*)   mucho
 lots of *adj.*   mucho, -a (-os, -as)
Louis   Luis
Louise   Luisa
lounge   la sala
love (**to**)   (*something*) encantar; (*someone*) querer (ie)
 everybody loved it   a todo el mundo le encantó
 I love it   me encanta
luck   la suerte
 have bad luck   tener mala suerte
lucky: be ___   tener suerte
lunch   el almuerzo
 eat (**have, take**) **lunch**   tomar el almuerzo, almorzar (ue)

M

ma'am   señora, señorita
machinery   la maquinaria
magazine   la revista
main   principal (*m. or f.*)
 main floor   el piso principal
make (**to**)   hacer
 make a date   hacer una cita
 make a reservation (**reservations**)   hacer reservas
 make an excursion   hacer una excursión
 make the (**a**) **trip**   hacer el (un) viaje
makes (**brands**)   las marcas
man   el hombre
 the (**two**) **young men**   los (dos) jóvenes
manager   el (la) gerente
many   muchos, -as
 how many?   ¿cuántos, -as?
 many people   mucha gente
 too many *adj.*   demasiados, -as
 very many *adj.*   muchísimos, -as
Margaret   Margarita
market   el mercado
married: get ___   casarse
Mary   María
master's   la maestría

master's degree   el título de maestría
match (*game*)   el partido
 final match   la final
 football (**soccer**) **match**   el partido de fútbol
 match (**the earrings**)   hacer juego con (los aretes)
matter: what's the ___ **with you** (*fam. sing.*)**?**   ¿qué tienes?
 what's the matter with (**Thomas**)**?**   ¿qué tiene (Tomás)?
May   mayo
may (*wish, indir. command*)   que + *pres. subj.*; *mark of the pres. subj. tense*
 may we see it (*m.*)**?**   ¿nos permite verlo?
me *dir. and indir. obj.*   me; *after prep.* mí
 with me   conmigo
meal   la comida
 meal hours (**schedule**)   el horario de las comidas
mean (**to**)   querer (ie) decir, querer (ie) + *inf.*
 we didn't mean to go   no queríamos ir
meddlesome   entremetido, -a
medicine   la medicina
 School of Medicine   la Escuela (Facultad) de Medicina
meet (**to**)   encontrar (ue); (*a person for the first time*) conocer
 nice to meet you (*formal sing. f.*)   mucho gusto en conocerla
memories   los recuerdos
merengue   el merengue
message   el recado
 leave a (**some**) **message for her**   dejarle algún recado
Mexican   mexicano, -a
Michael   Miguel
microwave oven   el horno microondas
millimeter   el milímetro
mine *pron.*   (el) mío, (la) mía, etc.
 of mine *adj.*   mío, -a
Miss   (la) señorita, (la) Srta.
mixer   la mezcladora
modern   moderno, -a
moment   el momento
 a few moments   un rato
Monday   el lunes
 on Monday   el lunes
money   el dinero
month   el mes
more   más
 more or less   más o menos
morning   la mañana

a morning flight un vuelo de la mañana
good morning buenos días
in the morning por la mañana
(on) Sunday morning el domingo por la mañana
one Sunday morning un domingo por la mañana
tomorrow morning mañana por la mañana
yesterday morning ayer por la mañana
most más
most of la mayor parte de
the most expensive one (*f.*) la más cara
mountain la montaña
movie (*place*) el cine; (*film*) la película
a musical movie una película musical
Mr. (el) señor, (el) Sr.
Mr. and Mrs. (Ramos) los señores (Ramos)
Mrs. (la) señora, (la) Sra.
much *adj.* mucho, -a; *adv.* mucho
as much (. . .) as tanto, -a (…) como
how much (. . .)? ¿cuánto, -a (…)?
so much *adj.* tanto, -a
so much as tanto como
very much *adv.* muchísimo
music la música
must deber, tener que + *inf.*; *for probability use future, future perf., or cond. tense*
one must (wait) hay que (esperar)
you (*fam. sing.*) **must see them** (*f.*) tienes que verlas
my mi(s)

N

near *adv.* cerca
near *prep.* cerca de, junto a
nearby *adj.* cercano, -a
nearly casi
necessary necesario, -a; preciso, -a
it is necessary to es necesario, hay que + *inf.*
it was necessary to era (fue) necesario *or* había (hubo) que
need (to) necesitar
neighborhood el barrio
never nunca
new nuevo, -a
news las noticias
newspaper el periódico
newspaper office la oficina del periódico

next próximo, -a
next year el próximo año
next (Wednesday, Friday) el (miércoles, viernes) próximo (*or* que viene)
next (week) la (semana) que viene, la próxima (semana)
on the next day al día siguiente
nice agradable (*m. or f.*)
nice to meet you (*formal sing. f.*) mucho gusto en conocerla
night la noche
at night de noche
every night todas las noches
last night anoche
one Sunday night un domingo por la noche
Saturday night el sábado por la noche
nine nueve
at half past nine a las nueve y media
at (up to) nine o'clock a (hasta) las nueve
forty-nine cuarenta y nueve
nine hundred novecientos, -as
nineteen diecinueve
be (nineteen) cumplir (diecinueve) años
no *adv.* no
none ninguno, -a; (*before m. sing. nouns*) ningún
no one nadie
North American norteamericano, -a
nose la nariz
nose drops las gotas para la nariz
not no
notebook el cuaderno
nothing nada
November noviembre
now ahora
nowadays hoy (en) día
number el número
dance number el número de baile

O

obtain (to) conseguir (i, i)
o'clock: at (nine) ___ a las (nueve)
at about one o'clock a eso de la una
at (five, twelve, two) o'clock a las (cinco, doce, dos)
of de
of course! ¡cómo no! ¡claro! ¡ya lo creo! ¡por supuesto!
offer (to) ofrecer
offering: they are ___ it (*m.*) **for** lo dan por

office la oficina
newspaper office la oficina del periódico
often a menudo
old: he will be eighteen (years old) tendrá (cumplirá) dieciocho años
how old is (Charles)? ¿cuántos años tiene (Carlos)?
on en, sobre
on (arriving) al (llegar)
on the following day al día siguiente
on (Thursday) el (jueves)
once: at ___ en seguida
once in a while de vez en cuando
one un (*before m. sing. nouns*), uno, -a; *indef. subject* se, uno, una
at about one o'clock a eso de la una
at one (o'clock) a la una
at one-thirty a la una y media
no one nadie
one another (*m.*) uno al otro
take leave of one another despedirse (i, i)
that one ése, ésa, aquél, aquélla
this one éste, ésta
this red one (*m.*) este rojo
which one? ¿cuál?
only sólo, solamente
open (to) abrir
opening: job ___ el puesto vacante, la vacante
opportunity la oportunidad
or o
order: in ___ that *conj.* para que
in order to *prep.* para
organize (to) organizar
other otro, -a
see each other verse
ought to deber
our nuestro(s), -a(s)
out: go ___ salir

P

P.M. de la tarde (noche)
at about (eight) P.M. a eso de las (ocho) de la noche
paella la paella
page la página
pair el par
paper el papel
parents los padres
parking el estacionamiento
participate (to) participar
party la fiesta
birthday party la fiesta de cumpleaños

have a party tener una fiesta
pass (to) pasar
past: (it is) half ___ (seven) (son) las (siete) y media
patience la paciencia
patient: be ___ tener paciencia
patio el patio
patrol car el carro patrulla
pay (to) pagar
peninsular peninsular (*m. or f.*)
people la gente (*requires sing. verb*)
   lots of people mucha gente
   many people mucha gente
   there are probably many people habrá mucha gente
   there were people había gente
   young people los jóvenes
per month al mes
percolator la cafetera
perhaps quizá(s), tal vez
permit (to) permitir
person la persona
   injured person (*m.*) el herido
pesetas las pesetas
photo la foto
   take (many) photos sacar (muchas) fotos (fotografías)
photograph la fotografía
   photographs in color las fotografías a colores
pieces of pottery los objetos de cerámica
pill la píldora
pillow la almohada
place el lugar
plan el plan
plan (to) pensar (ie) + *inf.*
plane el avión (*pl.* aviones)
   (going) by plane (yendo) en avión
   plane ticket el boleto de avión
play (*a game*) jugar (ue) (a + *obj.*); (*music*) tocar
   play tennis jugar (al) tenis
   (the match) is being played (el partido) se juega
player el jugador, la jugadora
player: compact disk player el tocadiscos para compactos
pleasant agradable (*m. or f.*)
   be pleasant ser agradable
please + *verb* hága(n)me or haga(n) Uds. el favor de + *inf.*; (*after request*) por favor
pleased: be (very) ___ estar (muy) contento, -a
   pleased to meet you (*m. pl.*) mucho gusto en conocerlos
pleasure el gusto
   what a pleasure! ¡qué gusto!
pneumonia la pulmonía

police (*force*) la policía
policeman el policía
pool la piscina
popular popular (*m. or f.*)
position el puesto, el trabajo
possible posible (*m. or f.*)
   it isn't possible no es posible
post office la casa de correos, el correo
poster el cartel
pottery: pieces of ___ los objetos de cerámica
practice (to) practicar
prefer (to) preferir (ie, i)
prepare (to) preparar
   (he) prepares to eat breakfast (él) se prepara para desayunarse (tomar el desayuno)
prescribe (to) recetar
prettiest el más bonito, la más bonita
   it is the prettiest (*m.*) **of them all** es el más bonito de todos
   the prettiest (*f.*) **of all** la más bonita de todas
pretty bonito, -a; hermoso, -a
   very pretty muy bonito, -a; hermoso, -a; bonitísimo, -a; hermosísimo, -a
price el precio
   at special prices a precio especial
   fixed price el precio fijo
   have fixed prices tener precio fijo
private privado, -a
probably probablemente
problem el problema
   he has had no problems él no ha tenido problemas
   there is no problem no hay problema
   unless they want to have problems a menos que quieran tener problemas
program el programa (*m.*)
   radio program el programa de radio
   television program el programa de televisión
promise (to) prometer
pronounce (to) pronunciar
provided that *conj.* con tal (de) que
pure puro, -a
put (to) poner
   put on (oneself) ponerse

Q

quarter el cuarto
   a quarter of an hour ago hace un cuarto de hora

   at a quarter to (ten) a las (diez) menos cuarto
quiet tranquilo, -a
quite bastante

R

radio el radio
   radio program el programa de radio
rain (to) llover (ue)
   it was raining cats and dogs llovía a cántaros
raincoat el impermeable
Raymond Ramón
read (to) leer
ready listo, -a
ready: to get ___ for prepararse para
   get ready for (the trip) prepararse para (el viaje)
receive (to) recibir
reception (area) el recibidor
receptionist el (la) recepcionista
recommend (to) recomendar (ie)
recommendation la recomendación
red rojo, -a
refrigerator el refrigerador
register (to) registrarse
remember (to) recordar (ue)
rent el alquiler
reply (to) contestar, responder
reservation la reserva
   make a reservation hacer (una) reserva
reside (to) residir
residence hall la residencia
   Michael's residence hall la residencia de Miguel
resign oneself (to) conformarse con, *reflex*
rest (to) descansar
restaurant el restaurante
return (to) volver (ue), regresar; (*give back*) devolver (ue)
rich rico, -a
   become rich hacerse rico, -a
   very rich (*pl.*) muy ricos, -as; riquísimos, -as
Richard Ricardo
right away en seguida
right: be ___ tener razón
ring el anillo
ring (to) sonar (ue)
Robert Roberto
room el cuarto, la habitación
   an empty room un cuarto desocupado
   dining room el comedor

living room   la sala
roommate   el compañero (la compañera) de cuarto
round-trip *adj.*   de ida y vuelta
round-trip ticket   el boleto de ida y vuelta
ruins   las ruinas
run (to)   correr
run across   encontrarse (ue) con
run into   encontrarse (ue) con

S

salad   la ensalada
sale: that are on ___   que se venden a precio especial
saleslady   la vendedora
sand   la arena
Sarah   Sara
Saturday   el sábado
next Saturday   el sábado próximo (*or* que viene)
on Saturday (morning)   el sábado (por la mañana)
on Saturday(s)   el (los) sábado(s)
Saturday night   el sábado por la noche
say (to)   decir
scarcely   apenas
had scarcely entered the room   apenas había entrado en el cuarto
scene   la escena
schedule: time ___   el horario
(university) time schedule   el horario (de la universidad)
scholarship   la beca
school   la escuela
high school   la escuela secundaria
School (*in a university*)   la Facultad
Engineering School   la Facultad de Ingeniería
School of Agricultural Engineering   la Facultad de Ingeniería Agrícola (*or* Facultad de Agronomía)
School of Business Administration   la Facultad de Administración de Negocios
School of Medicine   la Facultad de Medicina
sea   el mar
seat   el asiento
he has obtained seats   él ha conseguido asientos
no seats are (there are no seats) left   no quedan asientos
seated   sentado, -a
be seated   estar sentado, -a

second   segundo, -a
secretary   el secretario (*m.*), la secretaria (*f.*)
section   la sección (*pl.* secciones)
sports section   la sección de deportes
see (to)   ver
by seeing it (*m.*)   viéndolo
I'll see you (*fam. sing.*) **tomorrow**   te veo mañana
let's see   a ver
see each other   verse
see you soon   hasta pronto
we'll see you (*f. pl.*) **Sunday morning**   las vemos el domingo por la mañana
would that we see one another again soon!   ¡ojalá que nos veamos otra vez pronto!
seeing: by seeing it (*m.*)   viéndolo
seem (to)   parecer
it seems to (Sylvia)   le parece a (Silvia)
select (to)   escoger
sell (to)   vender
semifinal   la semifinal
send (to)   mandar, enviar
send (*fam. pl.*) **for Rita**   envíen Uds. por Rita
sentence   la oración (*pl.* oraciones)
serious   serio, -a; grave (*m. or f.*)
seven hundred   setecientos, -as
several   varios, -as
shall   *marker of the future tense; occasionally translated by the pres. ind. tense*
shall we sit down?   ¿nos sentamos?
sharp (*time*)   en punto
she   ella
sheet   la sábana
shirt   la camisa
shop: beauty ___   la peluquería
shopping: go ___   ir de compras
short   corto, -a
after a while   al poco rato
in short   en fin
shortly afterward   poco después
should *mark of cond. ind. and imp. subj.*   deber
he should practice   (él) debería practicar
the clothing they should take   la ropa que deben (debían) llevar
show (to)   enseñar, mostrar (ue)
showcase   la vitrina
since *conj.*   como, *prep.* desde
it is (a week) since (they came)   hace (una semana) que (vinieron) *or* (vinieron) hace (una semana)

sing (to)   cantar
siren   la sirena
sister   la hermana
sit down (to)   sentarse (ie), *reflex.*
let's sit down   sentémonos, vamos a sentarnos
shall we sit down?   ¿nos sentamos?
site   el lugar
six   seis
by six o'clock   para las seis
six thousand   seis mil
sixty   sesenta
size   (*dress*) la talla; (*shoes*) el tamaño
it's size eight (*dress*)   es de talla ocho
skate (to)   patinar
skirt   la falda
sky   el cielo
slacks (*pl.*)   los pantalones
sleep (to)   dormir (ue, u)
sleepy: be (very) ___   tener (mucho) sueño
slides   las transparencias
slow down (to)   moderar la marcha
slowly   despacio
small   pequeño, -a
snow (to)   nevar (ie)
snow   la nieve
so   tan
soccer   el fútbol
soccer match   el partido de fútbol
some *adj. and pron.* alguno, -a; (*before m. sing. nouns*) algún; *pl.* algunos, -as; unos, -as; *often not translated*
someone   alguien
something   algo
have (*or* take) **something to drink**   tomar algo
somewhat   algo
feel somewhat better   sentirse (ie, i) algo mejor
song   la canción (*pl.* canciones)
soon   pronto
as soon as possible   lo más pronto posible, tan pronto como (sea) posible
see you soon   hasta pronto
soonest: the ___ **possible**   lo más pronto posible
sorry: be ___   sentir (ie, i)
we are sorry that   sentimos que
south   el sur
South America   Suramérica
South American   suramericano, -a
to the south   al sur
Spain   España
Spanish *adj.* español, -ola; hispano, -a (*the language*) el español
Spanish American   hispanoamericano, -a

Spanish (**lesson**) la (lección) de español
speak (**to**) hablar
special especial (*m. or f.*)
spend (**to**) (*money*) gastar; (*time*) pasar
  after spending the summer después de pasar el verano
  spend several months pasar varios meses
sports los deportes
spring la primavera
  spring vacation las vacaciones de primavera
square la plaza
stadium el estadio
start (**to**) empezar (ie), comenzar (ie)
States: (the) United ___ los Estados Unidos
stay (**to**) quedarse
stone la piedra
store la tienda
  department store el almacén (*pl.* almacenes)
  jewelry store la joyería
storm la tormenta
strange extraño, -a; raro, -a
  it seems strange parece extraño (raro)
straw la paja
  straw hat el sombrero de paja
street la calle
  Constitution Street la calle Constitución
  Twenty-fourth Street la calle Veinticuarto
student el alumno (*m.*), la alumna (*f.*); el, la estudiante
  engineering student el, la estudiante de ingeniería
studies los estudios
study (**to**) estudiar
style el estilo
success el éxito
  be a success tener éxito
successful: be (**very**) ___ tener (mucho) éxito
suggest (**to**) sugerir (ie, i)
suit: bathing ___ el traje de baño
suitcase la maleta
summary el resumen (*pl.* resúmenes)
summer el verano
sun el sol
  the sun is shining hace (hay) sol
sunbathe: to ___ tomar el sol
sunbathing tomar el sol
Sunday el domingo
  (**on**) **Sunday** (**morning**) el domingo (por la mañana)
  on Sundays los domingos

one Sunday un domingo
one Sunday night un domingo por la noche
sunny: be ___ hacer sol
  it is sunny hace sol
supper: eat ___ cenar
sure seguro, -a
  be sure that estar seguro, -a de que
surely seguramente, por cierto
surprise la sorpresa
  what a pleasant surprise! ¡qué sorpresa tan (más) agradable!
surprise (**to**) extrañar
  John is surprised le extraña a Juan
sweater el suéter
swim (**to**) nadar
swimming pool la piscina
Sylvia Silvia
syrup: a cough ___ un jarabe para la tos

T

table la mesa
take tomar; (*carry*) llevar
  I'll take this one (*m.*) **with me** me llevo éste
  (**she**) **is taking them** (*f.*) **with her** (ella) se las lleva
  take a nap dormir (ue, u) la *or* una siesta
  take a (**the**) **trip** hacer un (el) viaje
  take a walk dar un paseo
  take breakfast tomar el desayuno, desayunarse
  take leave of despedirse (i, i) de
  take lunch tomar el almuerzo, almorzar (ue)
  take photos sacar fotos
  take something (*to drink*) tomar algo
talk (**to**) hablar
tanned bronceado, -a
  get tanned ponerse bronceado, -a
taxi driver el (la) taxista
teacher el profesor (*m.*), la profesora (*f.*)
  (**Spanish**) **teacher** el profesor *or* la profesora (de español)
team el equipo
telephone el teléfono
  call (*to the telephone*) avisar
telephone (**to**) llamar por teléfono
television la televisión
  on television en la televisión
  television program el programa de televisión

watch television mirar la televisión
tell (**to**) decir, contar (ue)
  he will be able to tell him él podrá decírselo
  tell (*fam. sing. command*) **us, Ann, what . . . ?** dinos, Ana, ¿qué… ?
ten diez
  at a quarter to ten P.M. a las diez menos cuarto de la noche
  at about ten o'clock a eso de las diez
  it must be half past ten serán las diez y media
  it's 10:40 son las once menos veinte
  (**until**) **ten o'clock** (hasta) las diez
  until 10:30 P.M. hasta las diez y media de la noche
tennis el tenis
terrible terrible (*m. or f.*)
than que; (*before numeral*) de
Thanksgiving Day el Día de Acción de Gracias
that *adj.* (*near person addressed*) ese, esa; (*distant*) aquel, aquella; *pron.* ése, ésa, aquél, aquélla; (*neuter*) eso, aquello; *relative pron.* que
  that of el (la) de
  that one *pron.* ése, ésa; aquél, aquélla
  that way así
the el, la, los, las
their *adj.* su(s)
theirs *pron.* (el) suyo, (la) suya, etc.; (el, la, los, las) de ellos (-as)
them *dir. obj.* los, las; *indir. obj.* les, se; *after prep.* ellos (-as)
then (*at that time*) entonces; (*next*) luego; (*well*) pues
there (*near person addressed*) ahí; (*distant*) allí; (*often after verb of motion*) alla
  there is (**are**) hay
  there was (**were**) había
these *adj.* estos, estas; *pron.* éstos, éstas
they ellos, ellas
thing la cosa
  how have things gone? ¿cómo lo han pasado?
think (**to**) creer, pensar (ie)
  think of pensar (ie) en
  what do you (*fam. sing.*) **think if . . . ?** ¿qué te parece si… ?
  what do you (*fam. sing.*) **think of these** (*m.*)**?** ¿qué te parecen éstos?

third   tercero, -a; (*before m. sing. nouns*) tercer

  the third floor (*Spain*)   el piso segundo (el segundo piso)

thirty   treinta

  on August thirtieth   el treinta de agosto

thirty-five   treinta y cinco

this *adj.*   este, esta

  this one *pron.*   éste, ésta

Thomas   Tomás

those   *adj.* (*near person addressed*) esos (-as); (*distant*) aquellos (-as); *pron.* ésos (-as); aquéllos (-as)

  those who work hard   los que (quienes) trabajan mucho

thousand: a (**one**) ____   mil

  (**six**) **thousand**   (seis) mil

  (**two**) **thousand**   (dos) mil

three   tres

three hundred and fifty   trescientos cincuenta

throat   la garganta

through   por

Thursday   el jueves

  on Thursday evening   el jueves por la noche

ticket   el boleto

  plane ticket   el boleto de avión

  round-trip ticket   el boleto de ida y vuelta

time   (*in general sense*) el tiempo; (*of day*) la hora; (*series*) la vez (*pl.* veces)

  arrive on time   llegar a tiempo

  at this (**that**) **time of the year**   en este (ese) tiempo del año

  at what time?   ¿a qué hora?

  be time to   ser hora de

  for a long time   hace mucho tiempo que *or* desde hace mucho tiempo

  have a good time   divertirse (ie, i)

  have time to   tener tiempo para

  how much time?   ¿cuánto tiempo?

  I wonder what time it is?   ¿qué hora será?

  on time   a tiempo

  the first (**second**) **time**   la primera (segunda) vez

  three or four times   tres o cuatro veces

  time schedule   el horario

  university time schedule   el horario de la universidad

  what time can it be?   ¿qué hora será?

  what time is it?   ¿qué hora es?

tired   cansado, -a

be (**quite**) **tired**   (**of** + *ing*)   estar (bastante) cansado, -a (de + *inf.*)

to   a, de, para, que, (*in time*) menos

  at a quarter to (**ten**)   a las (diez) menos cuarto

  have the opportunity to   tener la oportunidad de

  have time to   tener tiempo para

  have to + *verb*   tener que + *inf.*

  in order to *prep.*   para

  not to have anything to do   no tener nada que hacer

  up to *prep.*   hasta

toaster   la tostadora

today   hoy

tomorrow   mañana

  tomorrow afternoon (**morning**)   mañana por la tarde (mañana)

tonight   esta noche

too   también

too many *adj.*   demasiados, -as

topcoat   el abrigo

topic   el tema

tour   la excursión

  take a (**bicycle**) **tour**   hacer una excursión (en bicicleta)

town   el pueblo

traffic   el tráfico

translate (**to**)   traducir

travel (**to**)   viajar

  travel agency   la agencia de viajes

  travel in (**through**)   viajar por

travelling companion (*m.*)   el compañero de viaje

trip   el viaje

  business trips   los viajes de negocios

  have a good trip!   ¡buen viaje!

  make *or* **take the** (**a**) **trip**   hacer el (un) viaje

try (**to**)   tratar de + *inf.*

Tuesday   el martes

turn on (**to**)   poner

  shall I turn on the television?   ¿pongo la televisión?

  turn to   dirigirse a

turnover   la empanada

twelve   doce

  at twelve o'clock   a las doce

  twelve thousand   doce mil

twenty   veinte

twenty-one   veintiuno, -a; (*before m. nouns*) veintiún

twenty-four   veinticuatro

  Twenty-fourth Street   la calle Veinticuatro

two   dos

  at two o'clock   a las dos

typical   típico, -a

U

umbrella   el paraguas

unable: be ____   no poder (ue)

understand (**to**)   entender (ie)

unforgettable   inolvidable (*m. or f.*)

unfortunately   desgraciadamente

United States   (los) Estados Unidos

  in the United States   en los Estados Unidos

university   la universidad

  university cafeteria (**residence hall, time schedule**)   la cafetería (la residencia, el horario) de la universidad

  university tennis courts   las canchas de la universidad

unless *conj.*   a menos que

unoccupied   desocupado, -a

until *prep.*   hasta

up: get ____   levantarse

  go up (**to**)   subir (a)

  up to *prep.*   hasta

upon + -*ing*   al + *inf.*

urgent   urgente (*m. or f.*)

  be urgent   ser urgente

Uruguayan *adj.*   uruguayo, -a

use (**to**)   usar

used to + *inf.*   *indicates use of imp. ind. tense*

  the family used to live   la familia vivía

V

vacancy (*job*)   el puesto

vacation   las vacaciones

  Christmas vacation   las vacaciones de Navidad

  spring (**summer**) **vacation**   las vacaciones de primavera (de verano)

  Thanksgiving Day vacation   las vacaciones del Día de Acción de Gracias

vacuum cleaner   la aspiradora

Valencian   valenciano, -a

various   varios, -as

verse   el verso

very   *adv.* muy; *adj.* mucho, -a

video   el vídeo

  video camera   la (cámara) vídeo

view   la vista

village   el pueblo

viral   viral (*m. or f.*)

  viral pneumonia   una pulmonía viral

visit   la visita

be on a visit   estar de visita
visit (**to**)   visitar

W

wait for (**to**)   esperar
   wait long (**to**)   esperar mucho
waiter   el camarero (*m.*) (*Spain*), el mesero (*m.*) (*Mex.*)
walk   el paseo
   take a walk   dar un paseo
wall   la pared
want (**to**)   querer (ie), desear
wash (**to**)   lavar; (*oneself*) lavarse *reflex.*
water   el agua (*f.*)
way   el camino
   (**be**) **on one's** *or* **the way to**   (ir) camino de
   by the way   a propósito, por cierto
   in no way   de ninguna manera
   that way   así
we   nosotros, -as
weather   el tiempo
   the weather is fine today   hoy hace buen tiempo
wedding   la boda
   wedding gifts   los regalos de boda
Wednesday   el miércoles
   next Wednesday   el miércoles próximo (*or* que viene)
week   la semana
   every week   todas las semanas
   it is a week since (**they came**)   hace una semana que (vinieron) *or* (vinieron) hace una semana
   last week   la semana pasada
   next week   la semana próxima (*or* que viene)
   scarcely a week   apenas una semana
weekend   el fin de semana
weeks: a couple of ____   un par de semanas
welcome: you're ____   de nada, no hay de qué
well *adv.*   bien; bueno, pues

well: get ____   mejorarse
   feel well   sentirse (ie, i) bien
what?   ¿qué?
   what's new?   ¿qué hay de nuevo?
   what can I do for you (*pl.*)?   ¿en qué puedo servirles?
what a . . . !   ¡qué… !
when   cuando
where?   ¿dónde?; (*with verbs of motion*) ¿adónde?
   where is (**Louise**) **from?**   ¿de dónde es (Luisa)?
where   donde
whether   si
which   que; el (la, los, las) que; el (la) cual, los (las) cuales; lo que (cual)
while   el rato; *conj.* mientras (que)
   after a short while   al poco rato
white   blanco, -a
who   que: quien(es); el (la, los, las) que; el (la) cual, los (las) cuales
   those who work hard   los que (quienes) trabajan mucho
whom   que; a quien(es)
why?   ¿por qué?
will *marker of future tense*
   will you + *verb?*   ¿quiere Ud. (quieres) + *inf.*?
window   la ventana
windy: be ____   hacer viento
   it was windy   hacía viento
winter   el invierno
wish (**to**)   desear
with   con
wonder: I ____ **what time it is?**   ¿qué hora será?
word   la palabra
work (**to**)   trabajar
world   el mundo
   Hispanic world   el mundo hispánico
world   mundial *adj.* (*m. or f.*)
   World Cup   la Copa Mundial
worried   preocupado, -a
   be worried   estar preocupado, -a
worthwhile: be ____   valer la pena
would   *mark of imp. ind. or cond. tense*
would that . . . !   ¡ojalá (que) + *subj.!*

write (**to**)   escribir
written   escrito, -a

Y

year   el año
   at this time of the year   en este tiempo del año
   be (**eighteen**) **years old**   tener (*or* cumplir) (dieciocho) años
   last year   el año pasado
   next year   el próximo año
yesterday   ayer
   yesterday (**morning**)   ayer (por la mañana)
yet   todavía
you   (*formal*) *subject pron. and after prep.* usted (Ud. *or* Vd.), ustedes (Uds. *or* Vds.); *dir. obj.* lo (le), la, los, las; *indir. obj.* le, les, se
you   (*fam. sing.*) *subject pron.* tú, (*pl.*) vosotros, -as *or* ustedes (Uds. *or* Vds.) (*Am.*); *dir. obj.* te (*pl.*) os *or* los, las (*Am.*); *indir. obj.* te, (*pl.*) os *or* les, se (*Am.*); *after prep.* ti, (*pl.*) vosotros, -as *or* ustedes (Uds. *or* Vds.) (*Am.*)
young   joven (*m. or f., pl.* jóvenes)
   one of the young men   uno de los jóvenes
   the two young ladies   las dos jóvenes (*or* señoritas)
   the two young men   los dos jóvenes
   young people   los jóvenes
young-looking   juvenil (*m. or f.*)
your   *adj.* (*fam.*) tu(s), vuestro(s), -a(s); (*formal*) su(s), de Ud(s). *or* Vd(s).
yours   *pron.* (*fam.*) (el) tuyo, (la) tuya, (los) tuyos, (las) tuyas; (el) vuestro, (la) vuestra, (los) vuestros, (las) vuestras; (*formal*) (el) suyo, (la) suya, (los) suyos, (las) suyas; (el, la, los, las) de Ud(s). *or* Vd(s).
   of yours   *adj.* (*fam.*) tuyo(s), -a(s); vuestro(s), -a(s); (*formal*) suyo(s), -a(s); de Ud(s). *or* Vd(s).

Index

a
> **jugar a**, 52
> omission of personal, 109
> personal, 108
> preposition, 8–9
abrir, forms of, 32
absolute superlative, 68
acabar de, 23
accent. *See* written accent.
adjective clauses, subjunctive used with, 107, 109
adjectives
> comparison of, 64–65, 67–68
> irregular comparative forms, 64–65
> past participle used as, 35
> shortened forms of, 10
adverbial clauses, subjunctive used with, 121–123
adverbs
> comparison of, 66, 67–68
> denoting probability or conjecture, 50
> irregular comparative, 66
agreement
> of cardinal numbers, 10
> of ordinal numbers 10
alphabet, Spanish, 160
article, definite
> as a demonstrative pronoun, 125
> for the possessive, 30 (*footnote*), 59 (*footnote*)
> in comparison of adjectives, 65
> in dates, 11
> to form possessive pronouns, 124
> with nouns in apposition, 104 (*footnote*)
article, indefinite
> omission with **ciento** and **mil**, 10

become + adjective, 112

capitalization, 166
cardinal numbers, 9–10
> in dates, 11
-car verbs, 19, 63, 90, 175
-cer verbs, 176
cien / ciento, 10
-cir verbs, 176
clarification
> of **su, sus**, 8
> of **el suyo, la suya**, etc., 124
commands
> familiar, of reflexive verbs, 149
> familiar plural, 148–149
> familiar singular, irregular forms, 62–63
> familiar singular, negative forms, 76
> formal, 76
> formal, with spelling changes, 19
> indirect, 95–96

let, let's translated as, 96
> **nosotros**, 96
> position of object and reflexive pronouns with, 62–63, 76, 96
> **vamos a** + infinitive, 96
como si, 139
comparison
> irregular comparative adjectives, 64–65
> of adverbs, 66
> of equality, 67–68
> of inequality, 64–65, 66
compound verb tenses, 169–170
con: conmigo, contigo, 8
conditional perfect, 51, 170
conditional sentences, 122–123
conditional tense
> forms of, 46, 168
> irregular forms of, 47
> to express probability, 50
> uses of, 48–49, 50, 152
conjunctions
> that introduce clauses expressing condition, 123
> that introduce time clauses, 122
conocer, forms of, 78
consonants, Spanish, 161–162
contrary-to-fact sentences, 139
creer
> forms of, 37, 134
> uses of, 94
cualquier(a), cualesquier(a), 132 (*footnote*)
cubrir, forms of, 32

dar, forms of, 79, 134
dates, 11
deber, uses of, 49, 151–152
decir, forms of, 24, 32, 62, 78, 134
definite article. *See* article, definite.
dejar, uses of, 95
demonstrative pronouns, *See* pronouns.
devolver
> forms of, 32
> uses of, 23
diphthongs, Spanish, 162–163
direct object pronouns. *See* pronouns.
doler, 59 (*footnote*)
-ducir verbs, 105, 176

el cual, la cual, etc., 108, 125
el que, la que, etc., 108, 125
encontrarse + past participle, 35
envolver, forms of, 32
escribir, forms of, 32
estar, forms of, 79, 134
éste, etc., meaning *the latter*, 22

future perfect, 51, 170
future tense
    forms of, 45, 168
    irregular forms of, 47
    present indicative used instead of, 48
    to express probability, 50
    uses of, 48

-gar verbs, 19, 52, 63, 90, 175
-ger verbs, 120
get + adjective, 112
-gir verbs, 120
grammatical terms, 166–167
gran, grande, 64 (*footnote*)
-guir verbs, 91

haber
    forms of, 36, 48, 51, 79, 97, 134, 136
    impersonal expressions with **hay**, 35–36
    summary of uses of, 35–36
    to form perfect tenses, 32–33, 51, 97, 136,
        169–170
hacer
    forms of, 32, 62, 78, 134
    in expressions of time, 36, 110–111
    meaning *ago* or *since*, 36
hallarse + past participle, 35
hay
    hay que + infinitive, 36
    with impersonal expressions, 35–36

-iar verbs, 120–121, 177
imperative. *See* commands.
imperfect indicative
    of **hacer** in time clauses, 36, 110–111
    regular forms, 168
imperfect subjunctive. *See* subjunctive.
impersonal expressions, 35–36, 106
indefinite article. *See* article, indefinite.
indicative vs. subjunctive, 80–81, 92, 93–94, 95, 106, 109,
    121–123
indirect object pronouns. *See* pronouns.
infinitive
    after **acabar de**, 23
    after **hay que**, 36
    after impersonal expressions, 106
    after **para**, 154
    after prepositions, 4
    after verbs of perception (**oír, ver**, etc.), 112
    after **vamos a**, 96
    vs. subjunctive, 81–82
intonation, 163–165
ir
    forms of, 32, 62, 79, 134
    in **nosotros** commands, 96
    ir a + infinitive, 48
-ir verbs with stem change, 60–61
-ísimo, 68

jugar
    forms of, 52
    uses of, 52

latter, the, translation of, 22
leer, forms of, 37, 134
let, let's, 96
lo. *See* neuter **lo**.

must, 36

-ndo forms
    after **seguir**, 89 (*footnote*)
    forms of, 168
    irregular forms, 4, 61
    position of object and reflexive pronouns with, 6
neuter **lo**, 44 (*footnote*)
    lo cual, 108
    lo que, 108, 125 (*footnote*)
nosotros commands. *See* imperative.
numbers
    cardinal, 9–10
        in dates, 11
    ordinal, 10–11

oír
    followed by infinitive, 112
    forms of, 37, 78, 134
ojalá (que), 152
ordinal numbers. *See* numbers.

para, uses of, 123, 154–155
passive voice, 149–150
    se + verb used instead of, 7
past participle
    forms of, 31–32, 168
    in perfect tenses, 32–33, 51, 97, 136, 170
    irregular forms, 32, 170
    to express passive voice, 150
    used as adjective, 35
    used with **estar**, 35
pedir
    forms of, 61
    uses of, 61
permitir, uses of, 95
pero vs. **sino, sino que**, 126
personal **a**, 108
    omission of, 109
pluperfect
    indicative, 32–33, 170
    subjunctive, 136, 170
poder, uses of, 151–152
poner, forms of, 32, 62, 78
por
    idiomatic expressions with, 155
    uses of, 149, 154–155
possessive pronouns, 124
    clarification of **el suyo, la suya**, etc., 124
preguntar, uses of, 61

prepositions
   a, 8–9
   compound, 108
   con, 8–9
   de, 8–9
   infinitive used after, 4, 123
present indicative
   in simple conditions, 139–140
   of regular verbs, 168
   of stem-changing verbs, 60–61
   to express future time, 48
present perfect
   indicative, 32, 170
   position of object and reflexive pronouns with, 33
   subjunctive, 97, 170
present subjunctive. *See* subjunctive.
preterit
   irregular verbs with **i**-stems, 4
   irregular verbs with **j**-stems, 24
   irregular verbs with **u**-stem, 18
   of regular verbs, 168
   of stem-changing **-ir** verbs, 61
   verbs with spelling changes, 19
preterit perfect, forms of, 170
probability
   conditional to express, 50
   future to express, 50
pronouns
   demonstrative, 21–22
   direct object, 20
   indirect object, 20
   neuter demonstrative, 22
   position of, 6, 63, 96, 149
   possessive, 124
   prepositional, 8
   reflexive, 63, 149, 151
   relative, 107–108
   two object pronouns used together, 20
punctuation, 165
punctuation marks, 165

que
   relative pronoun, 107–108
   subordinate conjunction, 81
   with **hacer** in time expressions, 36
   with indirect commands, 96
¡qué! + adjective, 59 (*footnote*)
querer, uses of, 151
quien(es), relative pronoun, 108
quisiera, uses of, 151

reciprocal verbs, 151
reflexive pronouns. *See* pronouns.
reflexive verbs
   familiar plural command forms of, 149
   familiar singular command forms of, 149
reír(se), forms of, 61 (*footnote*)
relative pronouns, 107–108
reunirse, forms of, 153, 177 (*footnote*)

saber, forms of, 79
salir, forms of, 62, 78
se
   as indefinite subject, 7
   for **le** and **les**, 20
   se + verb for passive voice, 7
ser, forms of, 62, 79
si-clauses, 139–140
si meaning *whether*, 49, 140
sino, sino que vs. **pero**, 126
softened statements substituted for command forms
   using conditional tense, 48
   using subjunctive, 151–152
stem-changing verbs, 60–61, 63, 77, 134, 178–180
su, sus, clarification of, 8
subjunctive
   after impersonal expressions, 106
   after **ojalá (que)**, 152
   after **quizá(s)**, **tal vez**, 94
   after verbs of emotion, 91–92
   after verbs of persuasion, desire, request, etc., 81
   imperfect, forms of, 133–134, 168
   in adjective clauses, 107, 109
   in adverbial clauses, 121–123
   in conditional sentences, 122–123
   in formal commands, 76
   in implied commands, 83
   in indirect commands, 95–96
   in negative familiar commands, 76
   in **si**-clauses, 139–140
   in softened statements, 151–152
   pluperfect, forms of, 136, 170
   present, forms of, 76, 77, 78, 90, 168
   present perfect, forms of, 97, 170
   to express doubt or uncertainty, 93–94
   use of subjunctive tenses, 137–138
   vs. indicative, 80–81, 92, 93–94, 95, 106, 109, 121–123
superlative
   absolute superlative, 68
   of adjectives in comparisons of inequality, 65
suyo (-a, -os, -as), clarification of, 124
syllables. *See* word division.

tener
   forms of, 62, 78
tense. *See name of specific tense.*
traer, forms of, 24, 78

-uar verbs, 121, 177
-uir verbs, 153, 177
uno as indefinite subject, 8

valer, forms of, 141
venir, forms of, 62, 78
ver
   a ver, 96
   followed by infinitive, 112
   forms of, 32, 78
verb tenses. *See specific tense or verb; see also Appendix B.*
verse + past participle, 35

volver
    forms of, 32
    uses of, 23
vowels, Spanish, 160–161

will. See future tense.
word division, 163

would. See conditional tense.
written accent, 6, 20, 31, 37, 45, 46, 61 (*footnote*), 121, 149,
    153, 163

-zar verbs, 19, 63, 90, 175